LOGIC

THE THEORY OF INQUIRY

By

JOHN DEWEY

HOLT, RINEHART AND WINSTON
New York · Chicago · San Francisco
Toronto · London

965'76

21820-0118

PREFACE

THIS BOOK is a development of ideas regarding the nature of logical theory that were first presented, some forty years ago, in *Studies in Logical Theory;* that were somewhat expanded in *Essays in Experimental Logic* and were briefly summarized with special reference to education in *How We Think*. While basic ideas remain the same, there has naturally been considerable modification during the intervening years. While connection with the problematic is unchanged, express identification of reflective thought with objective inquiry makes possible, I think, a mode of statement less open to misapprehension than were the previous ones. The present work is marked in particular by application of the earlier ideas to interpretation of the forms and formal relations that constitute the standard material of logical tradition. This interpretation has at the same time involved a detailed development, critical and constructive, of the general standpoint and its underlying ideas.

In this connection, attention is called particularly to the principle of the continuum of inquiry, a principle whose importance, as far as I am aware, only Peirce had previously noted. Application of this principle enables an empirical account to be given of logical forms, whose necessity traditional empiricism overlooked or denied while at the same time it proves that the interpretation of them as *a priori* is unnecessary. The connection of the principle with generalization in its two forms—which are systematically distinguished throughout the work—and with the probability coefficient of all existential generalizations is, I suppose, sufficiently indicated in the chapters devoted to these topics. The basic conception of inquiry as determination of an indeterminate situation not only enables the vexed topic of the relation of judgment and propositions to obtain an objective solution, but, in connection with the conjugate relation of observed and conceptual material, enables a coherent account of the different propositional forms to be given.

The word "Pragmatism" does not, I think, occur in the text.

iii

Perhaps the word lends itself to misconception. At all events, so much misunderstanding and relatively futile controversy have gathered about the word that it seemed advisable to avoid its use. But in the proper interpretation of "pragmatic," namely the function of consequences as necessary tests of the validity of propositions, *provided* these consequences are operationally instituted and are such as to resolve the specific problem evoking the operations, the text that follows is thoroughly pragmatic.

In the present state of logic, the absence of any attempt at symbolic formulation will doubtless cause serious objection in the minds of many readers. This absence is not due to any aversion to such formulation. On the contrary, I am convinced that acceptance of the general principles set forth will enable a more complete and consistent set of symbolizations than now exists to be made. The absence of symbolization is due, first, to a point mentioned in the text, the need for development of a general theory of language in which form and matter are not separated; and, secondly, to the fact that an adequate set of symbols depends upon prior institution of valid ideas of the conceptions and relations that are symbolized. Without fulfilment of this condition, formal symbolization will (as so often happens at present) merely perpetuate existing mistakes while strengthening them by seeming to give them scientific standing.

Readers not particularly conversant with contemporary logical discussions may find portions of the text too technical, especially perhaps in Part III. I suggest that such readers interpret what is said by calling to mind what they themselves do, and the way they proceed in doing it, when they are confronted with some question or difficulty which they attempt to cope with in an intellectual way. If they pursue this course, I think the general principles will be sufficiently intelligible so that they will not be unduly troubled by technical details. It is possible that the same advice is applicable in the case of those whose very familiarity with current logical literature constitutes an obstruction to understanding a position that is at odds with most current theory.

As far as logical treatises and their authors are concerned, I hope the work itself affords sufficient indication of my chief lines of indebtedness. I should however state explicitly that, with the outstanding exception of Peirce, I have learned most from writers with whose positions I have in the end been compelled to disagree. Since it happens that there is no reference in the text to the writings of A. F. Bentley, I wish to record here how much I owe to them. My indebtedness to George H. Mead is also much greater than is indicated by the text.

With emphatic repetition of the disclaimer that is usual in the case of personal acknowledgments of indebtedness, it is a pleasure to mention some of them—my obligation to a succession of students for a period of more than a generation in which I have lectured on the themes of this volume can only be stated in this general way. Dr. Sidney Hook has read the several versions of all the chapters of this book and I have profited immensely by his suggestions and criticisms, both as to manner and substance of what was contained in these chapters. Dr. Joseph Ratner read many of the chapters and I am also indebted to him for suggestions and corrections. In some of the more technical chapters I have availed myself freely of the superior knowledge and competency of Dr. Ernest Nagel. It is my fault, not his, if avoidable errors still exist in the chapters referred to.

In conclusion, I want to say that the treatise that follows is introductory. It is a presentation of a point of view and method of approach. Although the statement of them has been maturing for over forty years, I am well aware that the presentation does not have and could not have the finish and completeness that are theoretically possible. But I am also convinced that the standpoint is so thoroughly sound that those who are willing to entertain it will in the coming years develop a theory of logic that is in thorough accord with all the best authenticated methods of attaining knowledge. My best wishes as well as my hopes are with those who engage in the profoundly important work of bringing logical theory into accord with scientific practice, no matter how much their conclusions may differ in detail from those presented in this book.

J. D.

Hubbards, Nova Scotia
August 24, 1938

CONTENTS

PART III

PROPOSITIONS AND TERMS

PART IV

THE LOGIC OF SCIENTIFIC METHOD

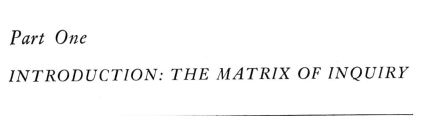

Part One

INTRODUCTION: THE MATRIX OF INQUIRY

CHAPTER 1

THE PROBLEM OF LOGICAL
SUBJECT-MATTER

CONTEMPORARY LOGICAL theory is marked by an apparent paradox. There is general agreement as to its proximate subject-matter. With respect to this proximate subject-matter no period shows a more confident advance. Its ultimate subject-matter, on the other hand, is involved in controversies which show little sign of abating. Proximate subject-matter is the domain of the relations of propositions to one another, such as affirmation-negation, inclusion-exclusion, particular-general, etc. No one doubts that the relations expressed by such words as *is, is-not, if-then, only (none but), and, or, some-all,* belong to the subject-matter of logic in a way so distinctive as to mark off a special field.

When, however, it is asked how and why the matters designated by these terms form the subject-matter of logic, dissension takes the place of consensus. Do they stand for pure forms, forms that have independent subsistence, or are the forms in question forms *of* subject-matter? If the latter, what is that of which they are forms, and what happens when subject-matter takes on logical form? How and why?

These are questions of what I called the ultimate subject-matter of logic; and about this subject-matter controversy is rife. Uncertainty about this question does not prevent valuable work in the field of proximate subject-matter. But the more developed this field becomes, the more pressing is the question as to what it is all about. Moreover, it is not true that there is *complete* agreement in the more limited field. On the contrary, in some important matters, there is conflict even here; and there is a possibility (which

1

will be shown in the sequel to be actualized) that the uncertainty and diversity that exists in the limited field is a reflection of the unsettled state of opinion about ultimate subject-matter.

To illustrate the existing uncertainty as to ultimate subject-matter, it is only necessary to enumerate some of the diverse conceptions about the nature of logic that now stand over against one another. It is said, for example, that logic is the science of necessary laws of thought, and that it is the theory of ordered relations—relations which are wholly independent of thought. There are at least three views held as to the nature of these latter relations: They are held (1) to constitute a realm of pure possibilities as such, where *pure* means independent of actuality; (2) to be ultimate invariant relations forming the *order* of nature; and (3) to constitute the rational structure of the universe. In the latter status, while independent of human thought, they are said to embody the rational structure of the universe which is reproduced in part by human reason. There is also the view that logic is concerned with processes of inference by which knowledge, especially scientific knowledge, is attained.

Of late, another conception of its subject-matter has appeared upon the scene. Logic is said to be concerned with the formal structure of language as a system of symbols. And even here there is division. Upon one view, logic is the theory of transformation of linguistic expressions, the criterion of transformation being identity of syntactical forms. According to another view, the symbolic system, which is the subject-matter of logic, is a universal algebra of existence.

In any case, as regards *ultimate* subject-matter, logic is a branch of philosophic theory; so that different views of its subject-matter are expressions of different ultimate philosophies, while logical conclusions are used in turn to support the underlying philosophies. In view of the fact that philosophizing must satisfy logical requirements there is something in this fact that should at least provoke curiosity; conceivably it affects unfavorably the autonomy of logical theory. On the face of the matter, it does not seem fitting that logical theory should be determined by philosophical realism or idealism, rationalism or empiricism, dualism or monism, atomistic or organic metaphysics. Yet even when writers on logic do not express their philosophic prepossessions, analysis discloses a connection. In some cases conceptions borrowed from one or another philosophic system are openly laid down as *foundations* of logic and even of mathematics.

This list of diverse views given above is put down by way of illustration. It is not exhaustive, but it suffices to justify one more endeavor to deal with proximate subject-matter in terms of a theory concerning the ultimate subject-matter of logic. In the present state of affairs, it is foolish to say that logic *must* be about this or that. Such assertions are verbal realisms, assuming that a word has such magical power that it can point to and select the subject to which it is applicable. Furthermore, any statement that logic *is* so-and-so, can, in the existing state of logical theory, be offered only as a hypothesis and an indication of a position to be developed.

Whatever is offered as a hypothesis must, however, satisfy certain conditions. It must be of the nature of a *vera causa*. Being a *vera causa*, does not mean, of course, that it is a *true* hypothesis, for if it were that, it would be more than a hypothesis. It means that whatever is offered as the ground of a theory must possess the property of verifiable existence in *some* domain, no matter how hypothetical it is in reference to the field in which it is proposed to apply it. It has no standing if it is drawn from the void and proffered simply *ad hoc*. The second condition that a hypothesis about ultimate logical subject-matter must satisfy is that it be able to order and account for what has been called the proximate subject-matter. If it cannot meet the test thus imposed, no amount of theoretical plausibility is of avail. In the third place, the hypothesis must be such as to account for the arguments that are advanced in support of other theories. This condition corresponds to the capacity of a theory in any field to explain apparent negative cases and exceptions. Unless this condition is fulfilled, conclusions reached in satisfaction of the second condition are subject to the fallacy of affirming an antecedent clause because the consequent is affirmed.

From these preliminary remarks I turn to statement of the position regarding logical subject-matter that is developed in this work. The theory, in summary form, is that all logical forms (with their characteristic properties) arise within the operation of inquiry and are concerned with control of inquiry so that it may yield warranted assertions. This conception implies much more than that logical forms are disclosed or come to light when we reflect upon processes of inquiry that are in use. Of course it means that; but it also means that the forms *originate* in operations of inquiry. To employ a convenient expression, it means that while inquiry into inquiry is the *causa cognoscendi* of logical forms, primary inquiry is itself *causa essendi* of the forms which inquiry into inquiry discloses.

It is not the task of this chapter to try to justify this hypothesis, or to show that it satisfies the three conditions laid down. That is the business of the work as a whole. But I wish to emphasize two points preparatory to expounding the *meaning* (not the justification) of the conception, an exposition that is the main task of the present chapter. One of them is that any revulsion against the position just indicated should be tempered by appreciation of the fact that all other conceptions of logical subject-matter that are now entertained are equally hypothetical. If they do not seem to be so, it is because of their familiarity. If sheer dogmatism is to be avoided, any hypothesis, no matter how unfamiliar, should have a fair chance and be judged by its results. The other point is that inquiries, numerous in variety and comprehensive in scope, do exist and are open to public examination. Inquiry is the life-blood of every science and is constantly employed in every art, craft and profession. In short, the hypothesis represents a *vera causa*, no matter what doubt may attend its applicability in the field of logic.

Further elucidation of the meaning of the position taken will proceed largely in terms of objections that are most likely to arise. The most basic of these objections is that the field indicated, that of inquiries, is already pre-empted. There is, it will be said, a recognized subject which deals with it. That subject is methodology; and there is a well recognized distinction between methodology and logic, the former being an application of the latter.

It certainly cannot be shown, short of the total development of the position taken, that this objection is not just. But it may be noted that assertion *in advance* of a fixed difference between logic and the methodology of scientific and practical inquiry begs the fundamental question at issue. The fact that most of the extant treatises upon methodology have been written upon the assumption of a fixed difference between the two does not prove that the difference exists. Moreover, the relative failure of works on logic that have identified logic and methodology (I may cite the logic of Mill as an example) does not prove that the identification is doomed to failure. For the failure *may* not be inherent. In any case, *a priori* assumption of a dualism between logic and methodology can only be prejudicial to unbiased examination both of methods of inquiry and logical subject-matter.

The plausibility of the view that sets up a dualism between logic and the methodology of inquiry, between logic and scientific method, is due to a fact that is not denied. Inquiry in order to reach valid conclusions must itself satisfy logical requirements. It is an easy inference from this fact to the idea that the logical requirements are imposed upon methods of inquiry from without. Since inquiries and methods are better and worse, logic involves a standard for criticizing and evaluating them. How, it will be asked, can inquiry which has to be evaluated by reference to a standard be itself the source of the standard? How can inquiry originate logical forms (as it has been stated that it does) and yet be subject to the requirements of these forms? The question is one that must be met. It can be adequately answered only in the course of the entire discussion that follows. But the meaning of the position taken may be clarified by indicating the direction in which the answer will be sought.

The problem reduced to its lowest terms is whether inquiry can develop in its own ongoing course the logical standards and forms to which *further* inquiry shall submit. One might reply by saying that it *can* because it has. One might even challenge the objector to produce a single instance of improvement in scientific methods not produced in and by the self-corrective process of inquiry; a single instance that is due to application of standards *ab extra*. But such a retort needs to be justified. Some kind of inquiry began presumably as soon as man appeared on earth. Of prehistoric methods of inquiry our knowledge is vague and speculative. But we know a good deal about different methods that have been used in historic times. We know that the methods which now control science are of comparatively recent origin in both physical and mathematical science.

Moreover, different methods have been not only tried, but they have been tried out; that is, tested. The developing course of science thus presents us with an immanent criticism of methods previously tried. Earlier methods failed in some important respect. In consequence of this failure, they were modified so that more dependable results were secured. Earlier methods yielded conclusions that could not stand the strain put upon them by further investigation. It is not merely that *conclusions* were found to be inadequate or false but that they were found to be so because of methods employed. Other methods of inquiry were found to be such that persistence in them not only produced conclusions that stood the strain of further inquiry but that tended to be self-rectifying. They were methods that improved with and by use.

It may be instructive to compare the improvement of scientific methods within inquiry with the improvement that has taken place in the progress of the arts. Is there any reason to suppose that advance in the art of metallurgy has been due to application of an external standard? The "norms" used at present have developed out of the processes by which metallic ores were formerly treated. There were needs to be satisfied; consequences to be reached. As they were reached, new needs and new possibilities opened to view and old processes were re-made to satisfy them. In short, some procedures worked; some succeeded in reaching the end intended; others failed. The latter were dropped; the former were retained and extended. It is quite true that modern improvements in technologies have been determined by advance in mathematics and physical science. But these advances in scientific knowledge are not external canons to which the arts have had automatically to submit themselves. They provided new instrumentalities, but the instrumentalities were not self-applying. They were used; and it was the result of their use, their failure and success in accomplishing ends and effecting consequences, that provided the final criterion of the value of scientific principles for carrying on determinate technological operations. What is said is not intended as *proof* that the logical principles involved in scientific method have themselves arisen in the progressive course of inquiry. But it is meant to show that the hypothesis that they have so arisen has a *prima facie* claim to be entertained, final decision being reserved.

I now return to exposition of the meaning of the position taken. That inquiry is related to doubt will, I suppose, be admitted. The admission carries with it an implication regarding the end of inquiry: *end* in both senses of the word, as end-in-view and as close or termination. If inquiry begins in doubt, it terminates in the institution of conditions which remove need for doubt. The latter state of affairs may be designated by the words *belief* and *knowledge*. For reasons that I shall state later I prefer the words "warranted assertibility."

Belief may be so understood as to be a fitting designation for the outcome of inquiry. Doubt is uneasy; it is tension that finds expression and outlet in the processes of inquiry. Inquiry terminates in reaching that which is settled. This settled condition is a demarcating characteristic of genuine belief. In so far, belief is an appropriate name for the end of inquiry. But belief is a "double-barreled" word. It is used objectively to name *what* is believed. In this sense, the outcome of inquiry is a settled objective state of affairs, so settled that we are ready to act upon it, overtly or in imagination. *Belief* here names the settled condition of objective subject-matter, together with readiness to act in a given way when, if, and as, that subject-matter is present in existence. But in popular usage, *belief* also means a personal matter; something that some human being entertains or holds; a position, which under the influence of psychology, is converted into the notion that belief is merely a mental or psychical state. Associations from this signification of the word *belief* are likely to creep in when it is said that the end of inquiry is settled belief. The objective meaning of *subject-matter* as that is settled through inquiry is then dimmed or even shut out. The ambiguity of the word thus renders its use inadvisable for the purpose in hand.

The word *knowledge* is also a suitable term to designate the objective and close of inquiry. But it, too, suffers from ambiguity. When it is said that attainment of knowledge, or truth, is the end of inquiry the statement, according to the position here taken, is a truism. That which satisfactorily terminates inquiry is, by definition, knowledge; it is knowledge because it *is* the appropriate close of inquiry. But the statement may be supposed, and has been supposed, to enunciate something significant instead of a tautology. As a truism, it defines knowledge *as* the outcome of competent and controlled inquiry. When, however, the statement is thought to enunciate something significant, the case is reversed. Knowledge is then supposed to have a meaning of its own apart from connection with and reference to inquiry. The theory of inquiry is then necessarily subordinated to this meaning as a fixed external end. The opposition between the two views is basic. The idea that any knowledge in particular can be instituted apart from its being the consummation of inquiry, and that knowledge in general can be defined apart from this connection is, moreover, one of the sources of confusion in logical theory. For the different varieties of realism, idealism and dualism have their diverse conceptions of what "knowledge" really is. In consequence, logical theory is rendered subservient to metaphysical and epistemological preconceptions, so that interpretation of logical forms varies with underlying metaphysical assumptions.

The position here taken holds that since every special case of knowledge is constituted as the outcome of some special inquiry, the conception of knowledge as such can only be a generalization of the properties discovered to belong to conclusions which are outcomes of inquiry. Knowledge, as an abstract term, is a name for the product of competent inquiries. Apart from this relation, its meaning is so empty that any content or filling may be arbitrarily poured in. The general conception of knowledge, when formulated in terms of the outcome of inquiry, has something important to say regarding the meaning of inquiry itself. For it indicates that inquiry is a *continuing* process in every field with which it is engaged. The "settlement" of a particular situation by a particular inquiry is no guarantee that *that* settled conclusion will always remain settled. The attainment of settled beliefs is a progressive matter; there is no belief so settled as not to be exposed to further inquiry. It is the convergent and cumulative effect of continued inquiry that defines knowledge in its general meaning. In scientific inquiry, the criterion of what is taken to be settled, or to be knowledge, is being *so* settled that it is available as a resource in further inquiry; not being settled in such a way as not to be subject to revision in further inquiry.

What has been said helps to explain why the term "warranted assertion" is preferred to the terms *belief* and *knowledge*. It is free from the ambiguity of these latter terms, and it involves reference to inquiry as that which warrants assertion. When knowledge is taken as a general abstract term related to inquiry in the abstract, it means "warranted assertibility." The use of a term that designates a potentiality rather than an actuality involves recognition that all special conclusions of special inquiries are parts of an enterprise that is continually renewed, or is a going concern.[1]

Up to this point, it may seem as if the criteria that emerge from the processes of continuous inquiry were only descriptive, and in that sense empirical. That they are empirical in one sense of that ambiguous word is undeniable. They have grown out of the experiences of actual inquiry. But they are not empirical in the sense in which "empirical" means devoid of rational standing. Through examination of the *relations* which exist between means (methods) employed and conclusions attained as their consequence, reasons are discovered why some methods succeed and other methods fail. It is implied in what has been said (as a corollary of the general hypothesis) that rationality is an affair of the relation of *means and consequences*, not of fixed first principles as ultimate premises or as contents of what the Neo-scholastics call *criteriology*.

Reasonableness or rationality is, according to the position here taken, as well as in its ordinary usage, an affair of the relation of means and consequences. In framing ends-in-view, it is unreasonable to set up those which have no connection with available means and without reference to the obstacles standing in the way of

[1] C. S. Peirce, after noting that our scientific propositions are subject to being brought in doubt by the results of further inquiries, adds, "We ought to construct our theories so as to provide for such [later] discoveries . . . by leaving room for the modifications that cannot be foreseen but which are pretty sure to prove needful." (*Collected Papers*, Vol. V., p. 376 *n.*) The readers who are acquainted with the logical writings of Peirce will note my great indebtedness to him in the general position taken. As far as I am aware, he was the first writer on logic to make inquiry and its methods the primary and ultimate source of logical subject-matter.

attaining the end. It is reasonable to search for and select the means that will, with the maximum probability, yield the consequences which are intended. It is highly unreasonable to employ as means, materials and processes which would be found, if they were examined, to be such that they produce consequences which are different from the intended end; so different that they preclude its attainment. Rationality as an abstract conception is precisely the generalized idea of the means-consequence relation as such. Hence, from this point of view, the descriptive statement of methods that achieve progressively stable beliefs, or warranted assertibility, is also a *rational* statement in case the relation between them as means and assertibility as consequence is ascertained.

Reasonableness or rationality has, however, been hypostatized. One of the oldest and most enduring traditions in logical theory has converted rationality into a faculty which, when it is actualized in perception of first truths, was called *reason* and later, *Intellectus Purus*. The idea of *reason* as the power which intuitively apprehends *a priori* ultimate first principles persists in logical philosophy. Whether explicitly affirmed or not, it is the ground of every view which holds that scientific method is dependent upon logical forms that are logically prior and external to inquiry. The original ground for this conception of reason has now been destroyed. This ground was the necessity for postulating a faculty that had the power of direct apprehension of "truths" that were axiomatic in the sense of being self-evident, or self-verifying, and self-contained, as the necessary grounds of all demonstrative reasoning. The notion was derived from the subject-matter that had attained the highest scientific formulation at the time the classic logic was formulated; namely, *Euclidean geometry*.

This conception of the nature of axioms is no longer held in mathematics nor in the logic of mathematics. Axioms are now held to be postulates, neither true nor false in themselves, and to have their meaning determined by the consequences that follow because of their implicatory relations to one another. The greatest freedom is permitted, or rather encouraged, in laying down postulates—a freedom subject only to the condition that they be rigorously fruitful of implied consequences.

The same principle holds in physics. Mathematical formulae have now taken the place in physics once occupied by propositions about eternal essences and the fixed species defined by these essences. The formulae are deductively developed by means of rules of implication. But the value of the deduced result for physical science is not determined by the correctness of the deduction.

The deductive conclusion is used to instigate and direct operations of experimental observation. The observable consequences of these operations in their systematic correlation with one another finally determine the scientific worth of the deduced principle. The latter takes its place as a means necessary to obtain the consequence of warranted assertibility. The position here taken, the general hypothesis advanced, is a generalization of the means-consequence relation characteristic of mathematical and physical inquiry. According to it, all logical forms, such as are represented by what has been called *proximate logical* subject-matter, are instances of a relation between means and consequences in properly controlled inquiry, the word "controlled" in this statement standing for the methods of inquiry that are developed and perfected in the processes of continuous inquiry. In this continuity, the conclusions of any special inquiry are subordinate to use in substantiation and maturation of methods of further inquiry. The general character of knowledge as an abstract term is determined by the nature of the methods used, not *vice versa*.

The character of the generalization of the relation of "first principles" and conclusions (in mathematical and physical science) may be illustrated by the meaning of first principles in logic; such as traditionally represented by the principles, say, of identity, contradiction and excluded middle. According to one view, such principles represent ultimate invariant properties of the *objects* with which methods of inquiry are concerned, and to which inquiry must conform. According to the view here expressed, they represent conditions which have been ascertained during the conduct of continued inquiry to be involved in its own successful pursuit. The two statements may seem to *amount* to the same thing. Theoretically, there is a radical difference between them. For the second position implies, as has already been stated, that the principles are generated in the very process of control of continued inquiry, while, according to the other view, they are *a priori* principles fixed antecedently to inquiry and conditioning it *ab extra*.[2]

Neither the existence nor the indispensability of primary logical principles is, then, denied. The question concerns their origin and use. In what is said upon this matter I follow in the main the account given by Peirce of "guiding" or "leading" principles. According to this view, every inferential conclusion that is drawn involves a habit (either by way of expressing it or initiating it) in the *organic* sense of habit, since life is impossible without ways of action sufficiently general to be properly named *habits*. At the outset, the habit that operates in an inference is purely biological. It operates without our being aware of it. We are aware at most of particular acts and particular consequences. Later, we are aware not only of *what* is done from time to time but of *how* it is done. Attention to the way of doing is, moreover, indispensable to control of what is done. The craftsman, for example, learns that if he operates in a certain *way* the result will take care of itself, certain materials being given. In like fashion, we discover that if we draw our inferences in a certain way, we shall, other things being equal, get dependable conclusions. The *idea* of a method of inquiry arises as an articulate expression of the habit that is involved in a class of inferences.

Since, moreover, the habits that operate are narrower and wider in scope, the formulations of methods that result from observing them have either restricted or extensive breadth. Peirce illustrates the narrower type of habit by the following case: A person has seen a rotating disk of copper come to rest when it is placed between magnets. He infers that another piece of copper will behave similarly under like conditions. At first such inferences are made without formulation of a principle.[3] The disposition that operates is limited in scope. It does not extend beyond pieces of copper. But when it is found that there are habits involved in

---

[2] This point is discussed in Ch. XVII.

[3] I do not recall that Peirce alludes to Hume's doctrine of habit, or to Mill's "propensity" to generalize. The fact involved seems to be the same. But Peirce connects the fact, as Hume and Mill did not, with basic organic or biological functions instead of leaving habit as an ultimate "mysterious" tie.

every inference, in spite of differences of subject-matter, and when these habits are noted and formulated, then the formulations are guiding or leading principles. The principles state habits operative in every inference that tend to yield conclusions that are stable and productive in further inquiries. Being free from connection with any *particular* subject-matter, they are formal, not material, though they are forms of material that is subjected to authentic inquiry.

Validity of the principles is determined by the coherency of the consequences produced by the habits they articulate. If the habit in question is such as generally produces conclusions that are sustained and developed in further inquiry, then it is valid even if in an occasional case it yields a conclusion that turns out invalid. In such cases, the trouble lies in the material dealt with rather than with the habit and general principle. This distinction obviously corresponds to the ordinary distinction between form and matter. But it does not involve the complete separation between them that is often set up in logical theories.

Any habit is a way or manner of action, not a particular act or deed. When it is formulated it becomes, as far as it is accepted, a rule, or more generally, a principle or "law" of action. It can hardly be denied that there are habits of inference and that they may be formulated as rules or principles. If there are such habits as are necessary to conduct every successful inferential inquiry, then the formulations that express them will be logical principles of all inquiries. In this statement "successful" means operative in a manner that tends in the long run, or in continuity of inquiry, to yield results that are either confirmed in further inquiry or that are corrected by use of the same procedures. These guiding logical principles are not *premises* of inference or argument. They are conditions to be satisfied such that knowledge of them provides a principle of direction and of testing. They are formulations of ways of treating subject-matter that have been found to be so determinative of sound conclusions in the past that they are taken to regulate further inquiry until definite grounds are found for questioning them. While they are derived from examination of methods previously used in their connection with the kind of conclusion they have produced, they are *operationally a priori* with respect to further inquiry.[4]

In the previous discussion I have made statements whose full force can become clear only in the more detailed development of logical themes in subsequent chapters. The discussion, as was said at the outset, is not intended to justify the position but to clarify its general meaning. In the remaining pages of this Introduction I shall set forth certain implications of the position for the theory of logic.

1. *Logic is a progressive discipline.* The reason for this is that logic rests upon analysis of the best methods of inquiry (being judged "best" by their results with respect to continued inquiry) that exist at a given time. As the methods of the sciences improve, corresponding changes take place in logic. An enormous change has taken place in logical theory since the classic logic formulated the methods of the science that existed in its period. It has occurred in consequence of the development of mathematical and physical science. If, however, present theory provided a coherent formulation of existing scientific methods, freed from a doctrine of logical forms inherited from a science that is no longer held, this treatise would have no reason for existence. When in the future methods of inquiry are further changed, logical theory will also change. There is no ground for supposing that logic has been or ever will be so perfected that, save, perhaps, for minor details, it will require no further modification. The idea that logic is capable of final formulation is an *eidolon* of the theater.

2. *The subject-matter of logic is determined operationally.*[5] This thesis is a verbal restatement of what was earlier said. The methods of inquiry are operations performed or to be performed. Logical forms are the conditions that inquiry, *qua* inquiry, has

---

[4] As has been indicated, the above account is a free rendering of Peirce. See particularly his *Collected Papers,* Vol. III, pp. 154–68, and Vol. V. pp. 365–370.

[5] The word "operational" is not a substitute for what is designated by the word "instrumental." It expresses the way in and by which the subject-matter of inquiry is rendered the means to the end of inquiry, the institution of determinate existential situations. As a general term, "instrumental" stands for the relation of *means-consequence,* as the basic category for interpretation of logical forms, while "operational" stands for the conditions by which subject-matter is (1) rendered fit to serve as means and (2) actually functions as such means in effecting the objective transformation which is the end of inquiry.

to meet. Operations, to anticipate, fall into two general types. There are operations that are performed upon and with existential material—as in experimental observation. There are operations performed with and upon symbols. But even in the latter case, "operation" is to be taken in as literal a sense as possible. There are operations like hunting for a lost coin or measuring land, and there are operations like drawing up a balance-sheet. The former are performed upon existential conditions; the latter upon symbols. But the symbols in the latter case stand for *possible* final existential conditions while the conclusion, when it is stated in symbols, is a pre-condition of further operations that deal with existences. Moreover, the operations involved in making a balance-sheet for a bank or any other business involve physical activities. The so-called "mental" element in operations of both these kinds has to be defined in terms of existential conditions and consequences, not *vice-versa*.

Operations involve both material and instrumentalities, including in the latter tools and techniques. The more material and instrumentalities are shaped in advance with a view to their operating in conjunction with each other as means to consequences, the better the operations performed are controlled. Refined steel, which is the matter of the operations by which a watch-spring is formed, is itself the product of a number of preparatory operations executed with reference to getting the material into the state that fits it to be the material of the final operation. The material is thus as instrumental, from an operational point of view, as are the tools and techniques by which it is brought into a required condition. On the other hand, old tools and techniques are modified in order that they may apply more effectively to new materials. The introduction, for example, of the lighter metals demanded different methods of treatment from those to which the heavier metals previously used were subjected. Or, stated from the other side, the development of electrolytic operations made possible the use of new materials as means to new consequences.

The illustration is drawn from the operations of industrial arts. But the principle holds of operations of inquiry. The latter also proceed by shaping on one hand subject-matter so that it lends itself to the application of conceptions as modes of operation; and, on the other hand, by development of such conceptual structures as are applicable to existential conditions. Since, as in the arts, both movements take place in strict correspondence with each other, the conceptions employed are to be understood as directly operational, while the existential material, in the degree in which the conditions of inquiry are satisfied, is determined both *by* operations and with an eye *to* operations still to be executed.

3. *Logical forms are postulational.* Inquiry in order to be inquiry in the complete sense has to satisfy certain demands that are capable of formal statement. According to the view that makes a basic difference between logic and methodology, the requirements in question subsist prior to and independent of inquiry. Upon that view, they are final in themselves, not intrinsically postulational. This conception of them is the ultimate ground of the idea that they are completely and inherently *a priori* and are disclosed to a faculty called *pure reason.* The position here taken holds that they are intrinsically postulates of and for inquiry, being formulations of conditions, discovered in the course of inquiry itself, which further inquiries must satisfy if they are to yield warranted assertibility as a consequence.

Stated in terms of the means-consequence relation, they are a generalization of the nature of the means that must be employed if assertibility is to be attained as an end. Certain demands have to be met by the operations that occur in the arts. A bridge is to be built to span a river under given conditions, so that the bridge, as the consequence of the operations, will sustain certain loads. There are local conditions set by the state of the banks, etc. But there are general conditions of distance, weights, stresses and strains, changes of temperature, etc. These are formal conditions. As such they are demands, requirements, postulates, to be fulfilled.

A postulate is also a stipulation. To engage in an inquiry is like entering into a contract. It commits the inquirer to observance of certain conditions. A stipulation is a statement of conditions that are agreed to in the conduct of some affair. The stipulations involved are at first implicit in the undertaking of inquiry. As they are formally acknowledged (formulated), they become logical forms of various degrees of generality. They make definite what is involved in a demand. Every demand is a request, but not every request is a postulate. For a postulate involves the assumption of responsibilities. The responsibilities that are assumed are stated in stipulations. They involve readiness to act in certain specified ways. On this account, postulates are not arbitrarily chosen. They present claims to be met in the sense in which a claim presents a title or has authority to receive due consideration.

In engaging in transactions, human beings are not at first aware of the responsibilities that are implicit; for laws, in the legal sense, are explicit statements of what was previously only implicit in customs: namely, formal recognition of duties and rights that were *practically* involved in acceptance of the customs. One of the highly generalized demands to be met in inquiry is the following: "If anything has a certain property, and whatever has this property has a certain other property, then the thing in question has this certain other property." This logical "law" is a stipulation. If you are going to inquire in a way which meets the requirements of inquiry, you must proceed in a way which observes this rule, just as when you make a business contract there are certain conditions to be fulfilled.

A postulate is thus neither arbitrary nor externally *a priori*. It is not the former because it issues from the relation of means to the end to be reached. It is not the latter, because it is not imposed upon inquiry from without, but is an acknowledgement of that to which the undertaking of inquiry commits us. It is empirically and temporally *a priori* in the same sense in which the law of contracts is a rule regulating in advance the making of certain kinds of business engagements. While it is derived from what is involved in inquiries that have been successful in the past, it imposes a condition to be satisfied in future inquiries, until the results of such inquiries show reason for modifying it.

Terming logical forms postulates is, thus, on the negative side, a way of calling attention to the fact that they are not given and imposed from without. Just as the postulates of, say, geometry are not self-evident first truths that are externally imposed premises but are formulations of the conditions that have to be satisfied in procedures that deal with a certain subject-matter, so with logical forms which hold for *every* inquiry. In a contract, the agreement involved is that between the consequences of the activities of two or more parties with respect to some specified affair. In inquiry, the agreement is between the consequences of a series of inquiries. But inquiry as such is not carried on by one person rather than another. When any one person engages in it, he is committed, in as far as his inquiry is genuinely such and not an insincere bluff, to stand by the results of similar inquiries by whomever conducted. "Similar" in this phrase means inquiries that submit to the same conditions or postulates.

The postulational character of logical theory requires, accordingly, the most complete and explicit formulation that is attainable of not only the subject-matter that is taken as evidential in a given inference, but also of general conditions, stated in the rules and principles of inference and discourse. A distinction of matter and form is thus instituted. But it is one in which subject-matter and form correspond strictly to each other. Hence, once more, postulates are not arbitrary or mere linguistic conventions. They must be such as control the determination and arrangement of subject-matter with respect to achieving enduringly stable beliefs. Only after inquiry has proceeded for a considerable time and has hit upon methods that work successfully, is it possible to extract the postulates that are involved. They are not presuppositions at large. They are abstract in the sense that they are derived from analytic survey of the relations between methods as means and conclusions as consequences—a principle that exemplifies the meaning of rationality.

The postulational nature of logical theory thus agrees with what has been said about logic as progressive and operational. Postulates alter as methods of inquiry are perfected; the logical forms that express modern scientific inquiry are in many respects quite unlike those that formulated the procedures of Greek science. An experimenter in the laboratory who publishes his results states the materials used, the setup of apparatus and the procedures employed. These specifications are limited postulates, demands and stipulations, for any inquirer who wishes to test the conclusion reached. Generalize this performance for procedures of inquiry as such, that is, with respect to the form of every inquiry, and logical forms as postulates are the outcome.

4. *Logic is a naturalistic theory.* The term "naturalistic" has

many meanings. As it is here employed it means, on one side, that there is no breach of continuity between operations of inquiry and biological operations and physical operations. "Continuity," on the other side, means that rational operations *grow out of* organic activities, without being identical with that from which they emerge. There is an adjustment of means to consequences in the activities of living creatures, even though not directed by deliberate purpose. Human beings in the ordinary or "natural" processes of living come to make these adjustments purposely, the purpose being limited at first to local situations as they arise. In the course of time (to repeat a principle already set forth) the intent is so generalized that inquiry is freed from limitation to special circumstances. The logic in question is also naturalistic in the sense of the observability, in the ordinary sense of the word, of activities of inquiry. Conceptions derived from a mystical faculty of *intuition* or anything that is so occult as not to be open to public inspection and verification (such as the purely psychical for example) are excluded.

5. *Logic is a social discipline.* One ambiguity attending the word "naturalistic" is that it may be understood to involve reduction of human behavior to the behavior of apes, amebae, or electrons and protons. But man is *naturally* a being that lives in association with others in communities possessing language, and therefore enjoying a transmitted culture. Inquiry is a mode of activity that is socially conditioned and that has cultural consequences. This fact has a narrower and a wider import. Its more limited import is expressed in the connection of logic with symbols. Those who are concerned with "symbolic logic" do not always recognize the need for giving an account of the reference and function of symbols. While the relations of symbols to one another is important, symbols as such must be finally understood in terms of the function which symbolization serves. The fact that all languages (which include much more than speech) consist of symbols, does not of itself settle the nature of symbolism as that is used in inquiry. But, upon any naturalistic basis, it assuredly forms the point of departure for the logical theory of symbols. Any theory of logic has to take some stand on the question whether symbols are ready-made clothing for meanings

that subsist independently, or whether they are necessary conditions for the existence of meanings—in terms often used, whether language is the dress of "thought" or is something without which "thought" cannot be.

The wider import is found in the fact that every inquiry grows out of a background of culture and takes effect in greater or less modification of the conditions out of which it arises. Merely physical contacts with physical surroundings occur. But in every interaction that involves intelligent direction, the physical environment is part of a more inclusive social or cultural environment. Just as logical texts usually remark incidentally that reflection grows out of the presence of a problem and then proceed as if this fact had no further interest for the theory of reflection, so they observe that science itself is culturally conditioned and then dismiss the fact from further consideration.[6] This wider aspect of the matter is connected with what was termed the narrower. Language in its widest sense—that is, including all means of communication such as, for example, monuments, rituals, and formalized arts—is the medium in which culture exists and through which it is transmitted. Phenomena that are not recorded cannot be even discussed. Language is the record that perpetuates occurrences and renders them amenable to public consideration. On the other hand, ideas or meanings that exist *only* in symbols that are not communicable are fantastic beyond imagination. The naturalistic conception of logic, which underlies the position here taken, is thus *cultural naturalism*. Neither inquiry nor the most abstractly formal set of symbols can escape from the cultural matrix in which they live, move and have their being.

6. *Logic is autonomous*. The position taken implies the ultimacy of inquiry in determination of the formal conditions of inquiry. Logic as inquiry into inquiry is, if you please, a circular process; it does not depend upon anything extraneous to inquiry. The force of this proposition may perhaps be most readily understood by noting what it precludes. It precludes the determination

---

[6] "Not even the physicist is wholly independent of the context of experience provided for him by the society within which he works." Stebbing, *A Modern Introduction to Logic*, p. 16. If one includes in "society" the community of scientific workers, it would seem as if "even" should be changed to read, "the physicist almost more than anyone else."

and selection of logical first principles by an *a priori* intuitional act, even when the intuition in question is said to be that of *Intellectus Purus*. It precludes resting logic upon metaphysical and epistemological assumptions and presuppositions. The latter are to be determined, if at all, by means of what is disclosed as the outcome of inquiry; they are not to be shoved under inquiry as its "foundation." On the epistemological side, it precludes, as was noted earlier in another connection, the assumption of a prior ready-made definition of knowledge which determines the character of inquiry. Knowledge is to be defined in terms of inquiry, not *vice-versa*, both in particular and universally.

The autonomy of logic also precludes the idea that its "foundations" are psychological. It is not necessary to reach conclusions about sensations, sense-data, ideas and thought, or mental faculties generally, as material that preconditions logic. On the contrary, just as the specific meaning of these matters is determined in specific inquiries, so generally their relation to the logic of inquiry is determined by discovering the relation that the subject-matters to which these names are given bear to the effective conduct of inquiry as such. The point may be illustrated by reference to "thought." It would have been possible in the preceding pages to use the term "reflective thought" where the word "inquiry" has been used. But if that word had been used, it is certain that some readers would have supposed that "reflective thought" designated something already sufficiently known so that "inquiry" was equated to a preexisting definition of thought. The opposite view is implied in the position taken. We do not know what meaning is to be assigned to "reflective thought" except in terms of what is discovered by inquiry into inquiry; at least we do not know what it means for the purposes of logic. Personally, I doubt whether there exists anything that may be called *thought* as a strictly psychical existence. But it is not necessary to go into that question here. For even if there be such a thing, it does not determine the meaning of "thought" for logic.

Either the word "thought" has no business at all in logic or else it is a synonym of "inquiry" and its meaning is determined by what we find out about inquiry. The latter would seem to be the reasonable alternative. These statements do not mean that a sound psychology may not be of decided advantage to logical theory. For history demonstrates that unsound psychology has done great damage. But its general relation to logic is found in the light that it, as a branch of inquiry, may throw upon what is involved in inquiry. Its *generic* relation to logic is similar to that of physics or biology. Specifically, for reasons that will appear in subsequent chapters, its findings stand closer to logical theory than do those of the other sciences. Occasional reference to psychological subject-matter is inevitable in any case; for, as will be shown later, some logical positions that pride themselves upon their complete indifference to psychological considerations in fact rest upon psychological notions that have become so current, so embedded in intellectual tradition, that they are accepted uncritically as if they were self-evident.

The remaining chapters of Part One are preparatory to the later and more detailed outline of what is implied in the propositions (1) that logical theory is the systematic formulation of controlled inquiry, and (2) that logical forms accrue in and because of control that yields conclusions which are warrantably assertible. Were the general point of view even moderately represented in current theory these chapters would not be needed. In the present state of logical discussion they seem to me to be necessary. Chapters II and III consider the naturalistic background of the theory, one upon its biological side, the other upon the cultural. Chapters IV and V endeavor to state the need and importance of a revision of logical theory in the direction that has been set forth.

CHAPTER II

THE EXISTENTIAL MATRIX OF INQUIRY:
BIOLOGICAL

THIS CHAPTER and the following one are occupied with development of the statement that logic is naturalistic. The present chapter is concerned with the biological natural foundations of inquiry. It is obvious without argument that when men inquire they employ their eyes and ears, their hands and their brains. These organs, sensory, motor or central, are biological. Hence, although biological operations and structures are not sufficient conditions of inquiry, they are necessary conditions. The fact that inquiry involves the use of biological factors is usually supposed to pose a special metaphysical or epistomological problem, that of the mind-body relation. When thus shunted off into a special domain, its import for logical theory is ignored. When, however, biological functions are recognized to be indispensable constituents of inquiry, logic does not need to get enmeshed in the intricacies of different theories regarding the relations of mind and body. It suffices to accept the undeniable fact that they are necessary factors in inquiry, and then consider how they operate in its conduct. The purpose of the following discussion is to show that biological functions and structures prepare the way for deliberate inquiry and how they foreshadow its pattern.

The primary postulate of a naturalistic theory of logic is continuity of the lower (less complex) and the higher (more complex) activities and forms. The idea of continuity is not self-explanatory. But its meaning excludes complete rupture on one side and mere repetition of identities on the other; it precludes reduction of the "higher" to the "lower" just as it precludes complete breaks and gaps. The growth and development of any living organism from seed to maturity illustrates the meaning of continuity. The method by which development takes place is some-

23

thing to be determined by a study of what actually occurs. It is not to be determined by prior conceptual constructions, even though such constructions may be helpful as hypotheses when they are used to direct observation and experimentation.

We cannot, for example, say in advance that development proceeds by minute increments or by abrupt mutations; that it proceeds from the part to the whole by means of compounding of elements, or that it proceeds by differentiation of gross wholes into definite related parts. None of these possibilities are excluded as *hypotheses* to be tested by the results of investigation. What is excluded by the postulate of continuity is the appearance upon the scene of a totally new outside force as a cause of changes that occur. Perhaps from mutations that are due to some form of radio-activity a strikingly new form emerges. But radio-activity is not invented *ad hoc* and introduced from without in order to account for such transformation. It is first known to exist in nature, and then, if this particular theory of the origin of mutations is confirmed, is found actually to occur in biological phenomena and to be operative among them in observable and describable fashion. On the other hand, should the conclusion of scientific investigation be that development proceeds by minute increments, no amount of addition of such increments will constitute *development* save when their cumulative effect generates something new and different.

The application of the postulate of continuity to discussion of logical subject-matter means, therefore, negatively, that in order to account for the distinctive, and unique, characters of logical subject-matter we shall not suddenly evoke a new power or faculty like Reason or Pure Intuition. Positively and concretely, it means that a reasonable account shall be given of the ways in which it is possible for the traits that differentiate deliberate inquiry to develop out of biological activities not marked by those traits. It is possible, of course, to deal with what was called proximate logical subject-matter without raising this question. But it is cause for surprise that writers who energetically reject the intervention of the supernatural or the non-natural in every other scientific field feel no hesitancy in invoking Reason and *a priori* Intuition in the domain of logical theory. It would seem to be more incumbent

pon logicians than upon others to make their position in logic
oherent with their beliefs about other matters.

If one denies the supernatural, then one has the intellectual re-
ponsibility of indicating how the logical may be connected with
he biological in a process of continuous development. This point
eserves emphasis, for if the following discussion fails to fulfil the
ask of pointing out satisfactorily the continuous path, then that
ailure becomes, for those who accept the naturalistic postulate,
ut a challenge to perform the task better.

Whatever else organic life is or is not, it is a process of activity
hat involves an environment. It is a transaction extending be-
ond the spatial limits of the organism. An organism does not live
n an environment; it lives by means of an environment. Breath-
ng, the ingestion of food, the ejection of waste products, are cases
f *direct* integration; the circulation of the blood and the energiz-
ng of the nervous system are relatively *indirect*. But every or-
anic function is an interaction of intra-organic and extra-organic
nergies, either directly or indirectly. For life involves expendi-
ure of energy and the energy expended can be replenished only
s the activities performed succeed in making return drafts upon
he environment—the only source of restoration of energy. Not
ven a hibernating animal can live indefinitely upon itself. The
nergy that is drawn is not forced in from without; it is a conse-
uence of energy expended. If there is a surplus balance, growth
ccurs. If there is a deficit balance, degeneration commences.
here are things in the world that are indifferent to the life-
ctivities of an organism. But they are not parts of *its* environ-
ent, save potentially. The processes of living are enacted by the
nvironment as truly as by the organism; for they *are* an integra-
on.

It follows that with every differentiation of structure the en-
ironment expands. For a new organ provides a new way of in-
eracting in which things in the world that were previously
ndifferent enter into life-functions. The environment of an ani-
al that is locomotor differs from that of a sessile plant; that of a
elly fish differs from that of a trout, and the environment of any
sh differs from that of a bird. So, to repeat what was just said,
he difference is not just that a fish lives *in* the water and a bird *in*

the air, but that the characteristic functions of these animals are what they are because of the special way in which water and air enter into their respective activities.

With differentiation of interactions comes the need of maintaining a balance among them; or, in objective terms, a unified environment. The balance has to be maintained by a mechanism that responds both to variations that occur within the organism and in surroundings. For example, such an apparently self-contained function as that of respiration is kept constant by means of active exchanges between the alkaline and carbon dioxide contents of changing pressures exerted by the blood and the carbon dioxide in the lungs. The lungs in turn are dependent upon interactions effected by kidneys and liver, which effect the interactions of the circulating blood with materials of the digestive tract. This whole system of accurately timed interchanges is regulated by changes in the nervous system.

The effect of this delicate and complex system of internal changes is the maintenance of a fairly uniform integration with the environment, or—what amounts to the same thing—a fairly unified environment. The interactions of inanimate things with their surroundings are not such as to maintain a stable relation between the things involved. The blow of a hammer, for example, breaks a stone into bits. But as long as life normally continues, the interactions in which organic and environmental energies enter are such as to maintain the conditions in both of them needed for later interactions. The processes, in other words, are self-maintaining, in a sense in which they are not in the case of the interactions of non-living things.

Capacity for maintenance of a constant form of interaction between organism and environment is not confined to the individual organism. It is manifested also, in the reproduction of similar organisms. The stone is presumably indifferent as to how it reacts mechanically and chemically (within the limits of its potentialities) to other things. The stone may lose its individuality but basic mechanical and chemical processes go on uninterruptedly. As long as life continues, its processes are such as continuously to maintain and restore the enduring relationship which is characteristic of the life-activities of a given organism.

Each particular activity prepares the way for the activity that follows. These form not a mere succession but a series. This seriated quality of life activities is effected through the delicate balance of the complex factors in each particular activity. When the balance within a given activity is disturbed—when there is a proportionate excess or deficit in some factor—then there is exhibited need, search and fulfilment (or satisfaction) in the objective meaning of those terms. The greater the differentiation of structures and their corresponding activities becomes, the more difficult it is to keep the balance. Indeed, living may be regarded as a continual rhythm of disequilibrations and recoveries of equilibrium. The "higher" the organism, the more serious become the disturbances and the more energetic (and often more prolonged) are the efforts necessary for its reestablishment. The state of disturbed equilibration constitutes *need*. The movement towards its restoration is search and exploration. The recovery is fulfilment or satisfaction.

Hunger, for example, is a manifestation of a state of imbalance between organic and environmental factors in that integration which is life. This disturbance is a consequence of lack of full responsive adaptation to one another of various organic functions. The function of digestion fails to meet the demands made upon it directly by the circulatory system which carries replenishing nutritive material to all the organs concerned in the performance of other functions, and the demands indirectly made by motor activities. A state of tension is set up which is an actual state (not mere feeling) of organic uneasiness and restlessness. This state of tension (which defines need) passes into search for material that will restore the condition of balance. In the lower organisms it is expressed in the bulgings and retractions of parts of the organism's periphery so that nutritive material is ingested. The matter ingested initiates activities throughout the rest of the animal that lead to a restoration of balance, which, as the outcome of the state of previous tension, is fulfilment.

Rignano, in an instructive discussion of the biological basis of thinking, says that every organism strives to stay in a stationary state. He gives evidence from the activity of lower organisms which shows that activities occurring when their state is disturbed are such as tend to restore the former stationary condition.[1] He also states that "a prior physiological state cannot be perfectly re-established and made to persist in normal activity until an animal by its movements has succeeded in getting again into an environment identical with its old one." His position may be interpreted so that what is said in this text is in agreement with it. But as his treatment stands, it emphasizes *restoration* of the previous *state of the organism* rather than the institution of an integrated *relation.* The establishment of the latter relation is compatible with definite changes in both the organism and the environment; it does not require that old and new states of either the organism or the environments be identical with one another. Hence the difference in the two views is of considerable theoretical importance.

If we take as an example the search for food found in connection with the higher organisms, it appears clear that the very search often leads the organism into an environment that differs from the old one, and that the appropriation of food under new conditions involves a modified state of the organism. The *form* of the relationship, of the interaction, is reinstated, not the identical conditions. Unless this fact is recognized, development becomes an abnormal or an unusual matter rather than the normal feature of life activities. Need remains a constant factor but it changes its quality. With change in need comes a change in exploratory and searching activities; and that change is followed by a changed fulfilment or satisfaction. The conservative tendency is doubtless strong; there is a tendency to get *back.* But in at least the more complex organisms, the activity of search involves modification of the old environment, if only by a change in the connection of the organism with it. Ability to make and retain a changed mode of adaptation in response to new conditions is the source of that more extensive development called organic evolution. Of human organisms it is especially true that activities carried on for satisfying needs so change the environment that new needs arise which demand still further change in the activities of the organism by which they are satisfied; and so on in a potentially endless chain.

In the lower organisms, interaction between organic and en-

---

[1] *The Psychology of Reasoning,* English translation, p. 6, p. 11 and p. 31.

iron-energies takes place for the most part through direct contact. The tension in the organism is that between its surface and its interior. In the organisms that have distance receptors and special organs of locomotion, the serial nature of life behavior demands that earlier acts in the series be such as to prepare the way for the later. The time between the occurrence of need and the occurrence of its satisfaction inevitably becomes longer when the interaction is not one of direct contact. For the attainment of an integral relation is then dependent upon establishing connections with the things at a distance which arouse exploratory activity through stimulation of eye and ear. A definite order of initial, of intermediate, and of final or closing activities, is thus instituted. The terminus *ab quo* is fixed by such a condition of imbalance in the organism that integration of organic factors cannot be attained by any material with which the organism is in direct contact. Certain of its activities tend in one direction; others move in a different direction. More particularly, its existing contact-activities and those aroused by its distance-receptors, are at odds with each other, and the outcome of this tension is that the latter activities dominate. A satiated animal is not stirred by the sight or smell of the prey that moves him when he is hungry. In the hungry creature activities of search become a definite intervening or intermediate series. At each intermediate stage there is still tension between contact activities and those responsive to stimuli through distance-receptors. Movement continues until integration is established between contact and visual and motor activities, as in the consummatory act of devouring food.

What has been said describes a difference between modes of environing-organical interactions to which the names excitation-reaction and stimulus-response may be applied. An animal at rest is moved to sniff, say, by a sensory excitation. If this special relation is isolated and complete in itself, or is taken to be such, there is simply excitation-reaction, as when a person jumps but does nothing else when he hears a sudden noise. The excitation is specific and so is the reaction. Now suppose an excitation comes from a remote object through a distance-receptor, as, the eye. There is also excitation-reaction. But if the animal is aroused to an act of pursuit the situation is quite different. The particular sensory excitation occurs, but it is coordinated with a larger number of other organic processes—those of its digestive and circulatory organs and its neuro-muscular system, autonomic, proprioceptor and central. This coordination, which is a state of the total organism, constitutes a *stimulus*. The difference between this condition (whatever name it be called by) and a specific sensory excitation, is enormous. The pursuit of prey is a response to the total state of the organism, not to a particular sensory excitation Indeed, the distinction between what has been called stimulus and response is made only by analytic reflection. The so-called stimulus, being the total state of the organism, moves of itself, because of the tensions contained, into those activities of pursuit which are called the response. The stimulus is simply the earlier part of the total coordinated serial behavior and the response the later part.

The principle involved in the distinction just drawn is more important than it may seem to be at first sight. If it is ignored, the sequential character of behavior is lost from view. Behavior then becomes simply a succession of isolated and independent units of excitation-reaction, which would be comparable, say, to a succession of muscular twitches due to a disordered nervous mechanism. When the stimulus is recognized to be the tension in the total organic activity (ultimately reducible to that between contact activities and those occasioned through distance-receptors), it is seen that the stimulus in its *relationship* to special activities persists throughout the entire pursuit, although it changes its actual content at each stage of the chase. As the animal runs, specific sensory excitations, those of contact and those that are olfactory and visual, alter with every change of position; with every change in the character of the ground; with changing objects (like bushes and rocks) that progressively intervene; and they also change in intensity with every change in distance from the hunted object.

The changing excitations are, however, integrated into a single stimulus by the total state of the organism. The theory that identifies stimuli with a succession of specific sensory excitations, cannot possibly account for such unified and continuous responses as hunting and stalking prey. On that theory the animal would have to make at each stage a new and isolated "response" (reaction) to everything that came across his path. He would be reacting to stones, bushes and to changes in the levels and character of the ground in so many independent acts that there would be no continuity of behavior. He would forget, as we say, what he was after in the multitude of separate reactions he would have to make to independent excitations. Because behavior is in fact a function of the total state of the organism in relation to environment, stimuli are functionally constant in spite of changes in specific content. Because of this fact, behavior is sequential, one act growing out of another and leading cumulatively to a further act until the consummatory fully integrated activity occurs.

Because organic behavior is what it is, and not a succession and compounding of independent discrete reflex-arc units, it has direction and cumulative force. There are special acts, like winking or the knee-jerk, that exemplify the isolated reflex-arc that is sometimes supposed to be the unit which, through compounding, constitutes behavior. But there is no evidence that such acts have played any role in development. On the contrary, the available evidence shows that they are end-points of highly specialized lines of development, or else are coincident by-products of the behavior of structures that have arisen developmentally.

What exists in normal behavior-development is thus a circuit of which the earlier or "open" phase is the tension of various elements of organic energy, while the final and "closed" phase is the institution of integrated interaction of organism and environment. This integration is represented upon the organic side by equilibration of organic energies, and upon the environmental side by the existence of satisfying conditions. In the behavior of higher organisms, the close of the circuit is not identical with the state out of which disequilibration and tension emerged. A certain modification of environment has also occurred, though it may be only a change in the conditions which future behavior must meet. On the other hand, there is change in the organic structures that conditions further behavior. This modification constitutes what is termed habit.

Habits are the basis of organic learning. According to the theory of independent successive units of excitation-reaction, habit-formation can mean only the increasing fixation of certain ways of behavior through repetition, and an attendant weakening of other behavioral activities.[2]

Developmental behavior shows, on the other hand, that in the higher organisms excitations are so diffusely linked with reactions that the sequel is affected by the state of the organism in relation to environment. In habit and learning the linkage is tightened up not by sheer repetition but by the institution of effective integrated interaction of organic-environing energies—the consummatory close of activities of exploration and search. In organisms of the higher order, the special and more definite pattern of recurrent behavior thus formed does not become completely rigid. It enters as a factorial agency, along with other patterns, in a total adaptive response, and hence retains a certain amount of flexible capacity to undergo further modifications as the organism meets new environing conditions.

There is, for example, reciprocal excitation between hand and eye activity; a movement of the hand is aroused by visual activity, then the movement of the hand is followed by a change in visual activity, and so on. Here is a definite recurring pattern of action. If the hand never did but one thing, say reach, then this habit-pattern might become rigidly set. But the hand also grabs, pushes, draws and manipulates. Visual behavior has to be responsive to the performance of a great variety of manual activities. It thus maintains flexibility and readaptability; the connection between hand and eye does not become a rigid bond.

The view that habits are formed by sheer repetition puts the cart before the horse. Ability to repeat is a result of a formation of a habit through the organic redispositions effected by attainment of a consummatory close. This modification is equivalent to giving some definite direction to future actions. As far as environing conditions remain much the same, the resulting act will look like a repetition of a previously performed act. But even then repetition will not be exact as far as conditions differ. Sheer repetition

---

[2] The effect of terminal success or consummatory satisfaction in determining habit has always been a stumbling-block to those who hold that there are elementary excitation-reaction "bonds." But this effect is just what should be expected on the ground of the view expounded in the text, since it is an expression of the fact that the stimulus-response relation is a function of the state of the organism as a whole.

s, in the case of the human organism, the product of conditions that are uniform because they have been made so mechanically—as in much school and factory "work." Such habits are limited in their manifestation to the rather artificial conditions in which they operate. They certainly do not provide the model upon which a theory of habit formation and operation should be framed.

From the foregoing considerations certain general conclusions follow as to the nature of the pattern of inquiry as a development out of certain aspects of the pattern of life-activities.[3]

1. Environmental conditions and energies are inherent in inquiry as a special mode of organic behavior. Any account of inquiry that supposes the factors involved in it, say, doubt, belief, observed qualities and ideas, to be referable to an isolated organism (subject, self, mind) is bound to destroy all ties between inquiry as reflective thought and as scientific method. Such isolation logically entails a view of inquiry which renders absurd the idea that there is a necessary connection between inquiry and logical theory. But the absurdity rests upon the acceptance of an unexamined premise which is the product of a local "subjectivistic" phase of European philosophy. If what is designated by such terms as doubt, belief, idea, conception, is to have any objective meaning, to say nothing of public verifiability, it must be located and described as behavior in which organism and environment act together, or *inter*-act.

The earlier discussion set out with the familiar common sense distinction of organism and environment, and went on to speak of their interaction. Unfortunately, however, a special philosophical interpretation may be unconsciously read into the common sense distinction. It will then be supposed that organism and environment are "given" as independent things and interaction is a third independent thing which finally intervenes. In fact, the distinction is a practical and temporal one, arising out of the state of tension in which the organism at a given time, in a given phase of life-activity, is set over against the environment as it then and there exists. There is, of course, a natural world that exists independently of the organism, but this world is *environment* only as it enters directly and indirectly into life-functions. The organism is

---

[3] The more specific points of connection are taken up in Ch. VI.

itself a part of the larger natural world and exists as organism only in active connections with its environment.

Integration is more fundamental than is the distinction designated by interaction of organism *and* environment. The latter is indicative of a partial disintegration of a prior integration, but one which is of such a dynamic nature that it moves (as long as life continues) toward redintegration.

2. The structure and course of life-behavior has a definite pattern, spatial and temporal. This pattern definitely foreshadows the general pattern of inquiry. For inquiry grows out of an earlier state of settled adjustment, which, because of disturbance, is indeterminate or problematic (corresponding to the first phase of tensional activity), and then passes into inquiry proper, (corresponding to the searching and exploring activities of an organism); when the search is successful, belief or assertion is the counterpart, upon this level, of redintegration upon the organic level.

A detailed account of the pattern of inquiry is given in Chapter VI. But the following considerations flow so directly from the pattern of life-behavior that they should be noted here:

a. There is no inquiry that does not involve the making of *some* change in environing conditions. This fact is exemplified in the indispensable place of experiment in inquiry, since experimentation is deliberate modification of prior conditions. Even in the pre-scientific stage, an individual moves head, eyes, often the entire body, in order to determine the conditions to be taken account of in forming a judgment; such movements effect a change in environmental relations. Active pressure by touch, the acts of pushing, pulling, pounding and manipulating to find out what things "are like" is an even more overt approach to scientific experimentation.

b. The pattern is serial or sequential. It has already been noted that this trait of life-behavior becomes more marked with the emergence of distance-receptors and of the neural apparatus necessary for coordinating their excitation with contact-receptors and with the muscular, circulatory and respiratory mechanisms which are involved in behavior. In the human organism, organic retention (or habit-patterns) give rise to recollection. Goals or consequences that are even more remote in time and space are then set up and the intervening process of search becomes more seriated in temporal span and in connecting links than in the case of the simple presence of distance-stimuli. Formation of an end-in-view, or consequence to be brought about, is conditioned by recollection; it requires making plans in conjunction with selection and ordering of the consecutive means by which the plan may become an actuality.

c. The serially connected processes and operations by means of which a consummatory close is brought into being are, by description, intermediate and instrumental. This distinctive characteristic prefigures, on the biological level, the interpretation that must be given, upon the level of inquiry, to operations of inference and discourse in their relation to final judgment as the consummation of inquiry.

d. The basic importance of the serial relation in logic is rooted in the conditions of life itself. Modification of both organic and environmental energies is involved in life-activity. This organic fact foreshadows learning and discovery, with the consequent outgrowth of new needs and new problematic situations. Inquiry, in settling the disturbed relation of organism-environment (which defines doubt) does not merely remove doubt by recurrence to a prior adaptive integration. It institutes new environing conditions that occasion new problems. What the organism learns during this process produces new powers that make new demands upon the environment. In short, as special problems are resolved, new ones tend to emerge. There is no such thing as a final settlement, because every settlement introduces the conditions of some degree of a new unsettling. In the stage of development marked by the emergence of science, deliberate institution of problems becomes an objective of inquiry. Philosophy, in case it has not lost touch with science, may play an important role in determining formulation of these problems and in suggesting hypothetical solutions. But the moment philosophy supposes it can find a final and comprehensive solution, it ceases to be inquiry and becomes either apologetics or propaganda.

e. From the postulate of naturalistic continuity, with its prime corollary that inquiry is a development out of organic-environmental integration and interaction, something follows regarding the relation of psychology and logic. The negative side of this conclusion has already been suggested. The assumptions of "mentalistic" psychology have no place in logical theory. The divorce between logic and scientific methodology, discussed in the previous chapter, has its basis largely in the belief that since inquiry involves doubt, suggestion, observation, conjecture, sagacious discernment, etc., and since it is assumed that all these things are "mentalistic," there is a gulf between inquiry (or reflective thinking) and logic. Given the assumption, the conclusion is just. But the recognition of the natural continuity of inquiry with organic behavior—the fact that it is a developed mode of such behavior—destroys the assumption. The student of intellectual history is aware of how the new scientific standpoint of the sixteenth and seventeenth centuries succeeded in setting up a gulf between the mental and the physical. The former was supposed to constitute a domain of existence of psychical "stuff" marked by processes totally unlike those of the external world which confronted "mind." The older Greek conception that the difference was one in the type of *organization* of common materials and processes, was lost from view. Psychology and epistemology accepted complete dualism, the "bifurcation" of nature, and the theory of thought and ideas was wrought into conformity with the dualistic assumption.

On the positive side, psychology is itself a special branch of inquiry. In general, it bears the same relation to the theory of logical inquiry that is sustained by physics or chemistry. But as it is more directly concerned with the focal center of initiation and execution of inquiry than are these other sciences, it may, if employed as servant and not as master of logic, make a contribution to logical theory which they cannot make. Personally, as has just been said, I doubt the existence of anything "mental" in the doctrinal sense alleged. But it is not necessary to go into that question, for, as was stated, if there is anything of this kind it is irrelevant to the theory of inquiry. Moreover, any investigation into it must itself be an inquiry that satisfies the logical conditions of all inquiry. Nevertheless, whatever throws any light upon the organic conditions and processes that are involved in the occurrence and conduct of inquiry (as a sound biological psychology cannot fail to do) can hardly fail to make valuable contributions to the results of inquiry into inquiry.

The points that have been made may be gathered together by consideration of the current meaning of "experience," especially in connection with the intensified ambiguity, due to historical changes, that is attached to "empirical." Experience has a favorable or honorific use, as when it is said that a certain conclusion or theory is experientially verified, and is thereby marked off from a wild fancy, a happy guess and from a *merely* theoretical construction. On the other hand, because of the influence of psychological epistemology of a subjective, private type, "experience" has been limited to conscious states and processes. The contrast of the two meanings is radical. When it is said that certain conclusions are experientially or empirically confirmed, a scientist means anything but that they rest upon mental and personal states of mind. Again, the word "empirical" is often set in opposition to the *rational,* and this opposition adds to the confusion. The early meaning of "empirical" limited the application of the word to conclusions that rest upon an accumulation of past experiences to exclusion of insight into principles.

Thus a medical practitioner may have skill in recognizing the symptoms of disease and skill in their treatment because of repeated past observations and customary modes of treatment, without understanding the etiology of disease and the reasons for the kind of treatment employed. The same thing holds of the skills of many mechanics and artisans. "Empirical" in this sense describes an actual fact and is justly distinguished from "rational" activity, meaning, by that word, conduct grounded in understanding of principles. But it is evident that when a scientific conclusion is said to be empirically established, no such exclusion of rationality or reasoning is intended or involved. On the contrary, every conclusion scientifically reached as to matters of fact involves reasoning with and from principles, usually mathematically expressed. To say, then, that it is empirically established is to say the opposite of what is said when "empirical" means only observations and habitual response to what is observed. The conversion of a justifiable distinction between empirical as defined in terms of the knowledge and action of artisans and rational as defined in terms of scientific understanding, into something absolute which sets every mode of experience in opposition to reason and the rational, depends accordingly, upon an arbitrary preconception as to what experience and its limits *must* be. Unfortunately, this arbitrary limitation still operates, as in many interpretations of the distinction between, say, temporal and eternal objects, perception and conception, and, more generally, matter and form.

It may be added that the honorific use of "experience" when it first appeared was undoubtedly overweighted upon the side of observation, as in the case of Bacon and Locke. This overweight is readily accounted for as a historic occurrence. For the classic tradition had degenerated into a form in which it was supposed that beliefs about matters of fact could and should be reached by reasoning alone; save as they were established by authority. Opposition to this extreme view evoked an equally one-sided notion that mere sense-perception could satisfactorily determine beliefs about matters of fact. It led in Bacon, as later in Mill, to a neglect of the role of mathematics in scientific inquiry, and in Locke to a pretty sharp division between knowledge of matters of fact and of relations between ideas. The latter, moreover, rested finally according to him upon sheer observation, "internal" or "external." The final outcome was a doctrine that reduced "experience" to "sensations" as the constituents of all observation, and "thought" to external associations among these elements, both sensations and associations being supposed to be merely mental or psychical.

The problem of the relation between material that is observed and subject-matter that is conceived or thought of is a real one, especially in respect to its logical equivalents. But the solution of the problem should not be compromised at the outset by a statement of it in terms of a fixed and absolute distinction between the experiential and the rational. Such a statement implies that there is no logical problem, but a separation absolutely and immediately given. Justification cannot be given at this stage of the discussion for the belief that, in a proper conception of experience, inference, reasoning and conceptual structures are as experiential as is observation, and that the fixed separation between the former and the latter has no warrant beyond an episode in the history of culture. Upon the basis of the naturalistic position here taken, there is a problem, which takes the following form: How does it come about that the development of organic behavior into controlled inquiry brings about the differentiation and cooperation of observational and conceptual operations?

The discussion of language and linguistic symbols in the following chapter lays the basis for an answer. But it must be repeated that adherence to a tradition that was formed before modern scientific inquiry (including the biological) had arisen or been subjected to independent analysis, should not be permitted to convert a problem that holds for all schools alike, into an alleged ready-made solution. For such a solution prevents the problem from being seen as a problem. Finally, while the position here taken implies that logic is empirical in that its subject-matter consists of inquiries that are publicly accessible and open to observation, it is not empirical in the sense in which Mill, for example, developed the ideas of Locke and Hume. It is experiential in the same way in which the subject-matter and conclusions of any natural science are empirical: experiential in the way any natural science is experiential, that is, as distinct from the merely speculative and from the *a priori* and intuitional.

I close with a reference to a predicament in which both organic behavior and deliberate inquiry are caught. There always exists a discrepancy between means that are employed and consequences that ensue; sometimes this discrepancy is so serious that its result is what we call mistake and error. The discrepancy exists because the means used, the organs and habits of biological behavior and the organs and conceptions employed in deliberate inquiry, must be present and actual, while consequences to be attained are future. Present actual means are the result of past conditions and past activities. They operate successfully, or "rightly," in (1) the degree in which existing environing conditions are very similar to those which contributed in the past to formation of the habits, and (2) in the degree in which habits retain enough flexibility to readapt themselves easily to new conditions. The latter condition is not readily fulfilled by lower organisms; when it is fulfilled a case of "evolution" occurs. The potential conditions for its fulfilment are present in the activities of human beings in much larger measure. But the inertial phase of habit is strong, and, so far as it is yielded to, human beings continue to live upon a relatively animal plane. Even the history of science has been marked by epochs in which observation and reflection have operated only within a predetermined conceptual framework—an example of the inertia-phase of habit. That the only way to avoid and avert the mistakes of this fixation is by recognition of the provisional and conditional nature (as respects any inquiry in process) of the facts that enter into it, and the hypothetical nature of the conceptions and theories employed, is a relatively late discovery. The meaning of the discovery has hardly penetrated yet into inquiry about the subjects of the greatest practical importance to man, religion, politics and morals.

The recognition of what Peirce called "fallibilism" in distinction from "infallibilism" is something more than a prudential maxim. It results of necessity from the possibility and probability of a discrepancy between means available for use and consequences that follow: between past and future conditions, not from mere weakness of mortal powers. Because we live in a world in process, the future, although continuous with the past, is not its bare repetition. The principle applies with peculiar force to inquiry about inquiry, including, needless to say, the inquiry presented in this treatise. The very words which must be used are words that have had their meanings fixed in the past to express ideas that are unlike those which they must now convey if they are to express what is intended. To those who are naturalistically inclined, the attendant "fallibility" will be but a spur to do better the work which this volume attempts to do. The present volume is an approach not a closed treatise. The aim it hopes to fulfil is that of being a sufficiently coherent and systematic approach to move others to undertake the long cooperative work (never-ending in any case as long as inquiry continues) needed to test and fill in the framework which is outlined in this book.

The important matter is that those who reject the doctrine of the intervention of some supernatural agency should not be led, by the fact that it is not customary to introduce biological considerations into the discussion of logical theory, to dismiss the chapter as irrelevant. Those who believe in such intervention have ground for belief in an *a priori* Reason upon which logical forms and principles depend; they are precommitted to belief in the irrelevancy of all considerations of the order of those here presented. But any thoroughgoing naturalist is equally committed by the logic of his position to belief in continuity of development, with its corrollary of community of factors in the respective patterns of logical and biological forms and procedures.

CHAPTER III

THE EXISTENTIAL MATRIX OF INQUIRY: CULTURAL

THE ENVIRONMENT in which human beings live, act and inquire, is not simply physical. It is cultural as well. Problems which induce inquiry grow out of the relations of fellow beings to one another, and the organs for dealing with these relations are not only the eye and ear, but the meanings which have developed in the course of living, together with the ways of forming and transmitting culture with all its constituents of tools, arts, institutions, traditions and customary beliefs.

I. To a very large extent the ways in which human beings respond even to physical conditions are influenced by their cultural environment. Light and fire are physical facts. But the occasions in which a human being responds to things as merely physical in purely physical ways are comparatively rare. Such occasions are the act of jumping when a sudden noise is heard, withdrawing the hand when something hot is touched, blinking in the presence of a sudden increase of light, animal-like basking in sunshine, etc. Such reactions are on the biological plane. But the typical cases of human behavior are not represented by such examples. The *use* of sound in speech and listening to speech, making and enjoying music; the kindling and tending of fire to cook and to keep warm; the production of light to carry on and regulate occupations and social enjoyments:—these things are representative of distinctively human activity.

To indicate the full scope of cultural determination of the conduct of living one would have to follow the behavior of an individual throughout at least a day; whether that of a day laborer, of a professional man, artist or scientist, and whether the individual be a growing child or a parent. For the result would show how thoroughly saturated behavior is with conditions and factors that

are of cultural origin and import. Of distinctively human behavior it may be said that the strictly physical environment is so
incorporated in a cultural environment that our interactions with
the former, the problems that arise with reference to it, and our
ways of dealing with these problems, are profoundly affected by
incorporation of the physical environment in the cultural.

Man, as Aristotle remarked, is a *social* animal. This fact introduces him into situations and originates problems and ways of
solving them that have no precedent upon the organic biological
level. For man is social in another sense than the bee and ant,
since his activities are encompassed in an environment that is culturally transmitted, so that what man does and how he acts, is determined not by organic structure and physical heredity alone but
by the influence of cultural heredity, embedded in traditions, institutions, customs and the purposes and beliefs they both carry
and inspire. Even the neuro-muscular structures of individuals
are modified through the influence of the cultural environment
upon the activities performed. The acquisition and understanding
of language with proficiency in the arts (that are foreign to other
animals than men) represent an incorporation within the physical
structure of human beings of the effects of cultural conditions, an
interpenetration so profound that resulting activities are as direct
and seemingly "natural" as are the first reactions of an infant. To
speak, to read, to exercise any art, industrial, fine or political, are
instances of modifications wrought *within* the biological organism
by the cultural environment.

This modification of organic behavior in and by the cultural environment accounts for, or rather is, the transformation of purely
organic behavior into behavior marked by intellectual properties
with which the present discussion is concerned. Intellectual operations are foreshadowed in behavior of the biological kind, and the
latter prepares the way for the former. But to foreshadow is not
to exemplify and to prepare is not to fulfil. Any theory that
rests upon a naturalistic postulate must face the problem of the
extraordinary differences that mark off the activities and achievements of human beings from those of other biological forms. It
is these differences that have led to the idea that man is completely
separated from other animals by properties that come from a non-

natural source. The conception to be developed in the present chapter is that the development of language (in its widest sense) out of prior biological activities is, in its connection with wider cultural forces, the key to this transformation. The problem, so viewed, is not the problem of the transition of organic behavior into something wholly discontinuous with it—as is the case when, for example, Reason, Intuition and the *A priori* are appealed to for explanation of the difference. It is a special form of the general problem of continuity of change and the emergence of new modes of activity—the problem of development at any level.

Viewing the problem from this angle, its constituents may be reduced to certain heads, three of which will be noted. Organic behavior is centered in *particular* organisms. This statement applies to inferring and reasoning as existential activities. But if inferences made and conclusions reached are to be valid, the subject-matter dealt with and the operations employed must be such as to yield identical results for all who infer and reason. If the same evidence leads different persons to different conclusions, then either the evidence is only speciously the same, or one conclusion (or both) is wrong. The *special* constitution of an individual organism which plays such a role in biological behavior is so irrelevant in controlled inquiry that it has to be discounted and mastered.

Another phase of the problem is brought out by the part played in human judgments by emotion and desire. These *personal* traits cook the evidence and determine the result that is reached. That is, upon the level of organic factors (which are the actively determining forces in the type of cases just mentioned), the individual with his individual peculiarities, whether native or acquired, is an active participant in producing ideas and beliefs, and yet the latter are logically grounded only when such peculiarities are deliberately precluded from taking effect. This point restates what was said in connection with the first point, but it indicates another phase of the matter. If, using accepted terminology, we say that the first difference is that between the singular and the general, the present point may be formulated as the difference between the subjective and the objective. To be intellectually "objective" is to discount and eliminate merely personal factors in the operations by which a conclusion is reached.

Organic behavior is a strictly temporal affair. But when behavior is *intellectually* formulated, in respect both to general ways of behavior and the special environing conditions in which they operate, propositions result and the terms of a proposition do not sustain a temporal relation to one another. It was a temporal event when someone landed on Robinson Crusoe's island. It was a temporal event when Crusoe found the footprint on the sands. It was a temporal event when Crusoe inferred the presence of a possibly dangerous stranger. But while the proposition was *about* something temporal, the *relation* of the observed fact as evidential to the inference drawn from it is non-temporal. The same holds of every logical relation in and of propositions.

In the following discussion it is maintained that the solution of the problem just stated in some of its phases, is intimately and directly connected with cultural subject-matter. Transformation from organic behavior to intellectual behavior, marked by logical properties, is a product of the fact that individuals live in a cultural environment. Such living compels them to assume in their behavior the standpoint of customs, beliefs, institutions, meanings and projects which are at least relatively general and objective.[1]

II. Language occupies a peculiarly significant place and exercises a peculiarly significant function in the complex that forms the cultural environment. It is itself a cultural institution, and, from one point of view, is but one among many such institutions. But it is (1) the agency by which other institutions and acquired habits are *transmitted*, and (2) it *permeates* both the forms and the contents of all other cultural activities. Moreover, (3) it has its own distinctive structure which is capable of abstraction as a *form*. This structure, when abstracted as a form, had a decisive influence historically upon the formulation of logical theory; the symbols which are appropriate to the form of language as an agency of inquiry (as distinct from its original function as a medium of communication) are still peculiarly relevant to logical theory. Consequently, further discussion will take the wider cultural environment for granted and confine itself to the especial function of language in effecting the transformation of the biological into the intellectual and the potentially logical.

---

[1] The non-temporal phase of propositions receives attention later.

In this further discussion, language is taken in its widest sense, a sense wider than oral and written speech. It includes the latter. But it includes also not only gestures but rites, ceremonies, monuments and the products of industrial and fine arts. A tool or machine, for example, is not simply a simple or complex physical object having its own physical properties and effects, but is also a mode of language. For it *says* something, to those who understand it, about operations of use and their consequences. To the members of a primitive community a loom operated by steam or electricity says nothing. It is composed in a foreign language, and so with most of the mechanical devices of modern civilization. In the present cultural setting, these objects are so intimately bound up with interests, occupations and purposes that they have an eloquent voice.

The importance of language as the necessary, and, in the end, sufficient condition of the existence and transmission of non-purely organic activities and their consequences lies in the fact that, on one side, it is a strictly biological mode of behavior, emerging in natural continuity from earlier organic activities, while, on the other hand, it compels one individual to take the standpoint of other individuals and to see and inquire from a standpoint that is not strictly personal but is common to them as participants or "parties" in a conjoint undertaking. It may be directed by and towards some physical existence. But it first has reference to some other person or persons with whom it institutes *communication*— the making of something common. Hence, to that extent its reference becomes general and "objective."

Language is made up of physical existences; sounds, or marks on paper, or a temple, statue, or loom. But these do not *operate* or function as mere physical things when they are media of communication. They operate in virtue of their *representative* capacity or *meaning*. The particular physical existence which has meaning is, in the case of speech, a conventional matter. But the convention or common consent which sets it apart as a means of recording and communicating meaning is that of agreement in *action*; of shared modes of responsive behavior and participation in their consequences. The physical sound or mark gets its meaning in and by conjoint community of functional use, not by any explicit convening in a "convention" or by passing resolutions that a certain sound or mark shall have a specified meaning. Even when the meaning of certain legal words is determined by a court, it is not the agreement of the judges which is finally decisive. For such assent does not finish the matter. It occurs for the sake of determining future agreements in associated *behavior*, and it is this subsequent behavior which finally settles the actual meaning of the words in question. Agreement in the proposition arrived at is significant only through this function in promoting agreement in action.

The reason for mentioning these considerations is that they prove that the meaning which a conventional symbol has is not itself conventional. For the meaning is established by agreements of different persons in existential activities having reference to existential consequences. The particular existential sound or mark that stands for *dog* or *justice* in different cultures is arbitrary or conventional in the sense that although it has *causes* there are no *reasons* for it. But *in so far* as it is a medium of communication, its meaning is common, because it is constituted by existential conditions. If a word varies in meaning in intercommunication between different cultural groups, then to that degree communication is blocked and misunderstanding results. Indeed, there ceases to be communication until variations of understanding can be translated, through the meaning of words, into a meaning that is the same to both parties. Whenever communication is blocked and yet is supposed to exist misunderstanding, not merely absence of understanding, is the result. It is an error to suppose that the misunderstanding is about the meaning of the *word* in isolation, just as it is fallacious to suppose that because two persons accept the same dictionary meaning of a word they have therefore come to agreement and understanding. For agreement and disagreement are determined by the consequences of conjoint activities. Harmony or the opposite exists in the effects produced by the several activities that are occasioned by the words used.

III. Reference to concord of consequences as the determinant of the meaning of any sound used as a medium of communication shows that there is no such thing as a *mere* word or *mere* symbol. The physical existence that is the vehicle of meaning may as a particular be called *mere;* the recitation of a number of such sounds or the stringing together of such marks may be called *mere* language. But in fact there is no word in the first case and no language in the second. The activities that occur and the consequences that result which are not determined by meaning, are, by description, only physical. A sound or mark of any physical existence is a part of *language* only in virtue of its *operational* force; that is, as it functions as a means of evoking different activities performed by different persons so as to produce consequences that are shared by all the participants in the conjoint undertaking. This fact is evident and direct in oral communication. It is indirect and disguised in written communication. Where written literature and literacy abound, the conception of language is likely to be framed upon their model. The intrinsic connection of language with community of action is then forgotten. Language is then supposed to be simply a means of expressing or communicating "thoughts"—a means of conveying ideas or meanings that are complete in themselves apart from communal operational force.

Much literature is read, moreover, simply for enjoyment, for esthetic purposes. In this case, language is a means of action only as it leads the reader to build up pictures and scenes to be enjoyed by himself. There ceases to be immediate inherent reference to conjoint activity and to consequences mutually participated in. Such is not the case, however, in reading to get at the meaning of the author; that is, in reading that is emphatically intellectual in distinction from esthetic. In the mere reading of a scientific treatise there is, indeed, no direct overt participation in action with another to produce consequences that are *common* in the sense of being immediately and personally shared. But there must be imaginative construction of the materials and operations which led the author to certain conclusions, and there must be agreement or disagreement with his conclusions as a consequence of following through conditions and operations that are imaginatively reinstated.

Connection with overt activities is in such a case indirect or mediated. But so far as definite grounded agreement or disagreement is reached, an attitude is formed which is a preparatory readiness to act in a responsive way when the conditions in question or others similar to them actually present themselves. The connection with action in question is, in other words, with *possible* ways of operation rather than with those found to be *actually* and immediately required.[2] But preparation for *possible* action in situations not as yet existent in actuality is an essential condition of, and factor in, all intelligent behavior. When persons meet together in conference to plan in advance of actual occasions and emergencies what shall later be done, or when an individual deliberates in advance regarding his possible behavior in a possible future contingency, something occurs, but more directly, of the same sort as happens in understanding intellectually the meaning of a scientific treatise.

I turn now to the positive implication of the fact that no sound, mark, product of art, is a word or part of language in isolation. Any word or phrase has the meaning which it has only as a member of a constellation of related meanings. Words as representatives are part of an inclusive code. The code may be public or private. A public code is illustrated in any language that is current in a given cultural group. A private code is one agreed upon by members of special groups so as to be unintelligible to those who have not been initiated. Between these two come argots of special groups in a community, and the technical codes invented for a restricted special purpose, like the one used by ships at sea. But in every case, a particular word has its meaning only in relation to the code of which it is one constituent. The distinction just drawn between meanings that are determined respectively in fairly direct connection with action in situations that are present or near at hand, and meanings determined for possible use in remote and contingent situations, provides the basis upon which language codes as systems may be differentiated into two main kinds.

While all language or symbol-meanings are what they are as parts of a system, it does not follow that they have been determined on the basis of their fitness to be such members of a system; much less on the basis of their membership in a comprehensive

---

[2] Literature and literary habits are a strong force in building up that conception of separation of ideas and theories from practical activity which is discussed in ensuing chapters.

system. The system may be simply the language in common use. Its meanings hang together not in virtue of their examined relationship to one another, but because they are current in the same set of group habits and expectations. They hang together because of group activities, group interests, customs and institutions. Scientific language, on the other hand, is subject to a test over and above this criterion. Each meaning that enters into the language is expressly determined in its relation to other members of the language system. In all reasoning or ordered discourse this criterion takes precedence over that instituted by connection with cultural habits.

The resulting difference in the two types of language-meanings fundamentally fixes the difference between what is called common sense and what is called science. In the former cases, the customs, the *ethos* and spirit of a group is the decisive factor in determining the system of meanings in use. The system is one in a practical and institutional sense rather than in an intellectual sense. Meanings that are formed on this basis are sure to contain much that is irrelevant and to exclude much that is required for intelligent control of activity. The meanings are coarse, and many of them are inconsistent with each other from a logical point of view. One meaning is appropriate to action under certain institutional group conditions; another, in some other situation, and there is no attempt to relate the different situations to one another in a coherent scheme. In an intellectual sense, there are many languages, though in a social sense there is but one. This multiplicity of language-meaning constellations is also a mark of our existing culture. A word means one thing in relation to a religious institution, still another thing in business, a third thing in law, and so on. This fact is the real Babel of communication. There is an attempt now making to propagate the idea that education which indoctrinates individuals into some special tradition provides the way out of this confusion. Aside from the fact that there are in fact a considerable number of traditions and that selection of some one of them, even though that one be internally consistent and extensively accepted, is arbitrary, the attempt reverses the *theoretical* state of the case. Genuine community of language or symbols can be achieved only through efforts that bring about community of activities under existing conditions. The ideal of scientific-language is construction of a system in which meanings are related to one another in inference and discourse and where the symbols are such as to indicate the relation.

I shall now introduce the word "symbol" giving it its signification as a synonym for a word *as* a word, that is, as a meaning carried by language in a system, whether the system be of the loose or the intellectual rigorous kind.[3] The especial point in the introduction of the word "symbol" is to institute the means by which discrimination between what is designated by it and what is now often designated by *sign* may be instituted. What I have called symbols are often called "artificial signs" in distinction from what are called *natural signs.*

IV. It is by agreement in conjoint action of the kind already described, that the *word* "smoke" stands in the English language for an object of certain qualities. In some other language the same vocable and mark may stand for something different, and an entirely different sound stand for "smoke." To such cases of representation the word *"artificial signs"* applies. When it is said that smoke as an actual existence points to, is evidence of, an existential fire, smoke is said to be a *natural* sign of fire. Similarly, heavy clouds of given qualities are a natural sign of probable rain, and so on. The representative capacity in question is attributed to *things in their connection with one another*, not to marks whose meaning depends upon agreement in social use. There is no doubt of the existence and the importance of the distinction designated by the words "natural" and "artificial" signs. But the fundamentally important difference is not brought out by these words. For reasons now to be given, I prefer to mark the difference by confining the application of *sign* to so-called "natural signs"—employing *symbol* to designate "artificial signs."

The difference just stated is actual. But it fails to note the distinctive intellectual property of what I call symbols. It is, so to

---

[3] This signification is narrower than the popular usage, according to which anything is a symbol that has representative *emotional* force even if that force be independent of its intellectual representational force. In this wider sense, a national flag, a crucifix, a mourning garb, etc., are symbols. The definition of the text is in so far arbitrary. But there is nothing arbitrary about the *subject-matters* to which the limited signification applies.

speak, an incidental and external fact, logically speaking, that certain things are given representative function by social agreement. The fact becomes logically relevant only because of the possibility of free and independent development of meanings in discourse which arises when once symbols are instituted. A "natural sign," by description, is something that exists in an actual spatial-temporal context. Smoke, as a thing having certain observed qualities, is a sign of fire only when the thing exists and is observed. Its representative capacity, taken by itself, is highly restricted, for it exists only under limited conditions. The situation is very different when the *meaning* "smoke" is embodied in an existence, like a sound or a mark on paper. The actual quality found in existence is then subordinate to a representative office. Not only can the sound be produced practically at will, so that we do not have to wait for the occurrence of the object; but, what is more important, the meaning when embodied in an indifferent or neutral existence is *liberated* with respect to its representative function. It is no longer tied down. It can be related to other meanings in the language-system; not only to that of fire but to such apparently unrelated meanings as friction, changes of temperature, oxygen, molecular constitution, and, by intervening meaning-symbols, to the laws of thermodynamics.

I shall, accordingly, in what follows, connect *sign* and *significance*, *symbol* and *meaning*, respectively, with each other, in order to have terms to designate two different kinds of representative capacity. Linguistically, the choice of terms is more or less arbitrary, although sign and significance have a common verbal root. This consideration is of no importance, however, compared with the necessity of having some words by which to designate the two kinds of representative function. For purposes of theory the important consideration is that existent things, as signs, are *evidence* of the existence of something else, this something being at the time *inferred* rather than observed.

But words, or symbols, provide no *evidence* of any existence. Yet what they lack in this capacity they make up for in creation of another dimension. They make possible ordered discourse or reasoning. For this may be carried on without any of the existences to which symbols apply being actually present: without, inleed, assurance that objects to which they apply anywhere actually exist, and, as in the case of mathematical discourse, without direct reference to existence at all.

Ideas as ideas, hypotheses as hypotheses, would not exist were t not for symbols and meanings as distinct from signs and significances. The greater capacity of symbols for manipulation is of practical importance. But it pales in comparison with the fact that symbols introduce into inquiry a dimension different from that of existence. Clouds of certain shapes, size and color may signify to us the probability of rain; they portend rain. But the *word* cloud when it is brought into connection with other words of a symbol-constellation enable us to relate the meaning of being a cloud with such different matters as differences of temperature and pressures, the rotation of the earth, the laws of motion, and so on.

The difference between sign-significance and symbol-meaning (in the sense defined) is brought out in the following incident.[4] A visitor in a savage tribe wanted on one occasion "the word for Table. There were five or six boys standing around, and tapping the table with my forefinger I asked 'What is this?' One boy said it was *dodela*, another that it was an *etanda*, a third stated that it was *bokali*, a fourth that it was *elamba*, and the fifth said it was *meza*." After congratulating himself on the richness of the vocabulary of the language the visitor found later "that one boy had thought he wanted the word for tapping; another understood we were seeking the word for the material of which the table was made; another had the idea that we required the word for hardness; another thought we wished the name for that which covered the table; and the last . . . gave us the word *meza*, table."

This story might have been quoted earlier as an illustration of the fact that there is not possible any such thing as a direct one-to-one correspondence of names with existential objects; that words mean what they mean in connection with conjoint activities that effect a common, or mutually participated in, consequence. The word sought for was involved in conjoint activities looking to a common end. The act of tapping in the illustration was isolated from any such situation. It was, in consequence,

[4] Quoted by and from Ogden and Richards, *The Meaning of Meaning*, p. 174.

wholly indeterminate in reference; it was no part of *communication*, by which alone acts get significance and accompanying words acquire meaning.[5] For the point in hand, the anecdote illustrates the lack of any evidential status in relation to existence of the symbols or representative values that have been given the name "meanings." Without the intervention of a specific kind of existential operation they cannot indicate or discriminate the *objects* to which they refer. Reasoning or ordered discourse, which is defined by development of symbol-meanings in relation to one another, may (and should) provide a basis for performing these operations, but of itself it determines no existence. This statement holds no matter how comprehensive the meaning-system and no matter how rigorous and cogent the relations of meanings to one another. On the other hand, the story illustrates how, in case the right word had been discovered, the meaning symbolized would have been capable of entering into relations with any number of other meanings independently of the actual presence at any given time of the object *table*. Just as the sign-significance relation defines *inference*, so the relation of meanings that constitutes propositions defines *implication* in discourse, if it satisfies the intellectual conditions for which it is instituted. Unless there are words which mark off the two kinds of relations in their distinctive capacities and offices, with reference to existence, there is danger that two things as logically unlike as inference and implication will be confused. As a matter of fact, the confusion, when inference is treated as identical with implication, has been a powerful agency in creating the doctrinal conception that logic is purely formal—for, as has been said, the relation of meanings (carried by symbols) to one another is, *as such*, independent of existential reference.[6]

V. So far the word "relation" has been rather indiscriminately employed. The discussion has now reached a point where it is necessary to deal with the ambiguity of the word as it is used not

---

[5] Another aspect of the same general principle, not directly connected with language, is brought out later in consideration of the meaning of any demonstrated object in relation to "*this*."

[6] A farther important logical aspect of this matter is dealt with below in the necessity of distinguishing *judgment* from propositions, and *involvement* from *implication*.

merely in ordinary speech but in logical texts. The word "relation" is used to cover three very different matters which in the interest of a coherent logical doctrine must be discriminated. (1) Symbols are "related" directly to one another; (2) they are "related" to existence by the mediating intervention of existential operations; (3) existences are "related" to one another in the evidential sign-signified function. That these three modes of "relation" are different from one another and that the use of one and the same word tends to cover up the difference and thereby create doctrinal confusion, is evident.

In order to avoid, negatively, the disastrous doctrinal confusion that arises from the ambiguity of the word *relation,* and in order to possess, positively, linguistic means of making clear the logical nature of the different subject-matters under discussion, I shall reserve the word *relation* to designate the kind of "relation" which symbol-meanings bear to one another *as* symbol-meanings. I shall use the term *reference* to designate the kind of relation they sustain to existence; and the words *connection* (and *involvement*) to designate that kind of relation sustained by *things* to one another in virtue of which *inference* is possible.

The differences, when once pointed out, should be so obvious as hardly to require illustration. Consider, however, propositions of mathematical physics. (1) As propositions they form a system of *related* symbol-meanings that may be considered and developed as such. (2) But as propositions of *physics,* not of mere mathematics, they have *reference* to existence; a reference which is realized in operations of *application.* (3) The final test of *valid* reference or applicability resides in the *connections* that exist among things. Existential involvement of things with one another alone warrants inference so as to enable further connections among things themselves to be discovered.

The question may be raised whether meaning-relations in discourse arise before or after significance-connections in existence. Did we first infer and then use the results to engage in discourse? Or did relations of meanings, instituted in discourse, enable us to detect the connections in things in virtue of which some things are evidential of other things? The question is rhetorical in that the question of historical priority cannot be settled. The question is asked, however, in order to indicate that in any case ability to treat things as signs would not go far did not symbols enable us to mark and retain just the qualities of things which are the ground of inference. Without, for example, words or symbols that discriminate and hold on to the experienced qualities of sight and smell that constitute a thing "smoke," thereby enabling it to serve as a sign of fire, we might react to the qualities in question in animal-like fashion and perform activities appropriate to them. But no inference could be made that was not blind and blundering. Moreover, since *what* is inferred, namely fire, is not present in observation, any anticipation that could be formed of it would be vague and indefinite, even supposing an anticipation could occur at all. If we compare and contrast the range and the depth of the signifying capacity of existential objects and events in a savage and a civilized group and the corresponding power of inference, we find a close correlation between it and the scope and the intimacy of the relations that obtain between symbol-meanings in discourse. Upon the whole, then, it is language, originating as a medium of communication in order to bring about deliberate co-operation and competition in conjoint activities, that has conferred upon existential things their signifying or evidential power.

VI. We are thus brought back to the original problem: namely, transformation of animal activities into intelligent behavior having the properties which, when formulated, are *logical* in nature. Associated behavior is characteristic not only of plants and animals, but of electrons, atoms and molecules; as far as we know of everything that exists in nature. Language did not originate association, but when it supervened, as a natural emergence from previous forms of animal activity, it reacted to transform prior forms and modes of associated behavior in such a way as to give experience a new dimension.

1. "Culture" and all that culture involves, as distinguished from "nature," is both a condition and a product of language. Since language is the only means of retaining and transmitting to subsequent generations *acquired* skills, acquired information and acquired habits, it is the latter. Since, however, meanings and the significance of events differ in different cultural groups, it is also the former.

2. Animal activities, such as eating and drinking, searching for food, copulation, etc., acquire new properties. Eating food becomes a group festival and celebration; procuring food, the art of agriculture and exchange; copulation passes into the institution of the family.

3. Apart from the existence of symbol-meanings the results of prior experience are retained only through strictly organic modifications. Moreover, these modifications once made, tend to become so fixed as to retard, if not to prevent, the occurrence of further modifications. The existence of symbols makes possible deliberate recollection and expectation, and thereby the institution of new combinations of selected elements of experiences having an intellectual dimension.

4. Organic biological activities end in overt actions, whose consequences are irretrievable. When an activity and its consequences can be rehearsed by representation in symbolic terms, there is no such final commitment. If the representation of the final consequence is of unwelcome quality, overt activity may be foregone, or the way of acting be replanned in such a way as to avoid the undesired outcome.[7]

These transformations and others which they suggest, are not of themselves equivalent to accrual of logical properties to behavior. But they provide requisite conditions for it. The use of meaning-symbols for institution of purposes or ends-in-view, for deliberation, as a rehearsal through such symbols of the activities by which the ends may be brought into being, is at least a rudimentary form of reasoning in connection with solution of problems. The habit of reasoning once instituted is capable of indefinite development on its own account. The ordered development of meanings in their relations to one another may become an engrossing interest. When this happens, implicit logical conditions are made explicit and then logical theory of some sort is born. It may be imperfect; it will be imperfect from the standpoint of the inquiries and symbol-meanings that later develop. But the first step, the one that costs and counts, was taken when some one began to

[7] Generalizing beyond the strict requirements of the position outlined, I would say that I am not aware of any so-called merely "mental" activity or result that cannot be described in the objective terms of an organic activity modified and directed by symbols-meaning, or language, in its broad sense.

reflect upon language, upon *logos*, in its syntactical structure and its wealth of meaning contents. Hypostization of *Logos* was the first result, and it held back for centuries the development of inquiries of a kind that are competent to deal with the problems of the existent world. But the hypostization was, nevertheless, a tribute to the power of language to generate reasoning and, through application of the meanings contained in it, to confer fuller and more ordered significance upon existence.

In later chapters we shall consider in some detail how a logic of ordered discourse, a logic that gathered in a system the relations which hold meanings consistently together in discourse, was taken to be the final model of logic and thereby obstructed the development of effective modes of inquiry into existence, preventing the necessary reconstruction and expansion of the very meanings that were used in discourse. For when these meanings in their ordered relations to one another were taken to be final in and of themselves, they were directly superimposed upon nature. The necessity of existential operations for application of meanings to natural existence was ignored. This failure reacted into the system of meanings as meanings. The result was the belief that the requirements of rational discourse constitute the measure of natural existence, the criterion of complete Being. It is true that logic emerged as the Greeks became aware of language as Logos with the attendant implication that a system of ordered meanings is involved.

This perception marked an enormous advance. But it suffered from two serious defects. Because of the superior status assigned to forms of rational discourse, they were isolated from the operations by means of which meanings originate, function and are tested. This isolation was equivalent to the hypostization of Reason. In the second place, the meanings that were recognized were ordered in a gradation derived from and controlled by a class-structure of Greek society. The means, procedures and kinds of organization that arose from active or "practical" participation in natural processes were given a low rank in the hierarchy of Being and Knowing. The scheme of knowledge and of Nature became, without conscious intent, a mirror of a social order in which craftsmen, mechanics, artisans generally, held a low position in comparison with a leisure class. Citizens as citizens were also occupied with doing, a doing instigated by need or lack. While possessed of a freedom denied to the artisan class, they were also taken to fail in completely self-contained and self-sufficient activity. The latter was exemplified only in the exercise of Pure Reason untainted by need for anything outside itself and hence independent of all operations of doing and making. The historic result was to give philosophic, even supposedly ontological, sanction to the cultural conditions which prevented the utilization of the immense potentialities for attainment of knowledge that were resident in the activities of the arts—resident in them because they involve operations of active modification of existing conditions which contain the procedures constituting the experimental method when once they are employed for the sake of obtaining knowledge, instead of being subordinated to a scheme of uses and enjoyments controlled by given socio-cultural conditions.

CHAPTER IV.

COMMON SENSE AND SCIENTIFIC INQUIRY

UPON THE biological level, organisms have to respond to conditions about them in ways that modify those conditions and the relations of organisms to them so as to restore the reciprocal adaptation that is required for the maintenance of life-functions. Human organisms are involved in the same sort of predicament. Because of the effect of cultural conditions, the problems involved not only have different contents but are capable of statement *as* problems so that inquiry can enter as a factor in their resolution. For in a cultural environment, physical conditions are modified by the complex of customs, traditions, occupations, interests and purposes which envelops them. Modes of response are correspondingly transformed. They avail themselves of the significance which things have acquired, and of the *meanings* provided by language. Obviously, rocks as minerals signify something more in a group that has learned to work iron than is signified either to sheep and tigers or to a pastoral or agricultural group. The meanings of related symbols, which form the language of a group, also, as was shown in the last chapter, introduce a new type of attitudes and hence of modes of response. I shall designate the environment in which human beings are *directly* involved the common sense environment or "world," and inquiries that take place in making the required adjustments in behavior common sense inquiries.

As is brought out later, the problems that arise in such situations of interaction may be reduced to problems of the use and enjoyment of the objects, activities and products, material and ideological, (or "ideal") of the world in which individuals live. Such inquiries are, accordingly, different from those which have knowledge as their goal. The attainment of knowledge of some things is necessarily involved in common sense inquiries, but it occurs 'or the sake of settlement of some issue of use and enjoyment, ind not, as in scientific inquiry, for its own sake. In the latter, 'here is no *direct* involvement of human beings in the *immediate* :nvironment—a fact which carries with it the ground of distin- ;uishing the theoretical from the practical.

The use of the term *common sense* is somewhat arbitrary from ι linguistic point of view. But the existence of the kinds of situa- :ions referred to and of the kind of inquiries that deal with the difficulties and predicaments they present cannot be doubted. They are those which continuously arise in the conduct of life and the ordering of day-by-day behavior. They are such as con-· stantly arise in the development of the young as they learn to make their way in the physical and social environments in which they live; they occur and recur in the life-activity of every adult, whether farmer, artisan, professional man, law-maker or adminis- trator; citizen of a state, husband, wife, or parent. On their very face they need to be discriminated from inquiries that are distinc- tively scientific, or that aim at attaining confirmed facts, "laws" and theories.

They need, accordingly, to be designated by some distinctive word, and *common sense* is used for that purpose. Moreover, the term is not wholly arbitrary even from the standpoint of linguis- tic usage. In the Oxford Dictionary, for example, is found the following definition of common sense: "Good sound practical sense; combined tact and readiness in dealing with the ordinary affairs of life." Common sense in this signification applies to be- havior in its connection with the *significance* of things.

There is, clearly, a distinctively intellectual content involved; *good sense* is, in ordinary language, good *judgment*. Sagacity is power to discriminate the factors that are relevant and important in significance in given situations; it is power of discernment; in a proverbial phrase, ability to tell a hawk from a hernshaw, chalk from cheese, and to bring the discriminations made to bear upon what is to be done and what is to be abstained from, in the "ordi- nary affairs of life." That which, in the opening paragraphs, was called the mode of inquiry dealing with situations of use and en- joyment, is, after all, but a formal way of saying what the dic- tionary states in its definition of common sense.

There is, however, another dictionary definition: "The general sense, feeling, judgment of mankind or a community." It is in this sense that we speak of the *deliverances* of common sense as if they were a body of settled truths. It applies not to things in their significance but to *meanings* accepted. When the Scottish school of Reid and Stewart erected "common sense" into an ultimate authority and arbiter of philosophic questions, they were carrying this signification to its limit. The reference to practical sagacity in dealing with problems of response and adaptation in use and enjoyment has now gone into the background. "Common" now means "*general.*" It designates the conceptions and beliefs that are currently accepted without question by a given group or by mankind in general. They are *common* in the sense of being widely, if not universally, accepted. They are *sense*, in the way in which we speak of the "sense of a meeting" and in which we say things do or do not "make sense." They have something of the same ultimacy and immediacy for a group that "sensation" and "feeling" have for an individual in his contact with surrounding objects. It is a commonplace that every cultural group possesses a set of meanings which are so deeply embedded in its customs, occupations, traditions and ways of interpreting its physical environment and group-life, that they form the basic categories of the language-system by which details are interpreted. Hence they are regulative and "normative" of specific beliefs and judgments.

There is a genuine difference between the two meanings of common sense. But from the standpoint of a given group there is a definite deposit of agreement. They are both of them connected with the conduct of life in relation to an existing environment: one of them in judging the significance of things and events with reference to what should be done; the other, in the ideas that are used to direct and justify activities and judgments. Tabus are, first, customary ways of activities. To us they are mistaken rather than sagacious ways of action. But the system of meanings embodied in the language that carries tradition gives them authority in such highly practical matters as the eating of food and the behavior that is proper in the presence of chieftains and members of the family configuration, so that they control the relations of males and females and persons of various kinship degrees. To us, such conceptions and beliefs are highly impractical; to those who held them they were matters of higher practical importance than were special modes of behavior in dealing with particular objects. For they set the standards for judging the latter and acting in reference to them. It is possible today, along with our knowledge of the enormous differences that characterize various cultures, to find some unified deposit of activities and of meanings in the "common sense and feeling of *mankind*," especially in matters of basic social cohesion.

In any case, the difference between the two meanings may be reduced, without doing violence to the facts, to the difference between phases and aspects of special practical situations that are looked into, questioned and examined with reference to what may or should be done at a particular time and place and the rules and precepts that are taken for granted in reaching all conclusions and in all socially correct behavior. Both are concerned, one directly and the other indirectly, with "the ordinary affairs of life," in the broad sense of life.

I do not suppose that a generalization of the inquiries and conclusions of this type under the caption of "use and enjoyment" needs much exposition for its support. Use and enjoyment are the ways in which human beings are directly connected with the world about them. Questions of food, shelter, protection, defense, etc., are questions of the use to be made of materials of the environment and of the attitudes to be taken practically towards members of the same group and to other groups taken as wholes. Use, in turn, is for the sake of some consummation or enjoyment. Some things that are far beyond the scope of direct use, like stars and dead ancestors, are objects of magical use, and of enjoyment in rites and legends. If we include the correlative negative ideas of disuse, of abstinence from use, and toleration and suffering, problems of use and enjoyment may be safely said to exhaust the domain of common sense inquiry.

There is direct connection between this fact and the concern of common sense with the *qualitative*. It is by discernment of qualities that the fitness and capacity of things and events for use is decided; that proper foodstuffs, for example, are told or discriminated from those that are unfit, poisonous or tabued. Tha enjoyment-suffering is qualitative through and through and is concerned with situations in their pervasive qualitative character, is almost too obvious for mention. Furthermore, the operations and responses that are engaged in use and enjoyment of situations are qualitatively marked off. Tanning skins is a process qualitatively different from that of weaving baskets or shaping clay into jars the rites that are responsive to death are qualitatively different from those appropriate to birth and weddings. Inferiors, superiors and equals are treated in modes of greeting and approach that are qualitatively unlike.

The reason for calling attention to these commonplace facts is that they bring out the basic difference between the subject-matters characteristic of common sense and of scientific inquiries; and they also indicate the differences between the problems and procedures of inquiry that are characteristic of common sense in different stages of culture. I shall first consider the latter point Common sense in respect to both its content of ideas and beliefs, and its methods of procedure, is anything but a constant. Both its content and its methods alter from time to time not merely in detail but in general pattern. Every invention of a new tool and utensil, every improvement in technique, makes some difference in what is used and enjoyed and in the inquiries that arise with reference to use and enjoyment, with respect to both significance and meaning. Changes in the regulative scheme of relations within a group, family, clan or nation, react even more intensively into some older system of uses and enjoyments.

One has only to note the enormous differences in the contents and methods of common sense in modes of life that are respectively dominantly nomadic, agricultural and industrial. Much that was once taken without question as a matter of common sense is forgotten or actively condemned. Other old conceptions and convictions continue to receive theoretical assent and strong emotional attachment because of their prestige. But they have little hold and application in the ordinary affairs of life. For example, ideas and practices which, in primitive tribes, were interwoven with practically every concern of ordinary affairs, are later relegated to a separate domain, religious or esthetic.

The business of one age becomes the sport and amusement of another age. Even scientific theories and interpretations continue to be affected by conceptions that have ceased to be determinative in the actual practice of inquiry. The special bearing of the fact that "common sense" is anything but a constant upon logical formulations, will concern us in the sequel. Here it is enough to call attention to a point which will later receive detailed examination: namely, the very fitness of the Aristotelian logical organon in respect to the culture and common sense of a certain group in the period in which it was formulated unfits it to be a logical formulation of not only the science but even of the common sense of the present cultural epoch.

I recur now to the bearing of the fact that common sense inquiries are concerned with qualitative matter and operations upon their distinction from scientific inquiries. Fundamentally, the distinction is that brought out in the previous chapter: Namely, that between significances and meanings that are determined in reference to pretty direct existential application and those that are determined on the ground of their systematic relations of coherence and consistency with one another. All that the present mode of statement adds is that, in the first case, "existential application" means application in *qualitative* use and enjoyment of the environment. On the other hand, both the history of science and the present state of science prove that the goal of the systematic relationship of facts and conceptions to one another is dependent upon *elimination* of the qualitative as such and upon reduction to non-qualitative formulation.

The problem of the relation of the domain of common sense to that of science has notoriously taken the form of opposition of the qualitative to the non-qualitative; largely, but not exclusively, the quantitative. The difference has often been formulated as the difference between perceptual material and a system of conceptual constructions. In this form it has constituted, in recent centuries, the chief theme of epistemology and metaphysics. From the standpoint that controls the present discussion, the problem is not epistemological (save as that word means the *logical*) nor is it metaphysical or ontological. In saying that it is logical, it is affirmed that the question at issue is that of the relation to each other of different kinds of *problems,* since difference in the type of problem demands different emphases in inquiry. It is because of this fact that different logical forms accrue to common sense and scientific objects. From this point of view, the question, summarily stated, is that of the relation to each other of the subject-matters of practical uses and concrete enjoyments and of scientific conclusions; not the subject matters of two different domains whether epistemological or ontological.

The conclusion to be later reached is here anticipated to serve as a guide in following the further discussion. (1) Scientific subject-matter and procedures grow out of the direct problems and methods of common sense, of practical uses and enjoyments, and (2) react into the latter in a way that enormously refines, expands and liberates the contents and the agencies at the disposal of common sense. The separation and opposition of scientific subject-matter to that of common sense, when it is taken to be final, generates those controversial problems of epistemology and metaphysics that still dog the course of philosophy. When scientific subject-matter is seen to bear genetic and functional relation to the subject-matter of common sense, these problems disappear. Scientific subject-matter is intermediate, not final and complete in itself.

I begin the discussion by introducing and explaining the denotative force of the word *situation.* Its import may perhaps be most readily indicated by means of a preliminary negative statement. What is designated by the word "situation" is *not* a single object or event or set of objects and events. For we never experience nor form judgments about objects and events in isolation, but only in connection with a contextual whole. This latter is what is called a "situation." I have mentioned the extent in which modern philosophy had been concerned with the problem of existence as perceptually and conceptually determined. The confusions and fallacies that attend the discussion of this problem have a direct and close connection with the difference between an object and a situation. Psychology has paid much attention to the question of the *process* of perception, and has for its purpose described the perceived object in terms of the results of analysis of the process.

I pass over the fact that, no matter how legitimate the virtual identification of process and product may be for the special purpose of *psychological* theory, the identification is thoroughly dubious as a generalized ground of philosophical discussion and theory. I do so in order to call attention to the fact that by the very nature of the case the psychological treatment takes a *singular* object or event for the subject-matter of its analysis. In actual experience, there is never any such isolated singular object or event; *an* object or event is always a special part, phase, or aspect, of an environing experienced world—a situation. The singular object stands out conspicuously because of its especially focal and crucial position at a given time in determination of some problem of use or enjoyment which the *total* complex environment presents. There is always a *field* in which observation of *this* or *that* object or event occurs. Observation of the latter is made for the sake of finding out what that *field* is with reference to some active adaptive response to be made in carrying forward a *course* of behavior. One has only to recur to animal perception, occurring by means of sense organs, to note that isolation of what is perceived from the course of life-behavior would be not only futile, but obstructive, in many cases fatally so.

A further conclusion follows. When the act and object of perception are isolated from their place and function in promoting and directing a successful course of activities in behalf of use-enjoyment, they are taken to be exclusively *cognitive*. The perceived object, orange, rock, piece of gold, or whatever, is taken to be an object of *knowledge per se*. In the sense of being discriminatingly noticed, it *is* an object of knowledge, but not of knowledge as ultimate and self-sufficient. It is noted or "known" only so far as guidance is thereby given to direction of behavior; so that the situation in which it is found can be appropriately enjoyed or some of its conditions be so used that enjoyment will result or suffering be obviated. It is only when an object of focal observation is regarded as an object of knowledge in isolation that there arises the notion that there are two kinds of knowledge, and two kinds of objects of knowledge, so opposed to each other that philosophy must either choose which is "real" or find some way of reconciling their respective "realities." When it is seen that in common sense inquiry there is no attempt made to know the object or event *as such* but only to determine what it signifies with respect to the way in which the entire situation should be dealt with, the opposition and conflict do not arise. The object or event in question is perceived as part of the environing world, not in and by itself; it is rightly (validly) perceived if and when it acts as clew and guide in use-enjoyment. We live and act in connection with the existing environment, not in connection with isolated objects, even though a singular thing may be crucially significant in deciding how to respond to total environment.

Recurring to the main topic, it is to be remarked that a situation is a whole in virtue of its immediately pervasive quality. When we describe it from the psychological side, we have to say that the situation as a qualitative whole is sensed or *felt*. Such an expression is, however, valuable only as it is taken negatively to indicate that it is *not*, as such, an object in *discourse*. Stating that it is *felt* is wholly misleading if it gives the impression that the situation *is* a feeling or an emotion or anything mentalistic. On the contrary, feeling, sensation and emotion have themselves to be identified and described in terms of the immediate presence of a total qualitative situation.

The pervasively qualitative is not only that which binds all constituents into a whole but it is also unique; it constitutes in each situation an *individual* situation, indivisible and unduplicable. Distinctions and relations are instituted *within* a situation; *they* are recurrent and repeatable in different situations. Discourse that is not controlled by reference to a situation is not discourse, but a meaningless jumble, just as a mass of pied type is not a font much less a sentence. A universe of experience is the precondition of a universe of discourse. Without its controlling presence, there is no way to determine the relevancy, weight or coherence of any designated distinction or relation. The universe of experience surrounds and regulates the universe of discourse but never appears as such within the latter. It may be objected that what was previously said contradicts this statement. For we have been discoursing about universes of experience and situations, so that the latter have been brought within the domain of symbols. The objection, when examined, serves to elicit an important consideration. It is a commonplace that a universe of discourse cannot be a term or element within itself. One universe of discourse may, however, be a term of discourse within *another* universe. The same principle applies in the case of universes of experience.

The reader, whether he agrees or not with what has been said, whether he understands it or not, *has*, as he reads the above passages, a uniquely qualified experienced situation, and his reflective understanding of what is said is controlled by the nature of that immediate situation. One cannot decline to *have* a situation for that is equivalent to having no experience, not even one of disagreement. The most that can be refused or declined is the having of that *specific* situation in which there is reflective recognition (discourse) of the presence of former situations of the kind stated. This very declination is, nevertheless, identical with initiation of another encompassing qualitative experience as a unique whole.

In other words, it *would* be a contradiction if I attempted to demonstrate by means of discourse, the existence of universes of experience. It is not a contradiction by means of discourse to *invite* the reader to have for himself that kind of an immediately experienced situation in which the presence of a situation as a universe of experience is seen to be the encompassing and regulating condition of all discourse.

There is another difficulty in grasping the meaning of what has been said. It concerns the use of the word "quality." The word is usually associated with something specific, like *red, hard, sweet;* that is, with distinctions made within a total experience. The intended contrasting meaning may be suggested, although not adequately exemplified, by considering such qualities as are designated by the terms distressing, perplexing, cheerful, disconsolate. For these words do not designate specific qualities in the way in which *hard*, say, designates a particular quality of a rock. For such qualities permeate and color *all* the objects and events that are involved in an experience. The phrase "tertiary qualities," happily introduced by Santayana, does not refer to a third quality like in kind to the "primary" and "secondary" qualities of Locke and merely happening to differ in content. For a tertiary quality qualifies *all* the constituents to which it applies in thoroughgoing fashion.

Probably the meaning of *quality*, in the sense in which quality is said to pervade all elements and relations that are or can be instituted in discourse and thereby to constitute them an individual whole, can be most readily apprehended by referring to the esthetic use of the word. A painting is said to have quality, or a particular painting to have a Titian or Rembrandt quality. The word thus used most certainly does not refer to any particular line, color or part of the painting. It is something that affects and modifies all the constituents of the picture and all of their relations. It is not anything that can be expressed in words for it is something that must be *had*. Discourse may, however, point out the qualities, lines and relations by means of which pervasive and unifying quality is achieved. But so far as this discourse is separated from *having* the immediate total experience, a reflective object takes the place of an esthetic one. Esthetic experience, in its emphatic sense, is mentioned as a way of calling attention to situations and universes of experience. The intended force of the illustration would be lost if esthetic experience as such were supposed to exhaust the scope and significance of a "situation." As has been said, a qualitative and qualifying situation is present as the background and the control of *every* experience. It was for a similar reason that it was earlier stated that reference to tertiary qualities was not adequately exemplary. For such qualities as are designated by "distressing," "cheerful," etc., are *general*, while the quality of distress and cheer that marks an existent situation is not general but is unique and inexpressible in words.

I give one further illustration from a different angle of approach. It is more or less a commonplace that it is possible to carry on observations that amass facts tirelessly and yet the observed "facts" lead nowhere. On the other hand, it is possible to have the work of observation so controlled by a conceptual framework fixed in advance that the very things which are genuinely decisive in the problem in hand and its solution, are completely overlooked. Everything is forced into the predetermined conceptual and theoretical scheme. The way, and the only way, to escape these two evils, is sensitivity to the quality of a situation as a whole. In ordinary language, a problem must be felt before it can be stated. If the unique quality of the situation is *had* immediately, then there is something that regulates the selection and the weighing of observed facts and their conceptual ordering.

The discussion has reached the point where the basic problem of the relation of common sense material and methods to that of scientific subject-material and method, can be explicitly discussed. In the first place, science takes its departure of necessity from the qualitative objects, processes, and instruments of the common sense world of use and concrete enjoyments and sufferings. The scientific theory of colors and light is extremely abstract and technical. But it is *about* the colors and light involved in every-day affairs. Upon the common sense level, light and colors are not experienced or inquired into as things in isolation nor yet as qualities of objects viewed in isolation. They are experienced, weighed and judged in reference to their place in the occupations and arts (including social ceremonial arts as well as fine arts) the group carries on. Light is a dominant factor in the daily routine of rising from sleep and going about one's business. Differences in the duration of the light of sun and moon interpenetrate almost every tribal custom. Colors are signs of what can be done and of how it should be done in some inclusive situation—such as, judging the prospects of the morrow's weather; selection of appropriate clothing for various occasions; dyeing, making rugs, baskets and jars; and so on in diverse ways too obvious and tedious to enumerate. They play their part either in practical decisions and activities or in enjoyed celebrations, dances, wakes, feasts, etc. What holds of light and color applies to all objects, events and qualities that enter into everyday common sense affairs.

Gradually and by processes that are more or less tortuous and originally unplanned, definite technical processes and instrumentalities are formed and transmitted. Information about things, their properties and behaviors, is amassed, independently of any particular immediate application. It becomes increasingly remote from the situations of use and enjoyment in which it originated. There is then a background of materials and operations available for the development of what we term science, although there is still no sharp dividing line between common sense and science. For purposes of illustration, it may be supposed that primitive astronomy and primitive methods of keeping track of time (closely connected with astronomical observations) grew out of the practical necessities of groups with herds in care of animals with respect to mating and reproduction, and of agricultural groups with reference to sowing, tilling and reaping. Observation of the change of position of constellations and stars, of the relation of the length of daylight to the sun's place in relation to the constellations along the line of the equinox provided the required information. Instrumental devices were developed in order that the observations might be made; definite techniques for using the instruments followed.

Measurement of angles of inclination and declination was a practical part of meeting a practical need. The illustration is, from a historical point of view, more or less speculative. But something of this general kind certainly effected the transition from what we call common sense to what we call science. If we were to take the practical needs of medicine in healing the sick and dealing with wounds, in their relation to the growth of physiological and anatomical knowledge, the case would be even clearer. In the early history of Greek reflective thought, art, or *techne*, and science, were synonymous.

But this is not the whole of the story. Oriental cultures, especially the Assyrian, Babylonian and Egyptian, developed a division between "lower" and "higher" techniques and kinds of knowledge. The lower, roughly speaking, was in possession of those who did the daily practical work; carpentering, dyeing, weaving, making pottery, trading, etc. The higher came to be the possession of a special class, priests and the successors of primitive medicine men. Their knowledge and techniques were "higher" because they were concerned with what were supposed to be matters of ultimate concern; the welfare of the people and especially its rulers—and this welfare involved transactions with the powers that ruled the universe. *Their* kind of practical activity was so different from that of artisans and traders, the objects involved were so different, the social status of the persons engaged in carrying on the activities in question was so enormously different, that the activity of the guardians and administrators of the higher knowledge and techniques was not "practical" in the sense of practical that applied to the ordinary useful worker.

These facts contained dualism in embryo, indeed in more or less mature form. This, when it was reflectively formulated, became the dualism of the empirical and rational, of theory and practice, and, in our own day, of common sense and science.[1]

The Greeks were much less subject to ecclesiastic and autocratic political control than were the peoples mentioned. The Greeks are pointed to with considerable justice as those who freed thought and knowledge from external control. But in one fundamentally important way they fixed, for subsequent intellectual history, the division just mentioned—although changing its direction and interpretation. Science and philosophy (which were still one) constituted the higher form of knowledge and activity. It alone was "rational" and alone deserved the names of knowledge and of activity that was "pure" because liberated from the constraints of practice. Experiential knowledge was confined to the artisan and trader, and their activity was "practical" because it was concerned with satisfaction of needs and desires—most of the latter, as in the case of the trader, being base and unworthy anyway.

The free citizen was not supposed to engage in any of these pursuits but to devote himself to politics and the defense of the city-state. Although the scientist-philosopher was compelled by constraint of the body to give some time and thought to satisfaction of wants, as a scientist-philosopher he was engaged in exercising his reason upon rational objects, thereby attaining the only possible complete freedom and perfect enjoyment. The definitely socio-practical division between workers and non-citizens who were servile, and the members of the leisure class who were free citizens, was converted by philosophic formulation into a division between practice and theory, experience and reason. Strictly scientific-philosophic knowledge and activity were finally conceived to be supra-social as well as supra-empirical. They connected those who pursued them with the divine and cut them off from their fellows.

I have engaged in what seems to be a historical excursus not for the sake of giving historical information but in order to indicate the origin of the distinction between empirical knowledge and practice on one hand and rational knowledge and pure activity on the other; between knowledge and practice that are

[1] See L. Hogben, *Mathematics for the Million*, Ch. 1.

admittedly of social origin and intent and the insight and activity that were supposed to have no social and practical bearings. This origin is itself social-cultural. Such is the irony of the situation. Relatively free as were the minds of Greek thinkers, momentous as were their accomplishments in certain directions, after Greek culture ceased to be a living thing and its products were carried over into different cultures, the inheritance from the Greeks became an incubus upon the progress of experience and of science, save in mathematics. Even in the latter field it kept mathematics for a long time subservient to strictly geometrical formulation.

The later revival of genuine science undoubtedly drew stimulus and inspiration from the products of Greek thought. But these products were reanimated by contact and interaction with just the things of ordinary experience and the instruments of use in practical arts which in classic Greek thought were supposed to contaminate the purity of science. There was a return to the conditions and factors mentioned earlier: qualitative materials, processes and instruments. Phenomena of heat, light and electricity became matters to be experienced under controlled conditions instead of matters to receive rational formulation through pure intellect. The lens and compass and a multitude of the tools and processes of the practical arts were borrowed and adapted to the needs of scientific inquiry. The ordinary processes that had long been at home in the arts, weakening and intensifying, combining and separating, dissolving and evaporating, precipitating and infusing, heating and cooling, etc. etc., were no longer scorned. They were adopted as means of finding out something about nature, instead of being employed only for the sake of accomplishing objects of use and enjoyment.

Symbolic instrumentalities, especially, underwent tremendous reconstruction; they were refined as well as expanded. On one hand they were constructed and related together on the basis of their applicability, through operations, to existence, and they were freed, on the other hand, from reference to direct application in use and enjoyment. The physical problems that emerged in pursuit of experiential knowledge of nature thus required and evoked new symbolic means of registration and manipulation. Analytic geometry and calculus became primary modes of conceptual response as quantity, change and motion were found to be not irrational accidents but the keys with which to solve the mysteries of natural existence. Language was, nonetheless, an old and familiar qualitative achievement. The most exact comprehensive mathematical language hardly compares as an achievement with the creation of intelligible speech by primitive peoples. Finally, the test of the validity of conceptions formulated and developed in rational discourse was found to reside in their applicability to existential qualitative material. They were no longer taken to be "true" as constituents of rational discourse in isolation but valid in the degree in which they were capable of organizing the qualitative materials of common sense and of instituting control over them. Those semantic-conceptual constructions that indicate with the greatest degree of definiteness the way in which they are to be applied are, even as conceptions, the most truly rational ones. At every point in the practice of scientific inquiry, the old separation between experience and reason, between theory and doing, was destroyed.

In consequence, the contents and techniques of common sense underwent a revolutionary change. It was noted earlier that common sense is not a constant. But the most revolutionary change it has ever undergone is that effected by the infiltration and incorporation of scientific conclusions and methods into itself. Even the procedures and materials that are connected with elementary environmental conditions of life, such things as food, clothing, shelter and locomotion, have undergone tremendous transformation, while unprecedented needs and unprecedented powers of satisfying them have also emerged. The effect of the embodiment of science in the common sense world and the activities that deal with it in the domain of human relationships is as great as that which has taken place in relation to physical nature. It is only necessary to mention the social changes and problems that have arisen from the new technologies of production and distribution of goods and services. For these technologies are the direct product of the new science. To relate in detail the ways in which science has affected the area of common sense in respect to the relationships of person to person, group to group, people to people, would be to relate the story of social change in the last few centuries. Applications of science in revolutionizing the forces and conditions of production, distribution and communication have of necessity tremendously modified the conditions under which human beings live and act in connection with one another, whether the conditions be those of interchange and friendly association or of opposition and war.

It is not intimated that the incorporation of scientific conclusions and operations into the common sense attitudes, beliefs and intellectual methods of what is now taken for granted as matters of common sense is as yet complete or coherent. The opposite is the case. In the most important matters the effect of science upon the content and procedures of common sense has been disintegrative. This disintegrative influence is a social, not a logical, fact. But it is the chief reason why it seems so easy, so "natural," to make a sharp division between common sense inquiry and its logic and scientific inquiry and its logic.

Two aspects of the disintegration which creates the semblance of complete opposition and conflict will be noted. One of them is the fact, already noted, that common sense is concerned with a field that is dominantly qualitative, while science is compelled by its own problems and goals to state its subject-matter in terms of magnitude and other mathematical relations which are non-qualitative. The other fact is that since common sense is concerned, directly and indirectly, with problems of use and enjoyment, it is inherently teleological. Science, on the other hand, has progressed by elimination of "final causes" from every domain with which it is concerned, substituting measured correspondences of change. It operates, to use the old terminology, in terms of "efficient causation," irrespective of ends and values. Upon the basis of the position here taken, these differences are due to the fact that different types of problems demand different modes of inquiry for their solution, not to any ultimate division in existential subject-matter.

The subject-matter of science is stated in symbol-constellations that are radically unlike those familiar to common sense; in what, in effect, is a different language. Moreover, there is much highly technical material that has not been incorporated into common sense even by way of technological application in "material" affairs. In the region of highest importance to common sense, namely, that of moral, political, economic ideas and beliefs, and the methods of forming and confirming them, science has had even less effect. Conceptions and methods in the field of human relationships are in much the same state as were the beliefs and methods of common sense in relation to physical nature before the rise of experimental science. These considerations fix the meaning of the statement that the difference that now exists between common sense and science is a social, rather than a logical, matter. If the word "language" is used not just formally, but to include its content of substantial meanings, the difference is a difference of languages.

The problems of science demand a set of data and a system of meanings and symbols so differentiated that science cannot rightly be called "organized common sense." But it is a potential organ for *organizing* common sense in its dealing with its own subject-matter and problems and this potentiality is far from actualization. In the techniques which affect human use of the materials of physical nature in production, science has become a powerful agency of organization. As far as issues of enjoyment, of consumption, are concerned, it has taken little effect. Morals and the problems of social control are hardly touched. Beliefs, conceptions, customs and institutions, whose rise antedated the modern period, still have possession of the field. The union of this fact with the highly technical and remote language of science creates and maintains the feeling and idea of a complete gap. The paths of communication between common sense and science are as yet largely one-way lanes. Science takes its departure from common sense, but the return road into common sense is devious and blocked by existing social conditions.

In the things of greatest import there is little intercommunication. Pre-scientific ideas and beliefs in morals and politics are, moreover, so deeply ingrained in tradition and habit and institutions, that the impact of scientific method is feared as something profoundly hostile to mankind's dearest and deepest interests and values. On the side of philosophical formulation, highly influential schools of thought are devoted to maintaining the domain of values, ideas and ideals as something wholly apart from any possibility of application of scientific methods. Earlier philosophic conceptions of the necessary separation between reason and experience, theory and practice, higher and lower activities, are used to justify the necessity of the division.

With respect to the second point, that of a seeming fundamental difference due to the fact that common sense is profoundly teleological in its controlling ideas and methods while science is deliberately indifferent to teleology, it must be noted that in spite of the theoretical difference, physical science has, in practical fact, liberated and vastly extended the range of ends open to common sense and has enormously increased the range and power of the means available for attaining them. In ancient thought, ends were fixed by nature; departure from those ends that were antecedently set and fixed by the very nature of things, was impossible; the attempt to institute ends of human devising was taken to be the sure road to confusion and chaos. In the moral field, this conception still exists and is even probably dominant. But in respect to "material" affairs, it has been completely abandoned. Inventions of new agencies and instruments create new ends; they create new consequences which stir men to form new purposes.

The original philosophical meaning of "ends" as fixed completions is almost forgotten. Instead of science eliminating ends and inquiries controlled by teleological considerations, it has, on the contrary, enormously freed and expanded activity and thought in telic matters. This effect is not a matter of opinion but of facts too obvious to be denied. The same sort of thing holds of the qualities with which common sense is inextricably concerned Multitudes of new qualities have been brought into existence by the applications of physical science, and, what is even more important, our power to bring qualities within actual experience when we so desire, has been intensified almost beyond the possibility of estimate. Consider, as one instance alone, our powers with respect to qualities generated by light and electricity.

The foregoing survey is made for a double purpose. On the one hand the outstanding problem of our civilization is set by the fact that common sense in its content, its "world" and methods, is a house divided against itself. It consists in part, and that part the most vital, of regulative meanings and procedures that antedate the rise of experimental science in its conclusions and methods. In another part, it is what it is because of application of science. This cleavage marks every phase and aspect of modern life: religious, economic, political, legal, and even artistic.

The existence of this split is put in evidence by those who condemn the "modern" and who hold that the only solution of the chaos in civilization is to revert to the intellectual beliefs and methods that were authoritative in past ages, as well as by radicals and "revolutionaries." Between the two stand the multitude that is confused and insecure. It is for this reason that it is here affirmed that the basic problem of present culture and associated living is that of effecting integration where division now exists. The problem cannot be solved apart from a unified logical method of attack and procedure. The attainment of unified method means that the fundamental unity of the structure of inquiry in common sense and science be recognized, their difference being one in the problems with which they are directly concerned, not in their respective logics. It is not urged that attainment of a unified logic, a theory of inquiry, will resolve the split in our beliefs and procedures. But it is affirmed that it will not be resolved without it.

On the other hand, the problem of unification is one in and for logical theory itself. At the present time logics in vogue do not claim for the most part to be logics of inquiry. In the main, we are asked to take our choice between the traditional logic, which was formulated not only long before the rise of science but when also the content and methods of science were in radical opposition to those of present science, and the new purely "symbolistic logic" that recognizes only mathematics, and even at that is not so much concerned with methods of mathematics as with linguistic formulation of its results. The logic of science is not only separated from common sense, but the best that can be done is to speak of logic *and* scientific method as two different and independent matters. Logic in being "purified" from all experiential taint has become so formalistic that it applies only to itself.

The next chapter deals explicitly with the traditional logic as derived from Aristotle, with a view to showing (1) that of necessity the scientific conditions under which it was formulated are so different from those of existing knowledge that it has been transformed from what it originally was, a logic of *knowledge*, into a purely formal affair, and (2) that there is a necessity for a logical theory based upon scientific conclusions and methods. These are so unlike those of classic science that the need is not revision and extension of the old logic here and there, but a radically different standpoint and a different treatment to be carried through all logical subject matter.

CHAPTER V

THE NEEDED REFORM OF LOGIC

THERE ARE not many today who would echo the saying of Kant about logic: "Since Aristotle it has not had to retrace a single step . . . and has not been able to make a single step in advance so that, to all appearance, it may be considered as complete and perfect." Nevertheless the prestige of that logic is still enormous. It forms the backbone of most logical texts that are taught in the schools, with additional chapters on "inductive logic" which are introduced, apparently, out of a feeling of need to pay some deference to what are supposed to be the methods of modern science.

Even those who realize the imperfections of classic logic in, for example, its assumption of the conception of fixed substances as necessary subjects of every proposition, do, nevertheless, pay homage even in their formal symbolic statements to traditional forms, contenting themselves with revisions and additions here and there. Those who, like John Stuart Mill, have systematically criticized the traditional theory and who have attempted to build a logic in accord with modern scientific practices, have disastrously compromised their case by basing their logical constructions ultimately upon psychological theories that reduced "experience" to mental states and external associations among them, instead of upon the actual conduct of scientific inquiry.

No apology is needed, therefore, for discussion of Aristotelian logic in relation to the theory of logic developed in this volume. For the former enters so vitally into present theories that consideration of it, instead of being historical in import, is a consideration of the contemporary logical scene. The competency of traditional logic as an organ of inquiry into existing problems of common sense and science is an urgent question. This chapter is, accordingly, a critical exposition of the main features of the Aristotelian logic in reference (1) to the conditions of science and culture which provided its background and substantial material, and (2) to their contrast with the conditions of culture and science which now obtain. The first point involves the attempt to show the intimate and organized way in which the classic logic reflected the science of the period in which it was formulated. The second point concerns the revolutionary change that has since taken place in science as the ground for a correspondingly radical change in logic.

A recent writer on logic has said: "Science seeks today to establish for the most part what are called 'laws of nature'; and these are generally answers rather to the question: 'Under what conditions does such and such a change take place?' or 'What are the most general principles exemplified in such and such a change?' than to the question, 'What is the definition of such and such a subject?', or 'What are its essential attributes?' It is more in respect of the problems to be answered, than of the logical character of the reasoning by which we must prove our answers to them, that Aristotle's views (as represented in the *Topics*) are antiquated." [1]

The implication of this passage, especially when it is extended to apply to logical works other than the *Topics*, would seem to be that a radical change in the problems and objects of inquiry (like the change from unchanging substances and their necessary essential forms to correlations of change) can take place with little change in logical forms. This implicit assumption is characteristic of much current logical writing. A contrary postulate is the ground for the present examination of Aristotelian logic in its relation to Greek science and culture in the fourth century B.C. The more adequate that logic was in its own day, the less fitted is it to form the framework of present logical theory.

Greek culture was extraordinarily rich in artistic accomplishment. It is noted also for acute and varied observations of natural phenomena and for comprehensive generalizations of what was observed. Medicine, music and astronomy, meteorology, language,

[1] H. W. Joseph, *An Introduction to Logic*, pp. 387–8.

and political institutions were all studied with the means at command in ways freer from external control than was the case in any previous civilization. Moreover, the special results in these varied fields were welded into that single comprehensive view which, following the Greek example, has ever since gone by the name of philosophy. Especially notable is the fact that, in the absence of the later sharp division between "subject" and "object," psychology was a science allied to biology which in turn was allied to physics, while morals and politics were parts of theory of Nature. Man was conceived in relation to nature, not as something set apart. Moral and political studies were not separated by sharp boundaries from cosmology. Mathematics, moreover, was thought to be an existential science.

Because of these facts, the conception that was entertained of *Nature* as a whole became the finally decisive consideration. One does not have to go into controversies that have arisen regarding the meaning of the word *nature* as used by the early scientist-philosophers, to be aware that earlier meanings finally bifurcated into two significant directions. "*Phusis*," the word translated as "nature" is etymologically connected with a root meaning "to grow." Now growth is change; it is coming into Being and passing out of Being, altering between the two extremes of birth and death. The adjective "physical" was employed by Aristotle to designate this aspect of Nature. The physical was not set over against the mental and psychical, for these were also "physical" in the sense of being marked by change. But, as we speak today of the "nature of things," so Nature in its most emphatic and eulogistic sense consisted of *unchanging* substances with their fixed essential characters or "natures." The distinction and relation of the permanent, the fixed, from and to the variable and changing, was the ultimate problem of science and philosophy. The philosophy of Aristotle is a systematic exposition and organized solution of this problem carried through all subjects with which inquiry was then concerned.

This basic fact has a fundamental connection with Aristotelian logic. On the negative side, this logic was not formal in the sense in which forms are independent of existential subject-matter. It was formal, but the forms were those of existence in so far as existence is known—*known* as distinct from being merely sensed, or discursively thought about, or an object of guess and opinion.

That the significance of the words "subject" and "object" has undergone reversal in the history of philosophic thought is a well known fact. What we call "objects" were in Greek terminology *subjects;* they were existences taken in their status as *subject*-matter of knowledge. Their logical forms were determined by the basic division supposed to exist in Nature between the changing and the eternal. Things that change are too unstable to be subjects of knowledge in its exact and complete sense. *Knowledge* as distinct from sense and opinion is fixed; truth does not alter. Hence its subjects ("objects" in our sense) must also be invariable. Seen from this point of view, Nature presented the scientific mind with an ordered grade or hierarchy of qualitative things from emptiness up to *Being* in its full sense.

That which truly *is* cannot change; the existence of change is thus proof of lack of complete Being, of what the Greeks sometimes called, because of emphasis upon lack of substantiality, *Nonbeing.* The various grades of intellectual apprehension corresponded, with their logical forms, point for point with the graded ranking of subjects in their qualitative degrees of Being.

Idiomatic speech today often uses the words *whole* and *perfect* as synonyms in contradistinction to the broken, the partial and imperfect. It is not too much to say that the implications of the identifications and the distinctions involved were determinative of Greek cosmology and theory of Being. Greek culture in its characteristic attitudes was definitely esthetic. Works of art are qualitative wholes; "pieces" of them are merely physical. The Greek urn as well as the Greek statue and temple were works of art; complete and, as we still say, *finished.* Measure, fixed limits, fixed ratio and proportions, are the mark of everything that truly is.

Such objects, or subjects, are *substances* having design and form in an objective sense. Change and susceptibility to variation lack, on the other hand, measure. They are marks of the presence of the *indefinite;* the finite, finished and complete are such because of fixed limits and measure. Change *as such* escapes intellectual apprehension. It can be *known* only in so far as it can be included within fixed boundaries which mark its beginning and its objective end or close; that is, as far as change tends to *move toward* a final and unchanging limit. Change is known, in other words, only as it is enclosed within fixed limits. From the side of knowledge and logical forms, the changing is sensible, particular or partial, while the measured whole, defined by limits, is the rational. The syllogism is the form of complete enclosure. It is of two types; in one, that which is enclosed as well as the limiting and enclosing is permanent; in the other, that which is held within bounds is itself in process of change or is "physical" not rational.

The first type of syllogism is that of rational knowledge, which is knowledge in its complete sense. This syllogistic form is strictly necessary and demonstrative in its contents. The other type of syllogism expresses *contingent* knowledge, which has various degrees of probability but in no case is necessary, because its subject-matter sometimes is and sometimes is not. The relation of *inclusion* is basic in both forms. Inclusion, however, involves exclusion. That which is fixed and permanent by nature excludes every other substance by its very nature. Being just what it is by reason of its eternal nature or essence, it is *not* anything else. Thus in addition to the fundamental logical form of universal (complete because dealing with what is *whole* by nature) and necessary propositions and relations of propositions, there are positive and negative propositions corresponding to ontological inclusions and exclusions.[2]

The so-called major and minor propositions respectively set forth the including and included "subjects," while the "middle term" is the *ratio* or logos, reason, the principle of measure and limit, which is the ground of inclusion or exclusion. It is indispensable in reasoning not because of any peculiar property of "thought" but because of the inherent connections in nature which bind "subjects" together and prevent their mingling. Since the middle term represents the principle of inclusion and exclusion in nature, it expresses a universal or whole. If it represented that which is particular (broken and partial) it could not be the ground or reason of that *con*clusion which is the exhibition in knowledge of *ex*clusions and *in*clusions in Nature.

---

[2] The technical scheme of figures of syllogisms and their relations to one another follows so directly that the topic will not be taken up.

That which is included or excluded is of necessity of a *kind* or *species*. For singular objects, *a* man, *a* rock, *a* particular community, come into being and pass out of being. They are particular (partial), not complete. The species or kind of which the singular is a part is eternal. Humanity is a species, and as a substantial species it does not originate nor pass away with the birth or death of Socrates, Alcibiades, Xenophon, etc. The substantial species is necessarily present in every particular or part, making it to be *what* it is, whether man, horse, oak tree or rock. That which belongs inherently and necessarily to a species is its nature or essence. *Definition* is the form which essence takes *qua* known. Far from being verbal or even a convenient process or product of "thought," definition is cognitive grasp of that which defines (marks out) ontological substance. It marks it off from everything else and grasps its eternal self-same character.

Species, moreover, form a graded hierarchy. There are "sensible species" represented by the qualities wet-dry, hot-cold, heavy-light. Here the phase of change, of the physical, is at its maximum. These qualities are always transient and always tending to pass into their opposites. Nevertheless, while particular existential qualities change, their kinds are fixed. Therefore, a lowest kind of cognitive apprehension, that of sense, can exist with respect to them. Even sense, in order to apprehend a quality, *red, hard*, must include it in its appropriate species—must *classify* it. At the other extreme, are species devoid of matter and change. The objects in which their essential nature is embodied, are constant and unswerving in their activities and movements.

The typical Aristotelian instance is that of the fixed stars, each of which pursues its eternal round without any variation. Between these two types of species come all the other kinds of phenomena and objects in the universe. To go into detail about them would be to rehearse the physics and cosmology of Aristotle. Suffice it to say that each kind is fixed in the order of Nature, and hence in degree of scientific or demonstrative knowledge, by the relative degree of variation to which it is subject. The latter trait marks the extent in which *matter*, the principle of instability and variation, is present. The higher species are marked by regularity of movement toward a fixed end or completion.

It is to be noted that the activities of *living* things are marked by an unusual degree of regular recurrence. This fact means that they are actuated by an unusual degree of *self-movement.* Their energy of self-movement is such that it resists change due to external circumstance much more than is the case not only with sense qualities (which are subject to change from all things about them) but also than in the case of such phenomena as weather and all inanimate things. This self-moving and self-governing trait of living creatures is of special importance because there is a qualitative hierarchy among living creatures. At the lower and inferior end are plants and their "vegetative functions," which consist in absorption and assimilation of food. Energy of self-movement marks also the various species of animal life.

At the apex is man. He retains both vegetative and animal functions; sensation, appetite, and locomotion. But in so far as man attains to rationality as such, pure in the sense of freedom from need, sensation and sense-perception, the energy of self-movement comes to completion. Reason *is* pure self-moving activity, having no dependence upon and no truck with anything outside itself. Such pure self-activity defines God and so far as mortals attain to it, they put off mortality.

From this survey, certain main points about the Aristotelian logic emerge. In the first place, the forms recognized are not formalistic. They are not independent of "subjects" known. On the contrary, they are the forms of these subjects as far as the latter are actualized in knowledge. In the second place, *knowledge*, in its logical forms, consists exclusively of definition and classification. Neither of these processes is linguistic, psychological, nor yet an aid in reflection. Definition is grasp of the essence which makes things to be what they truly are. Classification concerns the ontological exclusions and inclusions of real natural kinds or species. Definition and taxonomic classification are necessary forms of knowledge because they are expressions of necessary forms of Being.

In the third place, there is no room for any logic of discovery and invention. Discovery was thought of under the head of learning, and learning was merely coming into possession of that already known—as a pupil *comes to know* that already known by teacher and textbook. Learning belonged in the inferior region of change, and like every mode of change comes *to* something amounts to something, only as it falls within fixed limits of knowledge. In the case of learning (the sole form of discovery) the limits are apprehension of the species present in objects of perception on one hand and rational grasp of some essence defining a complete species or whole on the other hand. Learning merely brings these two antecedently given forms of knowledge into connection with each other. Similarly, invention of the new had no place. It had only its literal etymological meaning of *coming upon* something already there.

These considerations explain the ease with which a logical theory which was strictly ontological or existential in its original reference became a merely formal logic when the advance of science destroyed the background of essences and species upon which the original logic was based. The latter had no place for discursive or reflective operations save as processes of personal development (such as might now be called psychological but are rather pedagogical) by means of which individual persons arrived at direct apprehension of essences and of relations of inclusion and exclusion. Hence the perpetuation of the forms of the Aristotelian tradition, with elimination of the subject-matter of which they were the forms, also ruled out inquiry (which is effective reflection) from the proper scope of logic. The syllogism in the original logic was in no way a form of inferring or reasoning. It was immediate apprehension or vision of the relations of inclusion and exclusion that belong to real wholes in Nature.

In its final and complete sense all knowledge in the classic scheme is immediate rational apprehension, grasp or vision. Reflection and inquiry were of the nature of the maneuvering that an individual may be forced to engage in so as to get a better *view* of something already there, like making a journey to a museum to inspect the objects found in it. Form (*eidos*) and species are *views* of wholes. Because of the weakness of mortal flesh men have to engage in reflective inquiries, but the latter are of no inherent *logical* importance. Knowledge, when arrived at, is grasp and possession: of the nature of "intuition" in modern theory, only having none of the vagueness of "intuition" as that word is now used.

From our present point of view, Aristotle's saying that things of sense are better known in relation to us while rational objects are better known in themselves, is at least obscure. If, however, the etymological connection between *gignoskai, gnoscere* and *know* with *note* is borne in mind, the obscurity vanishes. To know was to *note*, and all that could be truly noted was that which already *marked* the subject of knowledge in Nature. Sensible and changing things are themselves noted, not merely notable, in relation to us; rational objects are noted and marked off in and of themselves, so that knowledge is attainment to vision of existential defining marks or objective notations.[3]

I come now to the fundamental difference between the Greek conception of Nature as it is expressed in Aristotelian cosmology, ontology and logic, and the modern conception as that has been determined in the scientific revolution. The most evident point of difference concerns the entirely different position given to the qualitative and the quantitative in their relations to one another. It is not merely that classic cosmology and science were constituted in terms of qualities, beginning with the four qualitative elements, earth, air, fire and water (themselves constituted by combinations of the contraries *wet-dry, cold-hot, heavy-light*), but that all quantitative determinations were relegated to the state of *accidents,* so that apprehension of them had no scientific standing. "Accident" is, of course, here a technical term. It does not imply that there is no cause for things existing in one amount rather than another, but that the cause is so external to the thing in question as not to be a *ground or reason* in knowledge.

The meaning of "accident" is determined by contrast with *essence.* That which is accidental is no part of essence and does not follow in any way from essence. Since the latter is the proper subject of knowledge, and since quantity (magnitude, amount) is wholly irrelevant to essence, consideration of it is outside the scope of *knowledge* in any grade except that of sense. As matter of sense it tends, moreover, to prevent ascent above sense to under-

---

[3] Were epistemological considerations pertinent, attention would have to be called to the fact that the classic logic cannot be understood in terms of the relation of subject and object, but only in that of the relation of potentiality and actuality, where change *as* potentiality occurs between the limits fixed in actuality by Nature.

standing. There was, therefore, on the basis of the Aristotelian theory of Nature and knowledge no point or purpose in making measurements except for lower "practical" ends. Quantity, the thing to be measured, fell wholly within the scope of more and less, fewer and greater, larger and smaller, or the *changing*. Measuring was useful to the artisan in dealing with physical things, but that very fact indicated the gulf which separated quantity and measuring from science and rationality. Observe by contrast the place occupied by measuring in modern knowledge.[4] Is it then credible that the logic of Greek knowledge has relevance to the logic of modern knowledge?

Another closely connected difference is found in the fact that because of the qualitative nature of the subject-matter of knowledge in the Greek conception of Nature, heterogeneity was postulated, as a matter of course, where modern science postulates homogeneity, endeavoring to substitute homogeneity for qualitative diversity. The difference is illustrated in the contrast between the present theory of "chemical" elements and the four qualitative elements (five, including the etherial substance of the fixed stars). The most striking instance, however, is found in the conception of qualitatively different kinds of *movement* that controlled science until, say, the sixteenth century. Instead of motion as measured change of position in space occupying a measured amount of time, circular movement, to and fro, and up and down, movements were conceived to be qualitatively exclusive of one another. They marked substances of different natures occupying places of different values in the hierarchy of species; different *ends* or completions respectively controlled them. Earth comes down or falls by its nature and by the nature of its *proper place;* fire and light move up for a similar reason. Levity is as much an inherent quality as is gravity, and so with the "essences" of other modes of movement.

Because of the teleological principle that *knowable* change tends toward a limiting fixed end, all motion was thought to tend naturally to come to a state of rest. This notion controlled science till, say, the time of Galileo. Note in contrast the place of homo-

---

[4] Measuring as something we do is radically other than the measure, or relation of fixed limits, that controls change.

geneous motion in modern science, a homogeneity differentiated by angular direction, momentum and velocity, which are all capable of measurement. The difference cannot be dismissed as simply a difference in the details of subject-matter and without relevance for logic. Self-returning qualitative movement is at the heart of the classic conception of reason and rational subjects. Its qualitative difference from other kinds of movement is the criterion by which forms of knowledge are graded. In addition, the difference of scientific concern with measurement and magnitude is involved.

A third closely connected difference is found in the fact that modern science is concerned with institution of *relations*, while classic logic is based on a theory of nature which treated all relations—save that of inclusion and exclusion of species (which was *not* conceived to be a relation) as accidental, in the same sense in which quantity is accidental. To be related meant in the Aristotelian scheme to be dependent upon something outside itself. But this dependence was not generalized and regarded as forming the very structure of a scientific object. On the contrary, it was put in sharp opposition to the independence, self-sufficiency and self-activity of "subjects" (substances) that are the only objects of scientific and demonstrative knowledge. *Now* to be here and *then* to be somewhere else was dismissed once for all as *the* sign of inferior *matter*, while in modern science such a change sets the problems of scientific inquiry.

Taking both measurement and relations into account, it is not too much to say that what Greek science and logic rejected are now the head corner-stone of science—although not yet of the theory of logical forms. Contemporary logic has moved far enough to criticize the old logic form. To recognition, for example, of propositions of the subject (substance)-predicate form it has added relational propositions. This is a marked advance. But up to a certain point the addition has increased confusion in logical theory as a whole, since no consistency of theory can be attained as long as the theory of antecedent subjects given ready-made to predication is retained.[5]

[5] Some specific instances of this confusion will be pointed out later. The underlying logical point at issue is not the *special* Aristotelian conception of substance, but the idea that *any* kind of subject, such as "this" or a sense datum, can be given ready-made to predication.

The next difference to be mentioned is found in the central place occupied by ends and teleology in Aristotelian logic. In converting that logic into a merely formal logic the teleological factor has disappeared. But teleology was so central in classic logic that it may be affirmed that with its disappearance, the reason for the Aristotelian logic has also vanished. Nothing is left but an empty shell; forms without subject-matter. In concluding this phase of the discussion I shall refer to the foundation of all the differences that have been mentioned—the reversed attitude of science toward change. *Completion* of the cycle of scientific reversal may be conveniently dated from the appearance of Darwin's *Origin of Species*. The very title of the book expresses a revolution in science, for the conception of biological species had been a conspicuous manifestation of the assumption of complete immutability. This conception had been banished before Darwin from every scientific subject save botany and zoology. But the latter had remained the bulwark of the old logic in scientific subject-matter.

When eternal essences and species are banished from scientific subject-matter, the forms that are appropriate to them have nothing left to which they apply; of necessity they are merely formal. They remain in *historic* fact as monuments of a culture and science that have disappeared, while in *logic* they remain as barren formalities to be formally manipulated. A striking illustration is afforded in the change that has taken place in the status of mathematics. In Greek logical theory, mathematics was an existential science. The discovery that the relation of the hypothenuse of a right-angled triangle whose other sides have the value of one is not numerically expressible, showed that magnitude and number as such are completely "irrational" or illogical. The fact that a ratio remained constant, no matter what the magnitude of the size and area of the triangle, together with the paradoxes of Zeno, helped to produce the doctrine of the "accidental" nature of quantity. It led to the notion that true *number*, as distinct from quantity, is geometrical in essence. For geometry was based on the conception of limiting measures, which determined the forms of objects in the sense of their configurations. The movement, represented at first in Cartesian algebraic geometry, that effected determination of all figures by formulae of generalized numerical coordinates was more than a new instrument of scientific analysis and record. It marked the beginning of the logical movement by which all mathematical propositions became formulae for dealing with possible objects, not descriptions of their existing properties—so that they are logically non-existential in their content, save when taken to prescribe operations of experimental observation.

The entire matter may be summed up by reference to the different conceptions of Nature that are involved respectively in ancient and modern science. In Greek science, Nature was a qualitative, a bounded and closed, whole. To know any special subject was to know it as a whole in its proper place in the comprehensively inclusive whole, Nature. It is not true that ancient science attempted to *deduce* knowledge of the included wholes from the conception of the final and complete whole. The notion that Greek science was deductive in this sense is a profound misapprehension. In the Greek scheme, knowledge consisted in *placing* each relative species, or whole, defined and identified by its own essence, in relation to other species within Nature as the final whole. The necessity of referring all special kinds and modes of knowledge to Nature as a closed whole explains why, in the classic conception, there could be no sharp distinction between science and philosophy. The subject-matter of modern natural science consists of changes formulated in correspondence *with one another*. This fact not only gives a radically different status to change but it radically affects the conception of Nature.

The formulation of correlated correspondences becomes more and more comprehensive in scope. But no scientist today would dream of setting up an all-inclusive formula for the universe as a whole. That job has been taken over by certain philosophic schools. The change in the conception of Nature is expressed in summary form in the idea that the universe is now conceived as open and in process while classical Greece thought of it as finite in the sense in which finite means finished, complete and perfect. The infinite was the *indefinite* in Greek science, and the indefinite, as such, could not be known.

It would be completely erroneous to regard the foregoing as a criticism of the Aristotelian logic in its original formulation in connection with Greek culture. As a *historic* document it deserves the admiration it has received. As a comprehensive, penetrating and thoroughgoing intellectual transcript of *discourse in isolation* from the operations in which discourse takes effect, it is above need for praise. What has been said is a criticism of the effort to maintain that logic, with revisions here and additions there, as adequate or even relevant to the science of today. As has already been said, the more final and complete it was for the class-culture of the epoch in which it was formulated, the less adapted is it to present conditions and demands of knowledge. The attempt to retain Aristotelian logical forms after their existential foundations have been repudiated is the main source of existing confusion in logical theory. It is the ultimate reason why logical forms are treated as *merely* formal.

But, as was earlier indicated, admiration for the comprehensive way in which classic logic accomplished its task even from the standpoint of its contemporary cultural context has to be qualified by recognition of the class-structure of that culture. In consequence, the formulation was partial even from the standpoint of the resources then and there available. The authors of the classic logic did not recognize that tools constitute a kind of language which is in more compelling connection with things of nature than are words, nor that the syntax of operations provides a model for the scheme of ordered knowledge more exacting than that of spoken and written language. Genuine scientific knowledge revived when inquiry adopted as part of its own procedure and for its own purpose the previously disregarded instrumentalities and procedures of productive workers. This adoption is the radical characteristic of the experimental method of science. The great role of mathematics in the conduct of science shows that discourse still has a fundamental role. But as far as existential knowledge is concerned, that role is now subordinate and not supreme. The confusion which marks logical theory is, then, a natural consequence of attempts to retain the forms of classical logical theory after the method of inquiry by which knowledge is obtained and beliefs are tested has undergone a radical change. Examples of the confusion will be given from time to time in subsequent chapters. It is fitting to give one instance here as an illustration. It concerns a matter no less important logically than the nature of the universal.

The meaning ascribed to universal and particular propositions in the classic logic is unambiguous and consistent. Universal propositions are about subjects (substances) which in and by Nature are self-contained existential wholes; particular propositions being about the things that are by nature partial, incomplete, because exposed to change. Species were the substantial wholes whose activity is self-actuated and self-regulated; incomplete things were dependent upon other things. The whole was the species fixed in nature, and is the precursor of the nondescript logical "class" of present logical theory. Things that are partial, because incomplete, in nature can only be spoken of *kathekaston* or in their severalty, for they are themselves severed.

According to present logic, as far as it takes account of scientific methods and their conclusions, universal and necessary propositions in their logical content are *non*-existential, while all *existential* propositions are singular or several. I am not objecting to the latter conception. It is the only view possible from the standpoint of present science. I am concerned with the confusion that results when an attempt is made to combine or "reconcile" this view with the one inherited from the classic logic. A simple example is found in the customary illustration that is given of the Aristotelian syllogism: All men are mortal; Socrates is a man; therefore, Socrates is mortal. I do not believe a single instance can be found in genuine Aristotelian writings in which a singular (which by its nature is an instance of severalty) appears as the minor premise in a rationally demonstrative syllogism. Its presence in such a syllogism would contradict the whole conception of demonstration as an actualized exhibition of a necessary relation of *fixed wholes* to one another.

The Aristotelian logic as far as its spirit, instead of its letter, is concerned, is nevertheless both generically and specifically significant for what needs to be done in logic in the contemporary situation. Generically, the need is for logic to do for present science and culture what Aristotle did for the science and culture of his time. Specifically, his logic is significant for present logic in that it included in a single unified scheme the contents of both the common sense and the science of his day.   The unification was effected in a way which is no longer possible.   We can no longer take the contents and procedures of both common sense and science as inherently fixed, differing only in qualitative grade and rank in a qualitatively fixed hierarchy.   The fixity of the contents and logical forms of both common sense and science in the Aristotelian scheme precluded the possibility of the reaction of science back into common sense and the possibility of the ever-continuing rise of new scientific problems and conceptions out of the material of common sense activities and materials.   All that science could do was to accept what was given and established in common sense and formulate it in its relation to the fixed subjects of higher rational knowledge.   The present need is for a unified logic that takes account of a two-way movement between common sense and science.

The common sense culture which was formulated was of a high order.   As far as free citizens—those who freely shared in the culture—were concerned, it was dominated by esthetic and artistic categories of harmony, measure, proportion, objective design and wholeness.   In addition, the leading conceptions of philosophic science were but translations into philosophic vocabulary of conceptions that dominate common sense in every period.   (1) The category of substance is the reflection of the conception that *things* exist in stable form in the world—an idea not only familiar to, but basic in, all those common sense beliefs that have not been modified by the impact of modern science.   These things are designated by the common nouns in general use.   (2) The category of fixed species corresponds to common sense belief in natural kinds, some of which are inclusive of others, while some are exclusive.   For common sense these natural kinds do not permit of transition from one to another nor of any overlapping.   The evidence for the existence of fixed natural kinds and of substantial objects is overwhelming from the standpoint of ordinary common sense.   (3) Common sense ideas, beliefs and judgments in every culture are controlled by teleological conceptions, by ends; in modern language, by considerations of *value*.   (4) Common sense thinks of the world of things and social relations in terms which, when they are reflectively organized, become the doctrine of graded ranks or hierarchies. Distinctions of low and high, inferior and superior, base and noble, and all manner of similar qualitative opposites of value, are almost the stuff of common sense beliefs which have not been transformed by the impact of science. They seem to be guaranteed by the obviously perceived structures of both nature and human society.

When I say that the philosophic science, of which logical theory was an integral member, organized these and like beliefs and ideas of common sense, it is not meant that the former merely mirrored the latter. The very idea of *reflective organization* negates such a notion. Not only were implications of which common sense was unaware made explicit, but the framework of conceptions was vastly extended by investigations of subjects with which common sense held no commerce. Above all, the very fact of organization involved an ordered arrangement foreign to common sense. Common sense, for example, would hardly have entertained the idea that the philosopher-scientist was higher in rank as to his objects and activities than the general and the statesman; or that the happiness of the former was of a godlike character in comparison with the happiness open to others. But none the less there were things involved in Athenian culture which, *when* they were put in ordered arrangement with one another, took the form of this conclusion.

We are brought back to the conclusions of the last chapter. The subject-matter and methods of modern science have no such direct affinity with those of common sense as existed when classic science and logic were formulated. Science is no longer an organization of meanings and modes of action that have their presence in the meanings and syntactical structures of ordinary language. Yet scientific conclusions and techniques have enormously altered the common sense relation of man to nature and to fellow-man. It can no longer be believed that they do not profoundly react to modify common sense, any more than it can now be supposed that they are but an intellectual organization of the latter.

Science has, however, affected the actual conditions under which men live, use, enjoy and suffer much more than (aside from material technologies) it has affected their habits of belief and inquiry. Especially is this true about the uses and enjoyments of final concern: religious, moral, legal, economic, political. The demand for reform of logic is the demand for a unified theory of inquiry through which the authentic pattern of experimental and operational inquiry of science shall become available for regulation of the habitual methods by which inquiries in the field of common sense are carried on; by which conclusions are reached and beliefs are formed and tested. In the next chapter the nature of this common pattern forms the theme of discussion.

Part Two

THE STRUCTURE OF INQUIRY AND THE CONSTRUCTION OF JUDGMENTS

CHAPTER VI

THE PATTERN OF INQUIRY

THE FIRST chapter set forth the fundamental thesis of this volume: Logical forms accrue to subject-matter when the latter is subjected to controlled inquiry. It also set forth some of the implications of this thesis for the nature of logical theory. The second and third chapters stated the independent grounds, biological and cultural, for holding that logic is a theory of experiential naturalistic subject-matter. The first of the next two chapters developed the theme with reference to the relations of the logic of common sense and science, while the second discussed Aristotelian logic as the organized formulation of the language of Greek life, when that language is regarded as the expression of the meanings of Greek culture and of the significance attributed to various forms of natural existence. It was held throughout these chapters that inquiry, in spite of the diverse subjects to which it applies, and the consequent diversity of its special techniques has a common structure or pattern: that this common structure is applied both in common sense and science, although because of the nature of the problems with which they are concerned, the emphasis upon the factors involved varies widely in the two modes. We now come to the consideration of the common pattern.

The fact that new formal properties accrue to subject-matter in virtue of its subjection to certain types of operation is familiar to us in certain fields, even though the idea corresponding to this fact is unfamiliar in logic. Two outstanding instances are provided by art and law. In music, the dance, painting, sculpture, literature and the other fine arts, subject-matters of everyday experience are *trans*formed by the development of forms which render certain products of doing and making objects of fine art. The materials of legal regulations are transactions occurring in the ordinary

activities of human beings and groups of human beings; transac
tions of a sort that are engaged in apart from law. As certain
aspects and phases of these transactions are legally formalized, con
ceptions such as misdemeanor, crime, torts, contracts and so on
arise. These formal conceptions arise out of the ordinary trans
actions; they are not imposed upon them from on high or from
any external and *a priori* source. But when they are formed they
are also *formative;* they regulate the proper conduct of the activi
ties out of which they develop.

All of these formal legal conceptions are operational in nature
They formulate and define *ways* of operation on the part of those
engaged in the transactions into which a number of persons or
groups enter as "parties," and the ways of operation followed by
those who have jurisdiction in deciding whether established forms
have been complied with, together with the existential consequences
of failure of observation. The forms in question are not fixed and
eternal. They change, though as a rule too slowly, with changes in
the habitual transactions in which individuals and groups engage
and the changes that occur in the consequences of these transac
tions. However hypothetical may be the conception that *logical*
forms accrue to existential materials in virtue of the control exer
cised over inquiries in order that they may fulfil their end, the con
ception is descriptive of something that verifiably exists. The de
velopment of forms in consequence of operations is an established
fact in some fields; it is not invented *ad hoc* in relation to logical
forms.

The existence of inquiries is not a matter of doubt. They enter
into every area of life and into every aspect of every area. In
everyday living, men examine; they turn things over intellectually;
they infer and judge as "naturally" as they reap and sow, produce
and exchange commodities. As a mode of conduct, inquiry is as
accessible to objective study as are these other modes of behavior.
Because of the intimate and decisive way in which inquiry and its
conclusions enter into the management of all affairs of life, no
study of the latter is adequate save as it is noted how they are af
fected by the methods and instruments of inquiry that currently
obtain. Quite apart, then, from the particular hypothesis about
logical forms that is put forth, study of the objective facts of in-

quiry is a matter of tremendous import, practically and intellectually. These materials provide the theory of logical forms with
a subject-matter that is not only objective but is objective in a
fashion that enables logic to avoid the three mistakes most characteristic of its history.

1. In virtue of its concern with objectively observable subject-
matter by reference to which reflective conclusions can be tried
and tested, dependence upon subjective and "mentalistic" states
and processes is eliminated.

2. The distinctive existence and nature of forms is acknowledged. Logic is not compelled, as historic "empirical" logic felt
compelled to do, to reduce logical forms to mere transcripts of the
empirical materials that antecede the existence of the former. Just
as art-forms and legal forms are capable of independent discussion and development, so are logical forms, even though the "independence" in question is intermediate, not final and complete.
As in the case of these other forms, they originate *out of* experiential material, and when constituted introduce new ways of operating with prior materials, which ways modify the material out of
which they develop.

3. Logical theory is liberated from the unobservable, trans-
cendental and "intuitional."

When methods and results of inquiry are studied as objective
data, the distinction that has often been drawn between noting
and reporting the ways in which men *do* think, and prescribing
the ways in which they *ought* to think, takes on a very different
interpretation from that usually given. The usual interpretation
is in terms of the difference between the psychological and the
logical, the latter consisting of "norms" provided from some source
wholly outside of and independent of "experience."

The way in which men *do* "think" denotes, as it is *here* interpreted, simply the ways in which men at a given time carry on
their inquiries. So far as it is used to register a difference from
the ways in which they *ought* to think, it denotes a difference like
that between good and bad farming or good and bad medical practice.[1] Men think in ways they should not when they follow methods of inquiry that experience of past inquiries shows are not

[1] *Cf.* pp. 6 and 10 of Introduction.

competent to reach the intended end of the inquiries in question

Everybody knows that today there are in vogue methods of farming generally followed in the past which compare very unfavorably in their results with those obtained by practices that have already been introduced and tested. When an expert tells a farmer he *should* do thus and so, he is not setting up for a bad farmer an ideal drawn from the blue. He is instructing him in methods that have been tried and that have proved successful in procuring results. In a similar way we are able to contrast various kinds of inquiry that are in use or that have been used in respect to their economy and efficiency in reaching warranted conclusions. We know that some methods of inquiry are better than others in just the same way in which we know that some methods of surgery, farming, road-making, navigating or what-not are better than others. It does not follow in any of these cases that the "better" methods are ideally perfect, or that they are regulative or "normative" because of conformity to some absolute form. They are the methods which experience up to the present time shows to be the best methods available for achieving certain results, while abstraction of these methods does supply a (relative) norm or standard for further undertakings.

The search for the pattern of inquiry is, accordingly, not one instituted in the dark or at large. It is checked and controlled by knowledge of the kinds of inquiry that have and that have not worked; methods which, as was pointed out earlier, can be so compared as to yield reasoned or rational conclusions. For, through comparison-contrast, we ascertain *how and why* certain means and agencies have provided warrantably assertible conclusions, while others have not and *cannot* do so in the sense in which "cannot" expresses an intrinsic incompatibility between means used and consequences attained.

We may now ask: What is the *definition* of Inquiry? That is, what is the most highly generalized conception of inquiry which can be justifiably formulated? The definition that will be expanded, directly in the present chapter and indirectly in the following chapters, is as follows: *Inquiry is the controlled or directed transformation of an indeterminate situation into one that is so determinate in its constituent distinctions and relations as to con-*

vert the elements of the original situation into a unified whole.[2]

The original indeterminate situation is not only "open" to inquiry, but it is open in the sense that its constituents do not hang together. The determinate situation on the other hand, *qua* outcome of inquiry, is a closed and, as it were, finished situation or "universe of experience." "Controlled or directed" in the above formula refers to the fact that inquiry is competent in any given case in the degree in which the operations involved in it actually do terminate in the establishment of an objectively unified existential situation. In the intermediate course of transition and transformation of the indeterminate situation, *dis*course through use of symbols is employed as means. In received logical terminology, propositions, or terms and the relations between them, are intrinsically involved.

I. *The Antecedent Conditions of Inquiry: The Indeterminate Situation.* Inquiry and questioning, up to a certain point, are synonymous terms. We inquire when we question; and we inquire when we seek for whatever will provide an answer to a question asked. Thus it is of the very nature of the indeterminate situation which evokes inquiry to be *questionable;* or, in terms of actuality instead of potentiality, to be uncertain, unsettled, disturbed. The peculiar quality of what pervades the given materials, constituting them a situation, is not just uncertainty at large; it is a unique doubtfulness which makes that situation to be just and only the situation it is. It is this unique quality that not only evokes the particular inquiry engaged in but that exercises control over its special procedures. Otherwise, one procedure in inquiry would be as likely to occur and to be effective as any other. Unless a situation is uniquely qualified in its very indeterminateness, there is a condition of complete panic; response to it takes the form of blind and wild overt activities. Stating the matter from the personal side, we have "lost our heads." A variety of names serves to characterize indeterminate situations. They are disturbed, troubled, ambiguous, confused, full of conflicting tendencies, obscure, etc.

It is the *situation* that has these traits. *We* are doubtful because

[2] The word "situation" is to be understood in the sense already expounded, *ante,* pp. 66–7.

the situation is inherently doubtful. Personal states of doubt that are not evoked by and are not relative to some existential situation are pathological; when they are extreme they constitute the mania of doubting. Consequently, situations that are disturbed and troubled, confused or obscure, cannot be straightened out, cleared up and put in order, by manipulation of our personal states of mind. The attempt to settle them by such manipulations involves what psychiatrists call "withdrawal from reality." Such an attempt is pathological as far as it goes, and when it goes far it is the source of some form of actual insanity. The habit of disposing of the doubtful as if it belonged only to *us* rather than to the existential situation in which we are caught and implicated is an inheritance from subjectivistic psychology. The biological antecedent conditions of an unsettled situation are involved in that state of imbalance in organic-environmental interactions which has already been described.[3] Restoration of integration can be effected, in one case as in the other, only by operations which actually modify existing conditions, not by merely "mental" processes.

It is, accordingly, a mistake to suppose that a situation is doubtful only in a "subjective" sense. The notion that in actual existence everything is completely determinate has been rendered questionable by the progress of physical science itself. Even if it had not been, complete determination would not hold of existences as an *environment*. For Nature is an environment only as it is involved in interaction with an organism, or self, or whatever name be used.[4]

Every such interaction is a temporal process, not a momentary cross-sectional occurrence. The situation in which it occurs is indeterminate, therefore, with respect to its *issue*. If we call it *confused*, then it is meant that its outcome cannot be anticipated. It is called *obscure* when its course of movement permits of final consequences that cannot be clearly made out. It is called *conflicting* when it tends to evoke discordant responses. Even were

---

[3] See, *ante,* pp. 26–7.

[4] Except of course a purely mentalistic name, like *consciousness*. The alleged problem of "interactionism" versus automatism, parallelism, etc., is a problem (and an insoluble one) because of the assumption involved in its statement—the assumption, namely, that the interaction in question is with something mental instead of with biological-cultural human beings.

existential conditions unqualifiedly determinate in and of themselves, they are indeterminate in *significance:* that is, in what they import and portend in their interaction with the organism. The organic responses that enter into the production of the state of affairs that is temporally later and sequential are just as existential as are environing conditions.

The immediate *locus* of the problem concerns, then, what kind of responses the organism shall make. It concerns the interaction of organic responses and environing conditions in their movement toward an existential issue. It is a commonplace that in any troubled state of affairs *things* will come out differently according to what is done. The farmer won't get grain unless he plants and tills; the general will win or lose the battle according to the way he conducts it, and so on. Neither the grain nor the tilling, neither the outcome of the battle nor the conduct of it, are "mental" events. Organic interaction becomes inquiry when existential consequences are anticipated; when environing conditions are examined with reference to their potentialities; and when responsive activities are selected and ordered with reference to actualization of some of the potentialities, rather than others, in a final existential situation. Resolution of the indeterminate situation is active and operational. If the inquiry is adequately directed, the final issue is the unified situation that has been mentioned.

II. *Institution of a Problem.* The unsettled or indeterminate situation might have been called a *problematic* situation. This name would have been, however, proleptic and anticipatory. The indeterminate situation becomes problematic in the very process of being subjected to inquiry. The indeterminate situation comes into existence from existential causes, just as does, say, the organic imbalance of hunger. There is nothing intellectual or cognitive in the existence of such situations, although they are the necessary condition of cognitive operations or inquiry. In themselves they are precognitive. The first result of evocation of inquiry is that the situation is taken, adjudged, to be problematic. To see that a situation requires inquiry is the initial step in inquiry.[5]

[5] If by "two-valued logic" is meant a logic that regards "true and false" as the sole logical values, then such a logic is necessarily so truncated that clearness and consistency in logical doctrine are impossible. Being the matter of a problem is primary logical property.

Qualification of a situation as problematic does not, however, carry inquiry far. It is but an initial step in institution of a problem. A problem is not a task to be performed which a person puts upon himself or that is placed upon him by others—like a so-called arithmetical "problem" in school work. *A* problem represents the partial transformation by inquiry of a problematic situation into a determinate situation. It is a familiar and significant saying that a problem well put is half-solved. To find out *what* the problem and problems are which a problematic situation presents to be inquired into, is to be well along in inquiry. To mistake the problem involved is to cause subsequent inquiry to be irrelevant or to go astray. Without a problem, there is blind groping in the dark. The way in which the problem is conceived decides what specific suggestions are entertained and which are dismissed; what data are selected and which rejected; it is the criterion for relevancy and irrelevancy of hypotheses and conceptual structures. On the other hand, to set up a problem that does not grow out of an actual situation is to start on a course of dead work, nonetheless dead because the work is "busy work." Problems that are self-set are mere excuses for seeming to do something intellectual, something that has the semblance but not the substance of scientific activity.

III. *The Determination of a Problem-Solution.* Statement of a problematic situation in terms of a problem has no meaning save as the problem instituted has, in the very terms of its statement, reference to a possible solution. Just because a problem well stated is on its way to solution, the determining of a genuine problem is a *progressive* inquiry; the cases in which a problem and its probable solution flash upon an inquirer are cases where much prior ingestion and digestion have occurred. If we assume, prematurely, that the problem involved is definite and clear, subsequent inquiry proceeds on the wrong track. Hence the question arises: How is the formation of a genuine problem so controlled that further inquiries will move toward a solution?

The first step in answering this question is to recognize that no situation which is *completely* indeterminate can possibly be converted into a problem having definite constituents. The first step then is to search out the *constituents* of a given situation which, as constituents, are settled. When an alarm of fire is sounded in a crowded assembly hall, there is much that is indeterminate as regards the activities that may produce a favorable issue. One may get out safely or one may be trampled and burned. The fire is characterized, however, by some settled traits. It is, for example, located *somewhere*. Then the aisles and exits are at fixed places. Since they are settled or determinate in *existence*, the first step in institution of a problem is to settle them in *observation*. There are other factors which, while they are not as temporally and spatially fixed, are yet observable constituents; for example, the behavior and movements of other members of the audience. All of these observed conditions taken together constitute "the facts of the case." They constitute the terms of the problem, because they are conditions that must be reckoned with or taken account of in any relevant solution that is proposed.

A *possible* relevant solution is then suggested by the determination of factual conditions which are secured by observation. The possible solution presents itself, therefore, as an *idea*, just as the terms of the problem (which are facts) are instituted by observation. Ideas are anticipated consequences (forecasts) of what will happen when certain operations are executed under and with respect to observed conditions.[6] Observation of facts and suggested meanings or ideas arise and develop in correspondence with each other. The more the facts of the case come to light in consequence of being subjected to observation, the clearer and more pertinent become the conceptions of the way the problem constituted by these facts is to be dealt with. On the other side, the clearer the idea, the more definite, as a truism, become the operations of observation and of execution that must be performed in order to resolve the situation.

An idea is first of all an anticipation of something that may happen; it marks a *possibility*. When it is said, as it sometimes is,

---

[6] The theory of *ideas* that has been held in psychology and epistemology since the time of Locke's successors is completely irrelevant and obstructive in logical theory. For in treating them as copies of perceptions or "impressions," it ignores the prospective and anticipatory character that defines *being* an idea. Failure to define ideas functionally, in the reference they have to a solution of a problem, is one reason they have been treated as merely "mental." The notion, on the other hand, that ideas are fantasies is a derivative. Fantasies arise when the function an idea performs is ruled out when it is entertained and developed.

that science is *prediction*, the anticipation that constitutes every idea an idea is grounded in a set of controlled observations and of regulated conceptual ways of interpreting them. Because inquiry is a progressive determination of a problem and its possible solution, ideas differ in grade according to the stage of inquiry reached. At first, save in highly familiar matters, they are vague. They occur at first simply as suggestions; suggestions just spring up, flash upon us, occur to us. They may then become stimuli to direct an overt activity but they have as yet no logical status. Every idea originates as a suggestion, but not every suggestion is an idea. The suggestion becomes an idea when it is examined with reference to its functional fitness; its capacity as a means of resolving the given situation.

This examination takes the form of reasoning, as a result of which we are able to appraise better than we were at the outset, the pertinency and weight of the meaning now entertained with respect to its functional capacity. But the final test of its possession of these properties is determined when it actually functions— that is, when it is put into operation so as to institute by means of observations facts not previously observed, and is then used to organize them with other facts into a coherent whole.

Because suggestions and ideas are of that which is not present in given existence, the meanings which they involve must be embodied in some symbol. Without some kind of symbol no idea; a meaning that is completely disembodied can not be entertained or used. Since an existence (which *is* an existence) is the support and vehicle of a meaning and is a symbol instead of a merely physical existence only in this respect, embodied meanings or ideas are capable of objective survey and development. To "look at an idea" is not a mere literary figure of speech.

"Suggestions" have received scant courtesy in logical theory. It is true that when they just "pop into our heads," because of the workings of the psycho-physical organism, they are not logical. But they are both the conditions and the primary stuff of logical ideas. The traditional empiristic theory reduced them, as has already been pointed out, to mental copies of physical things and assumed that they were *per se* identical with ideas. Consequently it ignored the function of ideas in directing observation and in ascertaining relevant facts. The rationalistic school, on the other hand, saw clearly that "facts" apart from ideas are trivial, that they acquire import and significance only in relation to ideas. But at the same time it failed to attend to the operative and functional nature of the latter. Hence, it treated ideas as equivalent to the ultimate structure of "Reality." The Kantian formula that apart from each other "perceptions are blind and conceptions empty" marks a profound logical insight. The insight, however, was radically distorted because perceptual and conceptual contents were supposed to originate from different sources and thus required a third activity, that of synthetic understanding, to bring them together. In logical fact, perceptual and conceptual materials are instituted in functional correlativity with each other, in such a manner that the former locates and describes the problem while the latter represents a possible method of solution. Both are determinations in and by inquiry of the original problematic situation whose pervasive quality controls their institution and their contents. Both are finally checked by their capacity to work together to introduce a resolved unified situation. As distinctions they represent logical divisions of labor.

IV. *Reasoning.* The necessity of developing the meaning-contents of ideas in their relations to one another has been incidentally noted. This process, operating with symbols (constituting propositions) is reasoning in the sense of ratiocination or rational discourse.[7] When a suggested meaning is immediately accepted, inquiry is cut short. Hence the conclusion reached is not grounded, even if it happens to be correct. The check upon immediate acceptance is the examination of the meaning as a meaning. This examination consists in noting what the meaning in question implies in relation to other meanings in the system of which it is a member, the formulated relation constituting a proposition. If such and such a relation of meanings is accepted, then we are committed to such and such other relations of meanings because of their membership in the same system. Through a series of intermediate meanings, a meaning is finally reached which

---

[7] "Reasoning" is sometimes used to designate *inference* as well as ratiocination. When so used in logic the tendency is to identify inference and implication and thereby seriously to confuse logical theory.

is more clearly *relevant* to the problem in hand than the originally suggested idea. It indicates operations which can be performed to test its applicability, whereas the original idea is usually too vague to determine crucial operations. In other words, the idea or meaning when developed in discourse directs the activities which, when executed, provide needed evidential material.

The point made can be most readily appreciated in connection with scientific reasoning. An hypothesis, once suggested and entertained, is developed in relation to other conceptual structures until it receives a form in which it can instigate and direct an experiment that will disclose precisely those conditions which have the maximum possible force in determining whether the hypothesis should be accepted or rejected. Or it may be that the experiment will indicate what modifications are required in the hypothesis so that it may be applicable, i.e., suited to interpret and organize the facts of the case. In many familiar situations, the meaning that is most relevant has been settled because of the eventuations of experiments in prior cases so that it is applicable almost immediately upon its occurrence. But, indirectly, if not directly, an idea or suggestion that is not developed in terms of the constellation of meanings to which it belongs can lead only to overt response. Since the latter terminates inquiry, there is then no adequate inquiry into the meaning that is used to settle the given situation, and the conclusion is in so far logically ungrounded.

V. *The Operational Character of Facts-Meanings.* It was stated that the observed facts of the case and the ideational contents expressed in ideas are related to each other, as, respectively, a clarification of the problem involved and the proposal of some possible solution; that they are, accordingly, functional divisions in the work of inquiry. Observed facts in their office of locating and describing the problem are existential; ideational subject-matter is non-existential. How, then, do they cooperate with each other in the resolution of an existential situation? The problem is insoluble save as it is recognized that both observed facts and entertained ideas are operational. Ideas are operational in that they instigate and direct further operations of observation; they are proposals and plans for acting upon existing conditions to bring new facts to light and to organize all the selected facts into a coherent whole.

What is meant by calling facts operational? Upon the negative side what is meant is that they are not self-sufficient and complete in themselves. They are selected and described, as we have seen, for a purpose, namely statement of the problem involved in such a way that its material both indicates a meaning relevant to resolution of the difficulty and serves to test its worth and validity. In regulated inquiry facts are selected and arranged with the express intent of fulfilling this office. They are not merely *results* of operations of observation which are executed with the aid of bodily organs and auxiliary instruments of art, but they are the particular facts and kinds of facts that will link up with one another in the definite ways that are required to produce a definite end. Those not found to connect with others in furtherance of this end are dropped and others are sought for. Being functional, they are necessarily operational. Their function is to serve as evidence and their evidential quality is judged on the basis of their capacity to form an ordered whole in response to operations prescribed by the ideas they occasion and support. If "the facts of the case" were final and complete in themselves, if they did not have a special operative force in resolution of the problematic situation, they could not serve as evidence.

The operative force of facts is apparent when we consider that no fact in isolation has evidential potency. Facts are evidential and are tests of an idea in so far as they are capable of being organized with one another. The organization can be achieved only as they *interact* with one another. When the problematic situation is such as to require extensive inquiries to effect its resolution, a series of interactions intervenes. Some observed facts point to an idea that stands for a possible solution. This idea evokes more observations. Some of the newly observed facts link up with those previously observed and are such as to rule out other observed things with respect to their evidential function. The new order of facts suggests a modified idea (or hypothesis) which occasions new observations whose result again determines a new order of facts, and so on until the existing order is both unified and complete. In the course of this serial process, the ideas that represent possible solutions are tested or "proved."

Meantime, the orders of fact, which present themselves in consequence of the experimental observations the ideas call out and direct, are *trial* facts. They are provisional. They are "facts" if they are observed by sound organs and techniques. But they are not on that account the *facts of the case.* They are tested or "proved" with respect to their evidential function just as much as ideas (hypotheses) are tested with reference to their power to exercise the function of resolution. The operative force of both ideas and facts is thus practically recognized in the degree in which they are connected with *experiment.* Naming them "operational" is but a theoretical recognition of what is involved when inquiry satisfies the conditions imposed by the necessity for experiment.

I recur, in this connection, to what has been said about the necessity for symbols in inquiry. It is obvious, on the face of matters, that a possible mode of solution must be carried in symbolic form since it is a possibility, not an assured present existence Observed facts, on the other hand, are existentially present. It might seem therefore, that symbols are not required for referring to them. But if they are not carried and treated by means of symbols, they lose their provisional character, and in losing this character they are categorically asserted and inquiry comes to an end. The carrying on of inquiry requires that the facts be taken as *re*presentative and not just as *pre*-sented. This demand is met by formulating them in propositions—that is, by means of symbols. Unless they are so represented they relapse into the total qualitative situation.

VI. *Common Sense and Scientific Inquiry.* The discussion up to this point has proceeded in general terms which recognizes no distinction between common sense and scientific inquiry. We have now reached a point where the community of pattern in these two distinctive modes of inquiry should receive explicit attention It was said in earlier chapters that the difference between them resides in their respective subject-matters, not in their basic logical forms and relations; that the difference in subject-matters is due to the difference in the problems respectively involved; and, finally, that this difference sets up a difference in the ends or objective consequences they are concerned to achieve. Because common sense problems and inquiries have to do with the interactions into which living creatures enter in connection with environing conditions in order to establish objects of use and enjoyment, the symbols employed are those which have been determined in the habitual culture of a group. They form a system but the system is practical rather than intellectual. It is constituted by the traditions, occupations, techniques, interests, and established institutions of the group. The meanings that compose it are carried in the common everyday language of communication between members of the group. The meanings involved in this common language system determine what individuals of the group may and may not do in relation to physical objects and in relations to one another. They regulate *what* can be used and enjoyed and *how* use and enjoyment shall occur.

Because the symbol-meaning systems involved are connected directly with cultural life-activities and are related to each other in virtue of this connection, the specific meanings which are present have reference to the specific and limited environing conditions under which the group lives. Only those things of the environment that are taken, according to custom and tradition, as having connection with and bearing upon this life, enter into the meaning system. There is no such thing as disinterested intellectual concern with either physical or social matters. For, until the rise of science, there were no problems of common sense that called for such inquiry. Disinterestedness existed practically in the demand that group interests and concerns be put above private needs and interests. But there was no intellectual disinterestedness beyond the activities, interests and concerns of the group. In other words, there was no science as such, although, as was earlier pointed out, there did exist information and techniques which were available for the purposes of scientific inquiry and out of which the latter subsequently grew.

In scientific inquiry, then, meanings are related to one another on the ground of their character *as* meanings, freed from direct reference to the concerns of a limited group. Their intellectual abstractness is a product of this liberation, just as the "concrete" is practically identified by directness of connection with environmental interactions. Consequently a new language, a new system of symbols related together on a new basis, comes into existence, and in this new language semantic coherence, as such, is the controlling consideration. To repeat what has already been said, connection with problems of use and enjoyment is the source of the dominant role of qualities, sensible and moral, and of ends in common sense.

In science, since meanings are determined on the ground of their relation as meanings to one another, *relations* become the objects of inquiry and qualities are relegated to a secondary status, playing a part only as far as they assist in institution of relations. They are subordinate because they have an instrumental office, instead of being themselves, as in prescientific common sense, the matters of final importance. The enduring hold of common sense is testified to historically by the long time it took before it was seen that scientific objects are strictly relational. First tertiary qualities were eliminated; it was recognized that moral qualities are not agencies in determining the structure of nature. Then secondary qualities, the wet-dry, hot-cold, light-heavy, which were the explanatory principles of physical phenomena in Greek science, were ejected. But so-called primary qualities took their place, as with Newton and the Lockeian formulation of Newtonian existential postulates. It was not until the threshold of our time was reached that scientific inquiries perceived that their own problems and methods required an interpretation of "primary qualities" in terms of relations, such as position, motion and temporal span. In the structure of distinctively scientific objects these relations are indifferent to qualities.

The foregoing is intended to indicate that the different objectives of common sense and of scientific inquiry demand different subject-matters and that this difference in subject-matters is not incompatible with the existence of a common pattern in both types. There are, of course, secondary logical forms which reflect the distinction of properties involved in the change from qualitative and teleological subject-matter to non-qualitative and non-teleological relations. But they occur and operate within the described community of pattern. They are explicable, and explicable only, on the ground of the distinctive problems generated by scientific subject-matter. The independence of scientific objects from limited and fairly direct reference to the environment as a factor in activities of use and enjoyment, is equivalent, as has already been intimated, to their *abstract* character. It is also equivalent to their *general* character in the sense in which the generalizations of science are different from the generalizations with which common sense is familiar. The generality of *all* scientific subject-matter as such means that it is freed from restriction to conditions which present themselves at particular times and places. Their reference is to *any* set of time and place conditions—a statement which is not to be confused with the doctrine that they have no reference to actual existential occasions. Reference to time-place of existence is necessarily involved, but it is reference to whatever set of existences fulfils the general relations laid down in and by the constitution of the scientific object.[8]

Summary. Since a number of points have been discussed, it will be well to round up conclusions reached about them in a summary statement of the structure of the common pattern of inquiry. Inquiry is the directed or controlled transformation of an indeterminate situation into a determinately unified one. The transition is achieved by means of operations of two kinds which are in functional correspondence with each other. One kind of operations deals with ideational or conceptual subject-matter. This subject-matter stands for possible ways and ends of resolution. It anticipates a solution, and is marked off from fancy because, or, in so far as, it becomes operative in instigation and direction of new observations yielding new factual material. The other kind of operations is made up of activities involving the techniques and organs of observation. Since these operations are existential they modify the prior existential situation, bring into high relief conditions previously obscure, and relegate to the background other aspects that were at the outset conspicuous.

---

[8] The consequences that follow are directly related to the statement in Ch. IV that the elimination of qualities and ends is intermediate; that, in fact, the construction of purely relational objects has enormously liberated and expanded common sense uses and enjoyments by conferring control over production of qualities, by enabling new ends to be realistically instituted, and by providing competent means for achieving them.

The ground and criterion of the execution of this work of emphasis, selection and arrangement is to delimit the problem in such a way that existential material may be provided with which to test the ideas that represent possible modes of solution. Symbols, defining terms and propositions, are necessarily required in order to retain and carry forward both ideational and existential subject-matters in order that they may serve their proper functions in the control of inquiry. Otherwise the problem is taken to be closed and inquiry ceases.

One fundamentally important phase of the transformation of the situation which constitutes inquiry is central in the treatment of judgment and its functions. The transformation is existential and hence temporal. The pre-cognitive unsettled situation can be settled only by modification of its constituents. Experimental operations change existing conditions. Reasoning, as such, can provide means for effecting the change of conditions but by itself cannot effect it. Only execution of existential operations directed by an idea in which ratiocination terminates can bring about the re-ordering of environing conditions required to produce a settled and unified situation. Since this principle also applies to the meanings that are elaborated in science, the experimental production and re-arrangement of physical conditions involved in natural science is further evidence of the unity of the pattern of inquiry. The temporal quality of inquiry means, then, something quite other than that the process of inquiry takes time. It means that the objective subject-matter of inquiry undergoes temporal modification.

Terminological. Were it not that knowledge is related to inquiry as a product to the operations by which it is produced, no distinctions requiring special differentiating designations would exist. Material would merely be a matter of knowledge or of ignorance and error; that would be all that could be said. The content of any given proposition would have the values "true" and "false" as final and exclusive attributes. But if knowledge is related to inquiry as its warrantably assertible product, and if inquiry is progressive and temporal, then the material inquired into reveals distinctive properties which need to be designated by distinctive names. As *undergoing* inquiry, the material has a different logical import from that which it has as the *outcome* of inquiry. In its first capacity and status, it will be called by the general name *subject-matter*. When it is necessary to refer to subject-matter in the context of either observation or ideation, the name *content* will be used, and, particularly on account of its *representative* character, content of propositions.

The name *objects* will be reserved for subject-matter so far as it has been produced and ordered in settled form by means of inquiry; proleptically, objects are the *objectives* of inquiry. The apparent ambiguity of using "objects" for this purpose (since the word is regularly applied to things that are observed or thought of) is only apparent. For things exist *as* objects for us only as they have been previously determined as outcomes of inquiries. When used in carrying on new inquiries in new problematic situations, they are known as objects in virtue of prior inquiries which warrant their assertibility. In the new situation, they are *means* of attaining knowledge of something else. In the strict sense, they are part of the *contents* of inquiry as the word content was defined above. But retrospectively (that is, as products of prior determination in inquiry) they are objects.

CHAPTER VII

THE CONSTRUCTION OF JUDGMENT [1]

IN TERMS of the ideas set forth in the last chapter, judgment may be identified as the settled outcome of inquiry. It is concerned with the concluding objects that emerge from inquiry in their status of being conclusive. Judgment in this sense is distinguished from *propositions*. The content of the latter is intermediate and representative and is carried by symbols; while judgment, as finally made, has *direct* existential import. The terms *affirmation* and *assertion* are employed in current speech interchangeably. But there is a difference, which should have linguistic recognition, between the logical status of intermediate subject-matters that are taken for use in connection with what they may lead to as means, and subject-matter which has been prepared to be final. I shall use *assertion* to designate the latter logical status and *affirmation* to name the former. Even from the standpoint of ordinary speech, *assertion* has a quality of insistence that is lacking in the connotation of the *word* "affirmation." We can usually substitute the phrase "it is *held*" or "it is *said*" for "*it is affirmed.*" However, the important matter is not the words, but the logical properties that are characteristic of different subject-matters.

A literal instance of judgment in the sense defined is provided by the judgment of a court of law in settling some issue which, up to that point, has been in controversy. 1. The occurrence of a trial-at-law is equivalent to the occurrence of a problematic situation which requires settlement. There is uncertainty and dispute about what shall be done because there is conflict about the *significance* of what has taken place, even if there is agreement about what has taken place as a matter of fact—which, of course, is not always the case. The judicial settlement is a settle-

---

[1] The word "construction" is here used to cover the operation of construction and the structure which results.

120

ment of an *issue* because it decides existential conditions in their bearing upon further activities: the essence of the significance of any state of facts.

2. This settlement or judgment is the outcome of inquiry conducted in the court-hearings. The inquiry exemplifies the pattern described in the last chapter. On the one hand, propositions are advanced about the state of facts involved. Witnesses testify to what they have heard and seen; written records are offered, etc. This subject-matter is capable of direct observation and has existential reference. As each party to the discussion produces its evidential material, the latter is intended to point to a determinate decision as a resolution of the as yet undetermined situation. The decision takes effect in a definite existential reconstruction. On the other hand, there are propositions about conceptual subject-matter; rules of law are adduced to determine the admissibility (relevancy) and the weight of facts offered as evidence. The *significance* of factual material is fixed by the rules of the existing juridical system; it is not carried by the facts independent of the conceptual structure which interprets them. And yet, the quality of the problematic situation determines which rules of the total system are selected. They are different in civil and criminal cases; in cases of trespass and of breach of contract. Conceptions have been organized in the past under definite rubrics which summarize the *kinds* of interpreting principles that past experience has shown to be applicable in the variety of special cases that normally arise. The theoretical ideal sought to guide judicial deliberation is a network of relations and procedures which express the closest possible correspondence between facts and the legal meanings that give them their significance: that is, settle the consequences which, in the existing social system, flow from them.

3. The final judgment arrived at is a settlement. The case is disposed of; the disposition takes effect in existential consequences. The sentence or proposition is not an end in itself but a decisive directive of future activities. The consequences of these activities bring about an existential determination of the prior situation which was indeterminate as to its issue. A man is set free, sent to prison, pays a fine, or has to execute an agreement or pay damages to an injured party. It is this resulting state of actual affairs—this changed situation—that is the matter of the final

settlement or judgment. The sentence itself is a proposition, differing, however, from the propositions formed during the trial, whether they concern matters of fact or legal conceptions, in that it takes overt effect in operations which construct a new qualitative situation. While prior propositions are means of instituting the sentence, the sentence is terminal as a means of instituting a definite existential situation.

Judgment figures, however, in determination of the intermediate propositions. When it is ruled that certain evidence is admissible and that certain rules of law (conceptual material) are applicable rather than others, *something* is settled. It is through a series of such intervening settlements that the final settlement is constructed. Judgment as final settlement is dependent upon a series of partial settlements. The judgments by which propositions are determined is recognized and marked off linguistically by such words as *estimates, appraisals, evaluations.* In resolution of problems that are of a looser quality than legal cases we call them *opinions* to distinguish them from a warranted judgment or assertion. But if the opinion held is grounded it is itself the product of inquiry and *in so far* is a judgment.[2] Estimates and appraisals are provisional; they are means, not ends. Even a judgment of appraisal by judges on the bench may be reversed in a higher court, while in freer conduct of scientific inquiry such judgments are expressly made subject to modification. The consequences they produce in the conduct of further inquiry is the criterion of their value. Judgments which intervene are ad-judgments.

I. *Final Judgment is Individual.* This caption is elliptical. It means that the subject-matter (objects) of final judgment is a *situation* in the sense in which the meaning of that word has been explained; it is a qualitative existential whole which is unique. "Individual" as here used has nothing to do with simplicity of constituents. On the contrary, every situation, when it is analyzed, is extensive containing within itself diverse distinctions and relations which, in spite of their diversity, form a unified qualitative whole. What is designated by the word *individual* has, accordingly, to be distinguished from that which is designated by

---

[2] *Opinion* in common speech often means a belief entertained without examination, being generated by custom, tradition or desire.

the word *singular*. Singulars are named by demonstratives, such as *this, that, here, now,* or in some cases by proper nouns. The difference between a singular and an individual is the same as that previously pointed out between *an* object (or set of objects in their severalty) and a situation.³ Singular objects exist and singular events occur within a field or situation. *This* or *that* star, man, rock or whatever, is always a discrimination or selection made for a purpose, or for the sake of some objective consequence within an inclusive field. The singular has no import save as a term of differentiation and contrast. If its object is taken to be complete in itself, loss of differential force destroys all power of reference on the part of the demonstrative act. The very existence of differentiation, on the other hand, shows that the singular exists within an extensive field.

It follows that determination of a singular is also instrumental in determination of a situation which is itself not complete and self-sufficient. It is a means of identifying a situation in reference to the problem set to inquiry. It represents, at a given stage of inquiry, that which is crucial, critical, differentiatingly significant. An artisan in carrying on his work at any given time takes note of certain aspects and phases of the situation in which his activities are involved. He notes *just that* object or occurrence which is decisive in the stage of development arrived at in the whole situation which is determinative of what is to be next. The objects which are *this* and *that*, to which his inquiry and activity are immediately directed, are, therefore, constantly changing. As one phase of the problem offered by his work is resolved, another phase, presented by a new object or occurrence, takes its place. Were not the sequence determined by an inclusive situation, whose qualitative nature pervades and holds together each successive step, activity would be a meaningless hop-skip-jump affair. Objects observed and dealt with would be a shifting panorama of sudden disconnected appearances and disappearances. Exactly the same account may be given of the succession of observations which deal with singular objects and occurrences in scientific inquiry. The singular is that upon which inquiry into an individual situation pivots under the special conditions that at a given time

³ *Ante*, pp. 66-7.

fix the problem with respect to the conditions to be dealt with forthwith.

The discriminative or differential aspect of the demonstrative act and its singular object is suggested in ordinary speech by the expression "pointing *out*." It is impossible merely to point *at* something.[4] For anything or everything in the line of vision or gesture may be equally pointed *at*. The act of pointing is wholly indeterminate as to its object. It is not selective within a situation, because it is not controlled by the problem which the situation sets and the necessity for determining the conditions which then and there point to the way in which it shall be resolved.

The point just made has its logical meaning in disclosure of the ambiguity of the word *given* as that is currently employed in logical texts. That which is "given" in the strict sense of the word "given," is the total field or situation. The given in the sense of the singular, whether object or quality, is the special aspect, phase or constituent of the existentially present situation that is selected to locate and identify its problematic features with reference to the inquiry then and there to be executed. In the strict sense, it is *taken* rather than given. This fact decides the logical status of *data*. They are not isolated, complete or self-sufficient. To be a datum is to have a special function in control of the subject-matter of inquiry. It embodies a fixation of the problem in a way which indicates a possible solution. It also helps to provide evidence which tests the solution that is hypothetically entertained. This theme will be developed in the discussion that follows of "thought," that is, inquiry.

II. *The Subject of Judgment*. What was said in the last chapter concerning the pattern of inquiry enables us to identify the structure of judgment as conjugate distinction and relation of subject-predicate. Observed facts of the case in their dual function of bringing the problem to light and of providing evidential material with respect to its solution constitute what has traditionally been called the *subject*. The conceptual contents which anticipate a possible solution and which direct observational operations constitute what has traditionally been called the *predicate*.

---

[4] Cf. the conditions and results of the pointing reported in the incident described on p. 53.

Their functional and operative correspondence with each other constitutes the *copula*.

In this section, I shall consider the *subject* of judgment. The bearing of the conclusions reached up to this point may be focalized by contrasting them with a doctrine current in logical theory. This latter view holds that the existential matter, which has ultimately the form of *this object* or *this quality*, is given or presented in a literal sense *to* judgment. Judgment proper is then confined to the work of predicating something of it, of characterizing what is handed out ready-made either to sense-perception or to judgment. I select one statement as typical: "In every proposition we are determining *in* thought the character of an object present to thought." [5] The contrasting position here taken holds that the subject-matters of subject and predicate are determined in correspondence with each other in and by the process of "thought," that is, inquiry.

Examination of the two opposed theories will start from the negative side. We begin by pointing out the difficulties, amounting to impossibilities, in the customary view advanced in many standard treatises. (1) It leaves judgment, as predication, and just at the point where its existential material is concerned, entirely at the mercy of the accidental flux of objects which happen to present themselves. It thereby destroys the possibility of sequential continuity in "thought." Predication would at one moment be characterizing one object, and at the next moment some other object, according as changes and shifts in environing conditions took place. The occurrence of successive "given" or "presented" singulars would be wholly determined by conditions outside of inquiry and therefore accidental and irrelevant. (2) The view would be another version of the old doctrine of passive receptivities, were it not that some active response is demanded in order to institute something to which a demonstrative term may be applied. Even then, there is nothing to ground the act of pointing so as to select one "this" rather than another. (3) Nor is there anything in a mere given "this" to ground one characterizing predicate rather than another. Either "this" is so empty that nothing can be said of it except "this is this" where

[5] W. E. Johnson, *Logic*, Part I, pages 9 and 11.

"this" signifies nothing beyond the mere presence of an indefinite somewhat, or else any one of a large number of predications can equally well be made. The truth is that the view criticized can be intelligibly stated only *after* inquiry has already made out some fact or set of facts and when the emphatic problem has become that of knowing how it should be characterized. The view owes whatever plausibility it appears to have to the fact that it begins its account of judgment after inquiry has been operative and has already established a partial judgment or appraisal. As was indicated in the prior chapter, in situations whose recognized constituents are similar to those of prior experiences, certain objects are likely to stand out sufficiently so as to afford clews. But (a) they do so as products of prior judgments, and (b) in any case they are provisional as evidential data. For they may be misleading clews because they turn out to be not "the facts *of the case*," or what is significant in respect to the present problem.

Suppose that in a given case, *this* is characterized "Washington Monument." The act of pointing does not determine any one "this" rather than another since everything in the line of pointing is pointed *at*. In the second place, even when we suppose that the act of pointing happens to land, so to speak, upon one singular rather than another, it is only a group of sensible qualities that is indicated. There is nothing in these qualities, apart from the control of their interpretation by an inclusive situation, to justify characterizing them as the Washington Monument—or as a memorial of any kind. The most that could be said is that the qualities observed in consequence of the demonstrative act are just the qualities they are. The nub of any existential identification or characterization of a thing as such-and-such lies in the ground it offers for giving the object a description in terms of what is *not* then and there observed. Apart from an inclusive situation which determines *in correspondence with each other* the material that constitutes the observed singular this and the kind of characterizing predicate applicable to it, predication is totally arbitrary or ungrounded. There must be some one *question* to which both the subject "this" and the predicate (say, *Washington Monument*) are relevant. That question grows out of and is controlled by some total situation. Otherwise propositions made are pointless.

Any proposition in which "this" appears is then instituted by a judgment of appraisal in which "this" is determined in order to provide evidential grounds for the qualification attached to it by the predicate. This fact is inconsistent with "this" being a *mere* this. There is, however, no incompatibility between the fact that *it* is just what it existentially is and the estimate that it is the needed evidential ground of a definite characterization. Stating the matter positively, the operations that institute a "this" as subject are always selective-restrictive of something from out of a larger field. What is selected and what is rejected flows from an estimate of their probable evidential significance.

III. *Subjects and Substances.* According to the original Aristotelian logic, certain objects, such as species, are logical subjects by Nature, since they are substances in Nature, so that only propositions having substances for their subjects can enter into rationally demonstrative knowledge or science. This theory of the nature of the logical subject at least recognizes that the logical subject has a determinate nature capable of grounding what is predicated of it. But the progress of science has destroyed the idea that objects as such are eternal substances, even such objects as the "fixed stars." [6] It also destroyed the notion of immutable kinds marked off from one another by fixed essences. The following problem accordingly arises: If the logical subject cannot be identified either with an object or sense-datum directly given to judgment for qualification through predication, nor yet with an ontological "substance," what is meant by being an object substantial *in any sense* that makes it capable of serving as a subject?

The answer to this question is implicit in what has been said. The subject is existential, either a singular *this*, or a set of singulars. But there are conditions of inquiry which must be satisfied by anything taken to be a subject. (1) It must delimit and describe the problem in such a way as to indicate a possible solution. (2) It must be such that new data, instituted by observational operations directed by the provisional predicate (representing a possible solution), will unite with its subject-matter to form a coherent whole.

[6] The Newtonian theory of atoms represented a survival of the old conception of changeless substances. Within the context of the theory, however, they were transferred from the region of common sense objects to that of strictly scientific objects.

The latter constitutes a substantial object in the logical sense of that term, or is on its way to becoming such an object. For it is union of connected distinctions so held together that it may be acted upon or with as a whole; and it is capable of incorporating into itself other predicated qualifications until it becomes, as such, a unity of inter-connected distinctions, or "properties."

Take, for an example, such an elementary proposition as "this is sweet." *This*, as has been shown, marks a selective-restriction, made for a definite purpose, within an inclusive qualitative problematic situation. The purpose is the final consequence of a resolved situation in attainment of which *"this"* has a special function to perform. If the predicate *"is sweet"* is an *anticipation* of the resolved situation, it means "this" *will sweeten* something if that operation is performed which is required to generate definite perceptible consequences. Or, it may record the achieved result of the execution of the operation: "This *has* sweetened something." When the operation is completed, *this* is definitely qualified as sweet. This fact is manifest not in a proposition (although a proposition may report it for purposes of record or communication of information) nor in symbols, but in a directly experienced existence. Henceforth, "this" is a sweet *somewhat*. The quality *sweet* does not stand alone but is definitely connected with other observed qualities. As thus characterized, it enters into further situations in which it incorporates into itself additional qualifications. It is a sweet, white, granular, more or less gritty thing or substance, say, *sugar*.

"Substance" represents therefore, a logical, not an ontological, determination. Sugar, for example, is a substance because through a number of partial judgments completed in operations which have existential consequences, a variety of qualifications so cohere as to form an object that may be used and enjoyed as a unified whole. Its substantial character is quite independent of its physical duration, to say nothing of its immutability. The object, *sugar*, may disappear in solution. It is then further qualified; it is a soluble object. In a chemical interaction its constitution may be so changed that it is no longer sugar. Capacity for undergoing this change is henceforth an additional qualification or property of anything that is sugar. The condition—and the sole condition that has to be satisfied in order that there may be substantiality, is that certain qualifications hang together as dependable signs that certain consequences will follow when certain interactions take place. This is what is meant when it is said that substantiality is a logical, not a primary ontological determination.

It is a form that accrues to original existence when the latter operates in a specified functional way as a consequence of operations of inquiry. It is not postulated that certain qualities always cohere in existence. It is postulated that they cohere as dependable evidential signs. The conjoined properties that mark off and identify a chair, a piece of granite, a meteor, are not sets of qualities given existentially as such and such. They are certain qualities which constitute in their ordered conjunction with one another valid signs of what will ensue when certain operations are performed. An object, in other words, is a set of qualities treated as *potentialities* for specified existential consequences. Powder is what will explode under certain conditions; water as a substantial object is that group of connected qualities which will quench thirst, and so on. The greater the number of interactions, of operations, and of consequences, the more complex is the constitution of a given substantial object. With the progress of technology, clay and iron have acquired new potentialities. A piece of iron is now a sign of many things of which it was not once a sign. When it was discovered that wood-pulp could be used for making paper if its material was subjected to operations in which it entered into new conditions of interaction, the *significance* of certain forms of lumber as objects changed. They did not become *entirely* new substantial objects because old potentialities for consequences remained. But neither was it the same old substance. The habit of supposing that it is the same all the time is the result of hypostatizing the logical character of being a sign or having significance into something inherent. Being a substantial object defines a specific function.

We speak regularly of chemical substances. A chemical substance is represented not by enumeration of qualities as such, but by a formula which provides a synoptic indication of the various types of consequences which will result. The perceptible qualities of table sugar and sugar of lead are much the same. Even common sense learns to distinguish them as different "substances" in virtue of some of the different consequences which ensue from their operational use. In the scientific statement of their chemical substance, even common sensible qualities are ignored. Different formulae enable us to anticipate differences which are not sensibly discernible at the time. To common sense, water is that which is pot*able*, which will cleanse, upon which many things will float, etc. Chemically, it is H_2O—a description in terms of a set of possible interactions and specified consequences. *Some* qualities are actually, sensibly, present. But as such they do not constitute an object. For common sense and for science alike, they constitute an *object* in virtue of the consequences of which the existent qualities, be they few or many, are signs, and of which they are the conditions *provided* operations institute certain interactions not then and there occurring.

The contrast between the conception of substance that has been set forth here with the Aristotelian ontological conception is, of course, intimately connected with the great change which has taken place in science, i.e., its complete shift from immutable objects to correspondences of changes. Aristotle said, "It is absurd to make the fact that the things of this earth change and never remain the same the basis of our judgments about the truth. For in pursuing the truth one must start from things that are always in the same state and never change. Such are the heavenly bodies; for they do not appear to be now of one nature and now of another, but are always manifestly the same and do not change." [7]

Such immutable things alone were complete substances and fit to be subjects of "true" propositions. In present science, on the other hand, such transitory events as lightning and such variable things as the weather become subjects of scientific judgments when they are determined as constituents of a systematic set of changes which as changes are in functional correspondence. Such facts exemplify what is meant by the functional nature of substantial objects. In the light of dependable inferences that can be drawn, of the correlations of changes that are established, an event like a flash of lightning has *logical* solidity and endurance in spite of its existential transitivity. It is substantial. It is representable by a

[7] Aristotle, *Metaphysics*, 1063 ª. Ross' translation.

substantive, which even when it is a verbal noun has constancy in discourse as a means of identification of the kind of which the singular is a specimen.

IV. *The Predicate of Judgment.* The logical meaning of *predicate* has been anticipated in the discussion of the logical subject, because of the strict correlativity of respective existential and ideational contents. The meanings which are suggested as possible solutions of a problem, which are then used to direct further operations of experimental observation, form the predicational content of judgments. The latter is related to the factual content, that is, the subject, as the possible to the actual. For example, in the illustration considered above, when *"this"* is estimated before the act of tasting to be *sweet*, a certain consequence is anticipated to which is assigned a definite connection in the total situation. If, however, it is at once asserted "this is sweet," the assertion is logically premature and ungrounded. The anticipation functions logically to instigate and direct an operation of experimental observation. When the consequences of the latter combine with facts already ascertained so as to constitute a unified total situation, inquiry comes to an end. But there is always danger that the congeniality or plausibility of the content of the predicate-meaning will lead directly to its acceptance. In that case, it is not operationally checked. It possesses *logical* status only as it is taken for what it is *qua* predicate—namely, a *method* of solution not itself a solution. There is also danger that pains will not be taken, even when an operation is performed, to scrutinize its results in order to ascertain whether the existential conditions actually cohere in a unified way. These two failures are the common source of premature, hasty, and therefore ungrounded assertion.

The essential error of the "rationalistic" tradition in logical theory consists in taking the consistency of the constituents of the conceptual contents (which form the predicate) as a final criterion of truth or assertibility. Subject-matter which, in its logical form, is a means for performing experimental activities to modify prior existences is mistaken to be final and complete in itself. Thereby an inherent ontological status is imputed to it. As has been pointed out, subject-matter endowed with "rational" form was treated in classic logic as constituting a superior realm of "Reality," in comparison with which material capable of sensible observation was by Nature metaphysically inferior. The latter was "known" only in so far as it could be directly subsumed under the conceptual material. A more recent tendency is to regard the conceptual subject-matter as constituting a realm of abstract possibility also taken as complete in itself, not as indicating possibilities of operations to be performed. While the resulting metaphysical status assigned is very different from that of classic ontology, there is nevertheless the same hypostization of a logical function into a supra-empirical entity. Meantime, the practice of scientific inquiry has provided the foundations for a correct logical interpretation.

The conceptual and "rational" contents are *hypotheses*. In their more comprehensive forms they are theories. As such they may be and usually are abstracted from application to this and that immediate existential situation. But on that very account. they are instruments of a wide, indefinite scope of operational application, actual application being made as special conditions present themselves. In reaction against the inherently "superior" position assigned to conceptual material, and because of its recognition of the necessity of observational experience to guarantee existential reference, "empiristic" logical tradition went to the other extreme. It denied the logical necessity of conceptual meanings and theories, reducing them to mere practical conveniences. Traditional empiricism supposed it was following the pattern set by scientific inquiry. But in fact it was engaged in corrupting formulation of scientific inquiry by subjecting the latter to uncritically accepted conclusions of a subjectivistic psychological theory.

V. *The Copula.* The logical import of copulation is involved in the prior account of subject and predicate. It is neither a separate and independent element nor yet does it affect the predicate alone, attaching the latter to an independently and externally given singular subject, whether the latter be taken to be an object, a quality, or a sense-datum. It does express the act of predication. But it also expresses the act or operation of "subjection"; that is, of constituting the subject. It is a name for the complex of operations by means of which (a) certain existences are re-strictively-selected to delimit a problem and provide evidential testing material, and by which (b) certain conceptual meanings, ideas, hypotheses, are used as characterizing predicates. It is a name for the functional correspondence between subject and predicate in their relation to each other. The operations which it expresses distinguish and relate at the same time.

The fact that judgment as such has a subject-predicate struc-ture, and that in this structure subject-and-predicate contents are at the same time distinguished and related, has been made a ground for holding that judgment has an inherently self-contradictory character.[8] This position is unanswerable unless it be recognized (1) that the copula stands for operations, and (2) that judgment is a process of temporal existential reconstitution.

1. Inquiry demands, as we have seen, operations of both observa-tion and ideation. There would be no control of the process of inquiry if each of these operations were not expressly formed with reference to the other. It is easy to see what would happen if observation were directed to material which had no connection with entertained ideas and hypotheses, and if the latter went off on a track of their own, having no connection with the material obtained by observation. In the process of reasoning, especially in scientific inquiry, there is often a considerable period in which conceptual material is developed on its own account, leaving observed material temporarily in abeyance. But none-theless in controlled inquiry, the entire object of this seemingly independent development is to obtain *that* meaning or conceptual structure which is best adapted to instigate and direct just those operations of observation that will secure as their consequence just those existential facts that are needed to solve the problem in hand.

2. Final judgment is attained through a series of partial judg-ments—those to which the name *estimates* or *appraisals* has been given. Judgment is not something occurring all at once. Since it is a manifestation of inquiry, it cannot be instantaneous and yet be inquiry. Short of attainment of a finally resolved situa-

---

[8] For example, by F. H. Bradley in both his *Logic* and his *Appearance and Reality*.

tion (the result of final judgment and assertion) respective subject-and-predicate contents are *provisionally* instituted in distinction from and correlation with each other. Were subject-and-predicate contents final rather than provisional, distinction and relation *would* constitute a state of irreconcilable opposition. Since they are functional and operative, there is no more conflict than there is in the fact that in the course of every complex productive activity, industrial or social, divisions of labor are instituted which nevertheless are functionally connected with one another. For they are instituted as cooperating means of a common unified outcome. Were a complex undertaking in which extensive division of labor prevailed arrested short of its temporal issue, and were the various activities and their respective partial products taken at the moment of arrest to provide a final interpretation of what is going on, the conclusion might not be that there was inherent contradiction among them, but the idea that irrelevancy and disorganization existed would be justified. The result of the discussion is, then, to show how indispensable it is to acknowledge that judgment, like inquiry, is temporal. It is temporal not in the external sense that the act of judging takes time, but in the sense that its subject-matter undergoes reconstitution in attaining the final state of determinate resolution and unification which is the objective that governs judgment.

It is necessarily involved in what has been said that the linguistic form which expresses, or is the symbol of, judgment is a true verb; that is, one expressing action and change.

When *is* appears in *judgment* it has temporal force, distinct from *was* or *will be*, and distinct from the "is" of a proposition where "is" designates a non-temporal or strictly logical relation between meanings. When it is stated that "the boy is running" the reference to change, time and place lies on the surface. When one says "this is red" the temporal reference is linguistically disguised. But the statement certainly does not mean that *this* is inherently red or is always red. Color quality changes to some extent with every change in light. It is red *now*, but only under a specifiable set of conditions, and a completely grounded judgment demands that the conditions be stated. "Is red" sets forth what in ordinary language is called an effect or a change brought about, or else a capacity to produce change, a power to redden other things.[9]

Etymologically, the word *is* derives from a root meaning to stand or to stay. To remain and endure is a mode of action. At least, it indicates a temporal equilibrium of interactions. Now a spatio-temporal change is existential. Consequently the copula in judgment, whether as a transitive or intransitive verb, or in the ambiguous form "is," has inherent existential reference. In such a proposition as "Justice is a virtue," *is*, on the other hand, stands for a relation between two abstractions or meanings, and accordingly is non-temporal. It is a mark of a logical relation such that in any proposition in which "justice" appears there is an implicatory relation to some proposition in which "virtue" appears.[10] The *situation* to which the sentence refers determines unambiguously whether "is" has an active force, expressing a change going on actually or potentially, or whether it stands for a relation between meanings or ideas. In a sentence having no contextual situation, its logical force is indeterminate. For any sentence isolated from place and function in inquiry is logically indeterminate.

The copula in a judgment, in distinction from the term of formal relation, expresses, accordingly, the actual transformation of the subject-matter of an indeterminate situation into a determinate one. So far is the copula from being an isolable constituent that it might be regarded as what sets the subject-and-predicate contents at work executing their functions in relation to one another. In complex undertakings a plan for division of functions is usually laid out on paper. But this plan is not the actual division of labor. The latter consists in the actual distribution of the active factors of what is doing in their cooperation with one another. The distribution, as well as the cooperation, is arranged with reference to an end or objective consequence.

The plan may be set forth and explained in propositions; its propositional exposition may be a means of criticism and of rearrangment of the plan of distribution. But the *actual* division can only be enacted. As just indicated, it may be stated in symbols, and symbolic representation of the division may be an indis-

---

[9] Cf. the previous analysis of "It is sweet."

[10] In other words, "the ambiguity of the copula," depends upon failure to determine whether in any given instance it has temporo-spatial reference or stands for a relation of meanings as such.

pensable means of an actual enactment. But it no more *is* a functioning division of labor than a blueprint is a house in process of building or a map is a journey. Blueprints and maps are propositions and they exemplify what it is to *be* propositional. Moreover, a map is no less a means of directing journeys because it is not constantly in use. Similarly, general propositions are no less a means of constructing judgments because they are not always operative in the existential work of reconstituting existential material.

Like a chart, indeed, like any physical tool or physiological organ, a proposition must be defined by its function. Furthermore, there is the same sort of advantage in having conceptual frameworks manufactured and on hand in advance of actual occasions for their use, as there is in having tools ready instead of improvising them when need arises. Just as a complex undertaking in any field demands prepared *materials* as well as prepared instrumentalities, so propositions which describe conjunctions of existential materials—ultimately reducible to space-time connections—are required in effective inquiry. At the outset substantial object-events serve this purpose as more or less secondary by-products or deposits from prior inquiries. But finally they are deliberately constituted by critical inquiry intended to produce objects that will operate as effective and economical means when they are needed—a differentia of common sense and scientific objects. Propositions about subject-contents, about spatial-temporal conjunctions of properties of existence, thus undergo independent development just as do propositions about meanings and their relations. The former will be called *material means* and the latter *procedural means*, it being remembered that both are operational since they are means of determining the final situation and judgment.

Despite the decay and abandonment of the cosmological foundation of the Aristotelian theory of the structure and the constituents of judgment, conceptions which were essential to it still play an important part in many logical texts under the name of the theory of predicables. That which can be predicated was classified in respect to its logical force or form under the following heads: essence, property, genus, differentia and accident. They expressed the ways in which predication can take place because of the different kinds of connection that were supposed to exist among things.

A substantial species is what it is in virtue of its eternal and fixed essence. To predicate an essence of a substance is accordingly to define it, definition being, as previously noted, neither verbal nor an aid in inquiry, but an apprehension ("re-marking" in a literal sense) of that which makes the substance to be what it is. A definition is stated and communicated by means of the predicables, genus and differentia, these being logical, not ontological like species and essence. A genus differed from a species; it was not, as in modern theory, simply a kind that is more comprehensive than the kinds called species. It has no existence while a species must *be*. It cannot, therefore, be the subject of any final judgment.[11]

Plane figure is generic as compared with triangle, and triangle is generic with respect to isosceles, scalene and equilateral triangles. But even the latter were only qualifications of species existing in nature. In setting forth a definition, in leading another to learn to grasp a defining essence or in enabling one's self to regrasp it, we start with the proximate genus and then give the differentia which distinguish a species within that genus from every other species falling within it. Thus the differentia of the genus plane figure in the case of a triangular figure is having three sides. A genus is the logical "matter" of definition, related to it as potentiality is to actuality in ontological material.

A property is no part of an essence but flows necessarily from it. It may, therefore, be predicated universally and necessarily of a subject just as the defining essence may be. It is not part of the essence of man to be a grammarian. But it flows necessarily from the essence of man as rational. Theorems that flow from the definitions and axioms of the Euclidean geometry have a similar logical status. But some things can only be predicated accidentally—that is, when they are neither part of an essence nor flow from it, nor are of the nature of genus and differentia. All changing things which cannot be enclosed within fixed limits

---

[11] Upon its logical side, the Aristotelian polemic against Platonic Ideas and Numbers (geometrical figures) was based upon the fact that the latter are genera, not species, and hence cannot exist by themselves, but only in thought.

are of this character. They bear a purely *contingent* relation to that of which they are predicated. It may be affirmed that "most blue-eyed persons are blonde"; "days in summer are warm as a rule or upon the whole"; etc. But there is no necessary connection between subject and predicate. They just happen, as it were, to be that way—not in the sense that there is no cause for their happening that way rather than in some other way, but in that the cause is itself another change, which also has a contingent relation to what is permanent, universal and necessary. There is no *reason* why accidents occur as they do in the sense of reason proper to the Aristotelian scheme.

This theory of the forms of predication was acute and comprehensive under the scientific conditions in which it was formulated. In the light of the theory and practice of modern scientific inquiry it has no validity. I shall take one instance as exemplary. Seeming exceptions to law or general principle ("accidents" in the old sense) are now the nutriment upon which scientific inquiry feeds. They have a ground or "reason" in the correlated conditions of their occurrence. General propositions are not only possible about these correlations but every existential general proposition or law *is* about them. In any other sense of the word, that which is "accidental" is that which is irrelevant in any given situation, and which, therefore, is to be ruled out because of absence of evidential function in the given problem. If not ruled out it is likely to carry inquiry into a wrong track. In short, there is no prior fixed and ready-made determination of what may be predicated and of ways of predication. Every predicate is ideational or conceptual. It must be so constituted as to direct operations whose consequences throw light upon the problem dealt with and provide additional evidence for its solution. Apart from the limits set by the problem in hand, there are no rules whatever for determining what may or should be predicated. As far as present logical texts still continue to talk about essences, properties and accidents as something *inherently* different from one another, they are repeating distinctions that once had an ontological meaning and that no longer have it. Anything is "essential" which is indispensable in a given inquiry and anything is "accidental" which is superfluous.

CHAPTER VIII

IMMEDIATE KNOWLEDGE:
UNDERSTANDING AND INFERENCE

THE CONSIDERATIONS adduced in discussion of the pattern of inquiry and of the structure of judgment, entail the conclusion that all knowledge as grounded assertion involves mediation. Mediation, in this context, means that an inferential function is involved in all warranted assertion. The position here defended runs counter to the belief that there is such a thing as immediate knowledge, and that such knowledge is an indispensable precondition of all mediated knowledge. Because of the wide currency of this latter doctrine and the intrinsic importance of the logical issue involved, this chapter will be devoted to the discussion of the theme of immediate knowledge.

Logical schools as opposed to each other as are the rationalistic and the empiristic agree in accepting the doctrine of immediate knowledge. On this point they differ only with respect to the objects and organs of such knowledge. Rationalist schools hold that ultimate principles of a universal character are the objects of immediate knowledge and that reason is the organ of their apprehension. Empiristic schools believe that sense-perception is the organ of knowledge and that the things immediately known are sensory qualities or, as they are now more usually called, sense-data. Some logical theories maintain that both kinds of immediate knowledge exist and that mediation and inferential knowledge result from the union of the two; a union in which *a priori* first truths and empirical material are brought into connection with each other.

The doctrine of immediate knowledge would not be so widely held unless there were *prima facie* grounds of great plausibility to suggest it and apparent evidence that can be marshalled in its support. I shall introduce critical discussion of the doctrine by stating how these grounds are to be interpreted from the standpoint of the position already taken in this book.

1. There is continuity in inquiry. The conclusions reached in one inquiry become means, material and procedural, of carrying on further inquiries. In the latter, the results of earlier inquiries are taken and used without being resubjected to examination. In uncritical reflection the net outcome is often an accumulation of error. But there are conceptual objects, and objects of perceptual experience, which have been so instituted and confirmed in the course of different inquiries, that it would be a waste of time and energy in further inquiries to make them objects of investigation before proceeding to take and use them. This immediate *use* of objects known in consequence of previous mediation is readily confused with immediate knowledge.

2. It was noted in the previous chapter that final judgment is constructed by a series of intermediate partial judgments, to which the name *estimates* or *appraisals* was given. The content of these intermediate judgments, which cover both matters of fact and conceptual structures, is carried in propositions. In any inquiry of extensive scope (because of the nature of the problem with which it is concerned) these propositions gain relative independence. While they are ultimately means for determining final judgment, for the time being they are absorbing ends; just as, we have seen, in physical production and construction, tools are apparently independent objects complete and self-sufficient in themselves. Their function and the potential consequence of the exercise of their function become completely integrated into their immediate structure. As soon as it is forgotten that they are means and that their value is determined by their efficacy as operative means, they appear to be objects of immediate knowledge instead of being means of attaining knowledge.

When, however, their functional character is recognized, the mistake which is committed in these interpretations is evident:

1. While the direct use of objects, factual and conceptual, which have been determined in the course of resolving prior problematic situations is of indispensable practical value in the

conduct of further inquiries, such objects are not exempt in new inquiries from need for reexamination and reconstitution. The fact that they have fulfilled the demands imposed upon them in previous inquiries is not a logical proof that, in the form in which they have emerged, they are organs and instrumentalities which will satisfy the demands of a new problematic situation. On the contrary, one of the commonest sources of error is the premature assumption that a new situation so closely resembles former ones that conclusions reached in these earlier cases can be directly carried over. Even the history of scientific inquiry shows how often this error has been made and for what long periods it has gone undetected. One indispensable condition of controlled inquiry is readiness and alertness to submit even the best grounded conclusions of prior inquiry to re-examination with reference to their applicability in new problems. There is a presumption in their favor but the presumption is no guarantee.

2. A similar order of considerations applies to propositional contents which are taken and used. They may have proved completely valid in dealing with some problems and yet not be the fit means for dealing with problems which *prima facie* present the same features. One may point to the revisions of the propositions of classic mechanics that were required when applied to extremely minute bodies of high velocities. For centuries, the axioms and definitions of Euclidean geometry were regarded as absolute first principles which could be accepted without question. Preoccupation with a new order of problems disclosed that they were both overlapping and deficient as logical grounds for a generalized geometry. The result has made it clear that instead of being "self-evident" truths immediately known, they are postulates adopted because of what follows from them. In fact, the belief that they are true by their intrinsic nature retarded the progress of mathematics because it prevented freedom of postulation. With this change in the conception of the character of mathematical axioms, one of the chief bulwarks of immediate knowledge of universal principles crumbled.

The denial of the existence of immediate knowledge does not then deny the existence of certain facts alleged to support the doctrine. It is the logical interpretation of these facts which is in question. Denial of the particular interpretation now under critical discussion was positively foreshadowed in the considerations which established the provisional and operational standing of the factual and conceptual contents of judgment. It is notorious that a hypothesis does not have to be true in order to be highly serviceable in the conduct of inquiry. Examination of the historical progress of any science will show that the same thing holds good of "facts": of what has been taken in the past as evidential. They were serviceable, not because they were true or false, but because, when they were taken to be provisional working means of advancing investigation, they led to discovery of other facts which proved more relevant and more weighty. Just as it would be hard to find an instance of a scientific hypothesis that turned out to be valid in precisely the same form in which it was first put forward, so it would be hard in any important scientific undertaking to find an initial proposition about the state of facts that has remained unchanged throughout the course of inquiry in respect to its content and its significance. Nevertheless, propositions about hypotheses and about conjunctions of existences have served an indispensable purpose because of their operational character as means. The history of science also shows that when hypotheses have been taken to be finally *true* and hence unquestionable, they have obstructed inquiry and kept science committed to doctrines that later turned out to be invalid.

These considerations dispose of a dialectical argument which has been used ever since the time of Aristotle, and is still current today. It is argued that inference must rest upon something known from which it starts, so that unless there are true premises which serve as such a basis it is impossible, no matter how adequate inference and discursive reasoning may be, to arrive at true conclusions. Hence the only way of avoiding a *regressus ad infinitum* is said to be the existence of truths immediately known. Even if the argument were dialectically unanswerable, it would still be confronted by the stubborn facts which show that correct conclusions have been progressively reached from incorrect "premises." But the dialectical reply is simple. It suffices to have hypothetical (conditional) material such that it directs inquiry into channels in which new material, factual and conceptual, is disclosed, ma-

erial which is more relevant, more weighted and confirmed, more
ruitful, than were the initial facts and conceptions which served
s the point of departure. This statement is but a restatement of
he functionally operative status of the contents of judgment up
o enactment of final judgment.

A certain ambiguity in words has played a very considerable
ole in fostering the doctrine of immediate knowledge. Knowl-
dge in its strictest and most honorific sense is identical with war-
anted assertion. But "knowledge" also means understanding, and
n object, or an act (and its object) that may be—and has been
—called *apprehension*. I can *understand* what the word and the
dea of centaur, sea-serpent, transmutation of chemical elements,
nean, without thereby knowing them in the sense of having
rounds for asserting their existence. No intelligent search for a
iew invention, no controlled inquiry to discover whether a certain
onception of, say, the nature of atoms is or is not borne out by
he facts, can be conducted without a direct grasp or understand-
ng of the meaning-content of some idea. As the very descrip-
ion of this kind of "knowledge" shows, it is not knowledge in the
ense of *justified assertion* that a state of existence *is* thus-and-so.
t is easy, however, as the history of philosophy illustrates, to
arry over the first meaning into the second. Since the first is
direct or immediate when it occurs, it is assumed that the second
lso has the same properties. Just as, after considerable experience,
ve understand meanings directly, as when we hear conversation
n a familiar subject or read a book, so because of experience we
ome to recognize objects on sight. I see or note directly that
his is a typewriter, *that* is a book, the other thing is a radiator,
tc. This kind of direct "knowledge" I shall call *apprehension;*
t is seizing or grasping, intellectually, without questioning. But
t is a product, mediated through certain organic mechanisms of
etention and habit, and it presupposes prior experiences and me-
liated conclusions drawn from them.

But the important point for the purpose of the present topic is
hat either an immediate overt response occurs, like using the
ypewriter or picking up the book (in which cases the situation
s not a cognitional one), or that the object directly noted is part
)f an act of inquiry directed toward knowledge as warranted

assertion. In the latter case, the fact of immediate apprehension is no logical guarantee that the object or event directly apprehended is that part of the "facts of the case" it is *prima facie* taken to be. There is no warrant for assuming that it is evidential with respect to the final assertion to be reached. It may be irrelevant in whole or part, or it may be trivial in its significance for the problem in hand. Its very familiarity may be obstructive, tending to fix indications that are suggested in old grooves when the need is to search for data which will start suggestions in an unaccustomed direction. In other words, immediate *ap*prehension of an object or event is no more identical with knowledge in the logical sense required than is immediate understanding or *com*prehension of a meaning. From these general considerations, turn to an examination of certain theories of immediate knowledge which have exercised historical influence.

I. *The Empiristic Theory of Mill*. Mill denies that there are *general* self-evident truths, or general *a priori* truths. Since he does not deny the existence of general truths, he is committed to a statement of a theory concerning their grounds or "proof." His position on this point is unambiguous. They not only arise genetically, in the course of sense perception, but they are *proved* if proved at all, by means of such particulars. These particulars in so far as they are ultimate, are then immediately known. For them to exist in sense-perception is identical with their being known. When this statement does not itself appear to be self-evidently true, it is said to be such because we are dealing with complexes of particulars, not with ultimate simple particulars. The latter Mill calls indifferently *sensations* or *feelings*, or even states of consciousness which are known when and because they exist. "Truths," he says, "are known in two ways: some are known directly, and of themselves; some through the medium of other truths. . . . The truths known by intuition are the original premises from which all others are inferred. . . . The province of logic must be restricted to that portion of our knowledge which consists of inferences from truths previously known. . . . Examples of truths known to us by immediate consciousness are our bodily sensations and mental feelings. I know directly and of

[1] John Stuart Mill, *Logic*, Introduction, Sec. 4.

my own knowledge, that I was vexed yesterday, or that I am hungry today."[2]

The question of whether states of consciousness exist which necessarily "know" themselves in virtue of being states of consciousness, Mill calls "metaphysical." In reality, the belief in their existence was part of a provincial psychological tradition; it no longer generally obtains. His position in respect to "immediate" knowledge of particulars can be discussed, however, without reference to any special assumption concerning the constitution of the particulars. Leaving out all reference to sensations and states of consciousness, it should be obvious that his examples fall far short of exemplifying what he alleges they illustrate.

Take the phrase "I was vexed yesterday." The meaning of "I" is so far from being immediately given that it has long been the theme of controversial discussion; an immediate knowledge of "yesterday" is certainly an extraordinary occurrence; differentiation of "vexation" from other emotional states is a rather slow acquisition in human development. The case is no different in principle from "I am hungry today." It is possible to *feel* hungry when one *is not* hungry; the "feeling" can be produced artificially without the organism being in a state of need for food. The discrimination between the two states may be a difficult problem. If "today" means anything more than the present moment, it involves a fairly elaborate intellectual construction, and any number of passages could be quoted from Mill himself to the effect that a given immediate state can be characterized as *hunger* only by going beyond that state and assimilating it inferentially to other states. That common sense directly grasps certain occurrences as having the *significance* of *vexation, hunger, yesterday, today*, is undeniable. But the "self-evidence" bred by familiarity, while a fact of *practical* importance, is very different from cognitive self-evidence, and often leads common sense astray even in practical matters. We are forced to the conclusion, which a more detailed analysis would bear out, that Mill's whole doctrine of immediate-knowledge is itself an *inference* from a psychological theory which is itself inferential. In its strictly logical bearing it rests upon the uncritical acceptance of the old notion that no

[2] John Stuart Mill, *Logic, loc. cit.*

proposition can be "proved" unless it follows from "truths" already known.

II. *The Lockeian Version.* Locke's account of immediate knowledge is important not only because of its historic influence, in that his original objective view of sensations and ideas was the source of their later transformation into states of consciousness, but because of his clear grasp of the epistemic issue involved—an issue that was obscured and dodged in later developments. He holds, on the one hand, that all knowledge of material existence depends upon sensation, and he points out, on the other hand, that sensations (which he takes to be bodily states) come between us and knowledge of objects in nature in such a way as to render impossible scientific knowledge of the latter. In the first place, most sensory qualities do not belong to natural objects, which possess only the primary qualities of figure, size, solidity and motion; in the second place, even the latter as experienced qualities do not enable us to get knowledge of the "real constitution" of objects.

"If," says Locke, "we could discover the figure, size, texture and motion of the minute constituent parts of any two bodies we should know without trial [experience] several of their operations upon one another as now we do know the properties of a square or triangle." But "if" here represents a condition contrary to fact. For we are destitute of senses acute enough to discover the minute particles of bodies and to give us ideas of their mechanical constitution. Nor is this the whole story. Even if we had senses acute enough to meet this condition (and it might now be argued that recent physics with the aid of artificial devices has supplied the lack), the dependence of knowledge of the real constitution of objects upon sense would still stand immovably in the way. "Knowledge about natural objects extends as far as the *present* testimony of the senses employed about particular objects that do *then* affect them and no further. Hence, we shall never be able to discover general, instructive, unquestionable truths about natural objects." [3] The italicized words, *present* and *then* indicate the impassable barrier existing between sense, which is particular and

[3] John Locke, *Essay on the Human Understanding*, Book IV, Ch. 3 on the Extent of Knowledge.

ransient, and objects which are permanent and have identical ultimate "constitutions" or structures.

This thoroughgoing negative conclusion of Locke, which necessarily follows from regarding sense-data as themselves objects of knowledge, might have acted as a warning to later theorists against assigning inherent cognitive import to sense-data; as a warning to examine any premise that leads to the conclusion that knowledge of physical objects is impossible. If sense-data, or any other data, are final and independent (isolated) objects of knowledge, *then* no predicates having objective existential reference can be warantably attached to them.

At times, when Locke rebels at his own conclusion, and is desirous of justifying the ways of God and Nature to man, he lays down a principle which, if he had followed it out consistently, might have set subsequent theory upon a different track. Upon occasion he says that qualities are marks of differences in things "whereby we are able to discern one thing from another, and so choose them for our necessities and apply them to our uses"—as, say, the quality of white, which enables us to tell milk from water.[4]

Had this mode of interpretation of sensory qualities been made fundamental, it would have appeared that they are not objects of cognition in themselves but that they acquire cognitive function when they are employed in specific situations as signs of something beyond themselves. Qualities are the sole means we have for discriminating objects and events. Their use in this capacity is constant. For *practical* purposes no harm results in identifying the function with the quality as an existence, just as no harm results from identifying an object as a *spade* because the operative use and the consequences of the use of the object are integrated with its existence. But failure for the purposes of *theory* to distinguish existence and function has been the source of continued doctrinal confusion.

III. *Atomic Realism.* Mill's interpretation suffered as we saw from two serious blemishes. It regarded qualities as states of consciousness and it treated such complex objects as *today, yesterday* and *vexation* as simple primitive data. Recent theory has avoided both of these errors. Qualities are given objective status

[4] *Ibid.,* Book IV, Ch. 4, on the Reality of Knowledge.

as sense-data, and the supposedly immediately given existentia contents of propositions are treated as complexes to be reduced to data that are irreducibly simple. Apprehension of immediate simple qualities constitutes propositions which are "atomic," while propositions containing an inferential coefficient are "molecular.' Such propositions as "This is red, hard, sweet," etc., are atomic According to the theory, *this* in such propositions is devoi of any *descriptive* qualification. For were *this* anything more than a bare demonstrative, it would be complex and hence, or the theory, not immediately given. In "This *ribbon* is red," wha is designated by *ribbon* is not given in the sense in which "this" and "red" are given. Some writers also include in the domain o atomic propositions, such propositions as "This is before that" a ρ simple and ultimate immediately given *relation.*

The notion that there is such a thing as a *merely* demonstrative "this" lacking all descriptive content has already been criticized According to the atomic logical theory, each *this*, as a subject of proposition, must be exactly identical logically (though not ir quality) with every other. Each is determined by the mere act o pointing *at* and each such act contains, by statement, nothing tha marks it off from any other demonstrative act. It follows that there is no ground or reason for *predicating* one quality of i rather than any other. The case is not bettered if it is said that "this red" is what is irreducibly given. For even here we have n proposition, only a bare "subject" which is the subject of n predicate. As in the first case, there is no ground whatever for any determinate predication.

It would not be denied, I suppose, that in fact it requires series of experimental operations, involving definite techniques to warrant the assertion that a given present quality is *red.* A scientific determination differs from a loose common sense asser tion of the existence of a specific quality just in the fact that such techniques are employed. A strictly grounded scientific de termination of red would, for example, involve the techniques by means of which the presence of a definite number of vibration per unit of time was ascertained. In other words, it is not held, take it, that the atomic quality is primitive in a psychological sense It is logically primitive in that any existential proposition finally rests upon determination of some simple quality. Now, while in most cases inquiry does not actually go as far as this, it is admitted that *in theory* experimental observation must proceed to determine an irreducible quality in order that an existential proposition be fully warranted. But the more clearly this fact is recognized the more clearly does it stand out that such a determination is not complete and final in itself but is a *means* to the resolution of some problem. It is a factor in the institution of what may warrantably be taken and used as evidence. For example, consider the case in which the utmost pains are taken in a case of spectrum analysis to reach a grounded proposition that such-and-such a color quality is present.

The fallacy in the theory of logically original complete and self-sufficient atomic propositions is thus an instance of the same fallacy that has been repeatedly noted: The conversion of a function in inquiry into an independent structure. It is an admitted fact that ideally, or in theory, propositions about irreducible qualities are necessary in order adequately to ground judgment having existential reference. What is denied is that such propositions have complete and self-sufficient logical character in isolation. For they are determinations of evidential material in order to locate the problem in hand and secure evidence to test a solution. The doctrine under criticism rules out the context in which such propositions occur and the logical end for which and logical ground upon which they are instituted. This may be verified by any one who calls to mind a case in which, either in common sense or science, such propositions are present and have weight. As to their ground, I call attention again to the fact that there is no *this* which is merely and exclusively *red* or any other single quality and that, therefore, there must be some ground for selection of one quality as predicate rather than another.

Although further discussion of the logical principles involved will require some retraversing of matters already gone over, the basic importance of the issue justifies repetition, especially as the territory will be surveyed from a somewhat different point of view. It has been usual for some time in philosophy (1) to view the common sense world in its distinction from the domain of scientific objects as strictly perceptual in character; (2) to regard perception as a mode of cognition; and (3) what is perceived whether object or quality, to be therefore cognitive in status and force. None of these assumptions is warranted. (a) The common-sense world includes, to be sure, perceived objects, but these are understood only in the context of an *environment*. An environment is constituted by the interactions between things and a living creature. It is primarily the scene of actions performed and of consequences undergone in processes of interaction; only secondarily do parts and aspects of it become objects of knowledge. Its constituents are first of all objects of use and enjoyment-suffering, not of knowledge. (b) In relation to perception, an environment forms an extensive temporal-spatial field. Only occasionally are reflexes directed in the life behavior of an organism toward isolated excitations. The maintenance of life is a continuous affair. It involves organs and habits acquired in the past. Actions performed have to be adapted to future conditions or death will speedily ensue. The material towards which behavior is *directly* impelled is but the focal aspect of an environing field. The kind of behavior which occurs must, in order to be adaptive and responsive, vary with the kind of field of which the immediate object is focal.

It follows, then, that when objects or qualities are cognitively apprehended, they are viewed in reference to the exigencies of the perceived field in which they occur. They then become objects of *observation*, observation being defined precisely as the restrictive-selective determination of a particular object or quality within a total environing field. Usually the total environing field is "understood," or taken for granted, because it is there as the standing condition of any *differential* activity to be performed. The psychological theory of perception has been framed in terms of what happens in these specific differential acts of observation-perception of *an* object or *a* quality, an orange, a patch of yellow. For the purpose of a report of just what occurs in an observation and for the *psychological* problem involved, it is not necessary to criticise this procedure. But when the results are carried over into logical theory and taken to provide the basis for a theory of data in their logical status and bearing, complete distortion results. For isolated objects or qualities are then taken in their isolation to be the *givens* or *data*.

For logical purposes, it makes no difference whether the data, when reduced to their simplest contents, are taken to be Lockeian simple ideas, sensations, Humeian impressions, the sense-data of contemporary theory, or "essences." For the same isolation, self-sufficiency, and completeness is ascribed to them in each case. What has actually occurred, then, in the formation of the contemporary theory of atomic propositions is that the conclusions of psychological theory, reached in dealing with a special psychological situation, have been bodily transferred into logic and made the basis of the entire doctrine of atomic propositions having existential reference. This uncritical adoption of psychological conclusions as the foundation of an important branch of the logical theory of propositions has occurred in spite of the fact that the logicians who proceed in this way are particularly urgent about the necessity of freeing logic completely from psychological matters.[5]

I turn now to certain popular and empirical considerations which are taken to substantiate the notion of immediate knowledge. 1. The distinction between acquaintance-knowledge and knowledge-about and the validity of the distinction is generally acknowledged. I am acquainted with my neighbor; I know something about Julius Caesar. Acquaintance-knowledge has a directness and intimacy lacking in knowledge-about. The latter can only be expressed in propositions *that* certain things are so-and-so. The former is expressed in actual commerce with the individual; it is marked by affection and dislikes. It takes effect in expectations as to the conduct of the person or object with which one is acquainted so that appropriate ways of overt conduct are ready in advance in the person having the acquaintance. I am acquainted, say, with the French language when I am prepared to speak and read it; I may know *about* its grammar and something of its vocabulary and yet have no ability to speak. The distinction between the two modes of knowledge was embodied in linguistic expressions long before theoretical attention was called to it: *Cognoscere* and *scire; connaitre* and *savoir; kennen* and *wissen;*

[5] A by-product of this dependence upon a special psychological analysis is that the doctrine of atomic propositions as ultimate existential propositions makes necessary the assumption of *a priori* universal propositions, for the atomic propositions, by description, are incapable of grounding inference and reasoning.

in earlier English idiom, to *ken* (with its association of *can*, ability to act) and to *wit*.

The existence and the importance of the difference is acknowledged. But it is far from supporting the logical theory of immediate knowledge. The immediacy involved is that of intimate connection with emotion and ability to act. In the first place, acquaintance-knowledge is not primitive, but acquired, and in so far depends upon prior experiences into which mediation has entered. In the second place (and of more importance for the present point), acquaintance-knowledge is frequently *not* knowledge in the sense of being warrantably assertible. It enables us to form practical expectations which are perhaps often fulfilled. But the familiarity that attends acquaintanceship often blinds us to things of primary importance in reaching conclusions. Acquaintance with certain habits of speech is no guarantee against blunders and solecisms; it may be their source. From a logical point of view acquaintance-knowledge is subject to critical inquiry and revision. As a rule, it invites it.

2. The existence of recognitions, which are practically instantaneous, is another empirical ground for the theory under examination. The same considerations apply here as in the case of acquaintance-knowledge. In fact, recognition may be regarded as a special limiting instance of the latter. We recognize persons with whom we have only slight acquaintance; we may recognize words in a foreign language without being so acquainted with the language that we can speak or read it. Recognition of an object is also (a) a product of experiences which have involved doubt and search, and (b) while of immense practical importance, is not exempt from the necessity of inquiries to determine the correctness of a given recognition and its pertinency to the problem in hand. Recognition is not re-cognition in the sense of a re-knowing. It is rather an *acknowledgement* of a certain object or event as having a specified place in a situation.

The doctrine that "simple apprehension" is complete in itself is often accompanied by a certain fallacy. It is supposed that because the *act* of apprehension is simple and single, therefore, the *object* apprehended must also be. But complex scenes are also apprehended simply—as when one returns to the scene of his childhood.

Moreover, relatively simple objects are important not in virtue of their inherently simple structure but because of some crucially evidential role their simplicity permits them to play—as for example, in the relation of finger-prints to personal identifications. Similarly, we recognize a familiar person by his voice alone without having to observe him in his physical entirety. It saves time and energy to be able to make the relatively simple a means of identification.

Such facts suggest the peculiar function of simples or elements in inquiry. The more complex the structure of an object, the greater the number of possible inferences that can be drawn from its presence; its different constituents point in different directions. The less complex a given object or event the more restricted it is in its constitution and hence the more *definite* is its indicative signifying capacity. There is abundant evidence in the history of science to show that reduction of objects to elements is one of the most effective means of both safeguarding and extending inferential inquiry. There is no evidence that such simple elements exist by themselves in nature. It is foolish to object to analysis and its outcome in institution of elements. But the very foolishness of this objection goes to show that the concept of "simple" and "element" is functional and that giving simples and elements independent existential standing, whether in physics, psychology, anatomy or politics, is but one more case of hypostization of an instrument.

IV. *Understanding and Comprehension.* So far the detailed discussion has been occupied with existential subject-matters, for grasp of which the word *apprehension* is generically employed. It is advisable to say something about direct grasp of meanings and conceptual structures for whose designation the words *understanding* or *comprehension* is used. We take, see, and "twig," the force of an argument; we have insight into general principles. The seeing and insight are often direct and practically instantaneous. A meaning, previously obscure, may come to us "in a flash." The same type of considerations adduced with respect to direct apprehension of objects and qualities applies in the case of the present topic, and discussion may be abbreviated. Attention has already been called to the fact that one meaning of *to know* is to understand, and that this meaning is not to be confused with warranted affirmation of validity. A person must understand the meaning of *authorship* in order to consider intelligently the application of that term to a given person, say, of the *Waverley Novels*. The understanding is a necessary condition of any particular ascription having validity. But evidently it is not a sufficient condition.

The series of propositions which constitute a chain of ordered discourse should be such that the meanings of their constituent terms are as unambiguous and determinate as possible. But fulfilment of this condition does not guarantee the validity of their application in a given problem. Hence *understanding*, like apprehension, is never final. No proposition about a relation of meanings, however determinate and adequate the proposition is, can stand alone logically. Nor is its incapacity to stand alone removed by union with other propositions of the same sort; although the union may result in getting meanings into such a shape that they are fitted for application.

The two doctrines, that there is an immediate knowledge of existential objects or of qualities as sense-data, and that there is an immediate knowledge of rational principles—necessarily go together. Atomistic empiricism and rational *a priorism* are correlative doctrines. Kant's categories of the *a priori* understanding are the logical counterpart of the doctrine of independent sense-material which he took over from Hume, just as T. H. Green's "necessary relations of thought" are required to balance the view of sensations he took over from the psychology of the school of the Mills. When the existential material of experience is reduced to immediately given atomic cases of "this," connection between the atoms (such as is involved in every molecular proposition), is impossible unless non-empirical or *a priori* propositions are recognized. Postulation of self-evident existential "facts" requires postulation of self-evident rational "truths."

A strictly logical formulation of this state of affairs is given by Bertrand Russell. After stating that "in every proposition and in every inference there is, besides the particular subject-matters concerned, a certain *form*, a way in which the constituents of the proposition are put together," he gives the following example of what is meant by form: "If anything has a certain property, and whatever has this property has a certain other property, then the thing in question has the other property." He then goes on to draw the theoretical conclusion considered in the next paragraph.[6]

The proposition cited as an example of form is said to be "absolutely general; it applies to all things and all properties, and it is quite self-evident." Moreover, it is *a priori:* "Since it does not mention any particular thing, or even any particular quality or relation, it is wholly independent of the accidental facts of the existent world, and can be known, theoretically, without any experience of particular things or their qualities and relations." This conclusion follows from its being laid down as a logical truth that "General truths cannot be inferred from particular truths alone, but must, if they are to be known, be either self-evident, or inferred from premises of which one at least is a general truth. But all *empirical* evidence is of particular truths. Hence if there is any knowledge of general truths at all there must be *some* knowledge of general truths which is independent of empirical evidence, i.e., does not depend upon sense-data."

In the latter passage there is not only an implicit but an explicit identification of ultimate ("primitive") existential propositions with atomic propositions. *If* empirical (here employed in the sense of existential) propositions are atomic, *then* it certainly follows that any propositions about the logical forms by which they are related to one another must be supra- and extra- empirical, or *a priori.* They must be known by some kind of rational intuition, a conception involved, although in a somewhat disguised way, in calling them "self-evident." The apodosis clause of the above *if-then* proposition follows with such neat necessity from the protasis clause that it invites attention to the latter. If the antecedent clause is invalid, the validity of the consequent clause is indeterminate, while if the consequent clause is false or doubtful, then so is that of the antecedent clause. In other words, the passage quoted sets forth a *problem.* The very necessity of the relation of the two clauses merely accentuates the importance of the problem. I shall not repeat here the reasons previously given

[6] Bertrand Russell, *Scientific Method in Philosophy,* and further quotations, p. 42, and pp. 56–7.

for rejecting the clause which postulates atomic existential propositions as primitive in independence of their function in inquiry. Nor shall I rehearse the reasons for doubting the existence of a faculty of pure reason independent of any and all experience, a faculty gifted with the power of infallible intuition.[7]

The points directly relevant to the problem are, first, that what is "self-evident" in the general logical proposition cited, is its *meaning*. To say that it is self-evident means that one who reflects upon it *in the meaning system of which it is a member* will apprehend its meaning in that relation—exactly as one might apprehend the meaning, say, of the empirical proposition "that ribbon is blue." The question of the logical force and function of the proposition, of the interpretation to be given it, remains open —just as does the *truth* of the empirical proposition after its *meaning* is grasped.

Secondly, the theoretical interpretation of the *significance* of the meaning directly apprehended is far from self-evident. There is, for example, the alternative represented by the theoretical position which was stated by Peirce, to the effect that all propositions about logical forms and relations are *leading principles*, not premises. They are, from this point of view, formulations of *operations*, which (a) are hypotheses about operations to be performed in all inquiries which lead to warranted conclusions; and (b) are hypotheses that have been confirmed without exception in all cases which have led to stable assertions; while (c) failure to observe the conditions set forth have been found, as a matter of experience of inquiries and their results, to lead to unstable conclusions.

Such propositions about logical forms as are exemplified in the dictum about possession of properties that are "independent" of the specific subject-matter of existential propositions are *not* (it is admitted) conclusions drawn merely from subject-matters as purely particular, and they are not *proved* by these particular propositions. But there is nothing in this admission inconsistent

---

[7] Attention may, however, be called to the fact that the assumption of both atomic existential propositions and of rationally intuited truths destroys the autonomy of logical theory, rendering it dependent upon psychological and epistemological considerations declared by definition to be outside the province of logic.

with their being drawn from *operations of inquiry* as existential and empirical occurrences. In the degree in which we understand what is done in inquiries that result in warranted assertions, we understand the operational conditions which have to be observed. These conditions, when formulated, are the content of general propositions about logical forms. The conditions of the required operations (required in order that a certain kind of consequence may issue) are as much matters of experience as are factual contents: which are themselves also discriminated in order to serve as conditions of a warranted outcome.

It is not claimed that this proposition about logical propositions is "self-evident" as to its truth. It *is* claimed that it has an intelligible meaning, capable of being directly grasped as a meaning, and that this meaning, when it is used or applied to the problems of logical theory serves to clarify and resolve them. The conception, on the other hand, that "experience" is reducible to immediately given atomic propositions, that are possessed of self-evident truth, introduces complications and confusions. Universal propositions about logical forms are propositional functions and as such are in themselves neither true nor false. They state modes of *procedure* in inquiry which are postulated as applicable and as required in any controlled inquiry. Like mathematical axioms, their meaning, or force, is determined and tested by what follows from their operative use.

As far as the doctrine of immediate knowledge is directly concerned, the discussion has reached an end. But there are certain things which may be added from the side of the mediated character of all knowledge in order to guard against misapprehension. (a) It is not held that inferred interpretations are tested, confirmed, verified (or the opposite) by particular objects in their particularity. On the contrary, it is the capacity of the inferred idea to order and organize particulars into a coherent whole that is the criterion. (b) It is not held that *inference* by itself exhausts logical functions and determines exclusively all logical forms. On the contrary, proof, in the sense of *test*, is an equally important function.

Moreover, inference, even in its connection with test, is not logically final and complete. The heart of the entire theory developed in this work is that the resolution of an indeterminate situation is the end, in the sense in which "end" means *end-in-view* and in the sense in which it means *close*. Upon this view, inference is subordinate although indispensable. It is not, as it is for example in the logic of John Stuart Mill, exhaustive and all-inclusive. It is a necessary but not a sufficient condition of warranted assertions.

CHAPTER IX

JUDGMENTS OF PRACTICE: EVALUATION

THE PREVIOUS chapter was devoted to enforcing the necessity of mediation in knowledge as warranted assertion. This necessity does not stand alone, for it is a necessary phase of the theory of inquiry and judgment that has been developed. It received separate development because of the traditional and still current doctrine of self-evident truths and self-grounded propositions. There is, however, another phase of our basic theory which stands equally (and possibly to a greater degree) in opposition to accepted logical theory, and which accordingly stands also in need of explicit treatment. For, contrary to current doctrine, the position here taken is that inquiry effects *existential* transformation and reconstruction of the material with which it deals; the result of the transformation, when it is grounded, being conversion of an indeterminate problematic situation into a determinate resolved one.

This emphasis upon requalification of antecedent existential material, and upon judgment as the resulting transformation, stands in sharp contrast with traditional theory. The latter holds that such modifications as may occur in even the best controlled inquiry are confined to states and processes of the knower—the one conducting the inquiry. They may, therefore, properly be called "subjective," mental or psychological, or by some similar name. They are without objective standing, and hence lack logical force and meaning. The position that is here taken is to the contrary effect: namely, that beliefs and mental states of the inquirer cannot be legitimately changed except as existential operations, rooted ultimately in organic activities, modify and requalify objective matter. Otherwise, "mental" changes are not only merely mental

159

(as the traditional theory holds) but are arbitrary and on the road to fantasy and delusion.

The traditional theory in both its empiricistic and rationalistic forms amounts to holding that all propositions are purely declaratory or enunciative of what antecedently exists or subsists, and that this declarative office is complete and final in itself. The position here taken holds, on the contrary, that declarative propositions, whether of facts or of conceptions (principles and laws) are intermediary means or instruments (respectively material and procedural) of effecting that controlled transformation of subject-matter which is the end-in-view (and final goal) of all declarative affirmations and negations. It is not, be it noted, the *occurrence* of purely declarative propositions that is denied. On the contrary, as will be shown later in detail, the existence of such propositions, setting forth relationships that obtain between factual data on one hand and between conceptual subject-matter on the other hand, is expressly affirmed. The point at issue concerns not their being but their function and interpretation.

The position may be stated in the following language: All controlled inquiry and all institution of grounded assertion necessarily contains a *practical* factor; an activity of doing and making which reshapes antecedent existential material which sets the problem of inquiry. That this view is not assumed *ad hoc* but represents what certainly occurs (or is a *vera causa*) in at least *some* cases, will be shown by considering some forms of common sense inquiry which aim at determining what is to be done in some practical predicament.

Inquiries of this type are neither exceptional nor infrequent. For the stock and staple of common sense inquiries and judgments are of this sort. The deliberations of daily life concern in largest measure questions of what to make or to do. Every art and every profession is faced with constantly recurring problems of this sort. To put their existence in doubt is equivalent to denying that any element of intelligence enters into any form of practice; to affirming that all decisions on practical matters are the arbitrary products of impulse, caprice, blind habit, or convention. Farmer, mechanic, painter, musician, writer, doctor, lawyer, merchant, captain of industry, administrator or manager, has constantly to inquire what it is better to do next. Unless the decision reached is arrived at blindly and arbitrarily it is obtained by gathering and surveying evidence appraised as to its weight and relevancy; and by framing and testing plans of action in their capacity as hypotheses: that is, as ideas.

By description, the situations which *evoke* deliberation resulting in decision, are themselves indeterminate with respect to what might and should be done. They require that *something* should be done. But *what* action is to be taken is just the thing in question. The problem of *how* the uncertain situation should be dealt with is urgent. But as merely urgent, it is so emotional as to impede and often to frustrate wise decision. The intellectual question is what sort of action the *situation* demands in order that it may receive a satisfactory objective reconstruction. This question can be answered only, I repeat, by operations of observation, collection of data and of inference, which are directed by ideas whose material is itself examined through operations of ideational comparison and organization.

I did not include the scientist in the list of persons who have to engage in inquiry in order to make judgments upon matters of practice. But a slight degree of reflection shows that he has to decide what researches to engage in and how to carry them on—a problem that involves the issue of what observations to undertake, what experiments to carry on, and what lines of reasoning and mathematical calculations to pursue. Moreover, he cannot settle these questions once and for all. He is continually having to judge what it is best to do next in order that his conclusion, no matter how abstract or theoretical it may be as a conclusion, shall be grounded when it is arrived at. In other words, the conduct of scientific inquiry, whether physical or mathematical, is a mode of *practice*; the working scientist is a practitioner above all else, and is constantly engaged in making practical judgments: decisions as to what to do and what means to employ in doing it.

The results of deliberation as to what it is *better to do* are, obviously, not identical with the final issue for the sake of which the deliberative inquiries are undertaken. For the final issue is some new situation in which the difficulties and troubles which elicited deliberation are done away with; in which they no longer *exist.* This objective end cannot be attained by conjuring with mental states. It is an end brought about only by means of existential changes. The question for deliberation is what to do in order to effect these changes. They are means to the required existential reconstruction; *a fortiori*, the inquiries and decisions which issue in performance of these acts are instrumental and intermediate. But what should be done depends upon the conditions that exist in the given situation and hence require a declarative or enunciatory proposition: "The actual conditions are so-and-so." These conditions are the ground of inference to a declarative proposition that such and such an act is the one best calculated to produce the desired issue under the factual conditions ascertained. Declarative propositions as to the state of facts involved set forth the obstacles and resources to be overcome and administered in reaching the intended goal. They state potentialities, positive and adverse. They function as instrumentalities. The propositions which set forth the way existing conditions should be dealt with stand in functional correlation with the enunciatory propositions which state existing conditions. The propositions as to procedure are not carriers of existential or factual materials. They are of the general form: "If such and such a course is adopted under the existing circumstances, such and such will be the probable result." Logically, the formation of these hypotheses as to methods of action involves reasoning, or a series of declarative propositions stating relationships of conceptual materials. For it is only rarely that the idea of the procedure which first suggests itself can be directly set to work. It has to be developed; this development constitutes rational discourse, which in scientific practice usually takes the form of mathematical calculation.

Preliminary to offering illustrations of what has been said, I shall summarize formally what is logically involved in every situation of deliberation and grounded decision in matters of practice. There is an existential situation such that (a) its constituents are changing so that in any case *something* different is going to happen in the future; and such that (b) just *what* will exist in the future depends in part upon introduction of *other* existential conditions interacting with those already existing, while (c) *what* new conditions are brought to bear depends upon what activities are undertaken, (d) the latter matter being influenced by the intervention of inquiry in the way of observation, inference and reasoning.

The illustration I shall employ to exemplify these four conditions is that of a person who, being ill, deliberates about the proper course to adopt in order to effect recovery. (1) Bodily changes are already going on which in any case will have *some* existential issue. (2) It is possible to introduce new conditions that will be factors in deciding the issue—the question for deliberation being whether they should be introduced and if so, which ones and how. (3) Deliberation convinces the one who is ill that he should see a physician. A proposition to this effect is equivalent to the conclusion that the consequences of the visit are calculated to introduce the interacting factors which will yield a desired issue. (4) Hence, the proposition when executed actually introduces intervening conditions which interact with antecedent existing conditions to modify their course and thus influence the issue. The latter is different from what it would have been if inquiry and judgment had not intervened—even if recovery of health is not attained.

Whenever there is genuine deliberation, there are alternatives at almost every step of the way. There is something to be said or tentatively affirmed at each step on both sides of the questions that come up. Reflection on past experience indicates that it is often well to let "nature take its course." But is the present case of that kind? The question of financial expense may enter in; that of whether a competent physician is available or what physician to consult; the question of the patient's engagements for the next few days and weeks, and the bearing of the physician's advice upon the patient's possibility of fulfilling them, etc., etc.

Such factual matters as these are examined and formulated in propositions. Each state of facts presented in a proposition suggests its own alternative course of action, and if there is genuine inquiry the suggestion has to be formulated. The formulation or proposition has then to be developed in terms of the probable consequences of adopting it. This development occurs in a series of *if-then* propositions. If the man finally decides to see such and such a doctor, the resulting proposition represents, in effect, an inference that this mode of procedure stands the better chance of introducing those factors which will yield, in their inter-action with existing conditions, a desired future existential situation: an inference that it will give to factors already in operation a direction that they would not take if left to themselves.

The contents of the propositions framed about matters of fact and about alternative courses of action (including the one adopted) are neither self-determined nor self-sufficient. They are determined with reference to an intended future issue and hence are instrumental and intermediate. They are not valid in and of themselves, for their validity depends upon the consequences which ensue from acting upon them—as far as these consequences actually ensue from the operations the propositions dictate and are not accidental accretions. Let the factual proposition be represented by "I am seriously ill." In the context indicated, the proposition is without point if taken to be final and complete. Its logical force consists in its potential connection with a future situation. The declarative proposition "I should or shall see a doctor" is similarly functional. It formulates the possible operation which, if performed, will aid in existential production of a future situation different in quality and significance from that which will exist if the indicated action is not taken. The same considerations will be found to apply to declarative propositions made by the attending physician about the facts which locate and describe the illness on the one hand, and the course of action he prescribes for dealing with the illness on the other.

This analysis, if accepted, carries with it recognition that declarative propositions (themselves the results of judgments of provisional appraisal) are factors which enter actively into the actual constitution of the existential subject-matter of the final judgment. This final subject-matter may not be that which was hoped for and intended. But in *any* case it is somewhat different from what it would have been if the operations, dependent upon intervening instrumental propositions, had not taken place. According to the commonly accepted interpretation of declarative propositions it is a straight contradiction that they should enter into the ultimate structure of the very situation they are "about." But the contradiction results from the theory which is accepted, not from the propositions themselves; it is a consequence of ignoring the intermediary and operational force of the propositions that are formed.

The standard account of the example discussed on the basis of traditional theory would be somewhat as follows: The propositions "I am ill" and "When one is ill, one should consult a doctor" are taken respectively as the minor and major premises of a syllogism from which the conclusion "I should see a doctor" necessarily follows. This interpretation rests upon taking advantage of an ambiguity. It may be but a linguistic rendering of a genuine judgment already made. In this case, the analysis of the text is confirmed. For then both major and minor state decisions reached in inquiry as to what the state of affairs should be in order to modify them in a given direction. Taken literally, however, the interpretation means that there was no inquiry and no judgment. It only means that the person in question, whenever he fancies he is ill has the *habit* of going automatically to a physician. There is no element of doubt or indeterminateness, no inquiry and no forming of propositions. There is a direct stimulus and it is responded to in accord with a previously formed habit. The alleged syllogism is but an externally imposed account of what has taken place in action in which no logical forms are involved.

This situation is of significance because it brings out by contrast the situations in which *judgment* does occur. A man may have a regular habit of consulting physicians because he is valetudinarian and on that account does not exercise judgment. Or he may have the tendency to go whenever his symptoms are severe and yet on this particular occasion be in doubt whether he is sufficiently ill to justify going. Then he engages in reflection. Moreover, in the concrete a man does not decide to see *a* doctor; he decides to see some given doctor, and he may need to investigate what physician to see. He may have reasons for thinking his financial state renders it better to take a chance about getting well, etc. The account which reduces a proposition of practice to a formal combination of a singular and a general proposition thus applies only to *ex post facto* linguistic analyses of either an act performed from habit without the intermediation of judgment or else of a judgment that has been completed. If deliberation and appraisals involving propositions actually intervene in reaching the decision "I shall see a physician," then a judgment of practice is a factor in the ultimate determination of the existential material which the preliminary judgments of appraisal are *about*.

The particular instance chosen can hardly be supposed to settle the larger question at issue. This problem is so important that I shall continue its discussion through a series of instances.

1. There are cases in which judgments of practice have to determine what to do next, "right away," in order to produce a specific existential situation as the result of the activity the judgment prescribes. One notes, for example, a motor car bearing down upon him. He may automatically swerve. In this case, there is no judgment and no proposition. But the situation may be such as to evoke deliberation. In this case, there will be observation of existing conditions (locating the problem) and formation of a plan of action to meet the emergency (solve the problem). The decisions made by an umpire in the course of a game afford an even better illustration. He has to form propositions about observed facts and about the rule that is applicable to their interpretation. Both his estimate of facts and of the rule that is applicable may be questioned, but in any case the final judgment of "Safe" or "Out" enters as a determining factor in the subsequent existential course of events. This fact shows that the action and position of, say, a runner in a baseball game are not that which is *judged*. The object of judgment is the total situation in which action occurs. Propositions about just what a batter or runner has done and about the rule (conception) which is applicable, are intermediate and instrumental, not final and complete.

The two instances cited illustrate what is meant by the phrase "procedural means" applied to the predicate of judgment. The subject-matter of the predicate represents an end-in-view, which is an anticipation of an existential consequence, an end in the sense of a fulfilling close and termination. The end-*in-view* of the man who sees an automobile approaching him is *getting to* a place of safety, not safety itself. The latter (or its opposite) is the *end* in the sense of close. Unless the anticipation or end-in-view is an idle fantasy, it takes the form of an operation to be performed. Similarly, the proposition "Out" or "Safe" in the case of the runner in the game is operational in that it decides what the runner shall then proceed to do and how the game shall go on. If the existential end in the sense of final outcome or close, were a term in a proposition, it would be taken to be already completed. Only if the end figures as a directive means to perform the action by which the actual termination is brought about is it other than self-defeating.

The predicate is not a "realistic" apprehension and enunciation of something already in existence; it is an estimate, based on realistic observation of facts *as conditions of possible issues*, of something to do. Likewise, the ideas of a goal for a runner in a race or of a target for an archer are obstructive not helpful unless they are translations of the final mark as an existence into *means whereby*—procedural means. The runner employs the *thought* of the goal as means of regulating his pace, etc., at different stages of his running; the archer uses the *thought* of the target, in connection with observations of the direction and force of wind, etc., as a guide or direction in *taking* aim. The difference between the two senses of *end*, namely, end-in-view and end as objective termination and completion, is striking proof of the fact that in inquiry the termination is not just realistically apprehended and enunciated but is stated as a way of procedure. Confusion of the two senses of "end" is the source of the notion that a judgment of practice is either purely declarative or else is so merely practical that it has no logical status.

2. Moral evaluations are also a case in point. The common, perhaps prevailing, assumption is that there are objects which are ends-in-themselves; that these ends are arranged in a hierarchy from the less to the more ultimate and have corresponding authority over conduct. It follows from this view that moral "judgment" consists simply in direct apprehension of an end-in-itself in its proper place in the scheme of fixed values. It is assumed that apart from this hierarchy of fixed ends, a moral agent has no alternative save to follow his desires as they come and go. According to the position here taken, ends as objective termini or as fulfilments function in judgment as representative of modes of operation that will resolve the doubtful situation which evokes and demands judgment. As *ends-in-view* they denote plans of action or purposes. The business of inquiry is to determine that

mode of operation which will resolve the predicament in which the agent finds himself involved, in correspondence with the observations which determine just what the facts of the predicament are.

The notion that a moral judgment merely apprehends and enunciates some predetermined end-in-itself is, in fact, but a way of denying the need for and existence of genuine moral judgments. For according to this notion there is no *situation* which is problematic. There is only a person who is in a state of subjective moral uncertainty or ignorance. His business, in that case, is not to judge the objective situation in order to determine what course of action is required in order that it may be transformed into one that is morally satisfactory and right, but simply to come into intellectual possession of a predetermined end-in-itself. Goods previously experienced assuredly are material means of reaching a judgment as to what to do. But they *are* means, not fixed ends. They are material to be surveyed and evaluated in reference to the kind of action needed in the *existing* situation.

The position which holds that moral judgment is concerned with an objective unsettled situation and that ends-in-view are framed in and by judgment as methods of resolving operations is consistent with the fact that, because of recurrence of similar situations, generic ends-in-view, as ways of acting, are built up and have a certain *prima facie* claim to recognition in new situations. But these standardized "prepared" propositions are not final; though highly valuable means, they are still means for examining the existing situation and appraising what mode of action it demands. The question of their applicability in the new situation, their relevancy and weight with respect to it, may and often does lead to their being re-appraised and re-framed.

3. *Interrogative Propositions.* Whether questions are propositions in any logical sense is not a matter often discussed. Logicians who do raise the problem usually take the position that they are not genuine propositions. Upon the position here taken, all *propositions* as distinct from judgment have an interrogative aspect. Since they are provisional, they are not only subject to being questioned but they themselves *raise* questions of pertinency, weight and applicability. When either facts or conceptions are taken to be completely assured (whether because of earlier suc-

cessful use or for any other reason), direct action, not judgment, ensues. It is a matter of great practical convenience that many facts and ideas may be so taken and directly used. But conversion of this practical value into assured logical status is one of the commonest ways of establishing the dogmatism which is the great enemy of free and continued inquiry.

Bosanquet is one of the comparatively few writers who has dealt expressly with the logical status of interrogations. He says they are only tentative and that "a tentative judgment lacks the differentia of judgment. It does not assert; it does not claim truth; a question as such cannot be an object of thought as such . . . it is not an attitude which the intellect can maintain within itself. . . . It is a demand for information; its essence is to be directed to a moral agent in which it may produce action." [1]

The passage quoted involves a point previously discussed, namely, the double character of judgment as provisional appraisal or estimate and as conclusive or final. What Bosanquet said evidently applies to judgment in its latter capacity. In ruling out from the meaning of judgment all preliminary estimates and evaluations concerning the force and relevancy of facts and ideas, his view leads to the conclusion he draws; namely, that inquiry is not a form of judgment and therefore as such is not logical in status. This position is of crucial significance in its far-reaching implications.

It is surely not unscientific to regard the actual work of science as one of inquiry. A position which rules science out of the field and scope of logic, save as a body of propositions that are accepted independently of the methods of inquiry by which they are reached, is with equal certainty not one to be lightly accepted. Ordinary language uses the expression "the matter in question" as a synonym for the subject-matter with which inquiry is occupied. From the standpoint of both science and common sense, it would seem more correct to say that a question (in the sense of a questionable and questioned subject-matter) is *the* object of "thought," than to say, with Mr. Bosanquet, that "a question cannot be the object of thought."

That a question is a demand for action on someone's part is

---

[1] *Logic*, Vol. I, p. 35.

a statement which, taken in isolation, is in full agreement with the position of this work.   Judgment as appraisal may enter even into the formation of questions addressed to another person, since just the question which should be asked is far from being a self-evident matter.   Nevertheless, the statement that a question by its nature is something addressed to another person, ignores the basic fact that questions are addressed to existential subject-matter.   A scientific inquiry may be regarded as a request "for information."   But the needed information is not handed out ready-made by nature.   It requires judgment to decide what questions should be asked of nature, since it is an affair of formulating the best methods of observation, experimentation and conceptual interpretation.

The last statement brings our discussion face to face with the problem concerning the relation of inquiry to judgments of practice.   For determination of what questions to ask and how to ask them is an affair of judging what should be done in order to secure the material, factual and conceptual, which is necessary and sufficient to resolve an unsettled situation.   One has only to bring to mind the procedure of a lawyer or a physician in any given case, to see how fundamentally his problem is one of framing right questions—the criterion of "rightness" being capacity to bring out the material which is relevant and effective in settling the situation that evokes inquiry.

4. *Deliberation* is involved in all the instances considered.   But one aspect of deliberation, in its emphatic sense, is so important that it is advisable to treat the topic in a separate heading.   Genuine deliberation proceeds by institution and examination of alternative courses of activity and consideration of their respective consequences.   This fact throws light upon the functional nature of disjunctive and hypothetical propositions.   Taxonomic systems, such as are exemplified in botany and zoology, are large scale examples of disjunctive propositions.   They were once regarded as marking the final goal of science—a view that followed consistently from the classic conception of fixed species.   They are now treated as useful means for the conduct of inquiry and of value only in this function; for any given taxonomic system is treated as flexible and subject to constant revision.   But unfor-

tunately, logical texts are given to treating disjunctive propositions as a separate theme. Consequently they employ, as illustrative material, disjunctions established by prior inquiry without reference to the inquiries *by which* they are established and without reference to those in which they further operate; while in the actual work of science taxonomic disjunctions are so regularly treated as purely instrumental devices as to lose all independent standing. It would hardly be an exaggeration to say that emphatic regard for taxonomy exposes a given scientific worker to something approaching contempt on the part of scientific workers in more advanced fields.

Disjunctive propositions are connected with practical judgment, for deliberation upon matters of policy requires (a) that alternative possibilities be instituted and explored, and (b) that they be such as to be readily comparable with one another. For example, a man who has come into possession of a large sum of money proceeds to deliberate as to what he shall do with it. His deliberation gets nowhere unless it takes the form of setting up alternative *possible* uses for the funds at command. Shall it be placed in a savings bank to draw interest? Invested in stocks, in bonds, in real estate? Or shall it be used for purposes of travel, or to buy books, apparatus, etc.? The problematic situation is made relatively determinate by analysis into alternatives, each of which is represented in a disjunctive proposition as a member of a system.

In the example given it is clear that each proposition is formed as a means of determining what to do, and that the resulting determination is a means of bringing into existence a certain eventual situation. Experts in special fields soon establish a set of alternatives. For new cases these alternatives are *prepared* materials, just as an artisan has at hand a set of tools relevant to his line of activity. In such cases, judgment goes rather to the question which one of the disjunctive set to employ rather than to *formation* of disjunctive propositions. But, nevertheless, the latter remain instruments. Hypostization of instruments into something final and complete places a restriction on further inquiry. For it subjects the conclusion to be reached to a preconception which is assumed to be beyond question and examination.

The relation of hypothetical to disjunctive propositions needs only to be suggested at this point. The meaning of each alternative mode of action is constructed in terms of the consequences which acting upon it will produce. The development of this meaning takes place through reasoning in the form "*If* such an alternative be adopted, *then* such and such and such consequences may be expected to follow." The derived consequences, compared with the consequences of other hypothetical propositions, provide the ground for tentative acceptance or rejection. In actual practice, the development of *if-then* propositions of this sort is often not carried far. But from the standpoint of warranted final judgment as to what should be done, disjunctives should be *exhaustive*, and development of each disjunctive member of the system, as a hypothesis, should be thorough.

5. *Evaluation.* A standing ambiguity in the word *value*, both as verb and noun, has frequently been pointed out. In one of its meanings "to value" is to enjoy and the resulting enjoyment is figuratively called *a* value. There is neither reflection nor inquiry in these cases of enjoyment as far as they occur spontaneously. The fact of an enjoyment may, however, be recorded and communicated linguistically. The resulting linguistic expression will have the outward form of a proposition. But unless a question has arisen it is a social communication rather than a proposition, unless the communication is made to provide a datum in resolving a new situation. If, however, the question is raised whether the subject-matter is *worthy* of being directly enjoyed; if, that is, the question is raised as to the existence of adequate grounds for the enjoyment, then there is a problematic situation involving inquiry and judgment. On such occasions *to value* means to weigh, appraise, estimate: *to evaluate*—a distinctly intellectual operation. Reasons and grounds one way and the other have to be sought for and formulated.

That such situations arise regarding persons once loved and admired, regarding objects upon which esteem (as distinct from estimation) was once lavished, is as indisputable as it is significant for the point at issue. For their occurrence shows that we evaluate only when a value, in the sense of material enjoyed, has become problematic. The propositions in this case are of a very different logical order from verbally similar sentences which only record and communicate the fact that a certain enjoyment, admiration or esteem has actually taken place. The latter "propositions" indeed record an occurrence, but if they have any logical status it is when they are material of an investigation conducted to reach a decision whether they were *justified* when they were enjoyed, or are justifiable in the present situation. Should we *now* commit ourselves to such an attitude? If we do, may we not regret it later?

Such questions arise in a wide range and variety of cases, from cases of eating a food which one knows from past experience will be immediately enjoyed, to serious moral predicaments. The only way of answering the questions, of resolving the doubts that have arisen, is to review the existential consequences which will probably occur *if* esteem, admiration, enjoyment are engaged in. For attitudes, esteem, etc., are active attitudes; they are *ways of acting* which produce consequences, and consequences can be *groundedly* anticipated only as consequences of conditions that are operative. The fact of enjoyment is only one of the operative conditions. It produces consequences—as in the act of eating the immediately enjoyed food—only through *interaction* with other existential conditions. The latter must, therefore, be independently surveyed. There is no way to estimate their probable consequences save in terms of what has happened in similar cases in the past, either one's personal past or in the recorded experience of others. On their bare face, existing conditions do not tell what their consequences will be. We have to investigate connections —usually that of cause-effect. Connections are then formulated in abstract generalized conceptual propositions, in rules, principles, laws. But the question of the *applicability* of the rules and principles at hand (however tested they *have* been) to the special situation in question always enters in. Choice has to be made among them. Consequently, in order to obtain a grounded final judgment there also has to be evaluation or appraisal of principles.

An evaluative proposition is not, then, merely declarative with respect either to facts or to conceptual subject-matter. The facts may be undoubted; I certainly have enjoyed this object in the past; I will get immediate enjoyment from it now. Certain general principles may be accepted as standards. But neither the facts nor the standardized rules as they present themselves are necessarily decisive in the evaluation being made. They are, respectively, material and procedural *means*. Their relevancy and weight in the present situation is the matter to be determined by inquiry before an evaluative appraisal can be grounded.

Such evaluative judgments are clearly an instance of judgments of practice; or, more strictly, all judgments of practice are evaluations, being occupied with judging what to do on the basis of estimated consequences of conditions which, since they are existential, are going to operate in any case. The more it is emphasized that direct enjoyment, liking, admiration, etc., are themselves emotional-motor in nature, the clearer is it that they are modes of action (of interaction). Hence a decision whether to engage or indulge in them in a given situation is a judgment of practice— of what should be done.

A point still more important for logical theory is that these evaluative judgments (as was brought out in the earlier discussion of judgment) enter into the formation of *all* final judgments. There is no inquiry that does not involve judgments of practice. The scientific worker has continually to appraise the information he gathers from his own observations and from the findings of others; he has to appraise its bearing upon what problems to undertake and what activities of observation, experimentation and calculation to carry out. While he "knows," in the sense of understanding, systems of conceptual materials, including laws, he has to estimate their relevancy and force as conditions of the particular inquiry undertaken. Probably the greatest source of the relative futility—or at least infertility—of that part of many logical texts which deal with scientific method, is failure to relate the material which they expound to the operations by which they are reached and the further operations they suggest, indicate and serve to direct.

6. *Appreciation.* The fact has been emphasized that a judgment of value is not identical with a statement that such and such a person arouses admiration and liking or that such and such an event or object was or is enjoyed. Such "propositions" have the property of truth only in a moral sense; that is, in opposition to being deliberate lies. Such propositions may, however, become constituents of a judgment of value, or an evaluation. They

take on this status when they are employed as material means of determining whether a given person or action *should* be admired or a given object enjoyed. When the statement "I like this picture" is changed into the proposition "This picture is beautiful," the issue shifts to the picture as *object*. To be valid, the latter proposition must be grounded upon discernible and verifiable qualities of the picture as an object. It depends, on one hand, upon discrimination of observable qualities and, on the other, upon the conceptual meanings which constitute, when they are made explicit, the definition of beauty. These statements are so far from being inconsistent with the existence of immediate non-judgmental esthetic experience that esthetic judgment must, to be genuine, grow out of the latter. But the immediate experience is not expressed in the statement "I like it." Its natural expression is rather the attitude of the observer or an interjection.

The last remarks bear upon the topic of appreciation. It is not bare enjoyment but enjoyment as *consummation* of previous processes and responses that constitutes appreciation. These previous states and operations involve reflective observation that partakes of the nature of analysis and synthesis, of discrimination and integration of relations. Appreciation, if genuine, is toward a subject-matter that is *representative*. It is not representative of something outside the appreciated object. The object in question is representative of that which has led up to it as fulfilment or consummatory close. Appreciation thus differs in a fundamental way from casual enjoyments that are just hit upon or let drop.

Words such as *climax, peak, culmination*, refer to consummatory objects. Any object or event that can be called by such names has an intrinsic reference to what went before. The words indicate that what preceded did not merely occur before the time of the peak but that they were such as to have the climacteric outcome as their own issue. Wherever there is appreciation there is the *heightened* quality produced by intrinsic connection of the object appreciated with its casual conditions. Its opposite is not dis-like or dis-enjoyment but de-preciation—disparagement of a result or product in its connection with the conditions and efforts of which it is the fruit. A man may take a drink of water almost automatically to quench thirst. If he is journeying in a barren land and forms an estimate of where he may find water and upon going to the spot quenches his thirst, he has a heightened quality of experience. Water is appreciated as he does not appreciate it when all he has to do is to turn a faucet and hold a tumbler under the stream that flows out. His experience has the representative quality of being an eventuation, a consummation.

There is, accordingly, an element of evaluation involved in appreciation. For such objects are not ends in the sense of being merely termini, but in the sense of being fulfilments: satisfactions in the literal sense in which that word means "*making suf*-ficient" something *de*-ficient. Consequently, judgments of appreciation are found wherever subject-matter undergoes such development and reconstruction as to result in a satisfying complete whole. Consider the following quotation as an illustrative of this point: "Classical thermo-dynamics forms a self-consistent and very elegant theory, and one might be inclined to think that no modification of it would be possible which did not introduce arbitrary features and completely spoil its beauty. This is not so since quantum mechanics has now reached a form in which it can be based on general laws, and is, although not yet quite complete, even more elegant and pleasing than the classic theory in the problems with which it deals." *

The words *beauty, elegance,* show clearly that here is a case of appreciation. Even slight analysis of the passage shows that the theory is elegant and has beauty because its subject-matter presents a consummated harmonious ordering of diverse facts and conceptions. Intellectual activity, science, has its phases of appreciation as truly as have the fine arts. They arise whenever inquiry has reached a close that fulfils the activities and conditions which led up to it. Without these phases, sometimes intense, no inquirer would have the experiential sign that his inquiry had reached its close.

Judgments of appreciation are not confined, however, to the *final* close. Every complex inquiry is marked by a series of stages that are *relative* completions. For complex inquiries involve a constellation of sub-problems, and the solution of each of them is a resolution of some tension. Each such solution is a heightening of

* Dirac, *Quantum Mechanics*, p. 1.

subject-matter, in direct ratio to the number and variety of discrepant and conflicting conditions that are brought to unification. The occurrence of these judgments of completion, not different in kind from those ordinarily called esthetic, constitutes a series of landmarks in the progress of any undertaking. They are signs of the achieved coherence of factual material and the consistency of conceptual material. They are indeed so important in their function of being clews and giving direction that the sense of harmony which attends them is too readily taken as evidence of *truth* of the subject-matter involved.[2] This error is due to isolating the feeling of harmony and congruity from the *operations* by which discrepant material is brought into harmonious union. The immediate experience of congruity, which is a valuable guide in conduct of inquiry, is converted into a criterion of objective truth.

This hypostization has affected the three most generalized forms of appreciation and produced the concepts of the Good, the True and the Beautiful as ontological absolutes. The actual basis of these absolutes is appreciation of concrete consummatory ends. In the case of intellectual, esthetic and moral experiences, the objective completion of certain unsettled existential conditions is brought about with such integrity that the final situation is possessed of peculiar excellence. There is the judgment "This is true, beautiful, good" in an emphatic sense. Generalizations are finally framed on the ground of a number of such concrete realizations. *Being* true, beautiful, or good, is recognized as a common character of subject-matters in spite of great differences in their actual constituents. They have, however, no meaning save as they indicate that certain subject-matters are outstanding consummatory completions of certain types of previously indeterminate situations by means of the execution of appropriate operations. Good, true, beautiful, are, in other words, abstract nouns designating characters which belong to three kinds of actually attained ends in their consummatory capacity.

Classic theory transformed ends attained into ends-in-themselves. It did so by ignoring the concrete conditions and operations by means of which the fulfilments in question are brought about.

---

[2] Cf. what was said in Chap. V about the esthetic nature of standards in Greek science, pp. 84, 96.

The traits which marked subject-matters in virtue of their being successful resolutions of problems of intellectual inquiry, of artistic construction and of moral conduct, were isolated from the conditions which gave them their standing and significance. Being thus isolated, they were necessarily hypostatized. In isolation from the means by which consequences are reached, they were taken to be the external ideals and standards of the very operations of inquiry, artistic creation and moral endeavor, of which in fact they are generalized results. This hypostization always happens when concrete ends in their terminal nature are erected into "ends-in-themselves."

The generalized and abstract conceptions of truth, beauty and goodness have a genuine value for inquiry, creation and conduct. They have, like all genuine ideals, a limiting and directive force. But in order to exercise their genuine function they must be taken as reminders of the concrete conditions and operations that have to be satisfied in actual cases. In serving as such generalized instruments, their meaning is exemplified in their further use, while it is also clarified and modified in this use. The *abstract* meaning of *truth*, of *being* true, for example, has changed with development of the methods of experimental inquiry.

In conclusion, the paradox that seems to attend the conception of judgments of practice which has been presented, will be recurred to. Irrespective of the question of paradox, there are but two alternatives regarding the intellectual status of deliberation: Either the intermediate and tentative propositions formed during the course of deliberation must be admitted to exercise a determining influence upon the very subject-matter they are about, or else all intellectual standing and bearing must be denied to them. The apparent paradox enters if the first interpretation is adopted. The idea is paradoxical, moreover, only from the standpoint of a prior conception of the nature of propositions: viz., that they are purely declaratory and are final and complete in this declaratory capacity. The problem takes on a very different aspect if it be admitted, even as a hypothesis, that *what* they declare is the need and advisability of performing certain operations as means of attaining a final subject-matter which may be groundedly asserted. For upon this basis, the idea that propositions are factors in determining the very subject-matter they are *about* is exactly what is to be expected instead of being paradoxical.

The issue will perhaps be clarified if we note in this connection that a certain ambiguity is attached to the word *about*. On the one hand, a proposition is said to be about something which does not appear as a term in the proposition. On the other, it is said to be about one of the terms of the proposition, usually about that term which is the grammatical subject of the sentence which expresses the affirmation or denial in question. For example, a man inquires into the subject-matter which relates to some perplexing question of foreign relations—his inquiry as a whole is about the perplexing situation. In the course of the inquiry, he makes propositions *about* states of fact and about rules of international law; the facts and rules are explicit constituents of the propositions. But these propositions are about (or refer to) subject-matters which are not a constituent of any of the propositions. Their point and force lies in that which they are about, the situation they serve to determine, and a situation that does not appear as a term in any proposition.

The net conclusion is that evaluations as judgments of practice are not a particular kind of judgment in the sense that they can be put over against other kinds, but are an inherent phase of judgment itself. In some cases, the immediate problem may so directly concern appraisal of existences in their capacity as means, positive-negative (resources and obstacles), and so directly concern appraisal of the relative importance of possible consequences that offer themselves as ends-in-view, that the evaluative aspect is the dominant one. In that case, there are judgments which in a *relative* sense may be called valuational in distinction from the subject-matter of other judgments where this aspect is subordinate. But since selection of existences to serve as subject-data and of ideas to serve as predicate-possibilities (or ends in view) is necessarily involved in every judgment, the valuation operation is inherent in judgment as such. The more problematic the situation and the more thorough the inquiry that has to be engaged in, the more explicit becomes the valuational phase. The identity of valuational judgment with judgments of practice is implicitly recognized in scientific inquiry in the necessity of experiment for determination of data and for the use of ideas and conceptions—including principles and laws—as directive hypotheses. In substance, the present chapter is then a plea that logical theory be made to conform with the realities of scientific practice, since in the latter there are no grounded determinations without operations of doing and making.

CHAPTER X

AFFIRMATION AND NEGATION:
JUDGMENT AS REQUALIFICATION

THERE IS a contrast between the traditional theory of positive and negative propositions and what occurs in the conduct of inquiry. The contrast invites examination. In scientific inquiry there is scrupulous attention to exceptions and whatever appear to be exceptions. The technique of inquiry is concerned as much with effective eliminations as with noting agreements. No amount of agreement among the traits of phenomena investigated suffices of itself to establish a conclusion; agreements have to be safeguarded at every point by observation of differences. Experimental operations are undertaken with the express object of instituting deliberate *variations* of conditions in order to bring out negative traits which serve to test currently accepted conclusions. Should logical theory take its cue for interpretation of affirmative and negative propositions from what happens in the conduct of inquiry, it would be evident that (1) such propositions are *functional* in resolution of a problematic situation, and are (2) conjugate or functionally correspondent in relation to each other.

Traditional theory, however, takes the propositions as given ready-made and hence as independent and complete in themselves. They are just there to be noticed, with description of whatever properties they present. This mode of treatment becomes intelligible when it is viewed in conjunction with its derivation from the onto-logical logic of Aristotle, whence it ultimately derives. In the latter logic, species or kinds are the ultimate qualitative wholes or real individuals. Some of these species are by nature, or by in-herent essence, exclusive of others. The negative proposition was thus a cognitive actualization of a fundamental ontological form. Species also are ordered hierarchically. Hence affirmation of inclusion of some species in species that are more comprehensive was also a cognitive actualization of the ontological.

Positive and negative propositions are on this basis immediate apprehensions or "notations" of what exists in and by nature. What has just been said applies also to universal propositions—i. e., to those about *wholes*. Similar considerations apply to particular propositions, and hence to the so-called square of opposition with its relations of contrariety, subcontrariety, contradiction and subalternation. Things that change are by inherent nature incomplete and partial. Hence they are apprehended in particular propositions. The connection between partial and particular was more than etymological. In traditional formal theory "some," the verbal mark of the particular, has come to mean "some, perhaps all." But in the Aristotelian theory, *some* meant *some only*. By the ontological nature of the case, wherever the affirmative "some are" applies, the negative proposition "some are not" holds also. The relation of subcontrariety was as ontological as was that of the contrariety of mutually exclusive universals. Particulars, or that which by nature is incomplete, because changing, can be known only through fixed limits imposed by the essence that defines a universal. Consequently, subalternation is in so far ontologically grounded. As for contradiction, it is evident that a proposition which is restricted by its ontological subject-matter to *some only* contradicts a proposition which by nature is about a whole.

The development of modern science destroyed the conceptions of fixed species, defined by fixed essences, upon which the Aristotelian logic rested. This destruction affected, therefore, the classic conceptions of universal and particular, whole and part, and the scheme of their relationships with one another. Modern logic, however, attempted to retain the scheme but with the understanding that it is purely formal, devoid of ontological import. The inevitable consequence is the mechanical way in which affirmative and negative propositions and their relationships are conceived in both traditional and modern formalistic logic. They have lost their ontological basis without gaining a functional relation to the conduct of inquiry.

The old designation, *quality* of propositions, is retained in connection with affirmative and negative propositions but is hardly more than a mechanical label. From the standpoint of the functional connection of positing and negating with determination of unsettled or indeterminate situations, they are means, through the operations of selection and elimination they respectively prescribe, of *re*qualifying the original indeterminate situation. Affirmative propositions represent the agreement of different subject-matters in their *evidential* capacity; they *agree* in that they support or are taken to support one another cumulatively in pointing in the same direction, in spite of the fact that existentially the subject-matters involved occur at different times and places. Negative propositions, on the other hand, represent subject-matters to be eliminated because of their irrelevancy or indifference to the evidential function of material in solution of a given problem. Ultimately, the fact that certain facts or ideas are excluded means that the original indeterminate situation can be transformed or requalified into a determinate one only through existential experimental operative elimination of some of its constituents; affirmation of certain data or ideas means that they are operatively selected to reinforce one another in institution of a unified situation. If these statements sound odd in contrast with the traditional interpretation of affirmation and denial, one has only to think of what happens in the conduct of scientific inquiry to see that they have a solid base and a pertinent meaning.

That inquiry selects appropriate evidential data by means of *comparison* of what is found to exist or occur in different existential cases is a commonplace. Without collection of phenomena observed at different times and places under different conditions, grounded inquiry, whether of common sense or science, can make no headway. Deliberate experimentation is resorted to for the express purpose of varying conditions, or so that observed consequences will so vary that comparison may have more extensive and more definite subject-matter to operate with. Collection of many cases with a view to institution of differences and agreements (in evidential force) is a kind of relatively uncontrolled experimentation. Comparison is so involved in all inquiries that reach grounded conclusions it is usually taken for granted.[1]

Now it is impossible to define comparison except operationally. It is a name for *all* operations in which identities and incompatibilities in evidential force are determined. It is a name for any and all of the operations by means of which alleged or provisional data are determined to *be* data with respect to the problem set by a given indeterminate situation; by which some facts are determined to be the "facts of the case" in hand and other facts not to be. It is impossible to give an independent definition of comparison and then derive the operations of establishing agreements and differences in evidential capacity from that definition. It is a blanket term for the entire complex of operations by which some existences are selectively instituted as data and other existential materials are eliminated as having nothing to do with the case; as, in fact, obstructive in the required work of requalification of the existential situation.

Mr. Bosanquet, one of the idealistic logicians referred to above, says "Comparison in the ordinary sense is a name applied to the intentional cross-reference of two or more given contents, in order to establish between these contents *as given*, a general or special identity, or partial identity (likeness)." [2] The view expressed in this passage serves to bring out, by contrast, the meaning of the position here held. The italicized words of the text cited, *as given*, involve, positively, an affirmation of the antecedent ontological basis of comparison and, negatively, a denial of the functional or operative force of propositions of identity—agreement—and difference—contrariety, subcontrariety, and contradictoriness. In contrast, the position of the text is that what is meant by comparison is institution of *selected* facts on the basis of equivalent (similar) evidential force in a variety of cases which are existentially different, this determination being grounded only as the operations of observation involved in the selection eliminate, *pari*

[1] Examination of logical texts will show that the word rarely appears. The exception to this statement is found in the case of the writings of logicians of the rational idealistic school. They are interested in it as a somewhat elementary exemplification of their ontological proposition that "reality" as such is always a system of differences-in-identity or identity-in-differences, or what is called the "concrete universal."

[2] *Logic*, Vol. II, p. 21, italics in original text.

passu, other existential constituents as irrelevant to the problem in hand; as non-evidential, and indeed misleading *unless* eliminated. The view of Mr. Bosanquet reduces comparison to an act that can be and is performed within the "mind." The view here taken is that it is operational in the existential sense of effecting modifications in what antecedently existed—as does controlled experimentation. "Similarity" is the *product* of *assimilating* different things with respect to their functional value in inference and reasoning. There is much common sense inference in which similarity is implicitly postulated. When the assumption is stated in a proposition (as it needs to be if the conclusion of inquiry is to be grounded) a proposition of *similarity* is, in effect, an affirmation that there is sufficient probability of equal values to serve as ground for tentative assimilation.

The foregoing discussion has contrasted a theory of affirmation and negation based upon the practice of present scientific inquiry with the Aristotelian doctrine and with that later formalization of his doctrine which emptied it of all content. The connection of our view with the general theory of judgment will now be considered. Indeterminate situations are marked by confusion, obscurity and conflict. They require clarification. An unsettled situation needs clarification because as it stands it gives no lead or cue to the way in which it may be resolved. We do not know, as we say, where to turn; we grope and fumble. We escape from this muddled condition only by turning to other situations and searching them for a cue. What is borrowed provides a new attitude as the means for directing observational operations—performed on the common sense level through sensorimotor organs. These operations make some aspects of the given situation stand out. The attitude, when made explicit, is an idea or conceptual meaning.

The very operations that select certain conditions, taken as potential clews to the problem to be dealt with, also rule out other conditions and qualities of the total given situation. Selection involves rejection and the latter act is rudimentary negation. The unsettled situation is also usually such as to evoke contrary modes of response. Attitudes and habitual modes of treating situations clash. This conflict is involved in confused and blind situations.

But sometimes the conflict is so uppermost that the main problem is that of reduction to unified significance rather than clarification. Some constituents stand out but point in opposed directions. To solve the problem resort must be had to other experienced situations. These suggest additions and eliminations which, when effected, will bring together the materials that first evoked conflicting responses.

The process of eliminating materials that are irrelevant and obstructive goes hand in hand with that of rendering other materials definite in their indicative force. Negation is thus the restrictive side of the selection involved in all determination of material as data. What is selected is provisionally positive. This positive phase is at first identical with *taking and using* the material in order to try it out. But *control* of this taking and using demands that the material be formulated. The propositions (that are the formulation) thus differ from the final assertion which is characteristic of judgment. Dependence of the rejection-selection operation upon suggestions supplied by other situations explains the emphasis put, in the traditional theory, upon "common" factors and upon agreement. Comparison is at the same time contrast, expressed in the rejection and the elimination of those elements and qualities in the situation which other situations indicate are irrelevant.

It is sometimes said that affirmation and negation cannot be made coordinate with each other because there then arises a *regressus ad infinitum*. Such would be the result if they trod upon each other's heels. But in fact they are strictly conjugate. Not only is all determination negation but all negation is (or moves in the direction of) positive determination. The relation of affirmation-negation is no more successive than the taking of food by an animal is prior to or after rejection of other materials as nonfood. Acts *which at one and the same time* accept for use and that shut out are not sequential.

The connection between organic selection-rejection and logical affirmation-negation is, moreover, a special case of a general principle already laid down. The organic function provides the existential basis of the logical. Transition from one to the other occurs when the direct existential commitment involved in organic acceptance-rejection is deferred till the functional capacity of materials has been determined in inquiry. This postponed determination is made possible by language, by propositions about final decisive action. There are, for example, historical reasons for believing that processes of blame and accusation in connection with attempts to support and refute allegations were a main factor in developing the positive-negative aspect of inquiry. Then came argumentation *pro and con* in relation to some proposal advanced for social adoption. Argument still means reasoning. *Crimen* means judgment in the Latin tongue, and its root is found in our words discrimination and crime. The Greek *aitia*, usually translated *cause*, had a definitely legal origin. Transition from the cultural to the logical status is manifest in the change from assent and dissent to affirmation and denial on specified grounds. To admit and to refuse to admit may be acts performed either for social reasons or because of reference to demands that are imposed by grounded inquiry. In the latter, they have explicit logical status. Affirmation is unambiguously a logical term. We *af*firm only that which we take to be capable of *con*firmation.

There is another objection to the idea that affirmation is logically coordinate with denial. When the functional nature of affirmative propositions is overlooked—that is, their office in institution of data and meanings to be operatively employed—they are given direct existential reference. They are taken to be declarative of what is existentially there. The same thing cannot be said of negative propositions. Hence it is denied by some writers that negative propositions have any logical import at all. They are at most, according to them, rejections of suggestions that have arisen in our own minds and hence they have only a personal or psychological standing. In the words of one writer on logic "There is no such thing as a negative copula but only a negated copula." [3]

Mere negation, however, reminds one unpleasantly of the disputes of children, consisting of reiterations of "'Tis, Tisn't." The important point is that the view in question follows from the postulate that all propositions about fact are complete and final because enunciative of antecedent existence. The doctrine which

[3] Sigwart, *Logic*, Vol. I, p. 122.

denies logical standing to denials thus gives indirect support to the position they are instrumental and functional. Existences and meanings are referred to, both in affirmation and negation, not just for the sake of mentioning them, but with respect to their function in requalification of an indeterminate situation; for this requalification can be effected (with respect to negation) only by elimination of obstructive materials and of suggestions that lead nowhere. If negative propositions are ruled out of the logical domain, comparison must go too.

In short, negation is other than mere omission or dropping out of certain considerations, factual and ideational. Some facts and some meanings have to be actively eliminated because they are obstacles that stand in the way of resolution of an unsettled situation. The idea that negation is connected with change, with becoming other or different, is at least as old as Plato. But in Plato change, altering or othering, has a direct ontological status. It is a sign of the defective ontological character of that which changes, its lack of full Being. The negative proposition, which dealt with change, was thus the counterpart in knowledge of the ontological inferiority of one kind of existential material. But in modern science, correlations or correspondences of change are the chief object of determination. It is no longer possible to treat the relation of the negative proposition to change and alteration as declarative of defective being. On the contrary, the negative proposition as such formulates a change *to be* effected in existing conditions by operations which the negative proposition sets forth. It is an indication of an experimental operation to be performed such that conditions will be so varied that the consequences of the operation will have an evidential significance lacking in the conditions as they existed at first.

The affirmative proposition also has intrinsic connection with change. Take the proposition "This is red." On its face, it is purely affirmative; it carries with it no suggestion of negation or elimination. But the bare existence of a red thing is not a sufficient ground for the affirmation that "It is red." To be grounded, alternative possibilities must be ruled out. There is no logical necessity why *this* should be red; it may have been some other color a moment ago and become another color a moment from now. The proposition is "synthetic" in the Kantian sense; it cannot be grounded in a mere intellectual analysis of *this*. Valid determination that "*this* is *red*" depends upon (1) exhaustive disjunction of alternative possibilities of color and (2) upon elimination of all other possibilities than the one affirmed, the elimination resulting (3) from a series of hypothetical propositions such as "If blue, then such and such consequences," etc., in contrast with the proposition "If red, then such and such other and differential consequences." I do not mean of course that as a matter of fact such an elaborate process of determination is often gone through. I do mean, however, that for complete logical validity there is required a proposition like the following: "*Only* if this is red, will observed phenomena be what they are." "*Only*" in this proposition depends upon a series of eliminations expressed in negative propositions. Whenever a scientific determination of color quality is required in solution of a scientific problem, inquiry proceeds in the direction of just such an exhaustive disjunctive system and of systematic elimination of all alternatives save one for which positive grounds are found.

The connection of this determination with deliberate institution of change should be obvious. A series of experimental operations has to be performed with and upon the existential material indicated by the demonstrative *this*. The changes which follow as consequences of the execution of these experimental operations provide grounds for denying that *it* is blue, yellow, purple, green, etc., and for affirming that it is red. If one is inclined to doubt this account, especially on the ground that the proposition in question, if not "self-evident," is at least not nearly as highly mediated as the account assumes, let him recall that scientifically color is determined only by operations which identify colors with certain rates of vibration, and red with one particular exclusive number. In other words, the proposition "This is red" means, logically, that a certain differential change has occurred or may be predicted to occur when certain operations are undertaken. In the latter case, the logical meaning is "This will become red or will redden something else," certain conditions being postulated. If the proposition be interpreted to mean "This has been red for a long time," even more extensive mediation is required to warrant a conclusion about the added trait of temporal duration. If it is taken to mean "It is red by nature or necessity," reference to change is excluded but this is the only case in which the proposition is not about a change.

Impersonal propositions such as "It is raining" have been the theme of more or less discussion. The natural interpretation of such propositions is that in them a total prior qualitative situation is negated-affirmed by specification of a change. "It" refers to the gross environing perceptual field; "rain" to the gross alteration it is undergoing. If the proposition is "It is only sprinkling" or "It is raining hard," the qualification is more differentiated because more specific negations have been introduced. Propositions of gross qualitative change are the starting points for a set of disjunctive propositions in which a single continuous change is formulated in terms of a scale or spectrum of degrees. It is not sufficient to take a gross change in its given discreteness. It has to be resolved into a series of changes, each of which is determined by reference to its position in a continuum of changes. Such determination involves a disjunctive set of propositions. In each determination of position in the scale a negation of all disjunctive possibilities except one is involved.[4]

After these general remarks, I come to the specific forms of the relations of affirmative and negative propositions designated as contrariety, subcontrariety and contradiction. From what has been said, it follows (1) that these relations have to be understood in the functional office they exercise in inquiry, (2) as correlative or conjugate determinations, not as independent sets of propositions which happen to sustain to each other the relation designated. (The ordinary square of opposition is likely to be interpreted in the latter sense, since failure to connect the propositions which are contrary, etc., with the process of inquiry has the effect of setting-up a purely mechanical scheme of propositions each logically independent of the other.)

I. Contrariety or logical opposition obtains between affirmative and negative propositions when both are general. The relation is such that only one can be valid and both may be invalid. The relation between "All marine vertebrates are cold-blooded" and

---

[4] The topic of scales receives further attention in the next chapter.

"No marine vertebrates are cold-blooded" exemplifies the relation of contrariety. *Contrariety of propositions sets the limits within which specific determinations must fall.* In themselves, they are indeterminate; that is, if they are taken as final and complete, rather than as expressing a certain necessary stage in the progress of controlled inquiry, they are logically defective. This logical defect is apparent in the fact that both may be invalid. Contraries are a stage in institution of the set of exhaustive disjunctives which, as we have seen, are required for adequate affirmative-negative determinations. They do not of themselves constitute the required disjunctives, for (as is evident in the illustration just given) they permit of alternatives, such as "*Some* are and *some* are not." But they set the limiting termini for intermediate alternatives. They serve to delimit the field of inquiry, and thereby to give direction to subsequent observational and ideational operations. The traditional *A* and *E* propositions represent the limits within which alternatives fall, but the fact that both may be invalid proves that they do not do more than that. As contraries, they represent, then, not conclusions but the results of a preliminary survey of the total problematic field, the survey being made to circumscribe the field within which further determinations must occur. A process of groping reaches its initial termination when we can state the extreme boundaries within which a solution must be sought.

We have, then, the following logical situation. (1) On the one hand, the field of possible propositions must be bounded or else inquiry will roam all over the lot. This delimitation is effected by means of contrary general propositions. (2) On the other hand, when the strictly functional nature of the propositions having the relation of contrariety to each other is overlooked, these delimiting propositions are supposed to exhaust possible alternatives. Then the rigid type of *Either-Or* reasoning results, a type which is common in thought about social and moral issues. *Either* "The Individual" *or* "Society" as a fixed entity; either freedom from all restraint or coercion from without; either the bourgeoisie or the proletariat; either change or the unchanging; either the continuous or the discrete, and so on. Only when the strictly functional nature of contrary propositions is seen do we escape from the unending and inherently endless round of controversies generated by this mode of thought. When their functional and instrumental nature is perceived, they are seen to be necessary, but necessary only because they set the boundaries within which a set of more determinate disjunctive alternatives are to be sought for. They are functional directives for further, more discriminating, determinations.[5]

In logical theory, the rigidity and hence apparent finality of contrary propositions is often enforced by use of symbols that have no meaning or content of their own. *A* and *Not-A* are, for example, such symbols. These purely formalistic contraries cannot possibly have directive force. For if, say, "virtue" be assigned to *A* as its meaning, then *Not-A* includes not only vice but triangles, horse races, symphonies and the precession of the equinoxes. Since the time of Aristotle, the nugatory nature of "infinitation of the negative" has been generally recognized. What has not been so generally recognized is (1) that failure to recognize the intermediary function of contrary proposition tends in the direction of infinitation, and (2) that any purely formalistic *either-or* formulation of contraries (such as *A* and *Not-A*) eliminates reference to any universe of discourse and, hence, when any value is assigned to the positive expression, renders the negative wholly indeterminate. Nevertheless, the institution of opposites in hypothetical form, *when interpreted as a means of fixing the limits within which determinate disjunctive alternatives fall,* is a necessary preparatory logical procedure.

II. Subcontrary propositions of the form "Some are . . ." and "Some are not" may both be valid while one must be valid, when they are determinate. "Some marine vertebrates are cold-blooded" and "Some are not" are subcontraries both of which are now known to be valid. The phrase "are now known" is related to

---

[5] The dialectic of thesis, antithesis and synthesis recognizes that the initial contraries are not final. But it suffers from the logical vice of supposing that the "synthesis" grows directly out of the contraries, instead of from determinate inquiries which the contraries indicate. In scientific inquiry, thesis and antithesis are never treated as generating a synthesis. For example, the relationship between "heredity" and "environment" as contraries sets an important problem, as at one time in physics a problem was set by the relation of centrifugal and centripetal "forces." But the scientific problem is handled by means of analysis of the subject-matter of these highly general terms into specific conditions, not by manipulation of the concepts.

the clause in the previous sentence "when they are determinate." The formal logical relation involved is, in other words, a form of existential contents determined by observation. However, like any form, it may be abstracted, while the abstract form has *logical* meaning only in its possible application to material contents. As far as mere form is concerned, both of the propositions cited might be invalid. For apart from what is existentially determined, the valid proposition might be "No marine vertebrates have blood." Only because a conjunction of the traits of possessing a spinal column and possessing blood has already been established, are the propositions subcontraries.

Subcontraries are more determinate than contraries but are still indeterminate as compared with final judgment. For fully determinate propositions regarding the subject-matter in question would be "*All* marine vertebrates *marked by-such-and-such traits* (say, bringing forth young alive and breathing with lungs) are warm-blooded" and "*All* marine vertebrates having such-and-such other differential traits are cold-blooded." If they were final and complete, subcontrary propositions as logical forms would be even more slovenly than contraries. As a matter of fact, however, they record the results of observation in such a way as to provide factual data that set a definite problem. The subcontrary propositions cited represented the state of zoology at a given date when the discovery of two kinds of marine vertebrates, marked off by differences in quality of blood, definitely set a problem; namely, the problem of discovering the conditions in which some marine animals are of one kind and others of another kind. It did so because of a *material* postulate, namely the postulate that blood plays such an important role in animal life that a difference with respect to it is, to a high degree of probability, bound up with other important characteristics. Propositions marked by "some," affirmative and negative, thus present the results of a relatively incomplete *empirical* state of inquiry, where "empirical" means a valid statement of results of actual observation without insight into the conditions upon which observed traits depend. The dependence of valid conclusions in existential matters upon factual observation shows that such propositions, while not final, represent a definite stage in the conduct of inquiry and perform a necessary office in carrying it forward to a conclusion.

Inquiry with respect to light is at the present time in this stage. There are grounds for holding that "Light in *some* respects is a radiant phenomenon and in *some* respects is not, being corpuscular." Granting the adequacy of the observations upon which these propositions rest, no one will deny that they mark a scientific advance. On the other hand, few would contend that scientific inquiry can be content with these propositions as final. They institute a definite problem for further investigation: Under what conditions is light vibratory and under what conditions is it discrete?

III. The discussion of subcontrariety leads up to the conception of subalternation. If it has once been determined that *all* marine vertebrates marked by a specified conjunction of traits are warm-blooded, the so-called subaltern that *some* such animals are warm-blooded is trivial. Reference to the general proposition may serve upon occasion as a reminder to some person who is temporarily forgetful, but it has no logical force. Suppose that inquiry at a certain stage has determined only that in the case of a shipwreck some passengers have been saved and some lost. Suppose further inquiry determines specifically the names of all who are saved and all who are lost. In the latter case, it is silly to recur to the weakened form "some" when the tabulated list of all of each kind is at hand. The name of any given person must appear in one list or the other. About a specified person there are no alternatives.

The real function of the proposition of the form of *some* is in the opposite direction from that of the traditional table. Instead of movement from "all" to "some," there is a reaction from *some* into *all*. At an early stage of inquiry that "some" are saved indicates that *perhaps* "all" on board have been saved. At the stage when the inquiry is completed, the transition is from the indefinite "some" of "*all*" who were on board, to *all* of a specified group. In a strictly empirical proposition (in the sense of "empirical" defined above), there is no difference in logical form between the proposition "All cases *so far observed* are such and such" and the proposition "Some cases out of all existential cases, past, present and future, are such and such." The logical sense of both linguistic forms is "*Perhaps* all cases are such and such." When the conditions under which phenomena are such and such have been *exclusively* determined (through a set of affirmative-negative propositions) then a general proposition in the form of a law is possible: Whenever conditions are such and such, consequences are such and such.[6]

IV. The foregoing analysis has one main purpose, namely to indicate, on one side, that when affirmative and negative propositions are taken to be final and complete (as they must be when their operative connection with the progressive conduct of inquiry is ignored) the forms in question are mechanical and arbitrary; and, on the other side, to indicate that when their functional capacity is taken into account the relations of contrariety, subcontrariety and subalternation mark definite stages in the advance of inquiry toward a final warranted judgment. These considerations come, as it were, to a head in the case of contradictory propositions, those that are such that if one is valid, the other is invalid, and if one is invalid the other is valid. In the traditional square of opposition this relation of contradiction is symbolized by the diagonal lines from the general affirmative to the negative particular (some, meaning one or more) and from the general negative to the affirmative particular. Formally speaking, it is certainly true that the proposition "all men are white" is contradicted if a single case of a colored person is observed, while the proposition "No men are red" was negated as soon as the first North American Indian was encountered.

But the essential logical point here is that the general (affirmative or negative) is negated not by the indeterminate "some" but by the determinate singular. "Some" is logically either excessive or deficient. It is excessive, if a singular case has been determined (not in fact an easy matter); it is defective, if "some" is understood in its strict logical force, namely, as an indication of a possibility, of the form "may be" or "perhaps." The fact that a given *I* or *O* proposition may be invalid is enough of itself to prove that it cannot contradict in any strict logical sense a general proposition of the opposite quality. The proposition "Some men are not white"

---

[6] The difference between the two kinds of general propositions in both of which the word *all* may appear is discussed in Chap. XIII.

indicates that an object *may be* colored and yet be a human being, or *may be* a human being and yet not be white. We are familiar with the warning against vague generalities. The warning is decidedly relevant at this point. "Some," *if unspecified* with reference to singulars, is of the nature of a vague generality. If it *is* specified, then it assumes one of two forms: "Such and such *determinate singulars* are of a given kind," which negates a general proposition that "all are of some other kind"; or, still more determinately, "*All* singulars marked by specified traits are of a certain kind." In either case, it is not an indeterminate "some" which contradicts the general *A* or *E* proposition.

As has already been indicated, the proposition about a number of (or *some*) singulars being such and such sets a *problem*. It suffices to negate a general proposition of the opposite quality. But the negation is in so far incomplete or indeterminate. It does not of itself establish a valid, universal proposition. It warrants a contradictory universal only when two logical conditions are satisfied: (1) Determination of a set of alternative disjunctives as exhaustively as possible, and (2) determination of the differential traits which are evidential signs of one and *not* another kind. At a given stage of scientific inquiry, an exception is discovered to some previously accepted generalization. If careful inquiry substantiates the authenticity of the exceptional singular, then the generalization in its previous form is certainly *negated*. But no scientific inquirer would suppose for a moment that this negation was equivalent to establishment of a valid universal proposition. The question at once arises as to the exact conditions under which the exceptional and negative case occurs. As soon as this is done, we have *another* generalization: "*All* cases marked by certain traits are such and such." In short, the discovery of singulars or a singular that negates a generalization is but the antecedently conditioning means to further inquiries. The proposition in which it is embodied is not final or complete, for it functions as occasion and stimulus of further inquiries with view to determining *how and why* the exception occurs. When these inquiries are satisfactorily concluded, then and only then do we have a final proposition, which takes the form of a new general proposition.

In no case of controlled inquiry is a flat negation of a generalization taken to be final. If it were so taken, a former generalization would simply be abandoned and that would be the end of the matter. What actually happens is that the prior generalization is modified and revised by discovery of the contradictory instance. Certain data discovered by using the Einsteinian theory of relativity contradicted the Newtonian formula of gravitation. If such negations had the independent and final logical status attributed to them by traditional formalistic logic, either the Newtonian formula would have been declared invalid and the matter would have ended there, or else the observational data would have been declared false and impossible because they contradicted the general proposition. Even in the cases in which an exception turns out to be apparent rather than actual, the older generalization is not simply confirmed, but gains a new shade of meaning because of its capacity to apply to the unusual and seemingly negative instance. It is in this sense that "the exception proves the rule."

The logic of the contradictory relation of propositions thus affords a crowning proof of the functional and operative import of affirmative-negative propositions. Nothing is more important in inquiry than institution of contradictory propositions. Since one must be valid and the other invalid, they are determinate in a way in which contraries and subcontraries are not. But if the traditional theory were sound, inquiry would have to stop right there. There would be no ground upon which to decide which one of the two is valid and which is invalid. Those who prefer to trust to the "evidence of the senses" would hold that the generalization had been proved false. Those who distrust sense and exalt "reason" would be inclined to reverse the conclusion and hold the singulars are not "really" what they seem to be. Institution of contradictories in the actual procedure of scientific inquiry is crucially important just because it does *not* adopt the canons of any theory that makes contradictories final and complete. In the conduct of inquiry, institution of a contradictory negation is treated as a step in the continuation of inquiry towards final judgment. The final effect is to revise the generalization reached in earlier inquiries. Through this modification a generalization becomes applicable to both the old evidential material which supported it and to the new evidential material which contradicts the earlier generalizations.

The original Aristotelian conception of affirmation and negation at least corresponded to what was supposed to be the ontological nature of the objects to which affirmative and negative propositions apply. The functional conception here advanced denies that affirmative and negative propositions have a one-to-one correspondence with objects as they are. But it gives them the operative and instrumental force of means of transforming an unsettled and doubtful existential situation into a resolved determinate one. The modern theory, derived, as has been said, from the attempt to retain forms after their material or existential content had been abandoned, is grounded in nothing and leads nowhere. It is formal only in the sense of being empty and mechanical. It neither reflects existence already known nor forwards inquiry into what may and should be known. It is a logical vermiform appendix.

In view of the fact that the metaphysical problem of the One and the Many has at various times had a very considerable influence upon logical theory, it may be appropriate, in concluding this chapter, to say a few words on that topic as it affects logical theory. Unity, or what is termed The One, is the existential counterpart of the product of operations which, by institution of agreement of different contents in evidential force, establish warranted identities. Negation, on the other hand, discriminates and produces differences. The latter when hypostatized constitute the Many. The problem when approached from the logical side is one of operations of unifying and discriminating. These operations have of course an existential basis and matrix. Integration and differentiation are biological processes foreshadowing the logical operations just mentioned. They are themselves prepared for and foreshadowed in physical processes of conjunction and separation. The insoluble problems which have led to speculative metaphysical constructions about the One and the Many arise from making entities, expressed in nouns, out of processes and operations properly designated by active verbs and adverbs.

CHAPTER XI

THE FUNCTION OF PROPOSITIONS OF
QUANTITY IN JUDGMENT

IN TRADITIONAL formal logic, the topic of quantity of propositions follows after that of quality. The traditional theory, applying to propositions with respect to both quality and quantity, holds that propositions are capable of interpretation on the basis of both extension and intension. In the former case, a proposition is of a relation of classes; in the latter, it states that members of a specified class are affirmed to be marked by a specified attribute. As applied to quantity, in extensive interpretation a proposition declares either that a class *as such* is contained in another class and then is general in quantity; or that *some* unspecified portion of it is so contained, and is particular in "quantity." When read in intension, a proposition states either that *any* member of the class has a certain "attribute" or that *some* unspecified portion of it has a given attribute. Thus, the "general" proposition "All men are mortal" means either that the class *men* is contained as a sub-class in the class *mortals,* or that *any man* whatever has the attribute *mortality.* In any case, quantity, so-called, is according to this doctrine marked by the two forms *all* (none, not any) and *some* (some-not), a distinction which, in combination with that of the affirmative-negative yields the four forms of *A E I O* propositions. The slightest inspection thus reveals that the distinction or form *called* quantity is, in fact, that of the *definite* class and an *indefinite* part of a class.

The extremely restricted conception of quantity involved in this theory hardly needs to be pointed out—restricted, that is, in comparison with propositions of common sense and of science which have quantitative marks. In common sense, there are "quantifications" such as *few-many*, *more-less*, *little-much*, *great small*, while "some" rarely appears except at an initial stage—as for example, in such sentences as, "Well *some*body has been here anyway," or "At all events, *some* beggars are honest." Moreover, even common sense propositions of quantity express result of measurement, as in the tables of weights and measurements that are in use in trade, industry and the crafts: "One cup holds half a pint; the suit cost $25; the plot of ground has an area of an acre, etc." No *scientific* proposition which records the processes and results of observation and experiment is complete unless processes and results are stated in numerical form.

The contrast of such propositions with those which are recognized in formal logic as marked by the form of quantity is so great as to demand explanation. The needed explanation is found on one side, in the fact that in common sense and science, propositions about quantitative distinctions and relations are always means to an objective end, not being final in themselves; and, on the other side, in the fact that a distinction which was material and necessary in the Aristotelian logic of science is now so irrelevant to the content of science that when retained it is purely formalistic, empty, and irrelevant, equally to Aristotle and to common sense and to science. That the modern formalism is wholly alien to the thought of Aristotle is seen in the fact that to him quantity was accidental, not essential. Hence it was the logical *ground* of distinction between universal and particular propositions, because it was a differential characteristic of the *particular over against* the universal in Nature. For him, *all* meant whole, qualitatively complete. Therefore, any proposition about the whole was *necessary*. *All* was neither collective nor *merely* general in logical force. Hence, strictly speaking, it was outside the domain of the category of quantity. For collective propositions are resolvable into a number of singulars and are consequently particular, no matter how extensive are the singulars contained in the count.

A *merely* general proposition is one which states that things are so-and-so as a rule, or *usually; upon* the whole; not *as* a whole. They too, then, fall in the category of particular propositions. Necessity and completeness, contingency and incompleteness, are the inherent logical forms of propositions marked by *all*

1d *some*. These logical forms were taken to be counterparts of 1tological properties. For some modes of Being *are;* they have ءeing in the complete sense of the word; they exist *always* without ١ariation or shadow of turning. About such objects, propositions ٢e made *to katholon*. But there are other things which change; ١ey are and are not; they come into Being and pass out of it. Of 1ch objects, propositions can only be made *to hekeston*, or in their ٢veralty since they are by nature severed and several. Given 1is cosmological and ontological framework, nothing could be ٥under and more comprehensive than the Aristotelian distinction ٤tween *all* and *some* as ultimate forms of propositions.

In such a scheme there is no special place for measurement and ٤termination of magnitude and degree. *More or less* is an in-٧vitable mark of some things; knowing that fact, one knows all ١at need be *known* about them. Measurement may assist practi-٤l activities which deal with changing materials, but it cannot in 1ny case lead to demonstrative knowledge. It is not necessary to ٧well upon the totally different situation which exists in the frame-٧ork of present science. The scientific object, *par excellence*, is correlation of functional correspondence of changes. There is ٠ way in which to determine the presence or absence of such ٥rrelations save by measurements whose results are numerically ٢ated. Hence in modern scientific context, particular proposi-١ons as such are determinations of the material of a *problem* for ٥rther investigation. They are not final; for they are not as far ٢ "thought" can possibly go in respect to objects that are 1complete or partial by nature. They are initial in inquiry. The ٤tention, then, of particular propositions marked by presence of ١e word *some* as a distinctive kind of proposition, is another 1stance of the formalization of a principle that once had material ١gnificance and that had its own relative scientific justification. ١he task of logical theory is to bring back the theory of proposi-١ons that are marked by quantity into connection with actual in-١uiry.

A beginning is made when it is pointed out that the connection ٥f quantitative determination with affirmation and negation is ٠ot external and mechanical but is intrinsic and organic. Neither ١quality" nor "quantity" can exist apart from comparison-contrast.

Given the latter, propositions are marked both by quality and quantity. For purposes of discussion we must deal with one aspect or the other separately, but the separation is made purely for the sake of discussion. It has no counterpart in the subject-matter which is the ground and result of comparison. The connection of the function of elimination with the work of comparison need not be gone over again. What is here significant is that all comparison is of the nature of *measurement*. Comparison obviously involves selection-rejection, for objects and events cannot be compared *in toto*. The positive import of this fact is that in order to be compared, subject-matters must be reduced to "*parts*"; that is, to constituents that are capable of being treated as of the same kind or homogeneous. To compare is to pair, and things that are paired are thereby made commensurate with respect to carrying out some operation in view.

The only difficulty standing in the way of recognition of the equipollence of comparison and measurement is the fact that the results of many measurements are stated qualitatively, not in numerical terms. There is at the very outset a fundamental ambiguity in the conception *whole-part*. In one sense, it is entirely qualitative. To be a whole is to be complete, finished; to be of seamless quality throughout. If *parts* are mentioned in connection with such a whole, nothing separable and removable is denoted. The most familiar instance of such "parts" are the organic members of a living body. If they are removed, they are no longer what they were *as* living "parts" of the living organism, while the latter is no longer a complete whole. It is not necessary, however, to go to so-called organic relations to find instances of qualitative whole-parts. In what is termed a *situation*, an immediate quality pervades everything that enters into that situation. If the situation experienced is that of being lost in a forest, the quality of being lost permeates and affects every detail that is observed and thought of. The "parts" are such only qualitatively.

The term "all" is still frequently employed in connection with qualitatively unified wholes: "It is not all of life to live," "All flesh is as grass which today is and tomorrow is cast into the fire," "It is all gone," "The fire is all out," "All the invited guests have now arrived" in the sense that the gathering is now complete—not in he sense of an enumeration. The quantitative meaning of whole-part is, on the other hand, either that of a collection or of an aggregation of homogeneous units such that the *whole* in question has its magnitude or amount determined by counting comprised units. There are cases of comparison-measurement which lie between the two limits set by the strictly qualitative and quantitative wholes. Common sense propositions marked by more-less, by the so-called *comparative* degree, as hotter-colder, taller-shorter, many-few, much-little, etc., are of this category. They represent measurements, but not measurements carried to the point of numerical determination. It is these intermediate cases which tend to obscure the connection of comparison with measurement.

From these introductory remarks, discussion proceeds to consideration of propositions marked by quantitative terms (1) to indicate more explicitly their connection with comparison, (2) to indicate their operational and intermediate force in determination of final judgment, and (3) to indicate the various logical forms they assume. The first topic is introduced by noting that the situation which evokes inquiry and which induces the formation of propositions as means to its final determination is indeterminate for the reason that, as it stands, it is both too wide and too narrow to provide the data that signify and that test proposed methods of resolution. The indeterminate situation is both deficient and redundant. Elimination of what is superfluous and obstructive and provision of what is lacking with respect to evidential capacity, are indispensable. The satisfaction of these requirements through the function of affirmation-negation has been dealt with. But redundancy and deficiency are also quantitative concepts in a quasi-qualitative form. What is termed in logic the *undistributed middle* is an instance of a too great width of subject-matter which incapacitates it to serve as ground; so also is the fallacy of affirming the antecedent because the consequent is affirmed.

The rule that from two particular propositions nothing can be inferred is on the other hand a warning that material in hand is too narrow to warrant a grounded inference. It is in effect a statement of the need for supplementation. In examples used in standard texts, the fallacies which result from too wide and too narrow subject-matter are readily detected, because they concern material already cooked or loaded. In actual inquiry a large part of the task is to determine just *what* subject-matter needs to be eliminated and provided and how. It required, for example, two centuries before the too great width of Newtonian conceptions of space and time was detected, and it took inquiry much more time than that to discover the narrowness of the ancient conception of atoms and corpuscles that unfitted it for scientific use. The only method for modifying subject-matter which is indeterminate because of overlappings and because of insufficiency is the weighting secured through measurement.

Measurement, as has been said, assumes at first a qualitative form. Propositions marked by such words as *much, little, few, many, a whole lot, scanty, abundant, small, great, high, low*, etc., etc., express measurement as far as they go. For there is nothing which is *much, little*, etc., absolutely or by itself. Moreover, these determinations not only involve comparison but they also involve the *means-consequence* relation. There is too much or too little for a specified end, not *per se;* "I should like to buy that article but I haven't enough money"; "Some people in this country have too much money for their own good and for that of the country." The *beginning* of the formation of a balance sheet in such cases takes the form of subcontrary propositions. "Some money is at hand and some is not." "Everybody needs *some* money, but no one needs *more* than a certain (not definitely specified) amount." Such propositions have rudimentary quantifications, but the quantities involved are still predominantly qualitative. Measurement or comparison becomes definite by means of counting and summing units. Then we have a whole-of-parts in specifically quantitative meanings of this term. Much becomes *how* much; many, *how* many.

It is not, however, to be inferred that in all cases qualitative measurement is so defective that, in order to be adequately determinate, it needs to pass into numerical measurement. For example, a painter at work upon a picture may decide that there is not enough red in a certain part of the picture to give the desired esthetic effect. He determines *how much* red should be added by "intuition" and trial, stopping when he gets the qualitatively unified whole he is after. He appraises or evaluates the amount eeded on the basis of a net qualitative outcome, not by weighing pigment upon a scale having numerical indices. Were the case one of regulated economical industrial production, the weighing of amounts would certainly take the form of numerical determination. In most moral as well as esthetic final judgments, qualitative measurement answers the end to be reached. Insistence upon numerical measurement, when it is not inherently required by the consequence to be effected, is a mark of respect for the ritual of scientific practice at the expense of its substance.

In the case of both qualitative and numerical measurement, something has to be taken away and something added. In this sense, measurement in qualitative terms, *more, less, enough,* etc., approximates the quantitative part-whole relation. The difference between the two cases concerns the method and criterion of measurement, not its presence or absence. The nature of the *end* to which measuring is relative determines both criterion and the method employed. It is as absurd to insist upon numerical measurement when the end to which the quantitative proposition is related as means to consequence is qualitative, as it is to be content with qualitative measurement (which is then guess-work) in the case of other ends-in-view.

In the case of the painter, the intended end is the picture as a qualitative whole. More of this color and less of that is therefore capable of measurement by direct qualitative observation. More red *here* affects not just the spatial part of the picture in which it is applied but the picture as a whole; other hues and shades are made qualitatively different by its application. In the case of a medical prescription, on the other hand, *too much* of an ingredient may change a medicine into a poison and too little may render it medically innocuous. Numerical measurement is then demanded by the end to be attained. It is ultimately the nature of the *problem* in hand which decides what sort of comparison-measurement is required in order to obtain a determinate solution. There are some persons who deplore the reduction by the scientist of all materials to numerical terms on the ground that it seems to them to destroy value which is qualitative. There are other persons who insist that every subject-matter must be reduced to numerical terms. Both are guilty of the same logical error. Both miss the logical meaning of measurement, which is determined by the instrumental reference of quantified propositions to an intended objective consequence. Both take propositions as ultimate and complete, when, in fact, they are intermediate and instrumental.

That one important difference between common sense and science is constituted by the tendency of the former to be satisfied with measurement that is dominantly qualitative is obvious. For *practical* ends it is enough to speak of a big crowd, or of the room growing warmer or colder, the day becoming brighter or duller, etc., whereas to satisfy the demands of technology, business, and science numerical comparisons are required. The box-office, for example, wants to know just *how* large or *how* small is the "crowd" in the theater; the careful householder wants a thermostat to keep variations of temperature within definite limits; the worker in the laboratory has to measure numerically just how much of each material and of each form of energy is involved in production of the phenomenon he is studying. All cases, however, whether of common sense, technology, business or science, explicitly reveal, when they are examined, the means-consequence relation, thereby disclosing the intermediate nature of propositions of quantity as instrumental in determinate resolution of an otherwise indeterminate situation.

It is often said that the conception of quantity rests upon complete indifference to quality. On this ground it is claimed, particularly by logicians of the idealistic school, that the concept of quantity so abstracts from the "real" world as to represent a low grade of "thought." This view is based upon failure to realize the operational character of propositions about quantity, whether extensive or intensive. But the notion of indifference to quality is also exposed to radical misconception. For the correct statement is that propositions about magnitude are based upon an *underlying* pervasive quality, and are indifferent only to differences *within* this basic quality; that is, they are indifferent to those qualities and only those qualities within the basic quality which are irrelevant as means to the consequences to be established. If, for example, a person is trying to frame a proposition about the number of sheep he owns or the area of the pasture in which they feed, he neglects qualitative differences that mark off individua sheep from one another and qualitative differences in different portions of the field in which they feed. But he has to *observe* the quality in virtue of which objects are sheep, or else he will count, say, dogs and stones. He has similarly to observe the quality in virtue of which grass-land is of the kind it is. The logical import of this commonplace remark is that it indicates in general (1) the control of propositions of magnitude by the quality of the *situation* to which the problem of inquiry is relevant, and in especial, (2) the importance and logical nature of *limits*.

The first point has already been sufficiently emphasized.[1] The import of the second point is at least suggested by the negative fact that the presence of limits in all counting and measurement that have existential reference (and it is only propositions having such reference that are under discussion) affords a complete answer to the objection brought by idealistic logicians against the validity of such propositions: viz., that they necessarily involve a *regressus ad infinitum*. Stated positively, all such measurement (including the case of enumeration) has its limits set, on one side, by the problematic subject-matter in hand and, on the other side, by the definite resolution which inquiry undertakes to effect. These considerations determine the meaning of the determinate *all* and of the indefinite *some*. They also fix the difference between two kinds of collective propositions in each of which the word *all* appears: "All the books on that shelf are novels"; "All the guests have arrived"; "The tide is all in or all out"—that is, is high or low; "The iron is *al*ready soft enough to work"; "The bowl is full of as much water as it will hold." In the last three cases qualitative wholeness predominates, though the propositions are certainly dependent upon comparison and involve measurement. In the first two cases, there has to be observation of each singular in order to warrant the propositions made though not in the later propositions.

Nevertheless, there is an aspect of totality involved and hence of inherent objective limitation in each instance. The propositions are not *collective* in the sense of mere *aggregates* of enumerated

---

[1] It is sufficient, however, to negate the idea that a scientific proposition is merely a numerical-index, to the exclusion of any symbol having reference to the qualitative.

units. The shelf is full of books of a kind; the quota of guests i complete. *All* in some other propositions has still a third meaning and this meaning, in spite of the word *all*, relegates the proposition in question to the category of the *particular* form. "All of th beans in this bag which have so far been examined are white." "N person who has as yet entered the hall is an acquaintance of mine." "Altogether the stamps in this collection number 874." In suc instances, the enumeration of singulars does not determine a limi nor yet even indicate that a limit has been reached; there is n intimation that anything having entirety is exhaustively deter mined. For logical purposes, the first proposition is equivalent t the proposition "some beans in this bag are white, and *perhaps a* are," the probability depending upon the number examined in it ratio to the total number in the bag—the latter setting a qualitativ limit. Confusion arises when application of the word *collectiv* to such propositions is used to assimilate them, in logical theory, t collections in which a limit is reached or set. That a regimen consists of so many companies and each company of so many men is a collective proposition in a very different sense from proposition about the number of books in a library or the numbe of stamps in a "collection," just as the proposition that "this room contains so many cubic feet" is different in form from the propo sition "this sand pile contains so many grains of sand." The dif ference will hereafter be noted by calling only the former *col lective*, while the latter will be called *aggregative*.

The distinction that has been drawn bears directly upon th status of propositions in which *some* is explicitly present. We may recur to the illustration in the last chapter regarding persons on shipwrecked vessel, placing the emphasis now not upon affirma tion, but upon *some* "are saved" and *some* "are lost." The affirma tion "Some are saved" and the negative proposition "Some are no saved" are clearly indeterminate; the indeterminacy is manifest i we suppose that a person having a friend on board is solicitou about his friend's fate. Until *singulars* are determined and the gathered together in a proposition that reaches an objective limi the propositions cited refer to indeterminate aggregates. When th needed operations are performed we have a collection that is othe than aggregative. "All the following persons (definitely specified

ere saved and all the following named persons were lost." There
now a double qualitative limitation. There is the qualitative limit
f completion set by the total number of persons on board and by
ie quality of being lost or saved.

So far it has been shown in what sense "all" is the mark of a
uantitative proposition, differentiating such a proposition, (1)
om mere aggregates (which in their indefiniteness do not differ
)gically from propositions in which "some" appears); and (2)
:om the "all" of non-existential propositions (such as "all triangles
ave the sum of their angles equal to right angles") which, when
alid, are *necessary* propositions; and (3) from "all" in such
:ropositions as "All men are mortal," where *all* applies to each and
very one of a specified kind although the singulars are not
apable of enumeration. That "all" has these four meanings is a
varning against using words as a clew to logical form apart from
1eir context in inquiry.

I now come to the topic of measurement by enumeration. A
1easured collection is identical with the kind of collection just
iid to have the property of totality in contrast with a *merely* num-
ered aggregate. In the latter, subject-matter sets no limits, and
onsequently fails to prescribe a whole. Measured collections in-
olve (1) limits from which to which; (2) something specified as a
nit for counting; and (3) progressive accumulation of these units
ntil the limit *ad quem* is reached. The word *accumulation* as here
sed involves something different from the *aggregation* found in the
1erely numerical set. When we measure the cubic capacity of a
quid container the successive addition of units is cumulative be-
ause it progressively tends toward a limit. Even if we were able
o count the number of drops of water that are contained, we
hould have at most simply an aggregation; as if it just happened
here are so many drops—no less, no more.

The cumulative aspect in genuine collective propositions signifies
hat such propositions depend upon some principle of arrangement
r order which is derived from the involved means-consequences
elation. Suppose, for example, that there are a number of ship-
vrecked persons in a boat. The number is definite; and there is a
lefinite amount of food and water on board, and the distance from
and is also approximately known. The length of stay on board,

the distance from a ship that might rescue them, weather-condi-
tions, etc., are, however, indeterminate, depending upon contingencies that cannot be accurately determined. Food and water
are measured not just for the sake of enumeration but as a means of
allotment, of distribution. Were there a store of food and water
at hand that would last beyond the remotest date that could be set
for rescue there would be no point in measuring. In the Garden
of Eden it may be presumed that waste and stringency were both
impossible. And in a similar situation no end is served by propositions as to quantity. But in cases of excess and deficiency, determined to be such by reference to an end to be reached as a
limit, apportionment is necessary if conduct is to be intelligent.
Allotting, meting out, involves a principle of distribution, and this
principle controls the subordinate operation of counting. There
must be *enough* if the end is to be attained and *just* enough in
the interest of economy and efficiency.

The illustrations have been taken from the field of common
sense, of situations of use-enjoyment. In this domain, control by
the qualitative is most clearly evident. Indeed, as was indicated
earlier, common sense propositions of quantity are likely to be
themselves semi-qualitative. Emergence from this state was
probably a slow historic process, being produced by exigencies of
technology, exchange and science. The word *few*, for example, is
derived from a root meaning *poor; many* from a root meaning
abundance, fullness. While physical science depends upon measurement by means of enumerated homogeneous units, it is equally
true of it that counting is for the sake of measuring and that
measuring is controlled by the problem set by some qualitative
situation, as one limit, and the objective consequence of a resolved
situation as the other limit. Mere counting and mere measuring are
childish (that is, immature) imitations of scientific procedure.

The homogeneous units that are required for numerically determinate measurement are fixed first in the case of bodies extended in space. An object that fills a span or stretch can be
readily marked off into sub-spans or sub-stretches of approximately
equal extent. Enumeration of these smaller intervals as units
measures the extent of the larger body. The span of the hand, the
pace in walking, were presumably the first such units evolved. A

ring can be doubled and redoubled and knots made at required points. By the use of a string knotted at approximately equal intervals notches can be cut in a stick, and the stick placed against some object. The length of the latter is measured by counting the number of notches in the superimposed rod as far as its extent and that of the object have the same ends or limits. The relatively qualitative *long* and *short* are refined into terms of *so* long or *so* short. Until the rise of geometry, however, the problem of complete reduction of the qualitative to quantitative relation was not solved—or even seen to be a problem. For the equality of intervals of the string and rod remained, after all, a matter of qualitative appraisal since it was conditioned by direct sensory-motor processes.

The measurement of discrete objects is the case that on its face comes closest to being *not* a case of measuring but of mere counting. One counts the number of chairs in the room; the shepherd counts the sheep in his flock; a man counts the number of bills or coins in his pocketbook. But if there is no end-in-view in the counting (in which case there *is* no measuring and weighing) such counting is like that of children who, after they have learned to count, count for the fun of it—and even then there is some limiting object, like seeing if they can count up to a million. The shepherd counts in order to see if his flock is "all there"; if it is increasing or decreasing, etc. A man keeps track of his funds because he has something to do with them, etc. More important is the fact that mere physical separation is not the ground of counting in the cases mentioned, provided "mere" means *apart* from consequence to be effected. So-called numerical identity is not something given *to* inquiry but is determined *in* inquiry. A book is the unit for one problem and purpose; a page for another; perhaps even a word or a letter is the unit as means to another end. A library, a whole set of books, may thus be the unit that has "numerical identity." The materials that appear in propositions as (numerical) identities are determined, like all other identifications, for and by operational use in solving some problem.

A derived but ultimately more important mode of measurement has for its object increase and decrease in *changes* which existentially are continuous—*intensive* as distinct from extensive quantity. That a body is getting colder or warmer, is moving a greater or less speed, (or in general is tending toward a contrar quality) are comparisons expressing vague qualitative measure ments that can be made on the basis of ordinary observations. Th problem of converting these qualitative estimates into definite, tha is to say, *numerical* form, involves overcoming difficulties that d not exist in the case of extended magnitudes. Continuous chang of quality does not lend itself to division into homogeneous unit since by description the quality is continuously becoming heter ogeneous to what it was. From the standpoint of the content o Greek science, with its disparaging view of change, all that wa necessary was to *classify* the diverse *kinds* of qualitative change tha occurred; as from warm to cold, wet to dry, soft to hard, up t down, and the reverse. In classic science it thus sufficed to say tha all qualities of sense-perception change between opposite limits cold and only cold is that which becomes warm and so on. Ther was no need for measurement and hence none for units by which t measure.

The concept of *series* is not found in Greek science or logic. I did not appear until change was found capable of reduction, fo the purpose of instituting controlled comparisons, to motion, an was thereby found capable of measurement in terms of homogeno ous units of space and time. Then the theory of celestial mechanic became for a time the model for all scientific descriptions and ex planations. The problem set to inquiry was that of translating con tinuous change of quality with which qualitative measurements ca deal only in terms of intensive degree (more-less, least-most) int numbered extent, direction, velocity and acceleration of motio correlated with numbered units of duration.

The problem was met by devices which permitted continuou qualitative change to be placed in functional correspondence wit continuous extended stretches marked off into discrete homo geneous units that can be counted. By the use of, say, a mercur thermometer, changes in the intensity of heat, which are no directly comparable with one another, are rendered comparabl with fixed units of extension—fixed, that is, as far as other condi tions can be kept constant. A numerical degree of temperature i a unit or sum of units of heat or cold indirectly. In itself it is th interval between two lines on a scale in which there is a column marked off on a glass tube containing, say, mercury. Change in temperature is measured by counting the number of such intervals and their fractional parts that are traversed by the enclosed mercury during a given time—which in turn is measured by a similar device in which the movement of an index or hand over a number of equally extended intervals on a dial or face yields enumerable units. The device is practicable because of the "law" of expansion and contraction of mercury, air or alcohol, with changes of temperature, conditions of pressure being maintained as constant as possible. The difference between *immediate* qualities of heat and cold is thus entirely eliminated, "absolute" or zero temperature being the point at which molecules cease to change position or move. The relation, or *ratio*, of qualitative changes *to one another* is thus determined through a *proportion* of which the other terms are the ratio which changes of position bear to one another.[2]

All of three types of comparison-measurement that have been discussed involve the operation of *matching*. In the first case, a certain extent of a rod is matched against an extent of a piece of cloth, side of a room, linear dimension of land, etc., etc. Measurement in the second case is made possible because objects can be matched against other objects taken as symbols—such sounds and marks, for example, as the numerals and figures *one, two, three, four*, etc. A word still in use, namely *digits*, suggests that the objects counted were first matched against toes and fingers. Although the latter are themselves existential, they are so when used in counting in the representative sense of sounds, and marks on paper, in linguistic communication. Toes and fingers *as thus used* are as symbolic as are the marks: 1, 2, 3, 4, etc. In the third case, changes in a continuum of change are matched against extended intervals, like those upon a glass tube or clock-face. In the first and third cases alike there is, in addition, a matching against *symbols,* such as are characteristic of the second case. The use of linguistic symbols, of number-*names,* is the invention which permitted quan-

<hr>

[2] The numerical determination of intelligence quotients will, for example, become scientifically significant in the degree with which they can be definitely correlated with *other* specified changes. By themselves they simply set a problem.

tity and number to become objects of independent or mathematical investigation. For the relations of symbols to one another in a meaning-symbol system can be examined on their own account, independent of the relations existential objects and changes sustain to one another.[3]

Matching or correspondence in some form is thus the basic operation in all propositions in which determination of quantity, having existential reference, appears. This fact explains the sense in which number and magnitude are *relational*. The relation involved is *complex*. For example, suppose a stick is measured off into twelve equal intervals. It can then be affirmed that the rod is twelve such intervals long and that each interval is one-twelfth as long as the entire stick. But if the matter ended here, there would be no measurement. The propositions are not only circular but trivial. The rod and its subdivisions become a *measure* only when applied to *other* objects so that the rod and its intervals are matched against differences of interval in these other things. Until a foot-rule is used to measure other things it is not a *rule*, but merely a stick that happens to be notched or lined in a certain rather curious fashion. Even when one foot-rule or yard-stick is compared with another, there is, as such, no measurement, but only a check upon the accuracy of the measuring capacity of one or other or both.

The standard meter is a bar of platinum kept under as constant conditions of temperature and pressure as possible in the city of Paris. But if that were the whole of the story, the word *meter* would not have the connection with measuring it actually has. By itself the bar is just a particular bar and nothing else; it is neither a standard of measurement nor is itself measured. It is a measure of length because (1) all other rods of a meter's length in use anywhere in the world may be checked by being matched against it, and (2) because, and *only* because, these other rods are themselves used in matching still *other things*. It is just as true that the length of the bar of platinum (or any other measuring rod) is determined by its application in measuring cloth, walls, sides of fields, etc., as that the length of the latter is determined by comparison with it.

[3] See, *ante*, pp. 54, 110. Discussion of the relations existing among symbols as such takes us out of the field of number and magnitude that have direct existential reference into the domain of mathematics. Hence it is no part of the subject-matter here considered. It is taken up in Chap. **XX**.

In short, when we apply the word *measure* to pounds, gallons, yards, etc., "measure" is an elliptic expression for *means of measuring*. Apart from operational use, the fact that pounds are relative to one another and to ounces and tons, has no measuring import. Moreover, *foot* and *yard* are not measures just because they can be matched against such qualitative objects as pieces of cloth (themselves qualitatively unlike), rolls of paper, boards, roads, fields, but are measures because this latter matching enables these other unlike qualitative things to be indirectly compared with respect to one another—just as, for example, matching dollar bills against a bushel of wheat would be of trivial importance if the matching of the bills against books, railway travel, groceries and houses did not enable *indirect* measurements or calculations to be undertaken about the values in exchange of these other things in relation to one another. The negation of quality or indifference to it which is sometimes ascribed to quantity and number (and a ground made for their disparagement) is not final but, on the contrary, *positive* means for controlled construction of new objects and institution of new qualities. Just as a piece of paper, enacted by law into legal tender, is a means for comparing values in exchange of things qualitatively unlike, thus promoting and controlling new transactions with qualitative objects—so *science* renders things qualitatively unlike (as sounds and colors, pressures, light and electricity) comparable with one another, in such ways that controlled *inter*changes are capable of being brought about.[4]

What has been said has a definite bearing upon so-called standards of value or more properly of valuation. It contradicts the notion that there are some entities that are standards "absolutely," that is, in themselves.[5] In the case of the platinum bar mentioned above no one would suppose that it is a standard measure of length because of some inherent property of absolute length. But in discussion of art, morals, economics and law it is a fairly usual assumption that critical evaluative judgments are impossible unless there is a standard of values which is such because of its own in-

---

[4] The ontological hypostization of a method, an instrumentality, of inquiry used to effect objective consequences, into something ontological, is the source of the mechanistic metaphysics of "reality."

[5] This notion is a twin of the notion of ends-in-themselves already criticised; see pp. 167–8.

herent constitution and properties. In economics it has been a fairly common assumption that gold is a standard measure of the value of other things because of its own "intrinsic" value. This idea appears almost always when paper money is denied the capacity to serve as a standard. Instead of a comparison of the capacity of gold and paper money to serve as standards on the ground of actual consequences operationally produced by their respective applications in determining exchange, an alleged absolute or "intrinsic" value in the case of gold is appealed to.

In morals, it is a common assumption that the fairness of particular actions cannot be determined unless there is some absolute standard with which they may be compared. *The* true and *the* beautiful are similarly hypostatized. But in fact, we institute standards of justice, truth, esthetic quality, etc., in order that different objects and events may be so intelligently compared *with one another* as to give direction to activities dealing with concrete objects and affairs:—exactly as we set up a platinum bar as a standard measurer of lengths. The standard is just as much subject to modification and revision in one case as in the other on the basis of the consequences of its operational application. Belief in magic is not confined to primitive peoples. The superiority of one conception of justice to another is of the same *order* as the superiority of the metric system to the more or less haphazard set of weights and measures it has replaced in scientific practice, although not of the same quality.

Yard and mile, ounce and pound, gill and gallon, are conceptual meanings of the same general type as common sense conceptions, which, as we have seen, are related to one another on socio-historic grounds. They are means of facilitating and executing all kinds of social transactions with reference to use and enjoyment. The metric system of measurements is rather of the type of the system of symbol-meanings which is framed on the basis of inter-relation and free translatability. The propositions that result from their application are still instrumental, although to a different end; in the latter case, that of facilitation of inquiry. Conceptions and principles that serve to measure or evaluate moral conduct and relations are logically of the same kind, and should be so treated in social practice.

It should be pointed out, by way at least of anticipation, that, according to the principle expounded, space and time are in science not *what* we measure but are themselves results of measurements of objects and events, in the interest of objective determination of problematic situations. This fact has, in the context of present discussion, definite bearing on the relation of discrete and continuous magnitude, as these are found in propositions having existential reference. A unit of measurement is, when it is taken as a unit of measurement, discrete. But it is *internally* continuous whether it be a millimetre or a kilometer. What is taken as discrete in one functional use is used as continuous in resolution of another problem and conversely. The same principle applies in propositions of temporal dates (discrete) and temporal durations (continuities). Even if there are, existentially, indivisible discrete pulses of change such that each change comes as a unitary whole, nevertheless, (1) such pulses must have *direction* if they can be used in determination of change as continuous, and (2) they are units of temporal measurement only when they are taken and used as means of comparison and measurement. Direction is necessary because it is required to effect that overlapping which is characteristic of all gross and observed change, since the latter could not arise by laying discrete pulses of change end to end.

These unitary pulses if they exist are as qualitative as is the bar of platinum referred to. They become units of magnitude only as they are functionally employed to connect into a unified scheme changes that by themselves are disparate and heterogeneous. Schematization of time as a straight line indefinitely extended in one direction may be useful for some purposes. But duration as it enters into an existential (non-mathematical) proposition has the *thickness* which is constituted by overlapping of sequential changes and by the fact that determination of any specific change requires reference to changes occurring contemporaneously. To say, for example, that a certain reign lasted from 1800 to 1830 would have no meaning if the interval in question had no other content than this reign.

It may be advisable to refer explicitly to the existential operations involved in comparison-measurements. In the matching characteristic of common sense it takes the obvious form of scoring and tallying, along with the activity of juxtaposing or superimposing. When the matching takes place by means of number-names, the names, even though they are but symbols, have to be pronounced or marked down, if counting is to be effected. Counting is as existential an operation as is whistling or singing. Calculations in scientific work may go on in the head as well as they may be written down on paper. But symbols as symbols do not have physical efficacy. They have to be existentially manipulated if calculation occurs. The habit of ruling out the existential acts of counting and calculation from the domain with which logic is concerned is simply another instance of the systematic neglect of operations, so characteristic of formalistic logic, a neglect which is due to the doctrine that propositions are merely enunciative or declarative of antecedent existence or subsistence.

Finally, qualitative control of existential propositions of number and magnitude is relevant to the difference between *unity* and a *unit*. Only that is unified or a unity which is a qualitative whole. In the language employed earlier in this chapter, it has members but is not an aggregate nor a collection of parts. When a qualitative whole is internally conflicting the pervasive whole affects the quality of the conflict, just as a civil war is what it is because it is disruption of and within a unity of a nation or people. The conflict can only be resolved and a new qualitative unified situation be produced by going outside the situation that is antecedently in existence so as to eliminate some of its factors and to introduce other new factors. Hence the necessity of comparison-contrast, which as we have seen is a name for the operations by which this elimination and introduction are effected. Control of the operations performed is exercised by the intent of production of a new unified situation. Propositions are the means by which the intent is carried out. The means are economical and effective (as in the reaching of any objective consequence) in the degree in which comparison takes the form of measuring and weighing. Without results secured by these operations, means employed either fail to bring about the intended end or they produce more than is intended, thereby creating a situation that perhaps is more troublesome and conflicting than the original one which the means used were intended to unify. Qualitative wholes *as such* are incommensurable, just because they are uniquely qualitative. But they are the limits or "ends" from which and to which propositions are means. As such limits they provide the criteria by which the relevancy and force of propositions of measurement, qualitative and quantitative, are measured.

CHAPTER XII

JUDGMENT AS SPATIAL-TEMPORAL
DETERMINATION: NARRATION-DESCRIPTION

JUDGMENT IS transformation of an antecedent existentially indeterminate or unsettled situation into a determinate one. As such, judgment is always individual in a sense in which individual is distinguished from both particular and singular, in that it refers to a total qualitative situation. In this sense there are no different kinds of judgment, but distinguishable phases or emphases of judgment, according to the aspect of its subject-matter that is emphasized.[1] In the opening statement existential transformation is the point of emphasis. Existential subject-matter as transformed has a temporal phase. Linguistically, this phase is expressed in narration. But all changes occur through interactions of conditions. What exists co-exists, and no change can either occur or be determined in inquiry in isolation from the connection of an existence with co-existing conditions. Hence the existential subject-matter of judgment has a spatial phase. Linguistically, this is expressed in description. For purposes of analysis and exposition the two phases must be distinguished. But there is no separation in the subject-matter which is analyzed. Whatever exists in and for judgment is temporal-spatial. In a given proposition, either the temporal or the spatial aspect may be uppermost. But every narration has a background which, if it were made explicit instead of being taken for granted, would be described; correspondingly, what is described exists within some temporal process to which "narration" applies.

---

[1] The two previous chapters have indicated, for example, that "quantity" and "quality" in judgment must be distinguished in discourse but that they cannot be separated.

220

I. I begin with consideration of that phase of the development of judgment in which temporal considerations are dominant. Their simplest form is found in propositions about changing present existential subject-matter linguistically expressed through active verbs in the present tense. Examples are such observations as "The Sun is rising; it is growing brighter; the room is getting cold; he is coming closer; the clock is striking; the fire is dying down, etc." In such a proposition as, "He was here a few minutes ago but has now gone," the subject-matter is of the same kind, but the words "was"—"ago" and "has gone" make explicit a reference to the past that is involved in the first set of sentences but that is there a matter of understood context. For it is indispensable to note that a limiting reference to both past and future is present in every existential proposition. There is reference to a limit *ab quo* and *ad quem*. Without this limitation, a change is not characterized or qualified. No *mere* flux can be noted, appraised or estimated. A change is characterized in terms of direction—*from* something *to* something. "The sun is rising"—that is, it was below the horizon, but is now moving further and further above the horizon. Such propositions as "It is sweet or red" state (as has already been noted) either that something is becoming or has become a changed quality, or else that it has the capacity to change—to redden or sweeten—something else.

The point just made has a fundamental importance for the theory of the temporal and historic phase of judgment which may not be apparent at first sight. For it signifies that the unitary subject-matter of every temporal proposition is a round, cycle, period, circuit, or *hora*. To judge is to render determinate; to determine is to order and organize, to relate in definite fashion. Temporal order is instituted through rhythms which involve periodicities, intervals, and limits; all of which are inter-involved. Absolute origins and absolute closes and termini are mythical. Each beginning and each ending is a delimitation of a cycle or round of qualitative change. A date, a moment or point of time, has no meaning except as such a delimitation.

That which exists is, as existent, indifferent to delimitation in respect to beginnings and endings. There are no absolute originations or initiations or absolute finalities and terminations in nature.

The "from which" and "to which" that determine the subject-matter of any particular narration-description are strictly relative to the objective intent set to inquiry by the problematic quality of a given situation. Such an event as, say, daybreak is the initial limit of subject-matter in one problem; the terminal limit in another, and an intermediate event in still a third problem—as, for example, in a proposition about the diurnal rotation of the earth. Generalized measures of temporal sequences, (such as are designated by the words second, minute, hour, day, year, century, period, epoch) stand for kinds of cycles which, like all measures, are procedural means of furthering and directing the inclusions-exclusions (affirmations-negations) by which determinate subject-matter of propositions is instituted.[2]

Since every change when it is subjected to inquiry is a round or cycle of events whose beginning and ending are determined by the indeterminate situation undergoing resolution (and hence are not absolute), every given change may be narrated in terms of an indefinite variety of included minor events as incidents, episodes or occurrences. To a layman a flash of lightning comes close to being an isolated instantaneous occurrence. A scientific account of it is a narration of a prolonged history of which the flash is one incident; with the growth of scientific knowledge the tale becomes longer. On the other hand, a mountain, which to the layman is a standing symbol of permanence, is to the geologist the scene of a drama of birth, growth, decay and ultimate death. Unless the difference between existential change as barely existential and as subject-matter of judgment is borne in mind, the nature of *event* becomes an inexplicable mystery. *Event* is a term of judgment, not of existence apart from judgment. The origin and development of the Appalachian Mountain Range is an event, and so is the loosening and rolling of a particular pebble on a particular ledge on a particular foot-hill. There may be a situation in which the latter sort of episode is much more important in judgment than is the history of long duration: as, for example, when a rolling pebble is

---

[2] The above considerations have definite bearing upon the probability-function of all existential propositions. For selection of events as initial and terminal with respect to solution of a given problem involves a risk which can never be completely eliminated. It also has a definite bearing (taken up in Chap. XXIII) upon the category of causation.

the "cause" of a sprained ankle. In the story of the cyclical weathering of the mountain, the roll of the pebble would hardly be *an* event at all; it would be but a specimen, unnoted in itself, of a *kind* of thing that is significant only *en masse*. An event is, strictly, that which comes out; that which issues forth; the net outstanding consequence, the eventuation. It involves a teleological concept; it is capable of description-narration only in terms of a delimiting beginning, an interval and a termination.

Propositions in which temporal connections enter explicitly into the formation of judgment may be conveniently considered under three heads: (1) Those about one's personal past, (2) those about special events not coming directly within one's own experience, and (3) consecutive historical narrations.

1. *Judgments of Recollection*. These are often disposed of by attributing them directly to a faculty of memory. This procedure consists in giving a name to the fact that judgments about one's past and history are possible and actual, and then treating the fact as if it were a causal force. To affirm that I did a given thing yesterday, or that I was ill last month, is to form an appraisal of a temporal sequence. It differs from any other historical reconstruction only in the fact that its subject-matter falls within my own biography. If the affirmation is grounded, it is mediated and hence depends upon evidential data instituted by observations. Like every mediated outcome, it is subject to error even though its subject-matter is something done or suffered five minutes ago. While in explicit *linguistic* statement the content of the proposition is usually a particular deed or something undergone at a particular time in the past, the actual *logical* object is a *course of events*, one limit of which is the present while the other is what happened at the specified past time.

The instance in question thus exemplifies the principle that a cycle or period is the object of every temporal proposition. Take the proposition "I went to Yonkers yesterday," or any other sentence about a particular act. On its face, it refers to an isolated occurrence. But "I" in this sentence has no meaning except as the *I* of today and of yesterday and of the days which preceded. Moreover, the particular act mentioned has background and foreground. If it were not involved in a continuing course of existence, out of which it grows and to which it contributes, that is, if it were completely isolated and self-enclosed, neither assigned date nor "I" would have the slightest meaning.

Some present state of affairs is always the *occasion* of the reconstruction of the past event. But as a mere occasion, it has no logical standing. By some organic mechanism (of the general nature of the physical modification called habit) it calls out or "suggests" something not present. This suggested something as such also lacks logical status. It may be a whimsy or castle in the air, and, in any case, if what is suggested is immediately accepted, without inquiry and test, as representative of something in my past history, there may be a proposition in the outer form of linguistic expression but not in its logical status. For the affirmation is without ground—a fact that is celebrated as a virtue by those who impute it to an intuition of the "faculty" of memory, but who in reality take the product of the working of a psycho-physiological mechanism as a case of knowledge. In order to figure in a proposition having logical character, the idea of a past event suggested by the associative mechanism has to be critically scrutinized. Did I really do thus and so? Or did I merely think of doing it? Or was it just something that I heard and that left a vivid impression on me? Or perhaps it is something that I now wish I had done?

Even those who hold that at least some "memory ideas" or "images" bring with them as part of themselves a tag to the effect that something corresponding to them actually happened in one's past experience, do not, nevertheless, go so far as to maintain that the idea or image brings the exact date of its occurrence with it. Since (1) the temporal place (date) of an occurrence in a sequential event is integrally involved in any recollection of one's past, and since (2) such temporal place, or date, is not an *inherent* part of what is suggested (since, that is, the suggested past event does not carry its date stamped upon it), the matter of the recollection is evidentially mediated; it is a matter of judgment. Its validity is as much dependent upon the material used as evidential data as is that of an inference about some event wholly outside of one's own personal past.

Dating, moreover, is nothing absolute. It depends upon conecting a particular occurrence with other events coming before and after in such a way that taken together they constitute a temporal series or history. If I say that "I was at home at five o'clock yesterday," I am in fact constructing as an object of grounded belief a sequential course of events. "Yesterday" has no significance save in connection with today, the day-before-yesterday and a series of tomorrows. "Five o'clock" has no significance save in connection with four and six o'clock, and so on. The problem presented by the enduring situation undergoing determination gives the date fixed upon its crucial significance. Were the facts as isolated and independent in existence as they appear to be in a sentence when the latter is separated from context, the latter would have no more meaning than if uttered by a parrot, and were the sentence uttered by a phonograph, its meaning would be fixed by the context, say of the story or dramatic reproduction in which it appears. Here, as in so many cases, the context is linguistically suppressed just because it is taken for granted.

If a memory-affirmation is questioned either by another or by one's self it is supported by making explicit the temporal contextual sequence. "At half past four I was leaving my office and it takes me just about half an hour to get home; I came straight back and remember looking at the clock as I came in and then I picked up the evening paper and was reading when so and so came in," and so on. Satisfactory as such a consecutive reconstruction may be for most *practical* purposes, it does not *logically* suffice. For these other incidents are also matters of recollection and themselves demand the same kind of grounded substantiation as the original judgment of recollection. It is at this point that the reference to *objective* evidential confirmation comes into play. The consistency of an account of an event alleged to have occurred with accounts of other specified events alleged to have occurred before and after is good as far as it goes, but is subject to the limitations that affect all cases of merely internal consistency. Paranoiac reconstructions of the past often have marvellous internal consistency. In crucial instances, such as sometimes present themselves, for example, in law courts, external evidence of documents, direct observations of other persons, etc., is imperatively demanded. Whenever there is reason to suspect collusion or common interest in establishing belief in a fictitious state of affairs, an even more external kind of evidence, more external in being independent of any personal element, will alone logically suffice— although, of course, in many cases we have to *act* upon evidence that falls far short of complete logical conclusiveness.

In other words, such judgments, like those about all existential matters, have probability, not "certainty." Hence the actions that are performed in consequence of accepting them are not logically *ex post facto* or mere practical appendages to a completed judgment. They are operations that provide additional evidence, which confirms, weakens, or in some way modifies, the provisionally accepted appraisal. Suppose I am in doubt whether I mailed a certain letter after writing it. I assume temporarily that I did mail it, and perform the operation of waiting for the reply which it called for. The consequence serves to determine the correctness of my assumption: I receive a reply or do not receive it. Or, I fear strongly that I did not mail the letter. I perform the operation of looking through all the places where I might probably have laid it. Not finding it I still am unwilling to accept as conclusive the idea that I mailed it. I write another letter inquiring to make sure whether it was mailed or not. What these illustrations bring out is that the consecutive qualitatively continuous history which is constructed is not confined to the past. Events occurring in the future stand in such relations of continuity to those that have occurred and those now occurring that they serve as evidential matter for testing provisional appraisals of recollection about what we have done and what has happened to us in the past.

A marked breach of continuity in the sequence of future or ensuing events with what we suppose happened in the past is enough, as a rule, to make us believe our belief invalid if not imaginary. On the other hand, the recurrent frequency with which subsequent events bear out reliance upon reconstructive temporal judgments gives us pragmatic confidence in their general dependability. Consequences of the method in the continuity of inquiry are the ground upon which data are relied upon when they themselves are *materially* inadequate. This confidence causes us as a matter of routine to act upon their accuracy without submitting them to special logical tests. The very cases which superficially viewed give rise to the belief that recollections of one's past are not mediated judgments, but are cases of "immediate or intuitive knowledge," are just the ones which, when they are closely examined, show *that they are instances of construction of extensive durational sequences of events*. Upon the whole, the trustworthiness of our reconstructions of personal past experience is so repeatedly confirmed by the course of ensuing events that we come to depend upon them without applying *special* tests. Only in cases of crucial doubt do we resort to the latter.

It may perhaps seem that much time has been spent in arguing a point that is quite obvious on its face, or that if not obvious, is in any case not a matter of much importance. Such is not the case. For the point that every temporal proposition is a *narrative* proposition means that the proposition is about a *course* of sequential events, not about an isolated event at an absolute point in time. This thesis is of such fundamental importance that it is necessary to establish it beyond reasonable doubt. The simplest instance is that of recollection. Since, as a result of borrowing from uncriticized psychological doctrine, the idea has become current that recollection is a case of "immediate" re-instatement of the past, it possesses crucial logical significance.

The net conclusion of the foregoing discussion will, accordingly, be formally set forth. A continuous course or round of events, a period marked by limits and interval, is the subject-matter undergoing determinate settlement in propositions of recollections of a personal past. In such determinations provisional judgments (of the nature of appraisals or estimates) have to be made about both present objects or events and past occurrences. Such judgments are not final and complete. They are the *means* by which conclusive and complete judgment about an entire course of sequential events, a history, extending from the past through the present into the future, is groundedly instituted. It is for the sake of resolving a total qualitative situation that the provisional judgments about past and present events—in the temporal sense of past and present—are made. When it is said that judgments of recollection are not complete in themselves but are instrumental means of requalifying a *present* situation, otherwise problematic, the word "present" does not mean a temporal event that may be contrasted with some other event as past. The situation that I am determining when I attempt to decide whether or not I mailed a certain letter is a "present" situation. But the present situation is not located in and confined to an event here and now occurring. It is an extensive duration, covering past, present and future events. The provisional judgments that I form about what is *temporally* present (as for example in going through my pockets now) are just as much means with respect to this total present *situation* as are the propositions formed about past events as past and as are estimates about ensuing events.[3]

2. *Judgments of Events Outside of Personal Recollections.* We constantly make judgments which reconstruct past scenes that are so completely outside of personal experience that there is no possibility of applying the doctrine of immediate or self-evident knowledge. A man is found dead under circumstances which *prima facie* provide no evidence as to the time and manner of his death. There are, however, conditions capable of observation. Analytic examination, employing available instruments and techniques, are brought into play. Present data are thus obtained as the basis of inference as to what took place in the past. Medical examination supplies data from which inference fixes approximately the time of the death and something concerning its immediate conditions; it happened, say, about eight hours before from a bullet fired from a revolver of a certain calibre, etc. The bare data do not, of themselves, provide these conclusions. The inferential conclusions drawn are an *interpretation* of directly observed facts mediated by conceptions drawn from prior experience; these conceptions being logically adequate in the degree that past experience has been critically analyzed. Moreover, the propositions that formulate the inferred conclusions are clearly intermediary, not final.

The data are such, we will say, as to preclude the possibility or idea of suicide. They suggest murder, but do not signify it. The man may have been shot accidentally or in self-defense during a struggle. Other investigations look for evidences of robbery; for

---

[3] The ambiguity of the term "present"—like that of "given"—has already been noted. See, *ante,* pp. 124–5.

men who had a motive for the act; for witnesses who may have heard a shot fired or seen a struggle, etc. When the dead body is identified, there is investigation of the person's movements when alive; whether he carried money; his enemies, previous threats against him, etc. Since it is not here a matter of writing a detective story, I only need to point out that evidential data consist (1) of facts that are *now* observable, stated in propositions that refer to temporally contemporaneous facts, and (2) of data derived from recollections of earlier observations. Given these propositions, the problem is to weave them into a grounded conclusion that the man in question met his death at the hands of another person at a certain time and under such circumstances as to bring the act under the legal conception of murder of the first degree. (For no matter how detailed are the material data they constitute a problem of this general logical type.) Solution of such a problem is impossible save upon the postulate that the subject-matter under inquiry is that of a temporal course of sequential events and upon the condition that the material in question satisfies this postulate. There are propositions on the one hand about things *now* observable; as, for example, there is no legal ground for accusing any one unless there is a *corpus delicti*. On the other hand, there are propositions about events that happened in the past. But neither set of propositions has probative force *unless temporal continuity can be reasonably established between their respective subject-matters*. It is the course of events constituting this history that is the object of logical determination. The propositions that are accumulated about past facts and facts now observable are but means to the formation of this historic narrative judgment. In themselves they are so many separate items. They are not complete and final. Moreover, the history under determination extends into the future. Something to ensue hangs upon the detection and conviction of a given person as the murderer: execution or imprisonment.

Take the case of a man who after a certain lapse of time presents himself as the legal claimant to an estate of a dead man, the estate having in the meantime been awarded to another person as the heir. The case, we will assume, is such that *if* the claimant is the man he claims he is, there is no doubt on the legal side that he is the one who is entitled to the estate. The problem is one, in short, of identification. A proposition to the effect that the claimant is or is not so-and-so, say Tichborne, is thus required to determine the matter in dispute, while this proposition does not represent the object of final determination. It is intermediate and instrumental to a judgment about the conclusive disposition of the estate. The proposition of identification operates as an instrumentality, moreover, only by instituting historic continuity or absence of such continuity between the given individual about whose past certain propositions are offered, and the individual about whom propositions are formed on the basis of contemporary observations. Here, as in our previous case, propositions have to be formed about contemporary facts and past events. But neither set of propositions proves anything nor do both of them together until they are filled out by propositions which bring their contents into temporal continuity with one another. Furthermore, a future consequence, the final disposition of the estate, is involved. This outcome also is historical, being the completion of a course of events. Taken in isolation, it is no more the object of determination than is the subject-matter constituted by past events or is that constituted by contemporary observable data:—such as, physical constitution, appearance, birthmarks, etc.

What is true in the two instances just mentioned is true of all judgments of events in their temporal qualifications. There is no such thing as *judgment* about a past event, one now taking place, or one to take place in the future in its isolation. The notion that there are such judgments arises from taking propositions that are indispensable material means to a completely determined situation as if they were complete in themselves.

3. *Judgments Recognized to be Historical.* The distinctively logical importance of the conclusions so far reached appears even more clearly when we come to the theme of historical judgments in the ordinary sense of history. In the latter case, there is no such need to dwell upon the issue of temporal continuity of subject-matter as there was in the topics that have been discussed. For history is admittedly history. The logical problem involved now takes a more restricted form: Given temporal continuity, what is the relation of propositions about an extensive past durational

sequence to propositions about the present and future? Can the historical continuum involved in admittedly historical propositions of the past be located in the past or does it reach out and include the present and future? There are of course, many technical methodological problems that have to be met by the historian. But the central logical problem involved in the existence of grounded judgment of historical subject-matter is, I take it, that which has just been stated. What conditions must be satisfied in order that there may be grounded propositions regarding a sequential course of past events? The question is not even whether judgments about remote events can be made with *complete* warrant much less is it whether "History can be a science." It is: Upon what grounds are some judgments about a course of past events more entitled to credence than are certain other ones?

That evidential data for all historical propositions must exist at the time the propositions are made and be contemporaneously observable is an evident fact. The data are such things as records and documents; legends and stories orally transmitted; graves and inscriptions; urns, coins, medals, seals; implements and ornaments; charters, diplomas, manuscripts; ruins, buildings and works of art; existing physiographical formations, and so on indefinitely. Where the past has left no trace or vestige of any sort that endures into the present its history is irrecoverable. Propositions about the things which can be contemporaneously observed are the ultimate data from which to infer the happenings of the past. This statement, in spite of its obviousness, needs to be made. Although it is taken for granted as a matter of course by those who work with source material, readers of the works which historians compose on the basis of available source-material are likely to suffer from an illusion of perspective. Readers have before them the ready-made products of inferential inquiry. If the historical writer has dramatic imagination, the past seems to be directly present to the reader. The scenes described and episodes narrated appear to be directly given instead of being inferred constructions. A reader takes conclusions as they are presented by the historian to be directly given almost as much as he does in reading a well constructed novel.

Logical theory is concerned with the relation existing between evidential data as grounds and inferences drawn as conclusions, and with the methods by which the latter may be grounded. With respect to logical theory, there is no existential proposition which does not operate either (1) as material for locating and delimiting a problem; or (2) as serving to point to an inference that may be drawn with some degree of probability; or (3) as aiding to weigh the evidential value of some data; or (4) as supporting and testing some conclusion hypothetically made. At every point, exactly as in conducting any inquiry into contemporary physical conditions, there has to be a search for relevant data; criteria for selection and rejection have to be formed as conceptual principles for estimating the weight and force of proposed data, and operations of ordering and arranging data which depend upon systematized conceptions have to be employed. It is because of these facts that the writing of history is an instance of judgment as a resolution through inquiry of a problematic situation.

The first task in historical inquiry, as in any inquiry, is that of controlled observations, both extensive and intensive—the collection of data and their confirmation as authentic. Modern historiography is notable for the pains taken in these matters and in development of special techniques for securing and checking data as to their authenticity and relative weight. Such disciplines as epigraphy, paleography, numismatics, linguistics, bibliography, have reached an extraordinary development as auxiliary techniques for accomplishing the historiographic function. The results of the auxiliary operations are stated in existential propositions about facts established under conditions of maximum possible control. These propositions are as indispensable as are those resulting from controlled observation in physical inquiry. But they are not final historical propositions in themselves. Indeed, strictly speaking they are not in their isolation historical propositions at all. They are propositions about what now exists; they are historical in their *function* since they serve as material data for inferential constructions. Like all data they are selected and weighed with reference to their capacity to fulfill the demands that are imposed by the evidential function.

In consequence, they are relative to a problem. Apart from connection with some problem, they are like materials of brick, stone and wood that a man might gather together who is intending to build a house but before he has made a plan for building it. He ranges and collects in the hope that some of the materials, he does not yet know just what, will come in usefully later after he has made his plan. Again, because of connection with a problem, actual or potential, propositions about observed facts correspond strictly with conceptual subject-matter by means of which they are ordered and interpreted. Ideas, meanings, as hypotheses, are as necessary to the construction of historical determinations as they are in any physical inquiry that leads to a definite conclusion. The formation of historical judgments lags behind that of physical judgments not only because of greater complexity and scantiness of the data, but also because to a large extent historians have not developed the habit of stating to themselves and to the public the systematic conceptual structures which they employ in organizing their data to anything like the extent in which physical inquirers expose their conceptual framework. Too often the conceptual framework is left as an implicit presupposition.

The slightest reflection shows that the conceptual material employed in writing history is that of the period in which a history is written. There is no material available for leading principles and hypotheses save that of the historic present. As culture changes, the conceptions that are dominant in a culture change. Of necessity new standpoints for viewing, appraising and ordering data arise. History is then rewritten. Material that had formerly been passed by, offers itself as data because the new conceptions propose new problems for solution, requiring new factual material for statement and test. At a given time, certain conceptions are so uppermost in the culture of a particular period that their application in constructing the events of the past seems to be justified by "facts" found in a ready-made past. This view puts the cart before the horse. Justification if it is had proceeds from the verification which the conceptions employed receive in the present; just as, for example, the warrant for the conceptual structures that are employed to reconstruct what went on in geological ages before the appearance of man or indeed of life on the earth, is found in verified laws of existing physical-chemical processes. For example, the institution of paleolithic, neolithic and bronze ages of "prehistoric times," with their subdivisions, rests upon a knowledge of the relation between technological improvements and changes in culture which is obtained and verified on the ground of contemporaneous conditions. Since differences in, say, the refinement of quality of the edges of stone implements do not bring their relative dates engraved upon them, it is clear that their use as signs of successive levels of culture is an inference from conceptions that are warranted, if at all, by facts that *now* exist. An extensive doctrinal apparatus is required in order to correlate with one another such varied data as fossil survivals, artefacts, ashes, bones, tools, cave-drawings, geographical distributions, and the material that is drawn from study of existing "primitive" peoples. Yet without these extensive correlations the reconstruction of "prehistoric" times could not proceed.

Recognition of change in social states and institutions is a precondition of the existence of historical judgment. This recognition in all probability came about slowly. In early days it was confined, we may suppose, to emergencies so great that change could not escape notice: such as mass migrations, plagues, great victories in war, etc. As long as these changes were supposed to constitute isolated episodes, history cannot be said to have emerged. It came into existence when changes were related together to constitute courses, cycles or stories having their beginnings and closings. Annals are material for history but hardly history itself. Since the idea of history involves cumulative continuity of movement in a given direction toward stated outcomes, the fundamental conception that controls determination of subject-matter as historical is that of a *direction* of movement. History cannot be written *en masse*. Strains of change have to be selected and material sequentially ordered according to the direction of change defining the strain which is selected. History is of peoples, of dynasties; is political, ecclesiastical, economic; is of art, science, religion and philosophy. Even when these strains are woven together into an effort to construct a comprehensive strand that covers a movement taken to be relatively complete, the various strains must first be segregated and each followed through its course.

From acceptance of the idea that inferential determinations of history depend upon prior selection of some direction of movement, there follows directly a consideration of basic logical importance. *All historical construction is necessarily selective.* Since the past cannot be reproduced *in toto* and lived over again, this principle might seem too obvious to be worthy of being called important. But it is of importance because its acknowledgment compels attention to the fact that everything in the writing of history depends upon the principle used to control selection. This principle decides the weight which shall be assigned to past events, what shall be admitted and what omitted; it also decides how the facts selected shall be arranged and ordered. Furthermore, if the fact of selection is acknowledged to be primary and basic, we are committed to the conclusion that all history is necessarily written from the standpoint of the present, and is, in an inescapable sense, the history not only of the present but of that which is contemporaneously judged to be important in the present.

Selection operates in a three-fold way. The first selection in order of time is made by the people of the past whose history is now written, during the very time when they lived. Herodotus wrote, he said, "in order that the things which have been done might not in time be forgotten." But what determined his selection of the things which should not be forgotten? To some minor extent, doubtless, his personal preferences and tastes; such factors cannot be wholly excluded in any case. But if these factors had been the only or main agency, his history would itself have soon been forgotten. The decisive agency was what was prized by the Athenian people for whom he directly wrote; the things this people judged worthy of commemoration in their own lives and achievements. They themselves had their appraisals of worth which were operating selectively. The legends they transmitted and the things they forgot to retell, their monuments, temples and other public buildings, their coins and their grave-stones, their celebrations and rites, are some of the selective evaluations they passed upon themselves. Memory is selective. The memories that are public and enduring, not private and transitory, are the primary material within which conscious and deliberate historians do their work. In more primitive peoples, folklore, implements, enduring relics, serve, in spite of the accidental ravages of time, the same function of self-appraisal that is passed by living peoples upon their own activities and accomplishments.

The historiographer adds a further principle of selection. He elects to write the history of a dynasty, of an enduring struggle, of the formation and growth of a science, an art or a religion, or the technology of production. In so doing, he postulates a career, a course and cycle of change. The selection is as truly a logical postulate as are those recognized as such in mathematical propositions. From this selection there follow selective appraisals as to (1) the relative weight and relevancy of materials at his disposal and (2) as to the way they are to be ordered in connection with one another. There is no event which ever happened that was *merely* dynastic, merely scientific or merely technological. As soon as the event takes its place as an incident in a particular history, an act of judgment has loosened it from the total complex of which it was a part, and has given it a place in a new context, the context and the place both being determinations made in inquiry, not native properties of original existence. Probably nowhere else is the work of judgment in discrimination and in creation of syntheses as marked as in historical evocations. Nowhere is it easier to find a more striking instance of the principle that new forms accrue to existential material when and because it is subjected to inquiry.

What has been said finds its conspicuous exemplification in the familiar commonplace of the double sense attached to the word *history*. History is that which happened in the past and it is the intellectual reconstruction of these happenings at a subsequent time. The notion that historical inquiry simply reinstates the events that once happened "as they actually happened" is incredibly naive. It is a valuable methodological canon when interpreted as a warning to avoid prejudice, to struggle for the greatest possible amount of objectivity and impartiality, and as an exhortation to exercise caution and scepticism in determining the authenticity of material proposed as potential data. Taken in any other sense, it is meaningless. For historical inquiry is an affair (1) of selection and arrangement, and (2) is controlled by the dominant problems and conceptions of the culture of the period in which it is written. It is certainly legitimate to say that a certain thing happened in a certain way at a certain time in the past, in case adequate data have been procured and critically handled. But the statement "It actually happened in this way" has its status and significance *within* the scope and perspective of historical writing. It does not determine the logical conditions of historical propositions, much less the identity of these propositions with events in their original occurrence. *Das geschichtliche Geschehen,* in the sense of original events in the existential occurrence, is called *"geschichtlich"* only proleptically; as that which is *subject* to selection and organization on the basis of existing problems and conceptions.

A further important principle is that the writing of history is itself an historical event. It is something which happens and which in its occurrence has existential consequences. Just as the legends, monuments, and transmitted records of, say, Athens, modified the subsequent course of Athenian life, so historical inquiry and construction are agencies in enacted history. The acute nationalism of the present era, for example, cannot be accounted for without reckoning with historical writing. The Marxian conception of the part played in the past by forces of production in determining property relations and of the role of class struggles in social life has itself, through the activities it set up, accelerated the power of forces of production to determine future social relations, and has increased the significance of class struggles. The fact that history as inquiry which issues in reconstruction of the past, is itself a part of what happens historically, is an important factor in giving *"history"* a double meaning. Finally, it is in connection with historical propositions that the logical significance of the emphasis placed upon temporal continuity of past-present-future in dealing with the first two themes of this chapter most fully comes to light.

Our entire discussion of historical determinations has disclosed the inadequacy and superficiality of the notion that since the *past* is its immediate and obvious object, therefore, the past is its exclusive and complete object. *Books* treat of the history of Israel, of Rome, of Medieval Europe, and so on and so on; of nations, institutions, social arrangements that existed in the past. If we derive our logical idea of history from what is contained within the covers of these books, we reach the conclusion that history is exclusively of the past. But the past is of logical necessity the past-of-the-present, and the present is the-past-of-a-future-living present. The idea of the continuity of history entails this conclusion necessarily. For, to repeat, changes become history, or acquire temporal significance, only when they are interpreted in terms of a direction *from* something *to* something. For the purposes of a particular inquiry, the *to* and *from* in question may be intelligently located at any chosen date and place. But it is evident that the limitation is relative to the purpose and problem of the inquiry; it is not inherent in the course of ongoing events. The *present* state of affairs is in some respect the *present* limit-*to*-which; but it is itself a moving limit. As historical, it is becoming something which a future historian may take as a limit *ab quo* in a temporal continuum.

That which is now past was once a living present, just as the now living present is already in course of becoming the past of another present. There is no history except in terms of movement toward some outcome, something taken as an issue, whether it be the Rise and Fall of the Roman Empire, Negro Slavery in the United States, the Polish Question, the Industrial Revolution or Land Tenure. The selection of outcome, of what is taken as the close, determines the selection and organization of subject-matter, due critical control being exercised, of course, with respect to the authenticity of evidential data. But the selection of the end or outcome marks an interest and the interest reaches into the future. It is a sign that the issue is not closed; that the close in question is not existentially final. The urgency of the social problems which are now developing out of the forces of industrial production and distribution is the source of a new interest in history from the economic point of view. When current problems seem dominantly political, the political aspect of history is uppermost. A person who becomes deeply interested in climatic changes readily finds occasion to write history from the standpoint of the effect of great changes that have taken place over large areas in, say, the distribution of rainfall.

There is accordingly, a double process. On the one hand, changes going on in the present, giving a new turn to social problems, throw the significance of what happened in the past into a new perspective. They set new issues from the standpoint of which to rewrite the story of the past. On the other hand, as judgment of the significance of past events is changed, we gain new instruments for estimating the force of present conditions as potentialities of the future. Intelligent understanding of past history is to some extent a lever for moving the present into a certain kind of future. No historic present is a mere redistribution, by means of permutations and combinations, of the elements of the past. Men are engaged neither in mechanical transposition of the conditions they have inherited, nor yet in simply preparing for something to come after. They have their own problems to solve; their own adaptations to make. They face the future, but for the sake of the present, not of the future. In using what has come to them as an inheritance from the past they are compelled to modify it to meet their own needs, and this process creates a new present in which the process continues. History cannot escape its own process. It will, therefore, always be rewritten. As the new present arises, the past is the past of a different present. Judgment in which emphasis falls upon the historic or temporal phase of redetermination of unsettled situations is thus a culminating evidence that judgment is not a bare enunciation of what already exists but is itself an existential requalification. That the requalifications that are made from time to time are subject to the conditions that all authentic inquiry has to meet goes without saying.

II. In what has been said attention has been given to the narrational propositions of existential judgment to the neglect of the descriptive. But things which happen take *place* in the literal sense of the word. The historian, as narrator, is *primarily* concerned with sequential occurrences with respect to their sequence. But he is quite aware that events do not occur just in time. They take place somewhere, and the conditions of this "somewhere" stand in coexistence with one another and also in coexistence with things taking place elsewhere. Locations, places, and sites are relative to one another; they co-exist. Abstract time as a mathematical entity may be conceived as a unilinear dimension. But events do not occur in an abstraction; the historic line of sequence consists of many dimensions. If only one event occurred in, say, 1492, the year 1492 would not be a date in a historical calendar but a purely mathematical conception, a pure number. It is not because of the sheer choice of historians nor because of literary quality and color that history cannot be written apart from geography, nor narration proceed without description.

Nor, on the other hand, has description significance apart from narration. In a biography, a portrait may be given by means of words or by a reproduction of a painting or a photograph. But the portrait is meaningless save in connection with a statement or estimate of the age of the person—whether explicitly given or inferred from the description, verbal or pictorial. A description consists always of coexisting characteristics that are so conjoined as to frame or outline an object or event in a way that affords the means for the identification of what is being described as the singular existence which it is. The terms of the description are evidential marks. Whatever is the literary or esthetic office of description, its sole logical function is to enable identification to be made for the sake of determining the relevancy of this and that proposition. A man is said to *answer* to a certain description; it is found that a certain arrangement of coexisting finger-whorls is the most effective means of identification. To describe a geometrical figure is to traverse its outline not for an esthetic purpose but to set forth just that conjunction of traits which enables it to be surely identified. A scientific description is logically adequate in the degree in which it consists of a group of coexistent traits which so identify an object that anything having these traits, and only those having them, is of such and such a kind. To be of such and such a description is to *be* of such and such a kind. In the Aristotelian scheme of science, as we saw, the proper description was also *ipso facto*, the proper and final *definition*. In modern science, proper description is strictly a means of identification, while the particular identifications made are relative to the problem in hand. It may be physical, psychological, or moral, according to the identification needed in order to warrant special predications. And any predication, as we have seen, is a requalification, or operational means of instituting a requalification, and so involves a change, which, when stated, is temporal-narrational.

Descriptions are, then, existential propositions which are means to judgment but are not themselves final and complete—not judgment itself. A single quality may serve as a diagnostic mark, as a certain quality of yellow in a flame is a sign of the presence of sodium. But a single trait is only the beginning of a description; it is an incomplete description. Thus "the man in the iron mask" is part of a description, but is not itself a description. It would be a description only if it were conjoined with other coexisting traits. The same thing is true of "the author of the letters of Junius"; "the man who invented the first wheel," and a multitude of other expressions. If the man in the iron mask should be identified (a complete description formed), then he would at once enter into a narrational sequence. When the partial description "the author of the Waverly Novels" was completed by uniting it with the characteristics of Sir Walter Scott, a large number of historical propositions about the author of the Waverly Novels at once became possible. If, however, "Sir Walter Scott" had no known characteristic except that of being the author of the Waverly Novels, there would be no coexistential conjunction, and we should be no better off than we were before. The sentence "Sir Walter Scott is the author of the Waverly Novels" is a complete proposition only because a number of *other* traits can be ascribed to him than that of being the author of the novels—a man born at a certain time, living in a certain place, having written poems, having a certain circle of friends, possessed of such and such qualities. From another point of view, the proposition links the life career of a certain man to the developing literature of the country—also a historical proposition.

A conjunction of traits or a description is the basis of institution of a kind, as will be shown in detail in the ensuing chapter. A proposition about a kind is general. Propositions which are linguistically expressed by proper names and by words like *this*, involve demonstrative reference to singulars. Hence it is often assumed in contemporary logical theory that there are such things as pure demonstrative propositions—"pure" in the sense that they involve no descriptive element. For example, in "That is a church," *that* would be called merely demonstrative, while in "That church is the Cathedral of St. John the Divine," *that church* would be called a mixed demonstrative descriptive term. While the notion of the logical difference between the two expressions rests heavily upon a mere linguistic difference, it also goes back to a logical error which has been dealt with in other connections.[4] It assumes that the subject-matter demonstratively present, which forms the logical subject, is immediately given. But determination of a singular or *this*, requires selective discrimination. This discrimination must have a ground. The ground involves *some* conjunction of traits and hence provides at least a minimum of description. Only functional position in a contextual situation can discriminate an actual *this* from an indefinite number of potential *thises*. No one can tell what is pointed *at* in a given act of demonstration unless there is an idea of what is to be pointed *out*— that is, discriminatively selected. *Mere* pointing is completely indeterminate.[5]

Supposing it is asked "What is that?" *That* is certainly highly indeterminate. Otherwise there would not be the question as to *what* it is. But there must be some minimum of descriptive determination involved, or otherwise neither the one asking the question nor the one of whom it is asked would know what the question was about. It might be any one of the great variety of objects that are in the general line of, say, the extended hand and index finger. In fact, *that* which is pointed to is that *dark* object or that suddenly *moving* thing, or is partially described, while the *question* shows that the descriptives *dark* or *suddenly moving* do not describe sufficiently to determine its kind in connection with the problem in hand. It is an *incomplete* description for this reason. But the instance does not show that *all* identifying and demarcating description is lacking, for such lack would be identical with complete absence of ground for further description. A person on a vessel at sea states, "There is a mountainous island." The person addressed replies, "No, it is a cloud." Unless there is *some* descriptive qualification that identifies what is meant by *there* and *it*, the two persons may be talking about entirely different objects. Common reference requires at least a minimum of description.[6] Given that minimum, the difference between qualification as "island" and as "cloud" is a direct invitation to further observations

[4] See *ante*, p. 124 and p. 148.
[5] Cf. the illustration given on p. 53.
[6] As is exemplified in the ambiguity of reference of pronouns in a non-declensional language.

which will so analyze *it* as to discover, if possible, traits which justify one descriptive qualification or another. The theory criticized confuses an inadequate description of *this* (which is the basis for further operations of observation in order to ascertain the conjunction of traits upon which rests identification of it as one of a kind) with total lack of descriptive qualification.

Propositions about a singular as one of a kind are dealt with later. At this juncture our discussion calls attention, in effect, to the double meaning of the words *demonstration* and *proof*. On the one hand, there is *rational* demonstration, an affair of rigorous sequence in discourse. On the other hand, there is *ostensive* demonstration. In the difference of opinion as to whether *that* is an island or a cloud, there is first an idea of the respective conjunctions of traits which describe the two kinds, and then there are the operations of observation which decide to which of the two descriptive prescriptions the object *answers*. If "this" does not turn out to be marked by traits which describe differentially the conceptions of mountains and islands, then *it* does not answer to that description. Were the theory of mere or pure demonstrative propositions sound, the failure to answer would have to be attributed to some property of the act of pointing—which is absurd. The important positive logical principle involved is that in all propositions of existential import, proof or demonstration is a matter of the execution of delimiting analytic operations of observation. *Evidence* not discourse is here what has probative force. The operations of observation executed are, however, controlled by conceptions or ideational considerations which define the conditions to be satisfied by *differential* traits in descriptive determination of kinds.

There is another mode of narrative-descriptive propositions the nature of which will be dealt with later.[7] Propositions that refer to courses of natural events are of this mode. The contents of physical laws and of the physical existences to which they refer are usually taken in logical theory to be non-historical. It is recognized, of course, that they are concerned with events that occur *in* time and *in* space. Although the conceptions of absolute time and space have been abandoned, the idea persists in logic that

[7] In Chapter XXII.

events *in* space-time can be regarded simply as specimen cases of laws. Because of this idea the determination of events is isolated in current logical formulation from the continuum of events with which they are constituents. This isolation is equivalent to ignoring the need for determining them as constituents of extensive historical events, in a sense in which "historical" has the same meaning that it has in determination of the course of human histories. The problem that is involved can be adequately discussed however, only in connection with discussion of methods of scientific inquiry. Consequently, consideration of it is deferred until that topic is taken up.

CHAPTER XIII

THE CONTINUUM OF JUDGMENT:
GENERAL PROPOSITIONS

EXPERIENCE HAS temporal continuity. There is an experiential continuum of content or subject-matter and of operations. The experiential continuum has definite biological basis. Organic structures, which are the physical conditions of experience, are enduring. Without, as well as with, conscious intent, they hold the different pulses of experience together so that the latter form a history in which every pulse looks to the past and affects the future. The structures, while enduring, are also subject to modification. Continuity is not bare repetition of identities. For every activity leaves a "trace" or record of itself in the organs engaged. Thereby, nervous structures taking part in an activity are modified to some extent so that further experiences are conditioned by changed organic structure. Moreover, every overt activity changes, to some extent, the environing conditions which are the occasions and stimuli of further experiences.

Hume, who carried the atomization of experiences to its extreme, was obliged on that account in order to obtain even a semblance of enduring objects, to introduce a counterbalancing principle, habit. Without this bond of connection neither memory nor expectation (to say nothing of inference and reasoning) could exist. Each new "impression" would be an isolated world of its own, without identifiable quality. He regarded habit as a "mysterious tie"—but a tie he had to have in order to account for even the illusion of stable objects and of a self that endured through the succession of experiences. The development of biological knowledge has now done away with the "mysterious" quality of the tie. Some sort of sequential connection is seen to be as inherent a quality of experience as are the distinctive pulses of experience that are bound together. Cultural conditions tend to multiply ties and to introduce new modes of tying experiences together.

The process of inquiry reflects and embodies the experiential continuum which is established by both biological and cultural conditions. Every special inquiry is, as we have seen, a process of progressive and cumulative re-organization of antecedent conditions. There is no such thing as an instantaneous inquiry; and there is, in consequence, no such thing as a judgment (the conclusion of inquiry) which is isolated from what goes before and comes after. The meaning of this thesis is not to be confused with the trivial, because external, fact that it takes time to form a judgment. What is affirmed is that inquiry, which yields judgment, is itself a process of temporal transition effected in existential materials. Otherwise, there is no resolution of a situation but only a substitution of one subjective unwarranted belief for another unwarranted one.

While continuity of inquiry is involved in the institution of any single warranted judgment, the application of the principle extends to the sequence of judgments constituting the body of knowledge. In this extension, definite characteristic forms are involved. Every inquiry utilizes the conclusions or judgments of prior inquiries in the degree in which it arrives at a warranted conclusion. Propositional formulations are the means of establishing conclusions. They consist of symbols of the contents that are derived from those phases and aspects of former inquiries that are taken to be relevant to the resolution of the given problematic situation. Scientific inquiry follows the same pattern as common sense inquiry in its utilization of facts and ideas (conceptual meanings) which are the products of earlier inquiries. It differs from common sense in the scrupulous care taken to ensure both that the earlier conclusions are fitted in advance to be means for regulation of later inquiries, and the care taken to ensure that the special facts and conceptions employed in the later ones are strictly relevant to the problem in hand. In common sense, the attitudes and habits formed in earlier experiences operate to a large extent in a *causal* way; but scientific inquiry is a deliberate endeavor to discover the grounds upon which attitudes and habits are entitled to operate causally in a given case.

That earlier conclusions have the function of preparing the way for later inquiries and judgments, and that the later are dependent upon facts and conceptions instituted in earlier ones, are commonplaces in the intellectual development of individuals and the historic growth of any science. That continuity is involved in the maturing of individuals and the building up of the procedures and conclusions of bodies of knowledge is too obvious to demand argument. It would even be too obvious to be worth mentioning were it not that this continuity is something more than an indispensable condition of intellectual growth. It is the only principle by which certain fundamentally important logical forms can be understood; namely, those of standardized general conceptions and of general propositions. The theme of the present chapter is then the connection between the continuum of inquiry and *generality* as a logical form.

Singular events and objects are recognized, or in logical language, identified and discriminated, as such-and-such, or so-and-so. "Such" designates relation to something else to which a singular is likened in respect to quality, degree or extent, or to which it stands in some relation of dependence. Illustrations of the *explicit* use of "such" in the first sense are found in such expressions as "such dire want"; "such soft music"; "such a hero"; "such opinions," etc. Examples of the second use are found wherever a comparison is made in which "as" (or so) and "such" are correlative: for example, "as is the teacher, so is the school," and other proverbial expressions, *such as*, "such the master, such the servant," while *so* as an equivalent of *hence* always indicates continuative logical force.

All propositions regarding *this* or any singular, having the formal "is" as connective, express assimilation of *this* to other singulars in quality, degree or extent, as in "This is red," "This is rust," "This is oxide of iron," or "This is a noise," "It is a bang," "It is the backfiring of an automobile." The predicates, when formally generalized as descriptive terms, are represented as "such and such." The singular is described (discriminated and identified) as one of a *kind* by means of a conjunction of traits which make it *like* certain other things already determined and that are likely to occur for determination in the future. These simple considerations are enough to establish a strong presumption of the connection between the general and the principle of continuity, while the meaning to be ascribed to "likeness" constitutes a problem for further discussion.

It is not uncommon to interpret the logical form under consideration by reference to a "common" factor which is instituted through *recurrence*. In some sense, this interpretation in terms of recurrence is justified since it marks recognition of some sort of continuity. But the problem is to ascertain the particular sense in which "recurrence" is to be taken. For when this conception is examined it is found to involve already the conception of *kind*, so that explanation of the conception of kind by that of recurrence is simply a substitution of one word for another. For example, a given singular event is followed by the proposition "This is a flash of lightning." *This flash* is certainly not recurrence in the sense of re-appearance of an *object* or event which has presented itself before and which has endured in existence during the interval. Clearly, recurrence here is practically synonymous with identification of the flash as *one of a kind*. We surely cannot, in this case, employ *recurrence* as something already understood by means of which to understand the conception of kind.

At best, the explanation of kinds, which are general, on the basis of recurrence would apply only in the case of enduring objects which reappear in experience from time to time. We see the same mountain over and over again under a great variety of changing circumstances. But this fact only guarantees the continuing existence of a *singular*. It leaves us without guidance or support in identifying another singular, not previously experienced, as a mountain, although it would support the inference that "*If* it is a mountain, it is enduring in temporal span." Recurrence is, in other words, one of the chief grounds for accepting belief in enduring objects which are not, like flashes of lightning, of very short duration. But it leaves the question of kinds just where it was.

Moreover, the difference in question is at most but one of length of duration. A mountain lasts longer than a cloud, but we know that mountains had an origin and that they will, given a sufficiently long time, decay and pass out of existence. We also know that the span of a given object's duration is not determined by an inherent eternal essence, but is a function of the existential conditions which produce it and which sustain it for a few seconds, or minutes, or many thousands of years. In existential principle, there is no difference between the passing rain and the "everlasting" ocean. Propositions about the length of the duration of an object are matters of evidence, not of deduction from the concept of substance.

It is said that there are savage peoples who believe that the light-bringing object which sets at night is not the same object as that which rises and brings light the next morning. They are said to believe that there is a new sun every day. Whether the belief is actually held or not makes no difference for the purpose of illustration. For in any case, the *experience* is unique and non-recurrent. On what grounds do we draw a distinction between its unique character and the identity of the object which is its subject-matter? It will be a year before the sun presents itself again in the same position in the heavens, and perhaps it will never appear again under exactly the same conditions. The question is not meant to suggest any doubt about the enduring quality of the object in question. It is meant to indicate that the reasons for the belief are matters of fact, of evidence, which warrant a conclusion as an *inference*.

Take the grounded proposition that the evening and the morning star are the same planet. This is not an idea or a fact given in immediate experience. It is not an aboriginal datum within the experience. It is warranted in and by a highly complex set of observations as these are systematized by certain conceptions of the structure of the solar system. The case of the identity of the sun is simpler but it is of the same order. The only conclusion which can be drawn for logical theory from these considerations is that the problem of the sameness of the singular object is of the same logical nature as the problem of kinds. Both are products of the continuity of experiential inquiry. Both involve mediating comparisons yielding exclusions and agreements and neither is a truth or datum given antecedent to inquiry.

They are not only products of the same operations of inquiry but are bound up together. *The determination that a singular is an enduring object is all one with the determination that it is one of a kind.* The identification of a sudden light as a flash of lightning, of a noise as the banging of a door, is not grounded upon existential qualities which immediately present themselves, but upon the qualities with respect to *the evidential function* or use in inquiry they subserve. What is recurrent, uniform, "common," is the power of immediate qualities to be *signs*. Immediate qualities in their immediacy are, as we have seen, unique, non-recurrent. But in spite of their existential uniqueness, they are capable, *in the continuum of inquiry*, of becoming distinguishing characteristics which mark off (circumscribe) and identify a *kind* of objects or events. As far as qualities are identical in their functional force, as means of identification and demarcation of kinds, objects are of the same kind no matter how unlike their immediate qualities. Scientific kinds are determined, for example, with extreme disregard of immediate sensible qualities. The latter are irrelevant and often obstructive in the institution of extensive systems of inference and hence are not employed to describe kinds.

A singular as a mere *this*, always sets a problem. The problem is resolved by ascertaining *what* it is—that is, the kind it is of. This fact alone is enough to show the identity of the two apparently different matters of determining the temporal endurance of an event and determining its kind. "This" is an intellectual puzzle until it is capable of being described in terms of what, linguistically, is a common noun. The description *is* qualification of the singular as one of a kind. The question, then, concerns the way in which the general form is instituted, it being noted that recurrence is connected with *inference* and not with existences apart from their function in inference.

A starting point for further discussion is found in the fact that verbal expressions which designate *activities* are not marked by the distinction between "singular" (proper) names and "common" names, which is required in the case of nouns. For what is designated by a verb is a *way* of changing and/or acting. A way, manner, mode, of change and activity is constant or uniform. It persists, although the singular deed done or the change taking place is unique. *An* act and *a* change can be demonstratively pointed out, and qualified as one of a kind, for example, *a* foot-race or *a* fire. But racing and burning are *ways* of acting and changing. They are exemplified in singulars but are not themselves singular. They may recur; they represent possibilities of recurrence. A way of operating employed to characterize a singular gives the latter potential generality. When the potential activity of, say, walking, is actualized, there comes into existence *a* walk. When the process of burning is actualized in a singular there is *a* fire. It is still a singular or *this* but it is a singular of a kind.

Because of the operation of tasting and touching, *this* is affirmed to be sweet and hard. The operation, being a constant, recurs. Its consequence may be that the particular *this* of a new experience is affirmed to be sour and soft. Discrimination occurs because of consequences of agreement and difference—because agreements and exclusions are instituted by recurring operations in the experiential continuum. The outcome is that the presence of certain immediate qualities is so conjoined with certain other non-immediate qualities that the latter may be inferred. When this further operation of inference takes place, the potential generality, due to the presence of the same modes of change and activity, is actualized. The resulting inference is *grounded* in the degree to which *differential* consequences are instituted so that some conjoined traits are inferable while other traits are excluded.

The connection of inference with expectation was correctly pointed out by Hume. He obtained a merely sceptical conclusion from this connection because (1) he never pursued his analysis of the "mysterious" principle of habit to the point of seeing its identity with a uniform mode of operation and change, and because (2) he failed to note that explicit *formulation* of an expectation renders it capable of being checked and tested by consequences, positive and agreeing, negative and excluding, while (3) such formulation transfers expectation from the field of existential causation to the logical realm. A generality is involved in every expectation as a case of a habit that institutes readiness to act (operate) in a specified way. This involvement yields what was called potential *logical* generality. Explicit formulation in propositional form of the expectation, together with active use of the formulation as a means of controlling and checking further operations in the continuum of inquiry, confers upon the potentiality a definite logical form.

The burnt child dreads the fire—an expectation and a *potential* generalization on the part of the child. The Egyptians looked forward to the occurrence of eclipses at specified dates. In so far as past occurrences had been analyzed sufficiently to furnish the ground for the expectation, the latter partook of the nature of inference. In as far, however, as merely *temporal* occurrences were the ground of the prediction, the latter was *not* inference in its definitive logical sense. It became such inference when certain constant modes of natural operation were ascertained to be the *reason* why certain conjunctions of circumstantial conditions could be used to ground a prediction.[1]

We are brought to the conclusion that it is modes of *active response* which are the ground of generality of logical form, not the existential immediate qualities of that which is responded to. Qualities which are extremely unlike one another in their immediate (or "sensible") occurrence, are assimilated to one another (or are assigned to the same kind) when the same mode of response is found to yield like consequences; that is, consequences subject to application of one and the same further operation. A flash of lightning is very different in its sensible setting from the electric spark which had been observed before the time of Franklin, as well as from the attraction exercised by amber when rubbed, as also from the tingling sensation experienced when under certain atmospheric conditions a person who has scuffed his feet touches another person. The assimilation of such phenomena and a great many others to one another, as of the kind *electro-magnetic*, did not come about by searching for and finding "common" immediate qualities. It was effected by employing modes of operation and noting their consequences. Similarly, the generalization of the three states of matter, solid, liquid and gaseous, was obtained by operations of experimental variation of temperature and pres-

---

[1] In the sense in which "empirical" is distinguished from "rational" on the ground of likeness of existential conditions, "empirical" inference is a mixture of expectations causally produced and inference in its logical sense.

sure and noting their consequences. Until this was done, certain things like air, seemed to be inherently or by their "essence" a gas. One has only to note the way in which scientific kinds are formed to be convinced that assimilation of different objects and events into kinds is not constituted by comparison of immediately given qualities along with "extraction" of those which are "common" but by the performance of operations which determine the presence of modes of interactions having specified consequences. "Common" designates, not qualities, but modes of operation.[2]

As has already been noticed, such expressions as "This is red, liquid, soluble, hard" are not primary, but express the consequences, actual or anticipated, of execution of operations. As qualifications, or as actual and possible predications, they are effected by the cumulative force of the recurrence of operations, similar and differentiating. The cumulative force of these observations issues in such propositions as "This is sugar," "That is a race horse," etc. In these propositions, the predicates represent potentialities which *will be actualized* when certain further operations are performed that produce interactions by introduction of new conditions. An actual, immediate quality thus becomes a sign of other qualities that will (or would) be actual *if* additional operations producing conditions for new modes of interaction were performed. When it is said, for example, "This is iron," the significance of the qualification *iron* consists of potentialities not then and there actualized. The qualities of "this" are actual. But they are taken not in their bare actuality but as evidential signs of consequences that will be actualized when further interactions are instituted. The importance of scrupulous determination, by observation, of existing qualities, is instrumental; it is a matter of instituting data for a controlled and grounded inference. Fulfilment of this condition demands, logically, variation of the operations of observation. The immediate qualities of iron pyrites *suggest* the proposition "This is gold." If the suggestion is immediately acted upon, the one who drew that conclusion finds himself, after a waste of time and energy, to be deluded. Care is taken in scientific inquiry, as distinct from the formation of common sense expectations, to

---

[2] Compare what was said earlier about exclusion and negative as *active* processes. See pp. 181 *seq.*

determine *in advance* whether given qualities are such as to be the differential traits which describe the thing as of a specified kind.[3]

The discussion has so far been occupied with *generals* in the form of a set of conjoined traits describing a *kind*. It has been shown that qualities become traits descriptive of a kind when they are the consequences of operations which are modes or *ways* of changing and acting. This fact indicates that the operations are themselves general, although in another sense from the generality attached to sets of conjoined traits. It indicates, indeed, that the type of generality which constitutes the logical form of the latter is derivative, depending upon the generality of the operations executed or possible. The discussion has thus arrived at a point where it is necessary to discriminate between two types or logical forms of generality. Historically, the generality of kinds came first. For men are customarily more concerned with the consequences, the "ends" or fruits of activity, than with the operations by means of which they are instituted. The direct result of this historical fact in logical theory was the conception of natural kinds or species (or "classes") and the construction of classificatory and taxonomic science. Even after the logical priority of operations in determination of kinds had become a commonplace of scientific *practice*, the priority and prestige of the conception of "classes" operated in logical theory to obscure recognition of the form of generality which is logically prior and conditioning. Indeed, it has done more than obscure it. It has resulted in the widespread confusion found in the attempt to interpret all logical generals on the ground of a theory of classes. Accordingly, not only the intrinsic merits of the case, but a prevalent confusion in logical theory, demands that special attention be given to the distinction and the relation of the two forms of generality.

The conclusion of the discussion of this point will be anticipated by the use of certain words to mark the distinction. Propositions about kinds and classes in the sense of kinds will be called

---

[3] The proposition "This is iron pyrites" is not *in such a case* itself an *inference* but an *expectation*. For the *proposition* is determined directly and sufficiently only by operations of experimental analysis which determine qualities as traits descriptive of a definitive kind. This point has important bearings upon the theory of induction, as is pointed out later. (See Chap. XXI)

generic propositions (in the sense in which species are also, as kinds, generic), while propositions whose subject-matter is provided by the operation by means of which a set of traits is determined to describe a kind, will be called *universal.* Correspondingly, the universals as such, will be called *categories,* in order to avoid the ambiguity found in the current use of the term "classes" in logical theory—the word "class" being used to designate both kinds and universals, which in logical function and form are distinct, as is shown later.

There are words in common use whose meaning is systematically ambiguous, for instance such words as "if, when, conditions." Sometimes they refer to the existential and sometimes to the ideational. When it is said, "If he doesn't come in five minutes I shan't wait any longer"—"*if*" refers to a set of contingent temporal-spatial circumstances. Similarly, when it is asked, "When does the sun rise tomorrow?" the reference is clearly to an occurrence in time. But the word "when" in the clause "*when* it is asked" has quite a different force. It means "whenever," or *if* at any time such a question should be asked, without implying that it has been asked or will, as a fact, ever be asked. The proposition "When angels appear, men are dumb" does not of itself imply that angels exist or will ever appear. In science, there are many propositions in which the clause introduced by "if" is known to be contrary to conditions set by existential circumstances; that is, to be such that they cannot be existentially satisfied, as "If a particle at rest is acted upon by a single moving particle, then," etc. In such propositions, *if* and *when* designate a connection of conceptual subject-matters, not of existential or temporo-spatial subject-matters. If the word "conditions" is used, it now refers to a logical relation, not to existential circumstances.

In certain contexts, the distinction is recognized in present logical theory: for example, in the doctrine that an *A* or *E* proposition does not imply an *I* or *O* proposition, and in the distinction made between mathematical and physical propositions. These considerations alone indicate the necessity of systematic recognition of two distinct logical forms of generality. The failure to carry the distinction through in a systematic way appears to be due to an attempt to reduce general propositions about kinds (under the name of classes) to the form of abstract universal propositions. The ultimate source of this attempt appears in turn to have its source in the fact that in the Aristotelian logic, kinds, as species, were interpreted as ontological universals. The development of modern logic, especially under the influence of mathematical science, has shown that universal propositions are abstract hypothetical propositions, or non-existential in import. Hence confusion arises in logical theory when propositions about kinds (general in the sense of *generic*) are identified with universal propositions.

Every modern text on logic points out the ambiguity in such propositions as "All men are mortal." In one interpretation, that sanctioned by tradition, it means that the class of men (in the sense of kind), is included within the class of mortal things. Stated explicitly in its existential import it means "All men have died or will die"—a spatio-temporal proposition. On the other hand, it means that "If any thing is human, *then* it is mortal": a necessary interrelation of the characters of *being* human and *being* mortal. Such a proposition does not imply nor postulate that either men or creatures who die actually exist. It would be valid, if valid at all, even if no men existed, since it expresses a *necessary* relation of abstract characters. On the other hand, the proposition "All men are mortal" interpreted in its existential reference is logically an *I* proposition, and being of the inductive order is subject to the contingencies of existence and of matter-of-fact knowledge. It is a proposition of a certain order of *probability*. The connection between the *fact* of life and the *fact* of death is of a different logical form from the relation between *being* human and *being* mortal. The latter is valid, as just stated, if valid at all, by definition of a conception. The former is a matter of evidence, determined by observations.

So far there is relatively clear sailing. But the distinction is often followed in contemporary logical texts by the assumption, explicit or implicit, that propositions about kinds are ultimately of the same logical dimension as are *if-then* universal propositions. The reasoning that leads to this assumption—or conclusion—is as follows. Propositions about kinds are not about the individuals of the kind, but about a relation of characteristic traits which determine the kind. The affirmation that "All individuals of the kind *men* are included in the more extensive kind *mortals*" does not involve acquaintance with all individuals, or even with a specified person. It applies to men not yet born as well as to an indefinite multitude of others with whom we have no acquaintance. Such propositions are therefore different in logical form from any proposition about a singular.

The proposition "Socrates is a man" is, for example, of a different logical form from the proposition "All Athenians are Greeks." The former is restricted to a singular who must, in order to warrant the proposition, be capable of *demonstrative* reference. The latter by its nature goes beyond singulars capable of being demonstratively referred to—this is the essence of its generality. The relation between the traits or distinguishing characteristics which determine the kind, men or Athenians, and the distinguishing characteristics which determine the kind, *mortals* or *Greeks*, is affirmed independently of demonstrative reference to any *particular given* singular. Hence it is frequently said to be affirmed independently of reference to singulars *as such*. It is assimilated in form to the abstract non-existential universal proposition.

The fallacy of the argument resides in identification of absence of reference to *specified* individuals or singulars with absence of reference to singulars as such. There is a clear difference between a proposition that refers to *each and every individual* who has certain characteristics (whether or not all individuals are known who have such characteristics), and a proposition that refers in its own content to *no* individual. It is true that the former is directly about a conjunction of characteristics and not about singulars as such. But it is equally true that it is about a set of characteristics that so describes a kind as to have reference to *all* (each and every) singular existences having the set of traits in question. "Each and every whale, whether observed or not, or whether now existent or not, is a mammal." "If an animal is cetacean, it is mammalian." When we compare these two propositions as to their logical form, it is evident that the latter expresses a necessary relation of characters and holds whether whales exist or not. The first proposition refers to each and every *existence* marked by a certain conjunction of traits. Independence of reference to that which exists at a *particular* time or place cannot be identified, save by radical confusion, with the absence of reference to spatial-temporal circumstances as such, the latter being inherent in the universal proposition.

The confusion is fostered by the logically ambiguous character of language—as in the double sense of "all" already mentioned. Linguistically, propositions about kinds are expressed by common nouns, and hypothetical universal propositions by means of abstract nouns; both of them being distinguished, of course, from proper nouns and from demonstratives like "this" and "here." But in many cases words in use fail to indicate by their linguistic form of which category they are. "Mankind," for example, designates explicitly a *kind;* "Humanity" may be an equivalent common noun or it may designate a relation of universal characters: the quality or state of *being* genuinely human. An even better example is "color." When it is said that red, green, blue, etc., are colors, the reference is clearly to kinds included in a more generic kind. But there is no abstract noun "colority" in common use. When Mill says that when it is affirmed "Snow is white, milk is white, linen is white, we do not mean that these things *are* a color but that they *have* a color," he speaks, of course, correctly. But then he proceeds to state "Whiteness is the name of the color exclusively." [4] Now a statement like Mill's implies that the difference between *having* a color and *being* colority is simply that between a quality referred to a thing as its property and the same quality taken without reference to a thing. But *whiteness* does not designate *a* color as a quality at all. It designates a certain way or mode of *being* colority, the abstract universal. A white thing may suggest *whiteness,* but *whiteness* is not a color which things have or can have. We may dwell upon a given quality of color without reference to other qualities indefinitely in isolation. But it still remains a quality, *white,* not *whiteness.* The scientific conception of colority is of a different logical dimension from that of colors and *a* color. Colority or being color is defined in terms of rates of vibration and white*ness* is defined as the functional correlation of the radiating-absorptive capacity of these vibrations combined in a stated proportion. It is in effect a definition of

[4] Mill, *Logic.* Book I, Ch. 2, Sec. 4.

conditions to be satisfied if a proposition, "This is white," is warranted.

Mill goes on to raise the question whether abstract words like whiteness are general or singular. Perplexed by certain considerations which will be presently noticed, he concludes that "the best course would probably be to consider these names as neither general nor individual, and to place them in a class apart." The conclusion does Mill's sense for logical forms credit: the "class apart" is, in fact, that of *abstract universals*. When he says they are not "general," he is using the word in the sense in which common nouns like *color* are general. His perplexity was then due to a belief that *some* abstract terms *are* names of an extensive kind. Color, for example, includes, according to him, whiteness, redness, blueness, etc.; and whiteness, in turn, includes various degrees. The same thing holds, he says, of magnitude and weight with reference to their various degrees. But such terms as equality, squareness, etc., designate, he says, an attribute "that is one and does not admit of plurality." Curiously enough he includes "visibility" in the same category—although it is evident that it does have degrees.

It is evident, I think, that Mill, when he speaks of abstract terms which, like common nouns, have extension of kinds or degrees, has slipped over from the abstract to existential objects and their qualities. *Objects* do have various sizes or degrees of magnitude and various weights. It is impossible to see how the abstract conception of magnitude or heaviness can have degrees any more than can squareness or equality. Since *different objects* may be equal to one another in magnitude, while they differ in size from some other objects, his reasoning in the case of magnitude would logically lead to the conclusion that equality is also a name "for a class of attributes," since objects have different sizes and yet some are nevertheless equal to others. With respect to magnitude, a big object exemplifies it in no other way than a small one; with respect to exemplification of weight in the abstract there is no difference between a heavy object and a light one. Redness, blueness, whiteness, are ways of *being* colority, not kinds of color (in the concrete), like red, blue and white.

The reference to Mill will be misunderstood if taken to apply to him peculiarly among writers on logic. He simply makes explicit a confusion that is implicit in many writers on logical theory. Exactly the same confusion exists when propositions like "All whales are mammals" are equated in logical form to propositions like "All squares are rectangular." For the latter proposition is not one about inclusion of *kinds*, but about a mode or way of *being* rectangular.[5]

I close this phase of the discussion by mentioning some distinctions of terminology which will be instituted and observed in order that there may be a suitable measure of linguistic protection against the confusion which has been described. As already stated, general propositions about kinds, or generals having existential reference, will be called *generic* propositions and terms. General propositions of the abstract *if-then* form will be called *universal* propositions. The word *class* is now used to designate both kinds and the different ways of being universal; for example, triangle is said to be a class including right-angled, scalene and isosceles triangles, thus making it much easier to confuse the logical form appropriate to kinds with the logical form appropriate to mathematical subject-matter. I propose to use the word *class*, when it is employed, as an equivalent of *kind*, and to use the word *category* for the other logical meaning. Triangularity, for example, is a category of which various ways of being triangular are subcategories. Qualities which descriptively determine (distinguish and identify) kinds, I shall indifferently call *traits* or *characteristics*, while the related contents of an abstract universal proposition are called *characters*.[6]

More will be said later about the ambiguity of the conception of "inclusion." When kinds are affirmed to be included in a kind

[5] The verbal ambiguity already mentioned is found in the word "square" when used mathematically. It looks like a concrete word, while in fact it means squareness, so that the proposition that reflects its logical meaning would be expressed in verbal form "Squareness is a mode of rectangularity." Similarly, "circle" in its *mathematical* use means circularity; its analytic expression in an equation obviously has no direct reference to objects or to qualities. The connection of the point here under discussion with the conception of operations developed in the first section of this chapter is taken up in the next chapter.

[6] Mill set the example of using the term "attributes" so loosely as to apply to qualities in the concrete, to traits and to what are here called characters. If the word "attributes" is used at all, it would be better, I think, to use it as a synonym for "characters."

of wider extension, the reference of "included" is clearly existential. But when a definition of polygon in geometry is said to "include" that of triangles, rectangles, etc., the meaning is very different. The Oxford Dictionary has a quotation which may be used to illustrate this type of meaning. "It is necessary to include in the idea of Labour all feelings of a disagreeable kind . . . connected with the employment of one's thought or muscles or both in a particular occupation."

"Inclusion" is here connected with definition of an idea or conception. The quotation is saying that any *definition* of labor (here employed as an abstract word) is defective which does not contain as an integral or necessary part of its conception the idea of disagreeableness. If, or when, the definition is accepted, it affords a necessary logical condition of determination whether a given occupation is of a kind to be included (in the other sense of inclusion) in the kind of occupations that are laborious. According to the definition, a proposition that such and such an occupation is or is not labor will depend for its *differentia* upon the presence or absence of a disagreeable quality attending its pursuit. A different definition or conception of labor might yield a different set of traits by which to assign an activity to a kind and to determine the relation of kinds. The instance illustrates the necessary relation subsisting between determination of generic propositions and the universal abstract propositions which are definitions of conceptual or ideational meanings. But it also involves their difference with respect to logical form, covering also the formal difference in the conceptions of inclusion and exclusion. A *rule* for inclusion and exclusion is not itself a case of the inclusions or exclusions which its application effects. To *preclude* or rule out by *definition* is a different logical matter from refusing on evidential grounds to place one kind within another kind.

In the next chapter, we shall return to a detailed consideration of generic and universal propositions in the light of the distinction of logical forms which has been formulated. In the state in which logical theory now exists, it is necessary, however, to engage in a discussion which would be an irrelevant *excursus* if the distinction were acknowledged and systematically adhered to. The present phase of the discussion may be concluded by saying that three logical motifs seem to have converged to bring about failure to recognize the distinction of logical forms. One of them is the influence of the Aristotelian identification of classes, as fixed ontological species defined by a formal essence, with the universal. The second is the desire to maintain the strictly formalistic conception of logic (ruling out of all existential and material references) by setting up mathematical propositions as the logical form normative for the interpretation of the form of all general propositions—a conception, however, which if it were rigorously maintained would demand elimination of all demonstrative reference and hence, ultimately, of singular and generic propositions. The third influence springs from a consideration inherent in inquiry itself, namely, the necessary function of universal propositions in determination of warranted singular and generic propositions, a point discussed at length in the ensuing chapter.

The problem of the nature of the general has been such a crucial issue in the history of both philosophic logic and metaphysical theory that a few words are added to indicate the traits which differentiate the position taken in this chapter from the views traditionally known as realism, conceptualism and nominalism—to *differentiate* it rather than here to argue for it and against the other interpretations. The theory agrees with the "realistic" interpretation of generals in affirming that *ways* of acting are as existential as are singular events and objects. It disagrees in that it holds that while these ways of interaction are necessary conditions, they are not sufficient conditions of *logical* generality, since the latter accrues only when and as the existentially general is used as a controlling function, in the continuity of inquiry, to attain warranted assertibility.

In consequence, the theory agrees with "nominalism" in holding not only that immediate qualities are the ground required for determination of a specified generality which is possessed of existential reference and also for test of its applicability in a given case, but (what is here more important) that the logically general, whether generic or universal, has necessarily the character of a *symbol*. For since it is not a literal transcription of a general in existence but is a utilization of the latter for the special purpose of inquiry (being, that is, a distinctively *logical* form), the status and function of a symbol is that of a required member of a *propositional* form, while propositional formulation is inherently necessary for controlled inquiry. It differs fundamentally from nominalism in holding not only that the general has its ground in existence (and hence is not a mere convenient memorandum or notation for a number of singulars), but that symbolization is a necessary condition of all inquiry and of all knowledge, instead of being a linguistic expression of something already known which needs symbols only for the purposes of convenient recall and communication.

Consequently, it agrees with "conceptualism" in the one point that the general *is* conceptual or ideational in nature. But it differs radically in its conception of what conceptions intrinsically are. Negatively, as has already been pointed out, it rejects completely the view that a conception represents simply a selection of material that is found to be antecedently "common" to a number of singulars. This rejection depends (1) upon interpreting the "common" in terms of the function performed by existential qualities in inference, and (2) upon the necessity of the abstract universal in order to warrant inferential use of qualities in any inquiry. The latter consideration is the more important in that it indicates the logical necessity of conceptions which, while they are *suggested* by singulars, are not *logically* derived from them, even from that which is common among them. For an idea or conception is of the nature of a *possibility* and hence is of a different dimension from actuality, no matter how frequently repeated or "common" the actual quality may be. This conceptual dimension is, furthermore, held to be logically an objective necessary condition in all determination of warranted beliefs or knowledge, not a psychological accretion—as seems to be implied in traditional conceptualism.

CHAPTER XIV

GENERIC AND UNIVERSAL PROPOSITIONS

I. *Introduction.* There are two forms of general propositions, the generic and the universal. Universal propositions are formulations of possible ways or modes of acting or operating. Propositional formulation is required for control of a way of acting that effects discrimination and ordering of existential material in its function as evidential data. Execution of the operation that is prescribed and directed by the universal proposition in serving this function also tests the force and relevancy of the universal proposition as a means of solution of the problem undergoing resolution. For the universal is stated as a relation of an antecedent *if* content and a consequent *then* clause. When its operational application determines existential conditions which agree with the contents of the *then* clause, the hypothesis is *in so far* confirmed. But its affirmation is not sufficiently warranted; agreement is a necessary but not sufficient test. For an affirmation of the antecedent merely because the consequent is affirmable is fallacious. Eliminations or negations have to be affected which determine that *only* if the antecedent is affirmed does the consequent follow.

Application to existential material of the operation that is formulated in the universal proposition determines the material in question to be of specified kinds, and, by means of conjoint execution of operations of inclusion-exclusion, determines the kinds to be the included members of an inclusive kind, and the *only* included kinds as far as the logical conditions of inclusion and exclusion are completely satisfied—a satisfaction which in fact can never be completely achieved because of the contingent nature of existential material, although the required satisfaction is approximated in the continuity of inquiry as a long run procedure.

There are organic activities upon the biological level which select and order existential conditions in a *de facto* way. If a lower organism were equipped with powers of symbolization the result would be its ability to refer some things to certain gross generalizations or kinds—to sort them out, for example, as foods, as inedibles, and as poisons; and into things harmful and adverse and things helpful and favorable—foes and friends. The cultural matrix not only supplies, through the medium of language, means for explicit formulation of kinds but also extends vastly the variety and number of kinds. For culture institutes and consists of a vast number of ways of dealing with things. Moreover, certain ways of action are formulated as standard and normative rules of action and of judgment on the part of members of the cultural group. As was shown earlier, common sense consists, in its generalized phase, of a body of such standardized conceptions which are regulative (or are rules) of the actions and beliefs of persons as to what is proper and improper, required, permitted and forbidden in respect to the objects of the physical and social environment. Thus things and persons are sorted out into distinctive kinds on the ground of allowable and prohibited modes of acting toward and with them: a practical foreshadowing of operations of inclusion and exclusion in the logical sense.

But there is only a foreshadowing. For human beings are "naturally" interested in consequences, outcomes and fruits, good and bad, rather than in the conditions, material and procedural, by which they are obtained. Moreover, the standardized conceptions and rules are for the most part products of habit and tradition. Hence they are so fixed that they are not themselves open to question or criticism. They operate practically to determine kinds but the grounds or reasons for the kinds that are acknowledged in practice are not investigated or weighed—it is enough that the customary rules are what they are. From the logical standpoint, there is a vicious circle. Fixed, unquestioned rules determine the recognized kinds, while kinds are so fixed by the rules that they do not serve to test and modify the ruling conceptions but are taken rather to exemplify and support the rules. At best, inquiry is confined to determining whether or not given objects have the traits that bring them under the scope of a given standardized conception—as still happens to a large extent in popular "judgments" in morals and politics.

The process of inquiry *as* inquiry consists, accordingly, of treating the general propositions that are formulations of ways of action as *hypotheses*—a mode of treatment that is equivalent to treating the formulated modes of action as *possible,* instead of as required or necessary. This way of treating conceptions has its direct impact also upon formation of kinds. For it demands that grounds for them be searched for, and the grounds must be such as to satisfy (inclusively and exclusively) the requirements of the hypothesis that has been adopted and employed. Since existence *is* existence and facts about it are stubborn, ascertained facts serve to test the hypothesis employed; so that when there is recurrent discrepancy of observed facts with the requirements of the conception (hypothesis or theory), the material ground is provided for modification of the hypothesis. Here also is a circular movement, but it is a movement within inquiry, controlled by the operations by means of which problematic situations are resolved.

II. *Inference from Case to Case.* It is convenient to begin the discussion by reference to the view of Mill, since he holds that generalizations proceed from singulars to other singulars and are *proved* by a sufficient number of particular cases, while he also admits that a "generalizing propensity" is involved when we proceed from one observed singular to others that are unobserved. "We conclude," he says, "from known to unknown cases by the impulse of the generalizing propensity." [1] The generalizing impulsive propensity may be fairly identified with the mode of action, organic or acquired, of which mention has been made. But in Mill's account of generalization, the need for propositional formulation of the active propensity is not recognized. Consequently, his account of the production and nature of general propositions sets forth, quite precisely, what happens in the case of those generalizations which *fail* to satisfy logical conditions: the generalizations (of which mention was made in the introductory paragraphs) that do not rest upon ascertained grounds and which, therefore, are unwarranted.

His well-known illustration of the village matron and her

[1] *Logic,* Book I, ch. 3, sec. 8.

neighbor's child affords, when it is analyzed, proof of this state-ment. The matron infers from case to case by virtue of a gen-eralizing propensity. Since this remedy cured my child, it will cure yours. No doubt there are many cases in which just this procedure is followed. If it were not, patent medicine testimonials would not have the vogue they have. But the fact that the pro-pensity operates simply as a propensity and not through the me-dium of a general proposition of the *if-then* form (and hence checked by the consequences that ensue from its operation) is precisely the reason for the relative worthlessness of the inferences which result. The propensity is a *cause* of the inferences that are made but is no sense their *ground*.

There is (1) no reason or ground for the village matron's as-sumption that it was the medicine recommended that in fact cured her own child. There is (2) no reason for the assumption that the disease of the neighbor's child is similar to—of the same kind —as the disease of her own Lucy. And yet that assumption was made, unless the matron carried her "propensity" to the point of recommending it for every case of illness in the village. Stated positively, inference from one case to other cases (which *is* a most important form of inference, being, as will be shown later, of the essence of the inductive function),[2] is grounded only through the intervention and intermediation of general propositions. Examina-tion of the two cases of illness in question is required to establish that they are similar or of the same kind. This examination is carried out by means of analytic comparison of both cases, a com-parison that establishes agreements and differences by using opera-tions that institute affirmative and negative propositions in strict correlation with each other. Moreover, this analytic comparison is effected (when it yields a grounded conclusion) by the oper-ative use of a conceptual apparatus of *if-then* propositions: If diphtheria, then certain characteristic traits; if typhoid, then cer-tain others; if measles, then certain others, and so on. Moreover, the conceptual apparatus is adequate only if the *if-then* proposi-tions that are employed form the content of a disjunctive system of propositions, theoretically (though not in practice) covering all possible cases of illness in such a way as to provide the procedural

[2] See Chap. XXI.

means of identifying and demarcating any case of illness whatever. For these reasons it was stated above that inference is made from one case to other cases only by the intermediary of general *propositions*, instead of saying by a single general proposition. For there is the proposition that this case is of a *kind*, and there is the generalization of the *if-then* form which is required to ground the proposition about a kind.

It will be noted that it is not denied that we do infer from one case to other cases. What is affirmed is that such inferences have logical standing—or are grounded—only as the inference takes place through the mediation of propositions of the generic and of the universal form.

III. *The Nature of Generic Propositions.* Every proposition that involves the conception of a kind is based upon a set of related traits or characteristics that are the necessary and sufficient conditions of describing a specified kind. These traits are selectively discriminated by observation out of the total perceived field. What is the criterion upon which some traits are taken and others are omitted and rejected? From the standpoint of existence, independently of its subjection to inquiry, there is no criterion. Everything in the world is like everything else in some respects, and is unlike anything else in other respects. From the existential point of view, comparison can form an infinite number of kinds and there is no ground whatever in any situation why one kind rather than another should be formed. For example, there are persons who have the quality of being cross-eyed, of being bald and being shoemakers. Why not form a kind on the basis of these qualities? The answer is that such a set of conjoined traits is practically worthless for the *purpose of inference*. This set of traits has no evidential value in respect to inferring other traits that are also conjoined but not observable at the time. It leads nowhere in inquiry.

Such a conjunction of qualities as viviparous, warm-blooded and lung-breathing is taken, on the other hand, to describe the kind *mammalian*, because and only because this conjunction of characteristics promotes and controls extensive inference. It permits grounded conclusions to be made regarding singulars. For singulars are affirmed or denied to be mammals according as to whether this conjunction of traits is or not found to exist upon observational inquiry. If it were not for the conception of related traits, the inquirer would not know what to look for or how to estimate what he found. The set of traits also enables inferences to be made regarding relations of kinds. The traits selected fall within, through additive determinants, the set of traits which describe the kind *vertebrates,* and is such as to enable demarcation to be made between the kind mammals and other kinds such as *fishes.* There was a time when the traits, walking, swimming, creeping and flying, were believed to provide the ground for identifying and differentiating diverse kinds of living creatures. In the continuum of experiential inquiry, it was found to be both too wide and too narrow. It put insects, birds and bats in one and the same kind; fish and seals in another kind; reptiles and worms in a third kind. Scientific inquiry showed that, on the contrary, seals, birds and reptiles should be included in one inclusive kind, because the traits by which that kind is descriptively determined enable inference to be ready and secure from case to case when they are found by directed observation to exist and sets barriers to inference when they are not found.

The theory which has been most generally current (or at least the most popular notion) about the formation of general conceptions is that they are formed by processes of comparison which extract elements that are *common* to many cases and drop out those that differ. The point already made, namely, that formation of kinds is rendered purely arbitrary, since everything is like and unlike other things, applies to this view. A more important objection in the present connection is that it puts the cart before the horse, taking for granted the very thing that is to be accounted for. Common qualities are *already* general qualities. For example, it is said that we form the general conception of a *horse* by comparing horses and taking the residuum of qualities they have in common. But generalization has already been effected when the singulars are adjudged to be horses.

If sound generalizations could be formed by placing, mentally, a number of singulars in a row and then throwing out unlike qualities until a number of "common" qualities remains, institution of kinds and of general conceptions would be an ultra-mechanical and easy operation. One only has to consider the traits that describe a kind in scientific inquiry to note that their institution is an arduous process, and does not proceed in the way that is here criticised. For scientific kinds, say that of *metals*, are instituted by operations that disclose traits that are *not* present to ordinary observation but are produced by operations of experimentation, as a manifestation of *interactions* that are taking place. For only qualities that are capable of being treated as signs of definite interactions facilitate and control inference.

We are thus brought back to the thesis that the traits which descriptively determine kinds are selected and ordered with reference to their *function* in promoting and controlling extensive inference. In other words, while every characteristic trait is a quality, not every quality is a trait. No quality is a trait in and of itself, or in virtue of existence. Qualities are existential and are produced and destroyed by existential conditions. For a quality to be a trait it must be used as an evidential sign or diagnostic mark. The very fact that qualities as traits are used to direct and to control inference is the reason why their fitness to perform the signifying function, to serve as evidential, is and must be itself a matter for careful investigation.

We habitually employ qualities as signs although we do not habitually or "naturally" investigate their qualifications to be so taken and used. As a rule only artists and those of strong esthetic inclinations pay much heed to qualities as qualities. A red light on a street corner is a traffic signal; except in this function little or no attention is paid to its intrinsic quality. Moreover, the quality as an existence is constantly changing. It varies with atmospheric conditions, with changes of sunlight, with the distance and optical apparatus of the percipient, etc. It is constant and uniform only in its function. Variations in its quality as existential are indifferent—until they pass a definite limit—to its function as a stop-signal.

It follows that the view that qualities are *themselves* general, as much so as relations and relationships, is as logically fallacious as is the doctrine that generals are determined by selection of "common" qualities. Nothing more intrinsically unique and non-general than a quality as an existence can be imagined. The

actual red of the traffic light is always varying, for existentially it
is a manifestation of a vast complex of changing conditions. The
function and only the function of a quality in grounding inference
is constant and general.

IV. *The Nature of Universal Propositions.* As has been said,
the existential basis of a universal proposition is a *mode of action.*
A universal proposition is not, however, *merely* a formulation of a
way of acting or operating. It is *such* a formulation as serves to
direct the operations by means of which existential material is
selectively discriminated and related (ordered) so that it functions
as the ground for warranted inferential conclusions. In other
words, a content of a proposition has the form of universality in
virtue of the distinctive function it performs in inquiry. Ways
of acting are, as has been pointed out repeatedly, at first practical
and actual. Through symbolization of propositional formulation
they represent *possible* ways of action. Entertained and developed
as possibilities of ways of acting which are *existentially* general
(because they are *ways* and not singular acts or deeds) they acquire
logical form.

In a universal proposition, possibility of a mode of operation
is expressed in an *if-then* form. *If* certain contents, *then* necessarily certain other contents. Traditionally, the *if* clause is called
the antecedent and the *then* clause the consequent. But the relation is purely logical, and the terms "antecedent" and "consequent"
are to be understood in a logical, not in an existential sense.
When an *if-then* proposition is formed in the process of deliberation about a specific matter of conduct, the two words have a more
literal sense. "If I first do this, then certain consequences may
be anticipated to follow." The relation in question is one of temporal priority and consequence. In the proposition, "If an act
of trespassing, then liability to a penalty," the terms are abstract
and the *relation* is non-temporal and non-existential, even though
the contents, the ideas of trespassing and penalty, have indirect
existential reference. When it is said "If a plane figure is a triangle, then the sum of its three interior angles is equal to two right
angles," not only is the *relation* non-existential, but the contents
are free from any prescribed existential reference even of the most
indirect sort. In such a proposition there is not even a semblance

of antecedent and consequent even in a logical sense. The meaning would be the same if the proposition read "If the sum of the three interior angles of a plane figure is equal to two right angles, the plane figure is a triangle."

In neither of the two cases cited does one clause *follow* from the other. For in their necessary interrelation they present the analysis of a conception into its integral and exhaustive contents. Hence it is misleading to say that one clause *implies* the other, not only because implication holds between propositions, not between clauses, but because such a statement obscures from view the primary logical consideration—namely, that the two clauses represent the analysis of a single conception into its complete and exclusive interrelated logical constituents. For this reason a universal hypothetical proposition has the form of a definition in its logical sense. Thus the proposition "If anything is a material body, it attracts other material bodies directly as its mass and indirectly as the square of the distance" may read equally well in the linguistic form "*All* material bodies, etc." It is a (partial) definition of *being* a material body. It expresses a condition which any observed thing must satisfy if the property "*material*" is groundedly applicable to it. On the other hand, if things are found that on grounds provided by *other* universal propositions are determined to be material which yet fail to answer to the requirements prescribed by the proposition quoted, then one or other of the involved universal propositions must be revised and reformulated.

The foregoing paragraphs are intended to show (1) what is meant by the functional character of the universal proposition and (2) in what special way it is functional. This special way may be restated as follows: A universal proposition prescribes the conditions to be satisfied by existential material, so that if singular it is determined to be one of a specified kind, or if a kind, it is included in and/or is inclusive of certain other specified kinds. It accomplishes this function by means of actual execution of the mode of operation which as a proposition it formulates. For an *actualized* operation is performed upon existential conditions and has consequences in the literal or existential sense. Simple agreement of these actual consequences with the content of the apodosis clause of the hypothetical universal is not, however, as already explained, a complete test of the hypothesis. The actual consequences must be shown, as nearly as possible, to be the *only* ones which would satisfy the requirements of the hypothesis. In order that determination of this mode of satisfaction can be approximately attained, the universal in question must be one of a system of interrelated universal propositions. A universal proposition which is not a member of a system could, at the most, only produce consequences that agree with the conditions it prescribes, without excluding the possibility of their also agreeing with conditions prescribed by other conceptions.

V. *The Conjugate Relation of Universal and Generic Propositions: Implication and Inference.* In the previous chapter it was said that "category" would be employed to designate the conceptions which are formulated in universal propositions instead of the word *class*, since the latter word is also used to denote generals of the form of kinds. Every conception which functions as representative of a possible mode of operation may be called a category. Although in the history of philosophy, the word has been used to a large extent to designate only the conceptions that were taken to be ultimate (even so with little regard to their operational nature), yet ordinary language uses the word more widely. When it is said, for example (taking the example from a dictionary quotation), that "this object falls within the category of machines," something more is meant than that it is included within the kind *machines*. What is meant is that it exemplifies the principle or order of principles by which *being* machinery is defined. A category is the logical equivalent of what practically is an attitude. It constitutes a point of view, a schedule, a program, a heading or caption, an orientation, a possible *mode of predication;* as, in Aristotle, to categorize is to predicate. Civil and criminal laws fall into kinds. But *being* civil or criminal law are categories. They are points of view from which certain forms of conduct are approached and regulated. A law is a formula for treatment. It determines whether certain agents can be brought before a court and how they shall be treated if and when so brought. Principles, prudential and moral, are categories. They are rules for conduct. While rules may themselves fall into classes in the sense of kinds, *being* a principle is not a kind but is a prescription for forming kinds and thus for determining whether a given action or line of conduct is of a specified kind.

Once it is recognized that a universal proposition is a formula of a possible operation, the chief logical problem about such propositions concerns their relation with generic propositions; that is, their relation with determination of the distinguishing traits which describe kinds. According to the view here stated, the relation is *conjugate*. Universals and generics bear the same relation to each other in inquiry that material and procedural means sustain to each other in institution of judgment. Propositions about kinds and singulars as of a specified kind provide the subject matter that forms the logical *subject* of final judgment. Propositions about the operations to be undertaken in order to effect the transformation of problematic subject-matter into a unified continuous existential situation provide the predicational subject-matter

An operation not formulated in a proposition is logically uncontrolled, no matter how useful it may be in habitual practice For until it is propositionally formulated, there is no ground for determining what consequences or what aspects of ensuing consequences are due to it and what consequences are due to extraneous unformulated conditions. The universal hypothetical states the relation between the operation and its consequences, the consequences being taken as themselves of operative force in the continuum of experience, not merely as final and hence isolated Thus they bear the same relation to propositions arranged in reasoning or ordered *discourse*, that propositions about kinds do to promotion and regulation of *inference*. *Particular* consequences do not of themselves lead on to further consequences. In deliberation, the "if" of any action proposed as possible will have for its "then" certain contemplated consequences. But what the further consequences of these consequences will be, remains a separate problem, and one readily lost from view, especially when the special consequences are agreeable. When the "consequences" are themselves possible operations, their formulation leads naturally to propositions about further operations with which they are related, or to discourse, until in mathematical discourse there is no set limit to the possibility of ensuing operations.

Recurring to the topic of conjugate relationship in its bearing upon the relation of generic and universal propositions, we have, first, the fact (already noted) that the operations which constitute the content of predicate subject-matter are such as determine evidential data. In the second place, the data which are thus constituted become the tests of operations already executed and the ground upon which new operations (or modifications of old ones) are suggested and executed. An executed operation first transforms antecedently existent material so that the material obtained becomes more indicative or signifying, and then this changed material calls for further operations, and so on until a resolved situation is instituted. In short, the *raison d'etre* of a given operation is that by it there is brought about approach towards the existential consequences that constitute a resolved situation. Propositional formulation of the operation in advance of its performance is a necessary condition of satisfactory execution of this office. On the other hand, scrupulous discriminative observation of the consequences of its actual performance, together with comparison of these consequences with those which are hypothetically determined, tests the validity (relevancy and force) of the propositional formulation of an operation, and thus reacts, when needful, to modify the operation and the proposition that are subsequently employed.

Stating this conclusion in formal terms:—No grounded generic propositions can be formed save as they are the products of the performance of operations indicated as possible by universal propositions. The problem of inference is, accordingly, to discriminate and conjoin those qualities of existential material that serve as distinguishing traits (inclusively and exclusively) of a determinate kind. The distinguishing traits that were once taken to describe the kind *metals* were peculiar lustre, opacity, malleability, high density and tenacity. The traits were observable qualities produced by the ordinary operations of the body, seeing, touching, etc., conjoined with activities of craftsmen in manipulating things for the ends of use and enjoyment. Valuable as the consequences of these activities were for strictly practical purposes, they failed to guide inquiry as inquiry. They gave no aid in searching for other metals than those ordinarily in use (then some seven in all);

they gave no aid in linking metals with non-metals in a common system of inferential conclusions; they did not even ensure accurate discrimination of a metal from an alloy. The net consequence was that, even from the standpoint of practical use, the art of metallurgy was restricted within narrow bounds.

The transition to the present scientific conception of being metallic and the determination of the traits by which the kind metals, and its subkinds (more than sixty) are described was brought about when the point of view changed. It changed from consequences connected with direct use and enjoyment to consequences brought about by *interactions of things with one another* human intervention consisting of the experimental operations that institute these interactions. The result was that immediate sensible qualities lost the significance previously given them as distinguishing traits. For example, an important element in the present definition of being metallic is "affinity" or capacity for interaction with certain non-metallic substances, especially oxygen, sulphur and chlorine, together with the capacity of oxides thus produced to interact as bases with acids to form salts. Another element is high positive electric capacity. It is obvious that such traits could never have been extracted as were lustre and opacity from immediate sensible qualities, or as tenacity and malleability were from operations executed by artisans. The traits are such as to promote (1) determination of previously unrecognized metals (2) accurate discrimination of subkinds; and, (3) above all, to relate inferences made about metals to inferences about all chemical changes in that extensive system which constitutes chemical science.

The illustration has been developed in some detail because it illustrates so clearly both the distinction and the relation of (1) definition and description; of (2) categories and kinds; of (3) characters and characteristics. In these distinctions, the first term in each of the three pairs refers to a possible operation of the nature of an interaction while the second refers to the existential consequences of the actual *execution* of the operation. As distinctions, they are inherently related. The relation is that of operations as procedural means to existential conditions as consequences. "*If metallic, then* certain specified characters; *if* iron, sodium, tungsten

. . . *then* certain additional differential consequences." The definition thus forms a rule for the performance of (1) an experimental operation and (2) for guiding further operations of discrimination. The latter are selective of special qualities as inclusive and exclusive evidential signs of subkinds within an inclusive kind.

The illustration up to this point has put its emphasis upon the dependence of propositions about kinds upon the definition provided by universal hypothetical propositions. Were the actual historical development of the latter in the progress of physico-chemical inquiry followed out, the conjugate role played by existential propositions of kinds in testing and revising previous universal conceptions would be equally evident. The later conceptions of being metallic, being iron, etc., did not appear out of the blue. They were *suggested* by conclusions as to matters-of-fact already obtained. The conversion of the suggestion into a proposition prescribed further operations, which yielded new matters-of-fact, and hence new ideas in the continuum of inquiry, until, on one side, the present conceptions and definitions were arrived at, and on the other side, the present set of differential descriptions and kinds. In short, the relation between the two forms of the universal and the generic is functional: it is exactly similar in logical status and function to the relation between the logical subject and predicate of final judgment.

The distinction of forms that has been discussed is, then, that between propositions facilitating and regulating *inference* and those constituting reasoning as ordered *discourse*. The movement from one existential proposition to another through inference depends, as we have seen, upon non-existential universal propositions as an instrumental intermediary—a consideration which demands that there be scrupulous attention to formation of the universal propositions employed in discourse. But the movement of inference cannot be identified with that of rational discourse without radical doctrinal confusion. Nor can either one of the two logical movements be identified with the *application* of the universal proposition to existential material. No amount of reasoning can do more than develop a universal proposition; it cannot, of itself, determine matters-of-fact. Only operational application can effect the latter determination. On the other hand, existential data cannot of themselves *prove* a universal. They can *suggest* it. But proof is effected by (1) the formulation of the idea suggested in a hypothetical proposition, and (2) by the transformation of data into a unified situation through execution of the operations presented by the hypothetical as a rule of action.

The condition to be satisfied in reasoning or discourse is constituted by the *implicatory* relation. Problems of discourse have to do with ascertainment of rigorous and productive implications. Inference, on the other hand, is conditioned upon an existential connection which may be called *involvement*. The problems of inference have to do with discovery of *what* conditions are involved with one another and *how* they are involved.[3] A person engaged in a business undertaking is involved *with* others *in* the conditions of the situation in which the undertaking is to be carried out. In a criminal conspiracy one person is involved *with* his accomplices *in* certain activities and consequences. But the scope of involvement is not confined to personal cases. An increase in the supply of gold involves, usually, a decrease in its price and an increase in the price of other commodities. The sudden and excessive rise of the customary level of a river is involved *in* heavy rain storms and involves *with* its occurrence perils to life and property, impassable roads, etc. An outbreak of bubonic plague involves a rise *in* death-rate *with*, perhaps, a campaign to exterminate rats. There is no need to multiply instances. Every case of the causal relation rests upon some involvement of existential conditions *with* one another in a joint interaction. The entire principle of functional correlations of changes rests upon involvements, as when, in the case of many substances, increase of heat is ground for an inference to their expansion; or when the volume of gases is said to be a function of pressure and heat. The essential consideration is that the relation is a strictly existential one, ultimately a matter of the brute structure of things.

Reasoning and calculation are necessary *instruments* for determining definite involvements. But the relations of terms and

---

[3] I owe the word "involvement" and explicit recognition of its logical import as the conjugate counterpart of *implication* to Dr. Percy Hughes. See his article, "Involvement and Implication," *Philosophical Review*, Vol. XLVII, (1938), pp. 267–274. He was kind enough to show me the manuscript in advance of publication.

propositions within reasoning and calculation (discourse) is implicatory and non-existential while description of kinds is a matter of involvement. Because the universal hypothetical propositions which constitute ordered discourse arise from analyses of single meanings or conceptions, their constituents sustain a necessary relation to each other. But propositions about objects and traits which are involved *with* one another *in* some interaction have reference to the contingencies of existence and hence are of some order of probability. Therefore, an indispensable factor of inquiry is determination of the order of probability presented in any given case. The traits or characteristics which describe a kind are taken to go together in existence. The ground of their selection is logical but the ground of their going together is existential. The ground is that, as a matter of existence, they do go together or are existentially so conjoined that when one varies the other varies. When no reason *why* they should go together is seen (such as forms the content of a universal hypothetical proposition), the ground for selection of a given conjunction may properly be called "empirical." In the degree in which the selection of a conjunction is determined by the operational application of a universal proposition (and this proposition in turn is one of a system of universal propositions which have been severally tested in experimental application) the probability of the validity of a given existential proposition is of a high order. But it never attains the status of inherent *logical* necessity. It remains a brute fact, even after a law has indicated why and how a proposition about the brute fact is fruitful in promotion and control of inquiry.

On the basis of the distinction and relation of existential involvement and logical implication, the point already made about the conjugate connection of generic and universal propositions may be illustrated as follows: One who is convicted of being an accomplice in a crime is so involved *with* the principals as to be involved *in* the consequences of the crime. But the involvement in, say, the penal consequences, results only because of the *definitions* of "crime," "principal" and "accomplice" instituted in a given legal system of conceptions. These definitions are categories set forth in *if-then* propositions. By application of these categories, the presence or absence of the conjunction of traits which indicates that a given action is of a kind involving specified consequences is decided. On the other hand, it is clear that the definitions and categories in question did not emerge from the blue, but were evolved and explicitly formulated in terms of conditions set by the need of dealing with actual cases of human action. As another example, one may scribble his name on a piece of paper and no legal consequences follow. But under conditions which are determined by an abstract definition, he may be held liable for payment of a given sum when he signs his name. Finally, the legal definitions and conceptions are evolved and are modified with respect to their function in regulation of situations which existentially arise in the field of human relationships. Effectiveness in regulation of human conduct is their final criterion of validity.

The functional correspondence, or conjugate relationship, of involvement and implication, kinds and categories, characteristics and characters, generic and universal propositions, signifies, to sum up, that they represent cooperative divisions of function in the inquiry which transforms a problematic situation into a resolved and unified one. The internecine logical war between empiricists of the type of Mill and the school of rationalism will continue as long as adherents of the one school and of the other fail to recognize the strictly intermediate and functional nature of the two forms of propositions as cooperative phases of inquiry. But the needed recognition cannot be effected until the field of logic is taken to be as broad as that of controlled inquiry. The relations of terms and propositions in discourse is such as to make possible purely formal statements—purely formal in the sense that it is the very nature of ordered discourse to deal with possibilities in abstraction from existential material. But any theory of "pure" logic which assumes that forms of discourse necessarily constitute the total subject-matter of logic is arbitrary. Fundamentally, it makes the personal interest which actuates a particular logician or group of logicians the criterion for logical subject-matter. In addition, it fails to provide the logical ground for discourse and its forms, and to provide a rational explanation of their applicability to existence, which remains a matter of a mysterious preestablished harmony between the possible—which is not efficacious—and the actual.

Part Three

PROPOSITIONS AND TERMS

CHAPTER XV

GENERAL THEORY OF PROPOSITIONS

JUDGMENT HAS been analyzed to show that it is a continuous process of resolving an indeterminate, unsettled situation into a determinately unified one, through operations which transform subject-matter originally given. Judgment, in distinction from propositions which are singular, plural, generic and universal, is *individual*, since it is concerned with unique qualitative situations. Comparison-contrast is, upon this position, the fundamental operation by which re-determination of prior situations is effected; "comparison" being a name for all the processes which institute cumulative continuity of subject-matter in the ongoing course of inquiry. Comparison-contrast has been shown to be involved in affirmation-negation, in measurement, whether qualitative or numerical, in description-narration, and in general propositions of the two forms, generic and universal. Moreover, it is a complex of operations by which existential conjunctions and eliminations, in conjugate connection with each other are effected—not a "mental" affair.

Propositions are logically distinct from judgment, and yet are the necessary logical instrumentalities of reaching final warranted determination or judgment. Only by means of symbolization (the peculiar differentia of propositions) can direct action be deferred until inquiry into conditions and procedures has been instituted. The overt activity, when it finally occurs, is, accordingly, intelligent instead of blind. Propositions as such are, consequently, provisional, intermediate and instrumental. Since their subject-matter concerns two kinds of means, material and procedural, they are of two main categories: (1) Existential, referring directly to actual conditions as determined by experimental observation, and (2) ideational or conceptual, consisting of interrelated meanings, which are non-existential in content in *direct* reference but which are applicable to existence through the operations they represent as possibilities. In constituting respectively material and procedural means, the two types of propositions are conjugate, or functionally correspondent. They form the fundamental divisions of labor in inquiry.

A contemporary movement in logical theory, known as logical positivism, eschews the use of "propositions" and "terms," substituting "sentences" and "words." The change is welcome in as far as it fixes attention upon the symbolic structure and content of propositions. For such recognition emancipates logical theory from bondage to preconceived ontological and metaphysical beliefs, permitting the theory to proceed autonomously in terms of the contents and functions of propositions as they actually present themselves to analysis. In emphasizing the symbolic element, it brings propositions into connection with language generically; and language, while *about* things directly or indirectly, is acknowledged to be of another dimension than that which it is about. Moreover, formulation of logical subject-matter in terms of symbols tends to free theory from dependence upon an alleged subjective realm of "sensations" and "ideas" set over against a realm of objects. For symbols and language are objective events in human experience.

A minor objection to the use of "sentences" and "words" to designate what have been called propositions and terms, is that unless carefully interpreted it narrows unduly the scope of symbols and language, since it is not customary to treat gestures and diagrams (maps, blueprints, etc.) as words or sentences. However, this difficulty may be guarded against. A more serious objection is that without careful statement, the new terminology does not discriminate between language that is adapted to the purposes of communication (what Locke called "civil" language) and language that is determined solely by prior inquiries related to the purposes of inquiry—the latter alone being logical in import. This serious difficulty cannot be overcome by considering sentences and words in isolation, for the distinction depends upon an intent which can be adjudged only by means of context.

In so far as it is not determined in a given case whether the intent is communication of something already known, or is use of what is already taken as known as means of inquiry into the as yet unknown and problematic, fallacies in logical theory are bound to arise. Take, for example, the matter of subject-predicate. The *grammatical* subject is the subject-matter that is taken to be common, agreed upon, "understood" as between the communicator and the one communicated to. The grammatical predicate is that which is taken to be in the knowledge or thought of the one giving information or advice, but not in the knowledge or thought of the receiver. Suppose the sentence to be "The dog is lost." The meaning of "the dog" is, or is supposed to be, common for all parties; that of "is lost" to be in possession of the speaker, and while relevant to the experience and beliefs of the hearer, not previously known by him.

Now if the logical theory of the subject-predicate is taken over from grammatical structure, it is likely, in fact, practically certain, to be concluded that the material of the logical subject is something already completely given independently of inquiry and of the need of inquiry, so that only the characterizations provided in predication have logically to be taken into account. Indeed, it is not too much to surmise that the direct movement from grammatical to logical structure had much to do with the Aristotelian formulation of the logical subject-predication relation. It led, on the one hand, to the theory that the ultimate subject is always some ontological substance and, on the other hand, to the classic theory of predicables. Again, it may not be too much to surmise that the doctrine, which has been criticized, regarding the immediately given character of the subject-content of propositions is an inheritance from the translation of grammatical into logical form, carried out under the influence of an uncriticized psychology of sensory-qualities as something immediately presented.

An even more serious objection is that logical positivism as usually formulated is so under the influence of logical formalism, derived from analysis of mathematics, as to make an over-sharp distinction between matter and form, under the captions of "meaning of words" and "syntactical relations." Now there is no question that logical theory must distinguish between form and matter. But the necessity for the distinction does not decide whether they are or are not independent of each other:—Whether they are or are not, for example, intrinsically related to each other in logical subject-matter and distinguishable only in theoretical analysis. While sentences or language invite making a distinction between the meanings of the words constituting its vocabulary and syntactical arrangements, this fact but poses in a new way the old fundamental problem of the relation, or absence of relation, between matter and form, or meanings and syntax. A tacit or explicit assumption that the distinction proves the independence of matter and form, identifying the logical simply with the latter, only begs the fundamental point at issue.

Ultimately, in spite of the nominal rejection of all "metaphysical" principles and assumptions, the idea that there is a sharp distinction, if not a separation, between form and matter, rests on a special purely metaphysical tradition. The admittedly formal character of mathematics does not prove the separation of form and matter; it rather poses that problem in a fundamental way. A more direct objection along the same line is that the identification of the logical with syntactical form is obliged to assume, as given, the distinctions between nouns, verbs, adjectives, prepositions and connectives, etc. No attempt has been made, and I do not see how one can successfully be made, to determine what words have the distinctive force postulated in the above classification (are nouns, verbs, etc.) without taking account of their meaning, which is a matter of material content.

It would be absurd, of course, to hold that the separation just mentioned is inherently involved in the substitution of "words" and "sentences" for "terms" and "propositions." But the fact that in the present state of logical theory the substitution *is* associated with the notion of this separation affords a reason for using the older terminology. This reason is linguistically reinforced by the fact, already mentioned, that the word "sentence" as ordinarily used expresses the close of inquiry rather than its initiation or continuing execution. The word "proposition," on the other hand, at least suggests something proposed, propounded for further consideration, and thereby something entering integrally into the continuum of inquiry.

The basic issue regarding the logic of propositions concerns the intrinsic conflict between the theory that holds to the intermediate and functional status of propositions in institution of final judgment, and the theories, traditional or contemporary, which isolate propositions from their contextual position and function in determination of final judgment. According to one variety of the latter position, judgment alone is logical and propositions are but linguistic expressions of them—a position which is consonant with the idea that logic is the theory of thought as mental. Another variety holds that since judgment is a mental attitude taken towards propositions, the latter alone are logical in nature. Sharp as is the opposition between these views, both of them hold that judgment—and "thought" generally—is mental. Both of them stand, accordingly, in opposition to the position here taken, which is that inquiry is concerned with objective transformations of objective subject-matter; that such inquiry defines the only sense in which "thought" is relevant to logic; and that propositions are products of provisional appraisals, evaluations, of existences and of conceptions as means of institution of final judgment which is objective resolution of a problematic situation. Accordingly, propositions are symbolizations, while symbolization is neither an external garb nor yet something complete and final in itself.

The view most current at the present time is probably that which regards propositions as the unitary material of logical theory. Propositions upon this view have their defining property in the property of formal truth-falsity. According to the position here taken, propositions are to be differentiated and identified on the ground of the function of their contents as *means*, procedural and material, further distinctions of forms of propositions being instituted on the ground of the special ways in which their respective characteristic subject-matters function as means. The latter point is the main theme of this chapter. But at this point it is pertinent to note that, since means as such are neither true nor false, truth-falsity is *not* a property of propositions. Means are either effective or ineffective; pertinent or irrelevant; wasteful or economical, the criterion for the difference being found in the consequences with which they are connected as means. On this basis, special propositions are *valid* (strong, effective) or *invalid* (weak, inadequate); loose or rigorous, etc.

Validity-invalidity is thus to be distinguished not only from truth-falsity but from formal correctness. Any given proposition is such that it promotes or retards the institution of final resolution. It cannot be logically adjudged, therefore, *merely* on the basis of its formal relations to other propositions. The syllogism "All satellites are made of green cheese; the moon is a satellite; therefore, it is made of green cheese" is formally correct. The propositions involved are, however, *invalid*, not just because they are "materially false," but because instead of promoting inquiry they would, if taken and used, retard and mislead it.[1]

The basic division of propositions has been said to rest upon their functional place in judgment. I return to this point. Grounded judgment depends upon the institution of facts which (1) locate and circumscribe the problem set by an indeterminate situation and which (2) provide the evidence which tests solutions that are suggested and proposed. Such propositions determine one of the two main divisions of propositions, those of subject-contents. But grounded judgment also depends upon meanings or conceptual structures which (1) represent possible solutions of the problem in hand, and which (2) prescribe operations which, when performed, yield new data tending in the direction of a determinate existential situation. These are propositions of predicate-contents—the other main division.

The subject-matter or content of the first main division of propositions consists of observed data or facts. They are termed *material* means. As such they are potentialities which, in interaction with other existential conditions produce, under the influence of an experimental operation, the ordered set of conditions which constitute a resolved situation. Objective interaction is the overt means by which the actualized situation is brought into existence. What was potential at a given time may be actualized at some later time by sheer change of circumstantial conditions, without intervention of any operation which has logical or intellectual intent, as when water freezes because of a specified change in temperature. But in inquiry a *deliberate* operation intervenes; first, to select the conditions that are operative, and secondly, to

---

[1] These remarks are not supposed to cover the whole ground of the relation of form and matter. That topic receives more extended consideration later.

institute the new conditions which interact with old ones. Both operations are so calculated that as close an approach as possible may be made to determining the exact *kind* of interaction, inclusively and exclusively, necessary to produce a determinate set of consequences. The *relation* between interacting conditions and actualized consequences is general, and is functionally formal, because it is freed from reference to any *particular* space-time actualization.

Potentialities are to be distinguished from abstract *possibilities*. The former are existential "powers" that are actualized under given conditions of existential interaction. Possibility, on the other hand, is a matter of an operation as such—it is operability. It is existentially actualized only when the operation is performed not with or upon symbols but upon existences. A strictly *possible* operation constitutes an idea or conception. Execution of the operation upon symbolized ideational material does not produce the consequences constituting resolution of tension. It produces them, as indicated in the previous paragraph, only by operationally introducing conditions that institute a determinate kind of interaction. The idea of taking a drink of water, for example, leads to actual drinking only because it institutes a change in prior conditions—if only by pouring from a pitcher or turning a spigot to bring water into connection with a new set of conditions. From these preliminary general statements discussion proceeds to consideration of the different kinds of propositions which are the sub-classes of the two main kinds just described.

I. EXISTENTIAL PROPOSITIONS

1. *Particular Propositions.* Propositions of the kind called particular represent the most rudimentary form of propositions of *subject*-content. They are propositions which qualify a singular, *this*, by a quality proceeding from an operation performed by means of a sense organ—for example, "This is sour, or soft, or red, etc." The word *"is"* in such instances as these has existential force not that of the timeless (because strictly logical) copula. "This is sour" means either that the actual performance of an operation of tasting has produced that quality in immediately experienced existence, or that it is predicted that if a certain operation is per-

formed it will produce a sour quality. "This is soft" means that *it* yields easily to pressure and will not cause most other things to yield when applied to them. When it is said of *this* "It is bright," an actual consequence of physical interaction with light is indicated. In short, the proposition is particular not because it applies to a singular but because the qualification is of *something taking place at a definite here and now*, or is of an immediate change. In the strictly particular proposition there is no ground for intimating that the *this* in question will remain sour, sticky, red, bright or whatever. "Is" is a verb of the strictly temporal present tense; or, if it is an anticipation of what will happen, it refers to an equally transitory local time in the future.

When the above propositions are called, as they sometimes are, *Propositions of Sense Perception*, there is confusion of the causal conditions under which the particular quality occurs with the logical form of the quality. For practical purposes it is highly important to know the causal conditions under which anything becomes hard, sour, or blue. Without this knowledge there are no means of controlling the occurrence of such qualities. But the *logical* import of a "particular" is determined by the strictly limited local and temporal occurrence of the quality in question. Hence such propositions represent the first stage in *determination of a problem;* they supply a datum which, when combined with other data, *may* indicate what sort of a problem the situation presents and thereby provide an item of evidence pointing to and testing a proposed solution. There are, however, instances in which the same *linguistic* expression has the force of a *singular* proposition—a form next discussed. In a given context of inquiry, "This is sweet" may not mean that some particular change is occurring which needs to be taken into account in formulating a problem. For in a special context, it may mark the resolution of some problem, as for example, a problem in which discovery of something which will sweeten something else is the object sought for. When a linguistic form is separated from the contextual matter of problem-inquiry it is impossible to decide of what *logical* form it is the expression.

2. *Singular Propositions.* Singular propositions are such as determine *this* to be one of a kind. Take the two possible meanings

of "This is sweet." When the proposition is particular, it indicates, as has been said, an immediate change that has occurred or is about to occur. The same expression when it presents the solution of a problem, means that "this" is one of the kind of sweet things: or that *this* has the potentialities which are properties of *any* sweet thing. The sweet quality is no longer simply a change which has occurred; it is a sign of a conjoined set of consequences that will occur when certain interactions take place. Take for example the propositions "He is cruel," or "He is kind." The qualification represented by "cruel" or "kind" marks a *disposition* to act in a certain way, not limited to a change occurring at a given time; what occurs at the time is being taken as evidence of the permanent traits which describe a kind. If the expression were phrased to read "He is a cruel *person*," the presence of traits describing a kind would be obvious.

Such propositions as "This is an elm tree," or "This is sugar, is granite, is a meteorite, etc.," unambiguously identify and demarcate a singular as one of a kind. It is not necessary here to repeat what has been said about the force of the conception or category of *kind* in promotion of grounded inferential conclusions. It may be necessary to point out that when an adjective, like "benevolent," "mammalian," has the same logical force as a common noun, there is postulated the existence of other qualifying characteristics in conjunction with the one explicitly stated. When it is said, "*This* is iron," *iron* clearly refers to traits not now immediately present, but which as potential consequences stand in conjunction with the immediately present quality of color or touch. Similarly, the *difference* between the propositions "He is (now and here) acting kindly" and "He is kind," is constituted by the fact that the latter involves inference from the immediate datum of change stated in the former to a set of traits not then and there observable.

The singular proposition thus takes us back to what was said in the previous chapter regarding the continuum of judgment. The propositions "This has vitreous lustre; cannot be scratched by a knife; scratches glass; is not fused by a blowpipe; breaks with conchoidal fractures" are propositions which, taken separately, set forth special modes of change. Applied concurrently and cumulatively to *this* they yield the set of conjoined traits describing the kind *quartz*. (1) *A* change is not merely noted as a brute fact, but the conditions are noted under which it occurs. (2) These changes are found to be so *involved* with one another that, in spite of variations in the circumstances in which they present themselves, the presence of one is a valid sign that the others will present themselves *if* specified interactions occur. Similarly, the proposition "This turns litmus paper red," *of and by itself*, records simply an isolated observation. In the course of cumulative progressive inquiries yielding other propositions about *this*, the proposition "*This* is an acid," (i.e., is one of a specified kind) is warranted. We are thus enabled to make definite the logical differences between quality, characteristic trait, and property which have previously been noted. "Turning paper red," is, as the object of a particular observation, a *quality*. As enabling reasonably safe inference to be made as to the occurrence of other qualities under certain conditions, it is a distinguishing trait or *characteristic* descriptive of a kind. It becomes a *property* when it is determined by negative as well as positive instances to be a constant dependable sign of other conjoined characteristics. It then *belongs* inherently to all cases of the kind.

Propositions of the class under consideration are often termed, in contemporary logical texts, propositions of *membership* in a kind. Membership, however, implies an articulation which is not involved. Propositions that "This is of specified kind," constitute "this" a *case* or representative of a kind, a specimen, rather than a member.[2] In one direction, determination of a singular as one of a kind involves a limitation of the singularity of *this*. It is no longer taken in its full qualitative existence, but is reduced to a characteristic which promotes identification and demarcation of it as *of* a kind. In another direction, namely, that of the range of grounded inferences that may be drawn, the limitation is conjugate with widening. Ordinary linguistic form is here, as in so many other instances, not a safe guide. "Paul was a Roman citizen," may merely state a particular historic fact, but in the context in which it was once uttered it signified that he was a representative of a *kind* of citizenship which carried with it certain rights. A mere

---

[2] The bearing of this distinction upon the concept of *extension* is considered below: See Chap. XVIII.

succession of particulars cannot, therefore, determine that an existence is one of a kind. The particular changes that occur must have *representative* capacity. This fact is fatal to the assumption often made that a quality like *red* and *hard*, is inherently general or universal. It becomes such in cumulative inference in the continuum of inquiry; that is, when determined to be capable of application to an indefinite number of singulars not actually present. In and of itself it is particular to the point of uniqueness.

Reference has been repeatedly made to contextual "conditions" as necessarily required for determination of the conceptions of characteristics, potentiality, and inference. The specific nature of these conditions is usually "understood" or taken for granted. Even in scientific inquiry and inference they are never completely stated. For a complete statement is impossible since it would have to exhaust practically everything. *Standardized* conditions are postulated, and are explicitly stated because, and as far as, they have *differential* effect. There are certain organic conditions under which sugar will not taste sweet and certain material conditions under which it will not sweeten another material. Only in special cases, is it necessary to state the conditions which cause consequences to be other than those normally postulated. For example, it is not safe to infer that a thing is sticky because it is sweet. But when differential conditions are adequately stated it is safe to infer that "This sweet thing is of the class of sticky things." Postulation, implicit or explicit, of the environing conditions that are required in a given case is equivalent to standardization of that set of conditions.[3]

3. *Propositions of Relationship of Kinds, or Generic Propositions.* It is now generally recognized that the proposition "Athenians are Greeks" is of different logical form from "Socrates is (was) an Athenian," and "This is iron" is of a different logical form from "Iron is a metal." The second proposition in each of the above pairs includes a lesser kind in a more extensive kind, as a species in a genus, while the first one of the pairs does not *include* the singular in a class or kind. In them the kind, described

---

[3] I owe to Dr. Nagel the observation that when formal symbols are employed to express this type of propositions, it is necessary to have a symbol standing for the postulated standardized conditions.

by means of specified traits, serves to identify and demarcate the singular, so that from directly observed characteristics other *characteristics*, not then observed or observable, may be inferred under given conditions. The membership of a kind in another kind not only extends enormously the number of characteristics that are inferable, but, what is even more important, it orders observed and inferred traits in a system. From the proposition "Roses are monocotyledonous angiosperms," it can be inferred that any object which is a rose has two seed leaves; that the parts of its flowers are not arranged by threes; that its leaves have reticulate venation, etc. And the wide range of inference is based upon general principles and not *simply* upon special observations.

This extension of the range of inference is then more than a fact of great practical importance, although it is that. It has definite logical import. For it reacts to determine the ground upon which conjoined characteristics are employed to describe *any* one of the kinds in question. It is not enough to select traits which permit inference within the limits of the specific kind directly involved. The traits must be selected and ordered so that as far as possible there will be a series of kinds each included in another until the most inclusive kind is reached. Not only are barriers to special inference broken down, but the extension of the range of inference depends upon formation of kinds in *systematic* relation to one another. Such systematization is one of the chief differences between common sense and scientific kinds. It is this systematic serial relationship which renders the category of *membership* or inclusion applicable to included kinds and not to the case in which a singular is simply identified and demarcated as one of a kind. The proposition of a relation of kinds thus provides the logical ground of the singular proposition. For in the proposition of the form "This is one of a kind," there is *implicitly* postulated that there are other kinds related to the one specified. For characteristics which suffice to ground the reference of *this* to a kind must be such as to demarcate it from other kinds. The adequate grounding of such a proposition demands, accordingly, that related but excluded kinds be determinately established. This condition is satisfied when (1) an inclusive kind is determined, and (2) when the differentia are ascertained which exclusively mark out included kinds from one another:—in other words, a set of conjoined affirmations-negations.[4]

Otherwise, the characteristics which are used to describe a kind may be such as either to overlap (and thereby the reference of the object or objects in question to *another* kind is possible) or else the characteristics taken are insufficient to justify reference to the kind specified: that is, they are too wide or too narrow. For example, when bats were assigned to the kind, *birds*, and whales to the kind, *fishes*, the characteristics of flying and swimming respectively were both too broad (inclusive) and too narrow (exclusive) to warrant the reference that was made. Only when coordinate kinds are determined, together with their differentia, and their subordination to (inclusion in) a more extensive kind, are logical conditions satisfied, and only then can inference proceed warrantably in the case of singular propositions.

The consideration that propositions of one of a kind and of a relation of kinds are related to inference is equivalent to surrender of the old system of rigid taxonomy; i.e., "classificatory" systems. As long as kinds were supposed to be ontological species marked off in nature, rigid taxonomic classification was inevitable. The substitution for such schemes of flexible relational kingdoms, orders, families, species, varieties, etc., in zoology and biology, was equivalent to determination of the relation of kinds on the ground of relationship to regulated systematic inference. The immediate effect of destruction of the idea of fixed natural species was, however, logically disintegrative. For it led to the idea, which still obtains in traditional empiristic logical theory, that all division into related kinds is *merely* a matter of practical convenience without intrinsic logical meaning. However, the discovery of progressive derivation, through differentiation under environing conditions, from a common ancestor, institutes an objective basis. In comparison with the theory of fixed species it marks restoration of an objective status of classification but upon a different basis. Externally, the difference is marked by the substitution of belief in "the origin of species" for the assumption of fixed natural kinds. The logical equivalent of this change is a working postulate—

[4] See Chap. X pp. 183–4, 197–8 and, below, the discussion of conjunctive-disjunctive functions, Chap. XVIII.

viz., that the arrangement of singulars in the classes which promote and control extensive inference, is that of genetic derivation or descent, where differentiation into kinds is conjoined with differentiations of environing conditions. On this basis, reptiles, for example, are found to be more nearly akin to birds than to toads and salamanders, with which they were originally classified. This change to a genetic principle of classification is identical, logically, with the shift from antecedents to consequences as the ground upon which to institute the conjunction of characteristics which describe kinds. It conforms to the emphasis placed upon interaction of conditions.

At this point, it is well to revert to the basic difference between generic propositions and universal propositions. It is not necessary here to repeat in detail what has been said about the ambiguity of "all" as sometimes having existential reference, in which case it represents an inference having at best a high order of probability, and sometimes having non-existential reference, when it stands for a necessary relation which follows, by definition, from analysis of a conception.[5] It is, however, in place to say something here about the contrast of the present logical interpretation and the traditional theory which holds that all propositions, except relational ones, are either classificatory or attributive, according as they are taken, at will, in "extension" or "intension." The contrast goes back to the fact that the position of the text affirms that all existential propositions are concerned with determination of *changes;* specifically of those changes which effect the transformation of an indeterminate unsettled situation into a determinate unified existential situation. Initial particular propositions, as we saw, are concerned with particular changes determined for the purpose of locating the *problem* set by a doubtful situation. These changes are linguistically expressed by verbs of action such as tastes, touches, hears, breaks, hits, runs, loves, moves, grows, stays,

---

[5] It would not, however, be hard to show that texts which recognize and explicitly state this ambiguity nevertheless tend to carry over the kind of generality marking the subject-matter of non-existential propositions to the subject-matter of existential generalizations. In this case they treat the probability property of the latter as a failure in logical status, since genuine logical form is defined on the basis of that necessity which is the property of rational discourse or the inter-relations of conceptions. Induction then becomes a logical scandal, since it is practically necessary and theoretically illegitimate.

etc., and then by adjectives which indicate the consequences of the change effected by the action expressed by a true verb. In the form in which a relation of kinds is determined, the changes in question become modes of *interaction*. The traditional interpretation of the classificatory nature of propositions rests upon ignoring connection with change. There is substituted for change a relation designated by *is* in the sense of a logical (non-existential) copula. "John runs," (expressing change) then becomes "John is a runner." "John runs," even when it takes the form "John *is* running," refers to some definite time and place; "is" in "is running" is a verb of action having tense and spatial reference; he is running *now and here*. "John is a runner," in the traditional interpretation, subordinates the singular, *John*, to a kind. It would hardly be a valid proposition unless John was by profession one who engaged in the sport of racing or at least showed a disposition to run on every suitable occasion.

Take again the proposition "John gives an apple to James." He does it at a certain time and place. The proposition marks an existential change then and there going on. The change may never have taken place before and may never occur again. But the proposition is often translated into the following: "John is a donor of an apple to James." The change is not merely verbal. It marks a shift in logical form. The relation of *donor and donee* is generic, and hence free from limitation to a *specified* time and place. Taken literally, the proposition in its translated form indicates that John makes a business of giving apples to James or at least that he is disposed to do so. Suppose, for example, we take the proposition "John Smith made a will in favor of George Jones." This is an act (change) which takes place at a given time and place. There must be witnesses, observers, of its occurrence. The relation between testator and legatee is, however, generic. Statement of the special act in terms of the relation brings the former within a system of legally defined categories whose application determines differential consequences. Apart from being one of the kind which is determined by legal categories, the special act could not be described as making a will. It would still be something which occurred at a given time and place, but might not be differentiated from scribbling one's name on a piece of paper.

In contrast with propositions just discussed, propositions affirming a relation of kinds such that one kind is included along with others in an extensive kind *are*, truistically, "classificatory." But it is a serious logical confusion to extend this classificatory character to singular propositions in intension as well as extension, when, truistically, they are supposed to be *attributive*. For logical confusion of forms occurs when it is concluded from the attributive character of the characteristics which determine a relation of kinds that "sweet" in the proposition "*This* is sweet," is attributive. Sweet is in no sense necessarily an *attribute* of "this." It may mark simply a *particular* change that has occurred, is now occurring, or that will occur at some particular time-place. So far, there is a restatement in other language of a point already made. We come to an additional point of logical importance when it is noted that the interpretation of all propositions in terms of classification or attribution (and of extension and intension) obscures their intermediary and functional nature.

The proposition "Iron is a metal" certainly means that the kind designated "iron" falls within the kind designated "metals." Or, stated attributively, it certainly means that the interrelation of characters by which being *metallic* is defined applies also to the interrelation of characters by which being *iron* is defined. But in whichever of the two ways the proposition is read, the proposition is instrumental to inference. And the sole logical ground for discrimination of the logical form thus presented from that of propositions such as "*This* is iron," resides in the kind of inference promoted. When an artisan determines "*This* is iron" he can infer what consequences will ensue if he treats it in a certain way: for example, that if he heats it, it will become soft enough to work. But the propositions "Iron is a metal" and "if anything is metallic it is a chemical element" are, as pointed out, grounds for inference of a different order.

4. *Contingent Conditional Propositions.* There is a type of propositions which are linguistically hypothetical and which nevertheless refer to singulars. The proposition "If this drought continues the harvest will be very poor" and "If that is dropped, an explosion will probably follow" refer to existential changes which are taken to be involved with one another. The same thing holds

of such a proposition as "If the rain continues, the scheduled ball game will be postponed." Such propositions exemplify a very common type of proposition. They are marked by the words "*If-then.*" But, as was remarked in an earlier chapter, in such cases there is postulated an existential connection between existential conditions in which the terms "antecedent" and "consequent" have literal or existential meaning. The drought, the bomb, are now in existence; if something happens (designated by "continues" and "dropped"), then certain physical results will follow in the temporal sense of *follow*. The connection is contingent and the propositions are of some order of probability. They are, moreover, preparatory. They are of the nature of advice or warning with respect to getting ready for future probable occurrences. "Get ready for a shortage of grain"; "Don't drop that thing unless you want an explosion to result"; "Don't take a trip to the ball park until you are sure about the weather." They are marked off from abstract universal hypotheticals in form, since they have specific spatio-temporal reference.

Logically speaking, such propositions are means of determining a *problem*. Take propositions of wider import, such as "If the *Phaedo* is historical, Socrates believed in the immortality of the soul," and "If the dialogue is dialectical, it does not necessarily follow that Socrates personally was committed to that belief." [6] The propositions decide nothing. But they indicate a problem. How far is Plato, in his dialogues in general and in this dialogue in particular, purporting to recount actual conversations that took place at definite dates and places? How far is he using the figure of Socrates to develop certain conceptions of his own? The propositions thus direct inquiry into channels where evidence for the solution of this problem may, it is hoped, be found. Both problem and solution, if the latter be found, are existential in reference. [7]

5. *Matter-of-fact or Contingent Disjunctive Propositions.* The necessity for determination, through negation and exclusion, of the

[6] The first of these propositions is taken from Joseph, *An Introduction to Logic*, p. 185.
[7] The difference in logical form from universal *if-then* propositions indicates the necessity for differential symbols when formal symbols are employed. "If *A*, then *B*" is wholly indeterminate in this respect.

characteristics that describe other kinds included along with the given kind in question in an including kind, has been pointed out. Observance of this condition generates existential disjunctive propositions. That "Iron is a metal" is not a proposition grounded *simply* by discovery that it possesses certain characteristics also found in tin, copper, lead, mercury, zinc, etc., for it is not grounded until the distinguishing characteristics which *exclusively* differentiate iron as a kind from those that describe other metals have been determined. Otherwise, iron might conceivably be an alloy like brass or bronze, since without exclusive or negative propositions not all the conditions are satisfied which are imposed by the definition of being a metal;—for example, that of being a chemical element. That a kind is *warrantably* included in another kind is thus dependent in logical ideal upon the formation of a set of exhaustive disjunctive propositions, such as "Metals are either . . . or . . . or . . . or . . , and these kinds are *all* the kinds of metals there are."

The dots (. . .) in the last sentence are meant to suggest that such disjunctive propositions are materially conditioned and hence are contingent, since there can be no guarantee that the formal condition of exhaustiveness is satisfied. The spectroscope has widened the area of observation. But until everything in all universes and galaxies has been analytically observed there is no assurance that the list of metals is complete. And even if this condition were fulfilled, it would still be a matter of fact, not of theory, that the disjunction is exhaustive. Only on the ground of theory which would prove that the existence of other metals is logically impossible, because involving contradictions, would the disjunctives be otherwise than contingent.

II. UNIVERSAL PROPOSITIONS

1. *Hypothetical Propositions.* The organic condition of predication is a mode of action, native or acquired, as in the case of a habit. A mode of active response, when it is inhibited from overt manifestation and expressed in a symbol, is a *suggested* meaning presenting a *possible* way of solving a problem. It retains its kinship with its organic source in standing for a way of active response, a way of dealing with existing conditions. It passes from

the status of suggestion to that of idea (in its logical sense) only as it is developed in relations to other symbols; that is, only as its meaning is developed in relation with other meanings. The first stage in this process is explicit formulation of the suggested meaning: its conversion into a proposition. The propositional form expands the idea into a relation of meanings. This expansion is not effected by conjoining or annexing an additional meaning to the original suggestion while leaving the latter unchanged. It consists of analysis of that which was first suggested. In an indeterminate situation, certain observed data suggest the presence of a man at a distance who is beckoning. If some other meaning were then merely added on, the effect would be that meanings would be accepted as they occur. This is the road that leads to phantasy. Inquiry or critical examination, such as is required to transform what is suggested into a logical idea or a meaning, must of necessity be applied to the constitution or structure of the suggested meaning: such a statement is truistic. The inquiry resolves it into related terms: *If* a man, *then* certain other things which are inherent constituents of *being* a man: that is, conversion of a conception into a definition.[8]

As soon as a meaning is treated *as* a meaning, it becomes a member of a system of meanings. This statement is implied in the remark of the previous paragraph that a meaning must be developed in relation with other meanings. This development constitutes reasoning or rational discourse—where discourse is a matter of sequential implications rather than communication of something already possessed. A universal proposition, in other words, has meaning as a member of a system not in isolation. The relation of implication is an expression of this fact, so that the development of an expanded meaning or hypothetic universal in terms of implied propositions, is the determination of *what* that meaning is. The emergence of contradictions, as in *reductio ad absurdum*, is proof that the original meaning was not what it was

[8] Among other things, this formulation is a safeguard against a current notion that the relation of antecedent and consequent is that of implication. Implication holds between propositions, not between constituents. The necessary relation obtaining between "antecedent" and "consequent" in the universal hypothetical is an expression of the fact that there is but one and the same meaning involved, the "antecedent" and "consequent" being taken to be its constituent parts. If the "taking" is correct the relation is (truistically or tautologically) *necessary*.

taken to be. The logical difference between universal and particular propositions is sharply marked at this point. The latter are determinations of the data that set the *problem* to be dealt with. Different particulars, independent in their material content, are connected with one another in that they all have the same function—that of logically determining a problem. In the earlier illustration, the determination "This is quartz" occurs through a cumulative series of materially independent operations of observation such as "This has vitreous lustre; it scratches glass but it is not scratched by a knife, etc." The force of these propositions is cumulatively evidential only in the degree in which their contents are *materially* independent, having no content in common with one another save "this." Exactly the opposite is the case with universal propositions. In the latter a break in community of meaning is a break in rigor of reasoning.

It has previously been shown that universal propositions are formulations of *possible* operations. As long as the operations are not executed, the subject-matter of such propositions is therefore abstract or non-existential. Take the proposition "Only if men are free, are they justly blamed." Neither the existence of freedom nor of just blame is affirmed. While it may be said that the existence of men is *postulated*, it is not implied nor is it expressly affirmed. The relation affirmed between freedom and just blame, if it is valid at all, will still be valid if all human beings are wiped out of existence. Freedom, justice and blame designate abstract characters. Nevertheless, the proposition formulates possible operations which, if actually performed, are *applied* to the actual conduct of men so as to direct observations into the conditions and consequences of actual cases of blame. Apart from such application, the proposition represents merely an abstract possibility depending upon a definition of freedom and justice which, as far as existence is concerned, might very well be arbitrary. The proposition may hence be countered by the contrary propositions "Only if men's actions are causally conditioned, can blame be effective, and only if it is effective is it justifiable."

Save as the two propositions are employed to direct operations of inquiry to systematic observation of the facts of human conduct (with respect to the conditions and consequences of blame) is there any ground for deciding in favor of one of these abstract possibilities rather than the other. Reasoning or dialectic (leaving the subject of mathematics for later discussion) thus has ultimately the function of directing operations of observation to the determination of the existential data which test proposed possible solutions, contrary propositions being (as we have seen) *means* of delimiting the field of inquiry.[9]

An even more crucial instance is provided by hypothetical universals contrary to fact such as are constantly employed in science, as for example the proposition "If bodies interact without friction, then . . ." or "If a body moves upon impact of one body only without being affected by other bodies, then. . . ." The value of such propositions is proved by their constant use in scientific calculations. Upon any other theory than that of the ultimate connection of hypothetical universals with conduct of observational experimental operations in inquiry, the proved utility of propositions contrary to fact presents an insoluble paradox. The attempt has been made to resolve the paradox by saying that while the propositions in question do not affirm anything of existence, they "ascribe to reality a character which is the *ground* of the connection stated in the hypothetical judgment." Regarding this mode of interpretation, it has been pertinently asked "How can there be the ground in the real universal of something which nevertheless does not exist?"[10] The seeming paradox completely disappears when it is seen that such propositions do not intend or purport to have reference to existence but to be relevant to *inquiry into existence*—a very different matter.

There is indeed something of the nature of contrary-to-factness in all definitions. For they are ideal as well as ideational. Like ideals, they are not intended to be themselves realized but are meant to direct our course to realization of potentialities in existent

---

[9] The formation of alternatives which are contrary to one another, as in the above instance, is required in order to conduct observations that yield negations or eliminations, while if negative propositions are neglected the final proposition is subject to the fallacy of affirming an antecedent because the consequent is affirmed. Dialectical reasoning, *provided* it proceeds disjunctively, can and should clarify the conceptions involved. But only systematic observation of cases of blame can decide which of two contrary abstract propositions in the disjunction can be converted into a valid proposition.

[10] Joseph, *Op. cit.,* p. 185.

conditions—potentialities which would escape notice were it not for the guidance which an ideal, or a definition, provides. We may not think the better of the mathematical circle because it cannot be matched by figures that exist, nor worse of actual figures because none of them possesses the roundness defined in the mathematical conception. To sanctify the ideal and to disparage the actual because it never copies the ideal, are two connected ways of missing the point of the *function* of ideal and actual. A vision is not a scene but it can enable us to construct scenes which would not exist without it. To suppose that a vision is worthless unless it can be directly determined to be a scene is for those who take the idea seriously, the high road to pessimism, and for others the road to fantasy. To ignore or depreciate the ideal because it cannot be literally translated into existence is to acquiesce not only to things "as they are"—as is sometimes said—but also to things "as they are not" because all things that *are* have potentialities.

Without retraversing ground already gone over, it may be pointed out that linguistic form, apart from content does not determine whether a sentence is logically about existential relationships or about abstract possibilities. Thus, "if grain is scarce, it is dear," may mean that in all known cases there is a conjunction of the characteristics of scant crops with high prices (both characteristics referring to actual occurrences), or it may mean that there is a necessary relation between the abstract characters *scarcity* and *dearness*. The ease with which the two forms of logical force are identified is explicable upon the basis of the conjugate relation or functional correspondence already mentioned. Unless it can be shown as matter of *theory* that there is an inherent relation between scarcity and dearness, the observed conjunction between small crops of grain and high prices may be circumstantial and coincidental. Stated from the other side, uniformity of an observed conjunction instigates search for the *reason* of the conjunction, which, when found, is stated in a proposition of relationship of abstract characters, in this instance, scarcity and dearness.

The conjugate relation of universal and generic propositions thus serves to explain an ambiguity in the meaning of *empirical*, and to throw light upon the logical relation of the empirical and the rational. In one sense, the more comprehensive one, *empirical* is identical with being proved (by means of controlled observational operations) to be existential. In this sense it is opposed to the *merely* ideational and *merely* theoretical. In a more restricted sense, *empirical* means that the subject-matter of a given proposition which has existential reference, represents merely a set of uniform conjunctions of traits repeatedly observed to exist, without an understanding of *why* the conjunction occurs; without a theory which states its *rationale*. In the latter sense only, is there opposition between the empirical and the rational. When the opposition exists, it sets a problem for further inquiry. It is a sign that propositions already formed do not satisfy the conditions which must be met in order to ground final judgment. Logical theories which fail to note the relativity of propositions to the given stage of inquiry attained, erect the distinction of empirical and rational into a rigid difference in the ontological natures of their respective subject-matters. The falsity of this interpretation is shown in the fact that observed uniformity of conjunction of traits is in every scientific case a stimulus to the formation of conceptions (expressed in hypothetical propositions) which indicate a reason for the observed uniformity of conjunction. On the other hand, the suggested reason is but an abstract possibility until its formulation, through the intermediary of experimental operations has produced existential consequences. These operations are conducted from a point of view different from those which yielded the previously observed conjunctions, since they are conducted to vary the conditions under which previous uniformities were observed. Hence, even when consequences reached agree with the phenomena previously observed, the probability that the conjunction is inherent and not merely circumstantial is greatly increased, since the new consequences are produced under conditions of conceptual experimental control. The clinching evidence is provided to the degree in which, by elimination or production of negative cases, other abstract possibilities are ruled out.[11]

2. *Disjunctive Universal Propositions.* Disjunctive form, in the case of universal propositions, is not to be identified with disjunc-

---

[11] It is hardly necessary to point out that there is an ambiguity in the words *rational* and *theoretical* which is the counterpart of that attending *empirical*.

tion in the case of generic propositions. The propositions that triangles are equilateral, scalene or isosceles is not of the same form as the proposition that metals are either tin, zinc, iron, mercury. . . . The difference is related with the ambiguity in "*included*" and "*including*" which has already been noted. Singular items are comprised in a *collection*. Singular objects indefinite in number, such that each and every one, having specified characteristics is one of a *class* (in the botanical and zoological sense of class) form or constitute the class of which they are *of*. To say that they are contained or included in it is but a back-handed way of saying they *constitute* it. They are certainly not contained existentially as pennies are contained in a box or cows enclosed in a field, nor are they contained as kinds are logically contained in a more extensive kind. To affirm that Mr. Franklin D. Roosevelt is "included" in the class of Presidents of the United States is only an awkward way of saying that he is one of the Presidents, past, present, and future, who make up the collection. For ultimately any class (as kind) is composed of an indefinite number of singulars.

A kind is properly said to be contained in another wider kind whenever the characteristics which describe the wider kind are a conjoined part of the set of characteristics which describe every included kind, and are also such as to enable, through a series of negative and disjunctive propositions, all included species to be exclusively demarcated from one another. The contrast with inclusion of singulars in a collection is seen in the absurdity of the notion that the conception of the "presidential" kind will enable different Presidents to be discriminated from one another. The relation of kinds to an inclusive kind and of included kinds to one another is suitably expressed by the traditional scheme of circles, the relation of the including genus to other genera being expressed by circles which lie entirely outside its boundaries. The sense in which "inclusion" applies to definitions and conceptions determines a different logical form. It cannot be symbolized by circles but may be symbolized appropriately by brackets or parentheses. Suppose it is a question of the definition of wealth in political economy. What shall be "included" in the conception? Shall wealth be defined in terms of utility as satisfaction of desire or as forwarding of purpose; or as exemption from "labor" in the sense of cost and sacrifice? Or, as power to command other commodities and services? There is here no question of kinds. But the conception or definition adopted will, when applied existentially, decide what things fall within and what without the kinds of things that are wealth. Similarly, *existential* figures may be classified as *kinds* of plane figures or of triangles. But, mathematically, "triangle" means triangularity, an abstract universal or category. As has been repeatedly stated, there are not three kinds of triangles but three modes of *being* triangular. Hence in the case of what is "included" in an idea or definition, any division of *being* such-and-such, if it is valid at all, is necessarily exhaustive, while in the case of kinds it is contingent. In the case of universals, to "include" means to be an integral part of an operative rule, which when applied determines what falls within the domain of operation. To exclude means to rule out, to debar; being a principle for determining inadmissability in the abstract. Exhaustiveness of disjunctions is, thus, a necessary character of abstract propositions. They must form an interrelated system.

III. RELATIONAL PROPOSITIONS

Logical theorists who retain as much of the Aristotelian logic as possible (although in a purely formalistic interpretation) criticise that logic because it recognizes only the subject-predicate form. They have shown the importance of relational propositions and of a logic of relatives. Relational propositions, like *if-then* propositions are, however, of two forms that must be distinguished. "This (town) is south of that"; "that table is farther away than this stand"; "*the* book you want is to the right of where you are looking," are relational. But they are singular and of existential reference. The word "is" in these propositions is the temporal verb, not the non-temporal logical copula. The relation is one of a spatio-temporal fact. Yesterday the table and stand and the books in question may have been differently situated with respect to that which is nearer or to the right of; they may be differently placed tomorrow. While the relative position of towns is not so readily shifted, there is nothing logically necessary in their present space-relationship. This principle holds of all singular relational propositions. For example, in the proposition "George is heavier (taller, darker, etc.) than James," *heavier* means weighing more; *taller* means subtending more space in a vertical direction. "Is" is not the logical copula for like all verbs of action it expresses a mode of action or interaction at a given time, just as *north-south, right-left* have to do with directions of *movement*. Logically speaking, there is no difference between the form of such propositions and the form of such propositions as "This is (growing, becoming) warm, red, soft, bright." They are *particular* propositions.

In other words (and this is the important consideration), all particular propositions are *relational*. They do not have a subject-predicate form save grammatically. "This is red" means, when it is analyzed from a logical point of view, that an object has changed from what it was, or is now changing into something else. It expresses a temporo-spatial connection as truly as do those which are relational in obvious grammatical form. Propositions of *one of a kind* are also relational. Their reference is not to a particular change taking place, but (as was shown earlier) to dispositions or potentialities of change. "This is iron" means that *this*, under specifiable conditions, will interact in certain ways and produce certain consequences. Only *grammatically* is "this" a subject and "iron" a predicate. Its relational character is seen in the fact that what is expressed can be put in the passive voice "Certain specified consequences will be produced by *"this"* under certain conditions." The grammatical form can be changed without changing the sense, just as "James strikes John" is completely equivalent to "John is struck by James."

Propositions about a *relation of kinds* are also relational, having no logical subject-predicate form. When it is said that "Iron is a metal" the proposition does not appear to be relational because we cannot convert it simply into "metal is iron." But the proposition as it stands is not logically a complete proposition. It does not indicate or even suggest its own grounds. At most it is either a sentence communicating information or is a proposition preliminary to further inquiries. The complete proposition is "Iron is a metal possessed of such-and-such differential characteristics." Any metal having these specified properties is iron, so that the proposition is logically, not verbally, a proposition regarding a *relation* of kinds.

The relational character of universal hypothetical propositions is also obscured by the fact that as they are reached and formulated they are often not completely determinate. In consequence, affirming the "consequent" is not a ground for affirming the "antecedent" nor denying the latter a ground for denying the former. Obviously, certain conditions necessary for complete logical reciprocity and equivalence are lacking. But this lack is not due to the *form* of the universal hypothetical; it marks a failure of its contents to satisfy logical conditions. The strictly formal character of such propositions (that is, their complete satisfaction of logical demands) is found when the proposition is so fully grounded that "only" is a proper qualifier. When the proposition is "Only if . . . then. . . ." the proposition is seen to be strictly relational.

This part of the discussion may be concluded by reverting to the distinction between contingent conditional and universal (necessary) hypothetical propositions. Take the proposition "If A is to the right of B and B to the right of C and C to the right of D, then D is to the left of A." If A, B, C and D are singulars, the proposition may be invalid. It is invalid, for example, if A, B, C and D are persons or chairs placed around a table. If, however, the proposition is understood to mean "Given a straight *linear* arrangement, then the relations are such that anything symbolized by D is to the left of whatever is symbolized by A," the proposition is in effect a definition of a specified form of space relationship and as such is necessary. A, B, C, D now stand not for singulars but for abstract characters.

The special import for logical theory of the present chapter is that the various forms of propositions discussed are shown to mark stages of progress in the conduct of inquiry. Current theory is given to taking the various forms of propositions as given ready-made, so that all theory has to do is to fix the appropriate labels on them; *particular, general, hypothetical,* etc. When they are considered functionally, as they have been considered in this chapter, (and throughout this work) it clearly appears that *particular* propositions function as instruments for determining the problem involved in an indeterminate situation, while the other forms listed represent stages in attainment of the logical means for solution of the problem. Only if propositions are related to each other as phases in the divisions of labor in the conduct of inquiry, can they be members of a coherent logical system. When their distinctive roles in the institution of final judgment is omitted from theoretical interpretation, it just happens that there appear to be a number of independent isolated propositional forms. A final point is that while the findings of this chapter regarding the relational character of *all* propositions were not developed in order to support the doctrine that all propositional forms are instrumental to judgment (which alone has subject-predicate form), nevertheless the findings are just what would be anticipated on the ground of the general theory advanced regarding propositions and judgment.

CHAPTER XVI

PROPOSITIONS ORDERED IN SETS AND SERIES

INQUIRY IS progressive and cumulative. Propositions are the instruments by which provisional conclusions of preparatory inquiries are summed up, recorded and retained for subsequent uses. In this way they function as effective means, material and procedural, in the conduct of inquiry, till the latter institutes subject-matter so unified in significance as to be warrantably assertible. It follows (1) that there is no such thing as an isolated proposition; or, positively stated, that propositions stand in ordered relations to one another; and (2) that there are two main types of such order, one referring to the factual or existential material which determines the final subject of judgment, the other referring to the ideational material, the conceptual meanings, which determine the predicate of final judgment. In the words of ordinary use, there are the propositions having the relation which constitutes *inference,* and the propositions having the serial relation which constitutes reasoning or *discourse.*

The following discussion is concerned, in respect to both types, with the logical order of propositions rather than with the temporal order of propositions in carrying on a given inquiry. In an inquiry of any high degree of difficulty many propositions are entertained during its course only to be discarded or modified in subsequent inquiry. For they are not propositions which *substantiate* the final conclusion even though in a given investigation an inquirer would not have reached that conclusion unless he had at one time entertained them. The order with which we are concerned is of the sort that can be instituted only *after* an inquirer has reached a valid conclusion and surveys the grounds upon which it is taken to be justified. The propositions in question are such, in other words, as are usually termed *premises* of a conclusion,

311

subject to the condition that there is no fixed limit to their number. This negative proviso is made because the theory of the syllogism reduces premises to two, called the major and minor. It will be shown later that the conception of but two premises, one universal and the other singular or generic, represents the logical structure of judgment as a union (copulation) of propositions of predicate and subject contents. The doctrine of a duality of premises thus provides an analysis of the logical conditions to be satisfied by a conclusion, rather than a statement of the premises upon which a conclusion actually rests. There is, I repeat, no fixed limitation upon the number of premises involved in substantiation of a conclusion.

1. *Dyadic and Polyadic Propositions.* If no proposition is a proposition in isolation, it follows that the related terms of a given proposition are ultimately determined by reference to the related terms of other propositions. This consideration applies to the number of terms in a given proposition as well as to its contents. Recent logical theory has paid much attention to the number of terms, distinguishing dyadic propositions, such as "Justice is a virtue"; triadic propositions, such as "The point M is the middle point between A and B"; tetradic propositions, such as "European nations owe the United States N dollars on account of war loans"; etc. Current theory, however, tends to take propositions as complete in isolation; hence, the current classification is made on linguistic rather than logical grounds. From a logical point of view, there are but two divisions, dyadic and polyadic. Propositions of predicate contents, or universal propositions, have but two terms, those of a definition and hypothesis. Propositions about factual data which serve as subject-content of judgment are, on the other hand, polyadic. Linguistically, there may be only two terms. But logically any existence has to be determined with respect to date and place. For example, "This is further away than that," "James is taller than John," express a relation between two-terms as far as words are concerned. But these propositions are not necessarily valid but hold of conditions at a particular time and locality. The first proposition, for example, obviously means further away from the speaker, hearer, or some specified object, thus involving a third term. Something of the same sort holds of

the proposition "A is the husband of B." A date is postulated if not expressed, since "is" here has a temporal present tense, not an intrinsic logical relation. Any proposition having direct existential reference applies to conditions or circumstances. "This is red" not always and necessarily, but under specifiable conditions. "Socrates is mortal" is not two-termed, because it means Socrates is (was) a human being living at some specific time and place, who died under specific temporal-spatial circumstances. However, there is no need to multiply instances.

On the other hand, "Man is mortal," is strictly dyadic, when it means "If anything is human, then it is mortal," for both terms are abstract and the relation affirmed is of abstract nonexistential character. The proposition states a relation between conceptual contents. The Newtonian formula for gravitation is equally two-termed, for it expresses a universal *if-then* relation between *being* material and *being* reciprocally "attracted" in a specified way. Regarding propositions of predicate contents, it is also needless to multiply examples. For they are (1) independent of space-time reference, and (2) state a necessary relation between antecedent and consequent. No matter how linguistically complex the formulation may be, no matter how many clauses and phrases are involved, the clauses and phrases belong to one or another of the two characters that are affirmed to be intrinsically related together. A mathematical equation or statement of a mathematical function may contain many symbols but they all fall on one side or the other of the function which is formulated.

2. *Equivalence of Propositions.* So far the discussion has dealt with logical properties belonging to both of the main types of propositional forms. I come now to a character which belongs only to propositions of conceptual or predicational contents, a character which marks them off from matter-of-fact propositions. When a problematic situation is present, some meaning is *suggested* as a possible mode of solution. Unless this meaning is formulated propositionally, it is at once accepted and inquiry ceases. The conclusion reached is then premature and ungrounded. But the meaning suggested is also a member of some constellation of meanings. Hence, it is not enough to formulate it in a separate proposition. The meaning has to be developed

in terms of a set of other propositions which formulate other meanings that are also members of the system to which it belongs. In a word there is reasoning, argument, or ratiocination: *Discourse*. Furthermore, the development of related propositions in discourse has *direction*. For it is regulated by the nature of the *problem* in which a meaning is to function as a manner or method of solution. Apart from reference to the use or application to be made of the meaning, a given proposition can be related to other propositions in the system of meanings to which it belongs in an indefinite or indeterminate variety of ways. But in any given discourse a meaning, propositionally formulated, is developed in that specially related series of propositions which have direction towards a proposition applicable in the stated conditions of the special problem in hand. Direction is such an obvious property of all reasoning and relevant discourse that it would be superfluous to note explicitly its presence were it not for its bearing upon the logical problem under discussion.

There are two logical conditions which ordered discourse must satisfy. The order of propositions must be *rigorous* and *productive*—a proposition in which "and" has other than enumerative force. The order must be productively rigorous and rigorously productive. To say that the order must be rigorous is to say that each proposition following from the initial one—"initial" in a logical but not temporal sense—must be equivalent in logical *force* to that which preceded it; otherwise it follows *after* but not *from*. The phrase "in logical force" is emphasized because of the equivocal meaning attaching to "tautology" in current logical theory. The principle of equivalence is not identical with that of tautology unless tautology is given a special meaning—a meaning which does not preclude but rather satisfies the condition of productivity. The *conceptions* or meanings found in subsequent propositions in the order of rational discourse are identical with those of antecedent propositions in operational force not in *content* and hence lead rigorously to meanings having *another* content. It is this difference of content that constitutes productivity in reasoning. The principle of *direction* is applicable at this point. What is demanded is a formulation of the meaning set forth in abstract universal form in the initial proposition *such that* it operatively leads to a proposition existentially applicable in a way in which the content of the initial proposition was not applicable. Satisfaction of the condition of rigor does *not* mean tautology in the sense that the dyadic terms of the initial abstract universal propositions are repeated in *linguistic* forms that are synonymous.

For example, in the proposition "An electric current is equal to the potential difference divided by the resistance," the term *potential divided by resistance* does not have the same immediate denotative or existential reference as "electric current." But the equivalence of conceptual contents affirmed in the proposition enables a *subsequent* proposition to be stated about something which is in turn equivalent to "potential divided by resistance," and so on. The term *current* does not appear in the proposition following it, and *potential divided by resistance* is replaced in the proposition which follows *it* by a relation between it and something else which is its equivalent. And so on until a proposition appears in a form operationally applicable in an experimental situation which yields material indispensable to the solution of the problem in hand, or at least to an improved statement of what the problem is. The conceptions of currents, of differences in the conductivity and resistance of metals, and of differences in the strength of currents, are ideas that must have arisen at a comparatively early time. They certainly arose long before the law mentioned above was arrived at. The statement of a determinate ratio or relation between previously independent conceptions was in effect a new way of conceiving *all* of them. It was, moreover, a way of conceiving them which enabled generalized relations to be followed out in a rigorous way. Equivalence is thus capacity for *substitution* of meanings in the series of propositions which constitute reasoning. There is, therefore, nothing miraculous in the fact that "deduction" yields propositions having contents which are other than that of those from which they were derived. For the propositions employed in demonstrative discourse or deduction are themselves framed with express reference to performance of this function. The trick of science, so to speak, does not consist in its dialectic or reasoning aspect, though here, too, sagacity is demanded save in all cases so familiar that calculation becomes mechanical. The chief difficulty and the chief insight in overcoming the difficulty consists in the formulation of related meanings such that equivalent propositions are progressively and productively (and yet rigorously) substitutable in development of propositions in series.

The conjugate relation already noted between propositions of abstract or ideational contents and matter-of-fact propositions arises from the fact that the subject-matter of a hypothesis is first suggested by the original problem and is then tested and revised on the ground of its consequences. The guiding criterion is the power of these consequences to promote solution of the problem in hand. The requirement set by continuity of inquiry is satisfied to the degree in which the range of substitutibility is enlarged. When equivalences are established only within a limited frame of existential reference, say, of problems of heat, or of mechanical changes (changes described in terms of motions spatially and temporally formulated) in isolation from each other, the domain of productive reasoning is in so far restricted, even though it is much wider than that of common sense. When hypotheses are formed so comprehensively in scope that they are applicable to the facts of temperature, electricity, light and mechanical motion, the degree of freedom enjoyed in the institution of equivalences, and therefore in reasoning, is enormously increased. Special "systems" then become members of a comprehensive system. Because of the conjugate relation of propositions of this form to matter-of-fact observational propositions the range of *inference* is correspondingly widened.

What has been said is directly applicable to the conception of indemonstrable propositions as the original ground of all rational demonstration. It is certainly true that in every instance of reasoning there is an initial proposition, not derived or "deduced" in that particular discourse, since to say that it is initial is the same as saying that it does not follow from predecessors. But (1) there is nothing inconsistent in its being initial in *that* set of propositions with its being a successor or final proposition in some other series. The continuity of inquiry involves, on the contrary, that conclusions in one problem or set of problems become starting points of discourse in dealing with new problems. The very conception of a system (alluded to in the previous paragraph) and of a system of sub-systems means just this sort of prepared possibilities of cross-reference, reciprocal borrowing and lending between different instances of reasoning. (2) The initial proposition is a hypothetical universal taken and used for the sake of what it will lead to. It is tested and retested *as* a hypothesis by its productive capacity in the institution of other universal propositions, while it is *finally* tested by the existential consequences of its application to matter-of-fact conditions. Its proof lies in these consequences, as the proof of a pudding is in the eating. When propositions are produced which contradict either an initial or a successor proposition, a new problem is set. In such cases it is usually found that the predecessor proposition in the series can be so modified as to meet the requirements of rigor only by meanings arising from new experimental operations.

It follows from what has been said that rigor-productivity are logical conditions which universal propositions in series have to satisfy; they are not, primarily, *properties* of any given series. They are rather limiting ideals which state the *intent* of any proposition of predicative content. They are not premises—save in logical theory itself—but are leading principles. The deliberate attempt to satisfy the formal conditions prescribed by rigor-productivity in abstraction from material subject-matter constitutes mathematics. This statement does not mean there is some domain marked off in advance to which mathematical propositions and reasoning apply. The meaning is the contrary: the regulated attempt to satisfy these conditions *is* mathematics.[1]

3. *Independence and Cumulative Force in Matter-of-Fact Propositions:* Propositions which determine the subject-content of final judgment are ordered by a different principle. One does not follow from another in the sense of being implied, or directly substitutable in logical force. On the contrary, the force of each such proposition is measured, first, by its having an *independent* subject-matter which is determined by an independent experimental operation; and, secondly, by its conjunction with other propositions about independent subject-matters by which *cumulative* convergence may be reached. Existential propositions are

---

[1] There is much in common between the account of the text and James' exposition of skipped intermediaries. See his *Psychology*, Vol. II, 645–51.

ordered because they are controlled by reference to the same problematic situation, and in so far as they promote its resolution. However, they do not form a series, but a set. In reasoning, serial propositions may be likened to the arrangement of the rungs of a ladder. Propositions about factual data, which serve to provide the evidence which grounds inference, are more like lines that intersect one another and which, in intersecting, describe a configurate area. In series of the ladder type sequential order is essential. With respect to propositions which determine evidential properties, ordinal position is not important. The logical order of the series (as distinct from the historical order of operations by which relevant and weighty data are secured) is constituted by the relations of inclusion (affirmation) and exclusion (negation, elimination) which define comparison. Operations of experimental observation (1) narrow the field of relevant evidential material and (2) effect intersections that converge towards a unified signifying force and hence to a unified conclusion.

For example, a physician in his diagnosis executes independent operations which yield a variety of independent data, regarding temperature, heart-beat, respiration, kidney excretions, state of the blood, metabolism, history of patient, perhaps his heredity, etc. These independent explorations are carried on as long as the significance of the data obtained by them remains obscure—that is, as long as they cumulatively fail to point in a determinate direction. What is usually called *correlation of data* is a matter of convergence in significance, of cumulative evidential force. Taken separately, such propositions have indicative force as to the nature of the problem and its possible solution. As they converge, they have probative force. Indicative force, when it is determined by elimination of alternative possible modes of solution, becomes *signifying* force. The conjugate connection of factual and conceptual propositions has the effect of enabling the conceptions already in hand (a matter depending upon the state of theory and the systematization of conceptions at the time), to determine the operations by means of which new, independent explorations are made and their results interpreted.

It is a familiar logical principle that affirmation of the consequent does not warrant complete affirmation of the antecedent. Denial of the consequent grounds, however, denial of the antecedent. When, therefore, operations yield data which contradict a deduced consequence, elimination of one alternative possibility is effected. Recurrent agreement of the indicative force of data, provided they are secured by independent experimental operations, gives cumulative weight to the affirmation of an antecedent whenever we can affirm the consequent. The affirmation of any given hypothesis proceeds in this way. But the possibility of the fallacy of affirming the antecedent still remains. Elimination of other possibilities progressively reduces the likelihood of fallacious inference. But there is never assurance that *all* alternative possibilities have been exhausted, because there is no assurance that the disjunction of alternatives is exhaustive. Hence *probability* is the mark of every proposition effected by inference from the set of matter-of-fact propositions, just as necessity—or rigor—is the mark of the non-existential proposition instituted through demonstrative discourse. Hence, exhaustiveness is not a *property* of any actual disjunctive set, but is a logical condition to be satisfied.

Comparison, as we saw, is a mode of measurement. It is determinate in the degree that measurement results in numerical statements. Measurement is possible because observed phenomena are enduring and extensive. The techniques of measurement translate endurance and spread, which are purely qualitative in immediate experience, into spatial-temporal relations, numerically formulated. It is of course a basic property of numbers that relations of equivalence can be instituted between them. In the actual practice of science, it is the agreement of numerical measurements of observed phenomena with those theoretically deduced from a hypothetical proposition which has the maximum of probative force. Qualitative endurances and extensive spreads run into one another. The existential conditions of any existence are indefinitely circumstantial. Otherwise stated, there can be no absolute guarantee that the selection of the phenomena which are numerically determined effects only those discriminations that are necessary to yield probative data. Hence precision of measurement and agreement of its results with deduced conclusions, is, as far as final evidential significance is concerned, subject to a condition which cannot be completely or absolutely controlled: namely, the validity of the original selective discrimination of the subject-matter of observation.[2]

Even were it possible to find a piece of gold that is *pure* gold, that is gold and nothing but gold, it could not be completely isolated from interactive connection with an indefinite variety of circumstantial conditions. A high degree of control of conditions is effected by the scientific techniques now available. But there always remains the *theoretical* possibility that *some* conditions which affect the observed phenomenon have not been brought under control. The postulate of a closed existential system is thus a limiting ideal for experimental inquiry. It is a logical ideal which points the direction in which inquiry must move but which cannot be completely attained. Hence, the statistical character of all factual generalizations is not a matter of defective techniques (although defective technique represents a failure to observe the conditions imposed by the logical condition to be satisfied), but is a matter of the intrinsic nature of the existential material dealt with.

The assumption that qualities literally recur (or are universals) is a fallacy (as was earlier noted) arising from confusing the constancy of evidential function—a product of continued inquiry—with immediate existential qualities. No quality as such occurs twice. What recurs is the constancy of the evidential force of existences which, as occurrences, are unique. When it is held that there is strict or implicatory necessity in the series of propositions "John is taller than James, James than William, and, therefore, John is taller than William"; it is overlooked that *tall* is a quality subject to change, by change in conditions. Practically speaking, no one would doubt that in *some* cases the conclusion is valid. But if we take the case of three things of approximately the same length, it is obvious that during the operation of measurement one of them may change its quality of length in spite of all efforts to maintain constant conditions. Hence, in *theory* the inference is of a certain order of probability, not necessary. The proposition "*If A* is longer than *B*, and *if B* is longer than *C, then A* is longer than *C*" is necessary when and since its contents are

---

[2] This fact agrees with the indefinitely extensive character of the perceptual field, and is in so far a confirmation of what was said earlier. See, *ante*, pp. 66-7.

abstract, not when A, B and C are singulars. The proposition is necessary *as* a definition. But that John, James and William as existences actually satisfy the conditions imposed by the definition does not follow from the definition. The conception that propositions about the *existences* in question, have the implicatory "transitivity" characteristic of the terms of the universal proposition is a fallacy depending upon doctrinal confusion of the logical properties of non-existential and existential propositions. It requires independent experimental operations to determine whether connections between existences satisfy the conditions laid down in a universal hypothetical proposition. In some cases, there is, as was just said, no practical difficulty in the way of performing the required operations. But the validity of the resulting conclusion rests wholly upon involvements among observed facts, not upon a necessary implicatory relation. The latter prescribes the operation to be performed, but is not *identical* with the circumstantial connection of existences with one another.

4. *Transposition of Terms.* Every logical text states the rules according to which the terms of a proposition may be transposed without affecting the logical force of a proposition. When a sentence is taken in isolation and not as a member of a serial arrangement in reasoning or inference such changes are merely grammatical. But every *proposition* in the logical sense of the term is a member of an ordered set or series of propositions. Every such set and series is framed with reference to the function to be served by either its final member or by cumulative convergence in effecting final judgment. Certain arrangements of terms *within* a proposition are more effective than are other arrangements in carrying forward the needed progression to a terminal proposition or else in giving it the form that best indicates its force in the set of independent propositions. This accounts for the logical importance of the changes in position called conversion, obversion, obverted converse, inversion, contraposition and obverted converse. It follows that no initial existential proposition can be converted simply. No one would suppose that the logical force of "All crows are black" is identical with that of "Any black thing is a crow." The legitimate transposition is "A black thing *may be* a crow." Stated in this form, the proposition has a

new functional force. It indicates an investigation to be undertaken with a view to finding out whether *black* in *this* case is or is not conjoined with other traits which describe the kind *crows*. *Blackness* is in some actual cases a *suggestion* worth developing. Such propositions as "Iron is a metal" are ambiguous apart from context. The more obvious interpretation is that it refers to a relation of kinds. It might, however, mean that "If anything has the characters which define *being* iron, then it has the characters which define *being* metallic." In the latter interpretation it is, as we have said, universal. In either case, convertibility depends upon the completeness of terms related in the proposition in question. As the proposition cited stands, the term *metal* is wider than the term iron, so that simple conversion is not possible. Conversion would then again give the transposed form the force of *may*, and so be a step in further observational investigations. But if the relations of sub-kinds with the kind *metal* have their differential traits already determined, as of iron with respect to tin, zinc, copper, etc., then the proposition is convertible simply, though with an order of probability dependent upon the exhaustiveness of the disjunction involved. That is, "metal" limited by specified differential traits is iron just as iron is a metal.[3]

The exact relation of what is called immediate inference to transposition of terms is a somewhat ambiguous matter. In some cases they are synonymous. Such is not the case in immediate inference by added determinants and by subimplication. In any significant instances of the two latter processes, inference is *not*, however, immediate. The ordinary textbook illustrations of "added determinants" are trivial because their subject-matter is familiar and standardized. The significant cases are those in which determinants are added because a proposition as it stands is too broad (or too *general* in the sense in which *general* means *vague*). In this case, an independent proposition or propositions is (are) required in order to determine whether the limiting determinant has an equivalent force when applied to both terms of the vague proposition. In such cases there is mediation. An example of subimplication is the following: "The sum of three angles of a Euclidean triangle is two right angles." Hence "The sum of the

---

[3] CF. *ante*, pp. 308–9.

three angles of a *scalene* triangle is two right angles." Here the second form does follow by implication; it is called *sub*implication simply because the particular inquiry in hand happens to call for a specific limitation or narrowing in the movement toward a terminal proposition. When however, logical texts state that the relation of a verifying case, expressed in an existential proposition, to a universal proposition (theoretical law or hypothetical formula) is that of subimplication, there is a plain fallacy involved. No non-existential proposition implies an existential one.

5. *The Syllogism.* A syllogism is an analysis of final judgment into its logically constituent propositional conditions. As has been pointed out, these logical constituents are (1) a proposition regarding matters-of-fact and, (2) a proposition regarding a relation of abstract characters, or conceptual contents. The formulation of the matter-of-fact ground constitutes the minor premise; that of ideational and hypothetic content constitutes the major premise. The syllogism is thus a generalized formula for logical conditions that must be satisfied if final judgment is to be grounded. It is, so to speak, a warning that in order to warrant a final judgment a conjugate connection between observed data and a conception, defined in a universal *if-then* form, must be instituted. Supposing the conclusion has been reached that a bat is a bird— the explicit minor would be "The bat has wings." In order to ground the conclusion "A bat is a bird" it would be necessary to lay down a general proposition to the effect that "all winged creatures are avian" where *all* has the force of a relation of characters. To warrant the conclusion completely, it would be necessary to establish the proposition "Birds and only birds are winged." Statement of the predicate-content in a proposition as a major premise is a necessary check upon drawing a conclusion. It functions as a directive for observational inquiries whose consequences tend in the direction of an inclusive-exclusive proposition.

The above account does not agree with the traditional theory. For the latter theory identifies, as a rule, the syllogistic with the ratiocinative or deductive form. It thus (1) leaves no room for an existential proposition and (2) makes a fetich of the idea that there can be only two "premises" in a ratiocinative series, an idea negated by every form of mathematical reasoning. The idea that a minor *existential* proposition can be deduced from a universal proposition represents a confusion which has been repeatedly commented upon.   No matter whether the minor proposition is singular (one of a kind) or is generic (a relation of kinds), it has to be instituted by independent operations of experimental observation. When the syllogism is of the *A A A* form, the proposition which is the minor premise is a *generic* but not a universal proposition since it is existential in reference.   In any *actual* case it is therefore of a certain order of probability, i.e., an *I* proposition.   This fact shows that the syllogism of the form of *Barbara* cannot, when the minor premise has existential reference, be regarded as setting forth *properties* possessed by any actual inference.   When treated, however, as a formula setting forth the logical conditions to be ideally satisfied by an inferential conclusion, the case is different. The general character of the minor proposition is then a way of stating that, ideally, or in strict theory, there should be a strictly conjugate relationship between the definition set forth in the major and the matters-of-fact constituting the minor premise. The syllogism, thus construed, means that a conclusion is logically warranted, and is only so warranted, when the operations involved in discourse and in experimental observation of existences, converge to yield a completely resolved determinate situation.

Such an interpretation gives the syllogism logical importance and indispensability.   It involves, however, a marked revision of the Aristotelian theory of the syllogism.   For in Aristotle's logic, the major premise, or definition, was the statement of an essence which ontologically determines a species, while the minor premise affirmed that some species fell existentially within that wider species—or else was an actualization of the logical potentiality represented by a genus.   Here, as in other cases previously mentioned, the bare form has been retained in traditional logic after its ontological ground (of fixed species and essences) has been repudiated.   Hence it was exposed to Mill's criticism.   However, Mill retained the logical error of the traditional theory although in a reversed direction.   The traditional theory holds that major and minor are of the same logical form, failing to recognize that one is non-existential and the other existential; and that, therefore, they have to be instituted by operations which are as different as are observation and rational discourse. Mill's theory makes the same error, save that now both major and minor are treated as existential, so that instead of assimilating the form of the minor to that of the major (as the traditional theory does), Mill assimilated the form of the major to that of the minor. That is to say, Mill holds that the major or general proposition is a summary memorandum of an indefinite number of particular existential propositions.

It is not correct to say, as is sometimes done, that Mill held that the syllogism involves a *petitio principii*. What he affirmed was that *if* the major be taken to prove the conclusion, *then* the conclusion of the syllogism begs the question, since in that case the latter is already included in the major premise. He says the major provides the formula "according to which but not by which the conclusion is drawn." It is, he says, "an assertion of the existence of evidence sufficient to prove any conclusion of a given description." [4] *Proof* on this view is provided exclusively by the various particular observed cases which the general or major premise sums up. Not an iota to probative force is added, he says, by the general as such. That he assimilates the form of the major to that of the minor is not only involved in his whole treatment but is explicitly affirmed, as when he says "the mortality of John, Thomas, and others, is, after all, the whole evidence we have for the mortality of the Duke of Wellington"—or any other person who has not as yet died. [5]

Mill's interpretation would be sound *if* evidential force were a matter of *self*-evidence; that is, if no principle or universal were required to decide what is evidence and what is not and how weighty and relevant are specific data in any given case. As it is, he begs the question by assuming that particulars as such are already equipped with adequate evidential capacity. In the language we have already used, particulars *suggest* a certain idea (which *is* general) but they do not validly *signify*, much less prove it. The whole problem of inquiry, upon the observational side, is to determine what observed conditions *are* evidential data or are "the facts of the case." What has already been determined to *be* evi-

[4] *Logic*, Book II, Chap. 3, Sec. IV and Sec. VI.
[5] *Ibid.*, Sec. III.

dence has probative force; that statement is a mere truism, since evidence and probative force are synonyms. What Mill fails to see is that observations, in order to yield evidential material, have to be directed by ideas and that these ideas have to be made explicit—formulated in propositions, and that these propositions are of the *if-then* universal form. What Mill has in mind by "sufficiency" of evidence is simply the number of particulars at hand, not the *principle* by which the evidential force of any particular is determined.

Mill's sense for fact leads him, however, into a deviation from—indeed, into a contradiction of—his official doctrine. This deviation approximates, if it is not identical with, the interpretation of the syllogistic form which has been given. The official doctrine is that the general proposition is "an aggregate of particular truths." But he also states that "Truth can only be successfully pursued by drawing inferences from experiences which, *if warrantable* at all, admit of being generalized, and which, *to test their warrantableness*, require to be exhibited in generalized form," [6] Again, instead of treating the general proposition as a bundle of particulars as particulars, he says at times that it states the "coexistence of *attributes*"—that is of *characters*, and expressly adds that "coexistence" is *not* to be understood in a temporal sense but in the sense of the property "of both being jointly attributes." [7]

Mill also states that the general or major is reached by induction, and while his theory of induction is confused, it assuredly involves operations of analyzing the material of gross observations together with operations of elimination, and of determination of agreement in evidential function, while he is obliged to admit the importance of hypotheses although he gives them only a "subsidiary" place.

Traditional theory affords another instance of the ambiguity of *all*, since it rests upon taking *all* in both an existential and nonexistential sense. Supposing it is said "All whales are mammals: all mammals are warm-blooded, therefore all whales are warm-blooded." If the example is an exemplification of analysis of a logically grounded judgment, then the major is an *if-then* uni-

---

[6] *Ibid.*, Sec. IX; italics not in original text.
[7] *Ibid.*, Sec. IV, and footnote.

versal proposition, affirming that there is a necessary relation between *being* mammalian and *being* cetacean such that a negation
of the relation involves contradiction. The proposition, if valid
at all, is valid even if whales have ceased to exist. As an operational proposition, it directs observation to ascertain whether in
the case of existential singulars the traits of suckling young, producing them alive, etc., are found in conjunction with one another.
On the other hand, *all* in the proposition "All whales are mammals" may mean that so far as singular whales have been observed,
they have been found to be, without exception, mammalian. This
proposition means "Whales *may* be mammals" and indicates that
possibility so strongly as to instigate search for the *reason* why the
traits are conjoined—that is, it instigates search for a relation of
characters which will institute an *if-then* proposition. Until some
reason is instituted capable of this formulation final judgment is
not reached. Inquiry is still in the propositional stage in which
singulars are observed and hypotheses are formed and tried out.

Upon examination it will be found that the difficulties which
have been alleged to inhere in the syllogistic form arise from
identifying it with properties possessed by reasoning or of inference taken in separation from each other. They vanish when it
is seen that it does not purport to be the form of either inference
or rational discourse. It is the form of the conjugate connection
of the factual and conceptual subject-matters of judgment, stated
in such a way as to indicate the conceptual and observational conditions to be fulfilled if judgment is to be adequately grounded.
Interpreted in this way, the "utility" of the syllogistic form
resides in the fact that it serves as a check in the case of specific
judgments, holding up the logical conditions that are to be satisfied.
It represents a limiting ideal. Even though no actual judgment
really satisfies the ideal conditions, a perception of failure to do so
occasions and directs further inquiry upon both the observational
and the conceptual sides. It promotes and supports the continuum
of inquiry.

CHAPTER XVII

FORMAL FUNCTIONS AND CANONS

ACCORDING TO the doctrine developed in previous chapters, every term (meaning) is what it is in virtue of its membership in a proposition (its relation to another term), and every proposition in turn is what it is in virtue of its membership in either the set of ordered propositions that ground inference or in the series of propositions that constitute discourse. It follows from this position that the logical content and force of terms and propositions are ultimately determined by their place in the set of propositions found in either inference or discourse. *Order* is thus the fundamental logical category with respect to determination of the meaning of terms, directly in propositions and indirectly in sets and series of propositions.

I. FORMAL RELATIONS OF TERMS

The fundamental rules of logical ordering of terms are known, technically, as *transitivity, symmetry and correlation,* while *connexity* is an important instance of their conjunction. Failure of terms to satisfy required logical conditions of order constitutes them *intransitive* and *asymmetrical,* while *non-transitive* and *non-symmetrical* characterize terms in their status as still indeterminate and problematic. The statement as respects intransitivity and asymmetry will be justified in later discussion. But it holds truistically in the case of *non*-transitivity and *non*-symmetry, since these relations by definition are of terms which may be either of one type or the other and hence are ambiguous in logical form.

The list, just given, of different types of relations sustained by terms to other terms, is one found in all modern logical treatises. The usual doctrinal interpretation is, however, quite different from that here given. For in current treatment, it is assumed that terms sustain these relations in and of themselves by the inherent nature of their own content. If this assumption is not always explicitly stated, it is implicit in failure to interpret terms on the ground of their functional force in satisfaction of the logical conditions of order that are imposed by the demands of valid inference and discourse. Stated positively, the doctrinal position expounded demands that formal *relations* of terms be interpreted as conditions which terms must satisfy in any inquiry that yields warranted conclusions, not as their inherent possession.

The reason why the relations that have been mentioned are usually illustrated by isolated terms is not far to seek. Many terms have been so standardized in the course of prior inquiries that their relational meaning can now be taken for granted and treated as if it belonged to them apart from their status and force in the conduct of continuous inquiry. This is strikingly true in the case of mathematical terms. It is also true in the case of such terms as *father of, wife of, spouse of*, etc. For their meaning is now settled by their place in some (contextual) ordered system of conceptions, which is so familiar that it is first taken for granted and then so completely ignored as to be virtually denied. There are said to be Australian tribes that do not have the conception of begetting, and in which therefore the conception "father of" can hardly be said to exist. There are many tribes in which "father of" expresses the relation called in our system "uncle of." Such facts indicate the relativity of these relative terms to a system of related meanings, biological or legal or both.

Before dealing severally with the different forms of relation, it is advisable, in the interest of avoiding doctrinal confusion, to recur to the basic logical distinction between terms having respectively existential and non-existential import. For *relation* and *related* are highly equivocal terms. There are terms that are *relative* but whose meaning is not exhausted in the relation specified. "Father of" is clearly a relative term; its meaning depends upon connection with another term, "offspring of." The same thing is true of terms like *short, small, rich, near, next, between*, etc. Indeed, it is true of all existential terms that have been prepared so as to function in inferential operations. But the singular who is *father of* has traits in excess of being a father; traits, moreover, that must exist independently of and antecedent to the "relation" in question.　Any one who is of the kind "fathers" must, for example, possess the independent characteristics of being an animal, a male, having sexual potency, etc.　Similarly, that which is short, small, near, etc., has an existence independent of the content expressed in these relative terms.　Abstract terms, however, like *fatherhood, length, magnitude, nearness, nextness,* are exhaustively and exclusively relational.　This exhaustiveness is what constitutes them abstract and universal terms.　The same thing holds of words that are pure connectives, like conjunctions, prepositions, and in general, what Chinese grammarians have aptly called "empty words."　It holds strikingly of all mathematical terms as such. In order to avoid the latent confusion present in the words "relative" and "related," the word *"relatives"* will here be reserved for existential terms that have a multitude of connections with a multitude of things other than that specified in the given related term—as a father is also, say, a citizen, a Republican, a Methodist, a farmer, etc., all of these words expressing relations which are logically independent of the relation designated by "father."　The term *"relational,"* on the other hand, will be used to designate abstract terms whose meaning is exhaustively contained in the terms.[1]

　　1. *Transitivity and Intransitivity.*　In order that inference may be grounded from one set of traits to another or from one kind to another, and in order that propositions may be so ordered in discourse that subsequent ones follow necessarily from antecedent ones, the terms involved must be ordered in that relation to one another known as transitivity.　Take such terms as "older than" (greater, brighter, etc.), or any property expressed linguistically by a comparative word.　If A is more (or less) in any designated trait than B, and B sustains this same relation to C, and C to D, and so on, then A sustains it to the last term in the series, whatever that may be.　The terms satisfy the condition of transitivity.　Intermediaries may be skipped whenever terms have been constituted to satisfy this form of order.　The relation is found also in terms that have to one another the serial order designated by *after* or *before,* in both the spatial and temporal sense of these words.

---

[1] The distinction is identical with that between *involvement* and *implication.*

The importance of serial orders *prepared* in advance in the case of relations designated by comparative terms and terms expressing spatial and temporal contiguities, together with the need of a principle that functions as a method or rule of so determining them, may be illustrated as follows: It would be theoretically possible to pick out members of a random crowd so as to rank them in the order of age from the oldest to the youngest. The transitive function expressed in "older than" would then be satisfied. But nothing would come of it. Nothing could be inferred as to any other traits of the singulars thus ordered. In similar fashion, take a row of books placed haphazardly on a shelf. Each book, after the first one, is "after" the one before so that the last book on the shelf is after every other one. Nothing, however, follows. When, on the other hand, singular persons insured in a life insurance company are arranged by yearly intervals in the order of *older than*, something does follow. There is inference to probable risks assumed, and hence to the amount of premiums to be paid by those occupying different positions in the series.

Take the case of *after* in its temporal sense. As I write, the sound of a motor car comes after the sound made by a typewriter key, and the sound of rustling leaves after that, and then the sound of a voice. Hence the last sound comes "after" that of the typewriter. The *logical* import of transitivity is obviously not satisfied by such a succession. It is artificial and trivial. One of the most pressing problems of scientific inquiry is to distinguish cases in which there is mere *succession* from those in which there is *sequence*. Repeated observation may determine an order of successions but an inference based upon it will be a case of the fallacy of *post hoc, ergo propter hoc*, unless some principle, stated in a universal proposition, gives, as it is operatively applied, a *reason* for the order. Such illustrations provide convincing evidence of the logical necessity for interpreting the relation of transitivity as a condition *to be* satisfied in the continuum of inquiry instead of being a relational property that just happens to belong to some terms.

The relation of transitivity is also exemplified in terms denoting *kinds* when, and only when, an extensive or inclusive *kind* has been determined with respect to included kinds in an order of progression. To take a simple example: When whales have been determined to be mammals and mammals to be vertebrates, there is warranted transitivity from whales to vertebrates. This transition is logically possible only when the set of conjoined characteristics that describe each kind has been previously inclusively-exclusively determined by the functions of affirmation-negation. Scientific natural inquiry is notoriously concerned to establish related kinds. This concern is not final, its purpose being to institute terms that satisfy the condition of transitivity, so that systematic inference is promoted and controlled.

So far, we have been concerned with transitivity as it affects terms, singular or generic, having existential reference. But the discussion has also shown that only terms that are serially ordered by means of a general principle can actually possess the relation in question. This principle is a *rule* for ordering, and is expressed in a universal proposition. This universal proposition must itself be in turn a member of a series of propositions in ordered discourse. Mathematical terms are typical examples of non-existential terms instituted so as to warrant transitivity in discourse. They are strictly *relational*, not merely *relative*. The abstract relational terms *fatherhood, sonship, unclehood, nephewship*, etc., in their distinction from the *relatives* "father-son, uncle-nephew," designate *relationships* which are independent of related existences. One cannot infer from the related term *father* the related terms *grandson* or *nephew*. The offspring in question may not themselves have offspring, and the fathers in question may not have brothers or sisters; and if they have, the persons in question may not have sons. The relations are intransitive. But paternity, grandfathership, brotherhood, uncleship, cousinship, etc., constitute a system of relationships such that each is transitively related to every other.

The nature of *intransitivity* is illustrated in the previous paragraph. Terms exemplifying this relation constitute as they stand the conditions of a *problem*. They suggest or indicate the need of operations which will transform them into terms that satisfy the requirement of transitivity. They indicate, on one side, the incompleteness of inquiry in a given case, and, on the other side, the operations by which the terms in question may be so ordered hat their meanings will be such as to fall into a determinate order. All terms designating particular *acts and changes* are logically intransitive. Take for example, the meanings of *A* and *B* as related in the proposition "*A* killed *B*," where "killed" stands for an act performed by a singular at a particular place and time which effects a change in something else. Every *particular* proposition (in the logical sense of "particular") is of this sort. Every such proposition expresses a problem or a special condition in the determination of a problem.[2]

Hence, such terms are intransitive not because of some peculiarity they possess in and of themselves, but precisely because as they stand they are not ordered with reference to determination of a spatial or temporal relation, or a relation of kinds, such that inference is warranted. When the act of killing is determined in connection with a graded series of kinds, as it is in a legal system, to be a case of accident, self-defense, or murder in a definite degree, it then acquires a meaning satisfying the condition of transitivity. Grounded inference is then possible to other previously unobserved traits, and to specified existential consequences. This transformation is effected, as has been previously shown, by ascertaining traits which are consequences of *modes* of interaction and employing them, instead of immediate qualities, as the ground of inference. For a *mode* of interaction is general, while *a* change is not. Hence the latter provides no ground for transition, while a *kind* of change which is a specified mode of a more extensive mode of *interaction* has the ordered relation necessary for transitivity. The equivalent of this condition in scientific inquiry is the requirement that every given *change* be determined to be a constituent of a definite set of *correlated* changes.

2. *Symmetry and Asymmetry.* Terms are relative to each other in the sense of symmetry when each one of the related pair bears the same relation to the other. "Partners," for example, is a symmetrical relation. If *A* is a partner of *B*, then *B* is a partner of *A*. "Spouse" is a term applied to objects each of which is symmetrically relative to the other. In other pairs, there exists the relation of *converse* symmetry. The relation of "husband-wife" is itself asymmetrical but the terms have the relation of converse symmetry.

[2] See, *ante*, pp. 201, 220.

"Testator-heir" are terms that sustain this relation to each other. The relation of converse symmetry exists in all cases of particular acts and changes, as in the examples of intransitivity given above. The relation is expressed grammatically by the active and passive voices of the verb. If *A* kills *B*, then *B* is killed by *A*. The same relation holds in the cases of action and of being acted *toward* (though not upon) linguistically expressed by intransitive verbs. The logical import of the relation of symmetry is constituted in its conjunction with transitivity. This conjunction is typically expressed in the formula: "Things that are equal to the same thing are equal to one another." The conjunction of symmetry and transitivity constitutes the meanings which validate substitutability in inference and discourse. Equality of magnitudes is an obvious case of terms that have symmetrical-transitive relativity.

The scope of the conjunction is not limited to quantities constituted by operations having existential reference. One who measures the floor of a room with reference to determining the amount of carpet to be purchased does so in order to institute terms having symmetrical transitive relations to each other. Algebraic equations exemplify terms having this conjunct relation in respects other than that of magnitude. Physical functions are generalizations which warrant substitutability in inference as to existential matters by satisfaction of conjunct symmetrical-transitivity. In short, the import of instituting meanings which have this conjoint relativity is that it is the logical ground of the fundamental logical category of *equivalence*. This consideration alone makes it unnecessary to dwell upon the fact that no term has this relation as its inherent property, but that the relation expresses a condition to be satisfied in institution of meanings entitled to function in controlled inquiry.

3. *Correlation.* For the purpose of inference and of ordered discourse, it is important in many problems that the relation between relata-referents be determinate with respect to its scope, or its range and comprehensiveness. *Correlation* is the name technically used to designate this form of order. In a monogamous legal system, the relation of husband-wife is *one-one;* in a polygamous system it is *one-many;* in a polyandrous system, it is *many-one.* A simple example of the force of the principle in inquiry is had

hen a man or woman is tried for bigamy. For it illustrates that
ie kind of "correlation" which holds among terms is conditioned
pon the extent to which a given *field* of subject-matter has been
ystematically determined in prior inquiry, a result that is brought
bout only through abstract universal propositions as rules of
peration. In the case cited, for example, only legal rules as to
narriage determine the import of a given relation so that conse-
uences may be inferred.

The relation of friend-friend is symmetrical in a given or speci-
ed case. But it is *many-many*. *A* and *B* are friends in a recipro-
al sense. But *A* may have *C, D, E* . . . as friends and *B* may
ave *N, O, P* . . . as friends. Nothing follows as to the relation
f friendship, indifference, or enmity existing among these other
erms as between friends of *B* and *A*. However, in the situation
lustrated in the saying "Love me, love my dog," the relation of
riend-friend is so conditioned that *B* cannot be a friend of *A*
inless *B* is also the friend of *C*, who is a friend of *A*. This type
f relation is exemplified in the case of some blood-kinship, blood-
rotherhood, and secret-society relations, where each related mem-
er is bound to defend and support every other member,
ndependently of prior acquaintance. The relation is still many-
nany, but a *system* is so constituted that the relation of *transitivity*
nolds between the elements of the system that have many-many
elations taken severally. When the relation is not determined by
:o-presence in a system, the many-many relation is too indeter-
ninate to permit of transitivity. Mathematics is the outstanding
:xemplar of a system in which terms have many-many relations
.o one another, and yet the rules of operations determining the
ystem are such that one-one relations can be instituted whenever
t is necessary.[3]

4. *Connexitivity*. Relational terms satisfy the condition of connexitivity whenever symmetrical terms are also transitive. Equivalence is, as we have seen, an instance of symmetrical transitivity,
grounding, as it were, back-and-forth movement in inference and
discourse. The term "connexitivity" may be extended to include
such cases. Asymmetrical transitivity is exemplified in such terms

---

[3] Any cardinal number, for example, is both a sum (product, power) and
also a unit factor and root with regards to other numbers.

as *greater-than*, *hotter-than*, and in comparative terms generally in which terms have the relation of *converse* symmetry. Connexitivity is not so much a coordinate relation as it is a complex of relations, the function of transitivity being basic in all modes of logical relation.

The discussion has been conducted upon the basis of distinctive forms of the relative and relational terms that are commonly recognized. But these forms have been interpreted upon the doctrinal ground that the relations in question indicate either (1) formal conditions that terms (meanings) must satisfy in order to function in inquiry yielding warranted conclusions, or (2) as warnings that the conditions required have *not* been fulfilled. An example of the latter would be the case of asymmetrical intransitivity or the many-many relations in which elements have not been determined to be elements in an ordered system. It is difficult to avoid the impression in reading some logical texts (even those in which the necessity of strict formalism is emphasized) that meanings (terms) are taken just as they happen to present themselves in isolation and certain labels are then placed upon them.

II. FORMAL RELATIONS OF PROPOSITIONS

It has been noted that (1) terms are logically related in a proposition only as the proposition of which they are related members is itself in ordered relation to other propositions, and that (2) certain terms have purely relational force, so that their meaning is wholly exhausted in their office of instituting relations between other terms. Terms that exemplify the latter condition are all the words that are grammatically called connectives, such as *and* *or*, *that* (which), *only* (none but), etc. These strictly relational terms appear in propositions. But their logical force and function in a proposition, in its severalty, have to do with the *function* of that proposition in a set or series of related propositions—a logical character expressed in contemporary logic by calling the propositions in which they appear "compound" propositions.[4] In other words, connectives represent satisfaction of the logical conditions

[4] According to the position developed in this book, the "simple" propositions, with which other propositions are contrasted as "compound," are logically incomplete, being instituted only for the sake of arriving at the complete propositions which are called compound.

hat are required to constitute *any given* proposition a member of
an ordered set or series of propositions.

It was shown in Chapter X that comparison-contrast is the
means by which contents are determined in that relation which
constitutes a proposition. It was also shown that comparison-
contrast can be defined only in terms of the institution of conjugately related affirmative and negative propositions, which
express the results of operations of inclusion-exclusion. The scope
and necessity of the latter operations in strict correspondence with
each other, is such that propositions logically related to one another
(in sets or series) must satisfy the formal conditions of conjugate
exclusiveness-inclusiveness, or be *conjunct-disjunct* in relation to
one another. The purely relational terms *and, or, that, only*, along
with other formally relational terms, such as, *if, then, either-one-
or-other-but not-both, some, is, is-not*, are the symbols by which
are designated the conjunctive-disjunctive functions which render
a given proposition formally capable of being a related member of
a set or series of ordered proposition. However, not all of the
relational terms listed stand on the same logical plane, or are of
coordinate force. Some of them mark a relation that satisfies (or
is taken as if it satisfied) the functions of conjunction-disjunction,
while others mark contents still in process of complete determination with respect to satisfaction of these functions—that is, meanings whose force is still problematic. "*Any*" is of the former type;
"*a or an*" (when not a synonym of "any") and "*some*" are of the
latter type, as are also "*this*," and "*the*" in the cases in which "the"
is a synonym of *this*.

The doctrinal conclusion reached may, accordingly, be formulated as follows: Sets and series of propositions are so ordered as
to constitute in their functional correspondence (conjugate relation) with each other a scientific system (one satisfying necessary
formal conditions) only when taken severally they are co-alternate
(exclusive) and, taken together, they are co-conjunct or inclusive
and exhaustive. This formulation is intended, on one side, to state
that the functions in question are not inherent properties of propositions but are logical conditions to be satisfied; and, on the other
side, that they are highly generalized logical "leading principles,"

since they set forth operations to be performed which are logically basic.

It remains only to introduce certain further distinctions, the most important of which are designated by words borrowed from mathematics but which are given logical meaning: namely, *additive* and *multiplicative*. Conjunction-disjunction is *additive* in application to *existential* subject-matter whether singular or generic; it is *multiplicative* in application to the interrelation of characters constituting abstract universal propositions. Illustrations will render the import of this statement evident. Additive summative conjunction is symbolized by *and* (of which a *comma* is often the logical equivalent) while additive alternate conjunction is expressed by *or*. In the case of singulars, "and" as an additive conjunction constitutes a collection, as "This regiment is composed of this and that and the other enumerated person" until every member is listed. An instance of alternate additive conjunction of singulars is found in the following: "Any member of the Cabinet of the Federal Government is either Secretary of State, or of the Treasury, of the Interior, or . . ." until all members of the collection are listed.

The logical force of *and-or* applied to *kinds* is different from this case of singulars. For example, such a proposition as that just stated (as to singulars composing a collection) is denied by denying the presence of any one of the singulars listed, while its completeness may be denied by affirming that some other singular should be added. In the case of kinds, denial applies to the *relation of conjunction* as such. The validity of the proposition "James, John, Robert and Henry were present on a given occasion" is impeached when it is shown that any one of the four was absent. The generic proposition "Birds, bats, butterflies are subkinds of one and the same inclusive kind" is invalidated whenever it is shown that the trait of being flying-creatures is not a conjunction of characteristics sufficient to determine an inclusive kind, and that differences in modes of flying are not sufficient to differentiate included kinds. Denial applies not to kinds taken severally but to the *relation* of inclusive-included; or, more strictly, to the set of generic differential characteristics by which kinds are determined as inclusive and included.

The proposition "Birds, fishes, reptiles, simians, human beings, . . are vertebrates," is a summative conjunctive proposition bout relations of kinds in forming an including kind. The alernate conjunctive form of proposition is "Vertebrates are birds or fishes or reptiles or simians or human beings or . . ." It might eem as if the difference were merely linguistic, not logical, consisting simply in the fact that in the case of summative addition (expressed by *and*) sub-species are enumerated first, and in the case of logical addition by alternates (expressed by *or*) the including kind is stated first. There is, however, a genuine logical difference. There is nothing in the case of summative addition taken apart from the alternative form to warrant either the completeness (sufficiency) of the included kinds in relation to the nclusive kind, or their non-overlapping character. The logical, as distinct from the verbal, force of *or* consists in satisfaction of the condition that the kinds which are summatively added do not overlap, being described by *differential* characteristics. Take for example, the proposition: "Birds and whales and mammals are vertebrates." Since whales and mammals are defined by the same set of traits, "and" does not here determine exclusion. The logical force of *or* means the necessity for institution of sub-kinds that are descriptively determined by traits that are so differential as to be reciprocally exclusive within the set of characteristics describing the including kind. Kinds connected by *and* may constitute propositions valid as far as they go but that are not sufficiently *inclusive*.

So far it has been assumed rather than shown that the additive function in its summative and alternative modes applies only to the relation of terms in propositions having existential reference. The simplest way of showing the validity of the position taken is to consider the relation of characters which constitute the content of a universal non-existential proposition. In the case of characteristics describing kinds, whether including or included, it is necessary that the traits employed be materially independent of one another and yet so involved that in cumulative conjunction they form a set of traits that suffice to determine kinds inclusively and exclusively. The relation of characters in an abstract proposition is, on the other hand, an *interrelation*. Only as the meaning of each character is constituted in reciprocal dependence upon all other characters involved does a universal proposition satisfy logical conditions. It is this form of relationship which is designated by the term *multiplicative*. The conjunction in question is not of contents that are capable of independent observation or independent determination. The "conjunction" is one of "natures" not of traits. The *necessity* of the relation marking universal propositions in distinction from the contingency of existential propositions is constituted by the *multiplicative* conjunction of its related characters.

Being mammalian, for example, is determined by the multiplicative conjunction of the characters, warm-blooded, viviparous and suckling young. If this universal proposition is valid as a definition, it is (1) independent of the existence of creatures marked by corresponding qualitative traits; while (2) it involves the idea that these characters are necessarily interrelated, so that any one of the three characters is meaningless *in the definition* apart from its modifying and being modified by the other terms. In other words, *if* warm-blooded, *then* viviparous, etc. Suppose, however a proposition about a relation of kinds were as follows: "Mammals are warm-blooded, and (or) viviparous, and (or) offspring-suckling." It is clear, on its face, that such a proposition is a disguised definition of *being* mammalian.

Alternate multiplication is necessary to determine *sufficiency* in the case of the relation of characters, as in the case of the conjunction of characters describing related kinds. Irrelevant and superfluous characters must be ruled out. In the case, say, of the conception of triangularity magnitude is excluded from the definition, while shape is no part of the conception outside the limits determined by the relations of the characters of right-angularity equilateralness and scaleness. This conception is now so standardized that elimination of these characters may seem too trivial to be worth mentioning. But there was a time when inquiry into geometrical relationships was retarded because size was thought to be a necessary property of triangles. For as long as triangles were supposed to have existential reference, size *was* a generic trait. If we take the relations of characters that define, say, being metallic, completeness of the characters in question can be determined only as they are disjoined from characters whose inter-relation defines being chemically elemental in other ways than being metallic as well as in ways that are reciprocally exclusive. To repeat in this context a point made in other contexts: When it is affirmed that triangularity is either right-angular, scalene or isosceles, it is affirmed (1) that these ways of being triangular exhaust all the possibilities of relationship of the lines and angles in question, and (2) that the relationships constituting being triangular are so *inter*related that these ways of being triangular are necessary to the conception of the triangular.

Functional *correspondence* of propositions which satisfy re-spectively the conditions of additive and multiplicative conjunc-tion-disjunction is necessary for final warranted judgment. Only copulation of propositions of subject-contents and predicate con-tents determines, on one side, that the universal propositions em-ployed are operationally relevant, and, on the other side, that the conjoined traits used to describe kinds are exclusive-inclusive be-cause of a ground or *reason*. For otherwise the basis of their conjunction is merely recurrent observations, so that the con-junction observed constitutes a *problem*. The logical form of the conjugate correspondence is expressed in the relational terms "either-one-or-other-but-not both." Take the following proposi-tion: "Mankind consists of Europeans, Africans, Australians, Americans . . ." where . . . indicates that addition is summa-tively exhaustive. There is nothing in the proposition as it stands to preclude hyphenated membership, or kinds that are, say, European-American. Only a rule expressed in a universal propo-sition can determine such kinds that this possibility is ruled out. Such a determination is not particularly important in the example selected, although the question of dual political citizenship may be an actual one. But there are scientific inquiries in which it is indispensable to determine that kinds are related so that any singular must be of one-or-another kind but-not-of-more-than-one. Indeed, satisfaction of this condition is necessary to any valid set of disjunctive propositions. It cannot be achieved except upon the basis of a set of disjunctive universal-hypothetical propo-sitions whose operational application determines kinds exclusive of one another within an exhaustive including kind.

1. Certain corollaries follow. It is usual in texts to find such propositions as have been considered termed "compound," where "compound" postulates "simple" propositions that are prior to and independent of the conjunctive-disjunctive function. But from the position taken (namely, that any symbolic expression has the logical status of being a proposition only as a member of an ordered set or series) it follows truistically that there are no "simple" propositions in the sense alleged. There are, of course, propositions that are *relatively* simple. But they have logical status only in institution of so-called "compound" propositions. For example, a *particular* proposition, one about *a* change which *at a given time* is incapable of analysis into a complex of interactions, is a simple or elementary proposition. But (1) it is only conditionally such, for its determination depends upon the available techniques of *experimental* observations. As these improve, changes which are more elementary may be discovered, while (2) in any case their simple nature is *functional*. For its content as simple is determined by its capacity to serve as a condition in delimitation of a problem. Hence the degree of "simplicity" required varies with the problem in hand.

2. Save as the conjugate nature of the functions of additive-multiplicative conjunction-disjunction is acknowledged there is no logical ground for making a distinction between division and classification. The process is then called "division" when it proceeds from the inclusive kind to the included kinds, and "classification" when the movement is in the reverse direction. Subject-matter is identical in both cases. If, however, "division" in its logical sense is reserved for discrimination of *differential* traits describing mutually exclusive kinds within the more comprehensive conjunction of traits that describe an including kind, it has a distinctive logical meaning. "Classification" would then be used to stand for the discriminated interrelation of *characters* that mark off "classes" (in the unambiguous sense of *categories*) within the *comprehension* of the category of the widest applicability. "Division" is applicable to kinds in extension and "classification" to conceptions in comprehension.

3. The classic theory of genus and fixed included species furnished an ontological ground for *definition*. The latter consisted

of statement of the genus and the differentia which together marked off and identified the species in question. Abandonment of the cosmological ground for this conception of definition left the logical status of definition in the air. It has been treated, for example, as a purely linguistic matter in which the meaning of a single word is set forth in a set of words whose several meanings are taken to be already understood. Taken literally, this conception leaves the *combination* of the defining words wholly unexplained and ungrounded. And yet it is in virtue of their conjunction, additive or multiplicative, that they form a definition, either in the sense of description of a kind or in the stricter sense of analysis of an abstract conception. That *symbols,* of which words in their ordinary sense are a limited kind, are necessary to definition, and that in a definition a single symbol having a total meaning is resolved into an *interrelation* of meanings is sound doctrine. It provides the element of plausibility in the merely linguistic interpretation of definition.

But the logical import of definition is radically different. Conceptual meanings are instituted in their office as representatives of *possibilities* of solution. They are capable of performing this office only as they are resolved into characters that are *necessarily* interrelated just because they are an analysis of a single conception. The value (validity) of any given analysis of any given conception (this analysis being the definition) is finally fixed by the power of the interrelated characters to institute a series of rigorous substitutions in discourse. Only such a conception of definition accounts for the indispensable role played by definitions in inquiry, and explains how and why a given selection and conjunction of the terms of a definition is logically grounded instead of being arbitrary.

III. FORMAL CANONS OF RELATIONS OF PROPOSITIONS

The functions of additive and multiplicative conjunction-disjunction go back, as we have seen, to the conjugate relation of affirmation-negation, inclusion-exclusion. Hence they may be further generalized. When so generalized, the fundamental functions involved take the form of logical principles to which the name *Canons* is traditionally applied. These canons are *Identity, Contradiction* and *Excluded Middle.* On the ground of the position taken, it follows truistically that they express certain ultimate conditions to be satisfied, instead of being properties of propositions as such. Upon the basis of the cosmological-ontological assumptions of the classic logic, it was a sound logical doctrine that treated identity, etc., as necessary *structural properties*. Species, which alone were capable of definition, classification, and scientific demonstration, were immutable. Hence they were inherently self-identical. Any species is always and necessarily just what it is. The canon of identity expressed symbolically in the form *A* is *A* was, accordingly, the proper form in which any proposition having scientific status should be stated. Species were also ontologically exclusive of one another. No transitions or derivations were possible among them because of their necessary ontological exclusion of one another. Hence, *tertium non datur*.[5]

1. *Identity*. From the standpoint of the position that it is necessary for propositions to satisfy conditions set by membership in a set or a series of propositions, *identity* means the logical requirement that meanings be stable in the inquiry-continuum. The direct and obvious meaning of this statement is that a meaning remain constant throughout a *given* inquiry, since any change in its content changes the force of the proposition of which it is a constituent, thus rendering it uncertain upon what meanings and relation of meanings the conclusion reached actually depends. Fulfilment of this condition does not mean, however, that a given symbol shall have the same meaning in *all* inquiries. If it did have this meaning, progress in knowledge would be impossible. But the judgment which is the final issue of inquiry modifies to some extent, sometimes crucially, the evidential import of some observed fact and the meaning previously possessed by some conception.

---

[5] That Aristotle's formulation of the principle of contradiction is somewhat equivocal is frequently noticed by modern exponents of his logical doctrine. It would seem to be a combination of two considerations; one, that any contradiction violates the principle of the necessary identity of a species; the other, that *contrary* propositions not only exist in the case of changes, as signs of lack of complete Being, but are inevitable, since in his cosmology it is the hot which becomes cold, the moist which alters into the dry, etc. Plato, without formulating the principle of contradiction, had argued against the *complete* reality of change on the ground that if it had a full measure of Being contradictory propositions were inevitable, since it then followed that something both was and was not. On the whole, contradiction seems to have been employed as evidence for the principle of identity rather than as an independent principle.

Unless *identity* has functional force in relation to the subject-matter undergoing inquiry, the canon of identity is violated in every scientific advance.

The deeper and underlying import of the principle of identity is, accordingly, constituted in the very continuum of judgment. In scientific inquiry, every conclusion reached, whether of fact or conception, is held subject to determination by its fate in further inquiries. Stability or "identity," of meanings is a limiting ideal, as a condition to be progressively satisfied. The conditional status of scientific conclusions (conditional in the sense of subjection to revision in further inquiry) is sometimes used by critics to disparage scientific "truths" in comparison with those which are alleged to be eternal and immutable. In fact, it is a necessary condition of continuous advance in apprehension and in understanding.[6]

2. *Contradiction.* The logical condition to be satisfied for the canon of contradiction is independent of that of identity, although necessarily conjunctive with it. Violation of the principle of identity *may* lead to contradiction. But the logically important instances are those in which *observance* of the principle of identity results in a contradiction. For establishment of propositions one of which must be valid if the other is invalid is an indispensable step in arriving at a grounded conclusion.[7] Contradiction is not then just an unfortunate accident which sometimes happens to come about. Complete exclusion, resulting in grounded disjunction, is not effected until propositions are determined as pairs such that if one is valid the other is invalid, and if one is invalid the other is valid. The principle of contradiction thus represents a condition to be satisfied. Direct inspection of two propositions does not determine whether or not they are related as contradic-

---

[6] The best definition of *truth* from the logical standpoint which is known to me is that of Peirce: "The opinion which is fated to be ultimately agreed to by all who investigate is what we mean by the truth, and the object represented by this opinion is the real." *Op. cit.*, Vol. V, p. 268. A more complete (and more suggestive) statement is the following: "Truth is that concordance of an abstract statement with the ideal limit towards which endless investigation would tend to bring scientific belief, which concordance the abstract statement may possess by virtue of the confession of its inaccuracy and one-sidedness, and this confession is an essential ingredient of truth." (*Ibid.*, pp. 394–5).

[7] Cf. *ante*, pp. 195–8 and pp. 337–41.

tories, as would be the case if contradiction were an inherent relational property. The contrary doctrine is often affirmed, as when it is said that the two propositions *A is M* and *A is not M* directly contradict each other. But unless *A* has already been determined conjunctively-disjunctively, by prior inquiry, some part of *A*, or *A* in some relation, may be *M*, and some other part of *A*, or *A* in some other relation, may be *not M*. The relation of *A* to *M* and *not M* can be determined only by operations of exclusion which reach their logical limit in the relation of contradiction.

3. *Excluded Middle.* It was stated earlier that complete satisfaction of the conditions of conjunctive-disjunctive functions, additive and multiplicative, is formally represented in the form *either-one-or-other-but-not-both*. The principle of excluded middle presents the completely generalized formulation of conjunctive-disjunctive functions in their conjugate relation. The notion that propositions are or can be, in and of themselves, such that the principle of excluded middle directly applies is probably the source of more fallacious reasoning in philosophical discourse and in moral and social inquiries than any other one sort of fallacy. That fact that disjunctions which were at one time taken to be both exhaustive and necessary have later been found to be incomplete (and sometimes even totally irrelevant) should long ago have been a warning that the principle of excluded middle sets forth a logical condition *to be* satisfied in the course of continuity of inquiry. It formulates the ultimate *goal* of inquiry in complete satisfaction of logical conditions. To determine subject-matters so that no alternative is possible is the most difficult task of inquiry.

It is frequently argued today that the three principles in question have become completely outmoded with the abandonment of their foundations in the Aristotelian logic. The Aristotelian interpretation of them as ontological, and any interpretation which regards them as inherent relational properties of given propositions, must certainly be abandoned. But as formulations of formal conditions (conjunctive-disjunctive) to be satisfied, they are valid as directive principles, as regulative limiting ideals of inquiry. An example sometimes put forward to show the meaninglessness of the principle of excluded middle is its inapplicability to existences in process of transition. Since all existences are in process of change it is concluded that the principle is totally inapplicable. For example, of water that is freezing and of ice that is melting, it cannot be said that water is either solid or liquid. To avoid this difficulty by saying that it is either solid, liquid or in a transitional state, is to beg the question at issue: namely, determination of the transitional intermediate state. The objection is wholly sound on any other ground than that the canon expresses a condition *to be* satisfied. But taken in the latter sense, it shows the scientific inadequacy of the common sense conceptions of *solid* and *liquid*. As scientific existential inquiry has become occupied with changes and correlations of change, the popular qualitative ideas of solid, liquid, gaseous states have been expelled. They are now replaced by correlations of units of mass, velocity and distance-direction formulated in terms of numerical measurements. The necessity of instituting exclusive disjunctions, satisfying the condition of excluded intermediates, has been a factor in bringing about this scientific change.

This chapter has been concerned with formal conditions which propositions must satisfy in order to fulfil their functions in inquiry. The logical conditions in question concern, on one side, sets of propositions in the relations which ground an *inferential* conclusion, and, on the other side, series of propositions in the relations that constitute ordered discourse. In each case, the concluding proposition is said to "follow" from preceding propositions while the reverse process is called "going or proceeding from." The nature of the "following" is different in inference and in discourse. The traditional (and essentially conventional) statement of the difference is that in the former we go from particular propositions to the general, and in the other from the general to the particular. This mode of statement had genuine import and foundation in the Aristotelian logic. But it lacks both ground and logical meaning in scientific inquiry as that is now carried on. A conclusion in mathematical discourse is as universal (since it is an abstract hypothetical proposition) as are those from which it follows. While it *may* have less comprehension, or scope of applicability, it may also have greater or less comprehension, according to the exigencies of the problem in hand. The idea that general propositions are arrived at by "going" from particular ones is more plausible, since particular propositions are necessary in order to formulate the problems that required general propositions for their solutions. But formulation of the operations that determine a generalization with respect to particulars is much more complex than can be covered by the words "following" or "going." The institution of the general proposition includes, for example, performance of operations prescribed by the idea of a possible solution such that facts not previously observed are their consequences. The *nature* of the "going" and the "following" which are involved constitutes a logical problem which carries logical discussion into the subject of the nature of scientific method. It involves specifically the problem of the nature of induction and deduction and their relations to each other. The field thus indicated forms the subject of Part IV and will be taken up after the discussion of Terms found in the next chapter.

CHAPTER XVIII

TERMS OR MEANINGS

IN OLDER logical texts it was the usual practice to deal first with terms, then with propositions and finally with propositions ordered in relation to one another. According to the position developed in this book, the procedure is reversed, for inquiry, involving propositions so determined and arranged as to yield final judgment, is the logical whole upon which propositions depend, while terms as such are logically conditioned by propositions. It follows that the discussion of terms undertaken in this chapter introduces no new principles. Special discussion of terms may, however, serve to review and clarify some of the conclusions already arrived at. The word "term" was used by Aristotle to designate an elementary constituent of a proposition as its *boundary;* and the word *term* is derived from the Latin *terminus* meaning both *boundary* and terminal *limit.* Like other boundaries, for example those of political institutions and tracts of real estate, terms both demarcate and connect, and hence no term has logical force save in distinction from and relation to other terms.

This statement is not contradicted by the fact that all familiar words carry some meaning even when uttered in isolation. They have such meaning because they are used in a context in which relation to other words is involved; furthermore, their meaning is potential rather than actual until they are linked to other words. If the words *sun, parabola, Julius Caesar,* etc., are uttered, a line of direction is given to observation or discourse. But the objective of the direction is indeterminate until it is *distinguished* from alternative possible terminations, and is thus *identified* by means of relation to another term. Uncertainty as to boundaries is the source of disputes and conflicts about meanings. Indeterminate terms either claim too much and are loose because overlapping, or are too restricted and result in an unoccupied no-man's-land. In other words, no term can be fully determinate save as the terms to which it is related are also determinate in both conjunctive and disjunctive reference. Terms, as logical limits, look, like other boundaries, in two directions. They are settled as the outcome of prior activities and they exercise jurisdiction in further inquiries. They possess both of these traits and exercise both of these functions in their capacity of instruments. Like all instrumentalities they are modifiable in further use.

Traditional texts on logic have usually distinguished between terms as concrete and abstract; denotative and connotative; extensive and intensive; singular (plural), collective and general. These recognized distinctions will be taken as the material of discussion. But their interpretation on the ground of the principles formulated in previous chapters will necessarily differ in important respects from that which is traditional. It will also involve introduction of some additional distinctions, as for example, resolution of general terms into generic and universal. In its departure from traditional interpretations, the discussion also involves disagreement with some recent texts that have also departed from tradition. For example, some texts make a sharp distinction between *names* and *terms* on the ground that names are designations of subject-matters which are irrelevant to strict logic while terms are purely formal. Strictly adhered to, this position would eliminate completely all so-called "concrete" terms and would also exclude all existential propositions since the latter ultimately involve either proper names or some equivalent expression such as the demonstrative "this."

The texts in question are never wholly consistent in this matter. In further distinction from them the position here taken involves the impossibility of making a sharp division between form and subject-matter. For it holds that subject-matter is what it is in virtue of its determination by the forms which make inquiry to be what it is, while forms in turn are adapted to institution of subject-matters such as serve the requirements of controlled inquiry. There are other schools that limit the application of *names* to existential things and which therefore assign to *terms* a wider scope. But names are designations by means of symbols. And while it is fundamentally important to note whether what is designated by a symbol is material or is formal (as in the case of *and-or*), it is purely arbitrary to hold that the latter words do not designate or name what they do designate, namely formal relations. It seems to be a superstition taken over from traditional grammar that a name must designate something concrete. In fact every symbol names something; otherwise it is totally without meaning and is not a symbol. A diagram or a map has some reference and designative force, even though linguistic usage does not treat either of them as a name.

The basic distinction of terms which is here proposed follows from the theory of judgment. Any given term applies ultimately to the content of either subject or predicate of judgment; it is either existential or conceptual in reference. All other distinctions are either aspects of this fundamental distinction in logical office or are derived from it. A simple example of this distinction occurs between the following terms.

1. *Concrete and Abstract Terms.* Words designating immediately experienced qualities are concrete *par excellence*. For example, *sweet, hard, red, loud* when they are used to characterize observed subject-matter so as to discriminate and identify it: that is, as evidential marks or signs. Demonstrative words, *this, that, now, then, here, there,* are also concrete. So are common nouns which designate kinds, and such adjectives as designate characteristics by which kinds are identified and discriminated. Abstract words are such as stand for conceptions, including relations which are taken without reference to actual application to things, for example, *sweetness, solidity, redness, loudness, presence, absence, position, location, fatherhood, angularity,* etc. While certain endings, such as *ity, ness, tion,* differentiate abstract nouns from common nouns, there are many words which are abstract or concrete according to the context in which they function, independently of verbal endings. Color and sound, for example, are concrete when they refer to traits that are properties of existential objects, but in science they are abstract, meaning colority or visibility and audibility as possibilities. In order to be applicable in directing scientific inquiry they are defined in terms of numerical rates. Many adjectives are striking instances of indeter-

minateness with respect to the difference in question. As applied directly to things they are of course existential, but they may also stand for simple possibilities. The words *circular* or *oblong* are concrete when used to describe actual objects, as in "circular saw" or "oblong table." In mathematics, circle means circularity, and oblong means rectilangularity. As the example shows, nouns that are formed from adjectives may be abstract in use without indicating that form when the word does not function in a given proposition. Thus "solid" may be used to characterize things in distinction from "liquid," while in mathematics it designates a *character* which defines possible ways of *being* figurate in distinction from the way designated by *plane*.

Traditional nominalistic empiricism has tended to treat abstraction as such as "vicious" when taken to be other than a convenient linguistic procedure for referring to a number of singulars having a "common quality." Even now, it is regarded as a mark of sophistication to contemn an abstract word because a concrete "referent" cannot be pointed out. There is without doubt great abuse of abstractions, but it is to be corrected by noting that their referents are possible modes of operating. The counterpart logical error is that an abstraction is mere selection of a universal quality already possessed by objects. Then it is said that the abstract idea of smoothness arises from apprehending the quality "smooth" apart from any particular thing that possesses it. The universal, *smoothness,* according to this view is logically prior to the concrete *smooth,* the latter being an embodiment of the universal in a singular. Generalized, this view holds that all qualities and all relations are intrinsically universal, even such qualities as *sweet, hard, red,* etc., as well as such relations as are expressed by active verbs which connect existential objects together, as *kill, eat, give.* In "Brutus murdered Caesar" for example "murdered" is regarded as having the same logical form as *is* has when it is affirmed that "Honesty is a virtue"; or that the form of "different from" is identical when it is affirmed that "Pride is different from conceit," as it is when it is said "This object is different from that in shape, or size," etc.

We cannot arrive at the abstract from the concrete merely by considering a quality apart from other qualities with which it is conjoined in a thing. There exists, we shall say, a horse which is roan, male, five years old and fifteen hands high. We can select any one of these qualities for further consideration without thinking of, or inquiring into, other qualities. For example, if a buyer is considering buying a horse to form one of a team, his inquiry may attach itself either to color or height or age as matters which decide whether or not the two horses will "go well" together. But the quality still remains "concrete." Roan is not roanness; so-many-years-old is not age as an abstraction; so-high is not tallness. The comparison in which a given quality is selected out of a complex is a *condition* of abstraction, but the quality selected is not, on that account, a universal. Moreover, a quality is not a universal merely because it characterizes a number of singulars. In that capacity it serves, like any trait, to describe a kind. To become a universal it must be so defined as to indicate a possible mode of operation. Its function is to determine the characteristics which must be found to exist in order to warrant the inference that a given singular is of specified kind. Genuine illustrations of abstraction are found in the conception of heat as a mode of molecular motion; just as a pseudo-abstraction is found in the old conception that heat is califoricity—which only repeats in an abstract *word* the experienced quality. The quality *smooth* is warrantably affirmed of objects only as the universal, *smoothness*, is such as to prescribe operations of technical measurement. The common sense conception of smoothness, derived from operations executed by touch and sight, serves many ordinary practical ends but is in no sense a scientific conception. Only a mathematical formula *defines* smoothness. It can no more be derived from directly experienced qualities by selection, inspection and comparison of them than the definition of heat as molecular motion can be derived from direct inspection and comparison of the *quality* of various hot things.

2. *Singular, Generic and Universal Terms.* Each conceptual term of predicative force is universal since it designates an operation *possible of performance*, independently of whether the conditions to which it applies are actually observed or not. Singular and generic terms are existential in reference and are conjugate. The *individual* as such is a unique nonrepeatable qualitative

situation. The singular, represented, say, by *this*, is a subject-matter discriminately selected from a total qualitative situation so as to serve the function of determining a problem and providing facts which, as evidence, test any proposed solution. As has been previously said, qualities are not recurrent in themselves but in their evidential function. *As* evidential, they are characteristics which describe a kind. Consequently, singular and generic represent two emphases of a subject-matter of a proposition which has existential import. "*This* is a meteorite" is singular with respect to *this;* generic with respect to meteorite. Context determines upon which of the conjugate forms emphasis falls in a given case. When meteorites are included within a more extensive kind, the proposition is that of a relation of kinds. There is no *explicit* reference to a singular or *this;* the proposition holds, if valid, independently of whether any meteorite is observed to exist at this or that particular time and place. But the proposition postulates that meteorites do exist at *some* time and place. Thus it possesses a conjugate, although indirect, reference to singulars. The case is not otherwise when it is said that "Ogres are fabulous animals." It postulates the existence of fabulous or mythical beliefs, and affirms that *belief* in ogres has existed and that such beliefs are of the kind called fabulous, since observation has not established the existence of ogres although it warrants affirmation of the existence of beliefs about them.

"General" as a logical term is ambivalent. As has been repeatedly noted, it is employed to designate both the generic and the universal. The confusion of the two and its consequences in logical doctrine, namely, failure to observe the logical difference of the existential and non-existential, the factual and ideational, have been dealt with. We append, however, some comments upon the double meaning of the word *law*. It is employed to designate the content of physical generalizations both when (1) a specified conjunction of traits has been observed and confirmed without an exception being found, and (2) when the relation in question is itself a member of a system of interrelated universal propositions. In the former case, it designates what we call a general fact, such as "tin melts at the temperature of 232° C." There is no objection to the double use of the word "law." But the use should not be allowed to disguise the fact that *law* in one case is existential in reference, while in the other it is definitely non-existential in reference. A law in mathematical physics is universal in as far as its mathematical content enables deduction to other propositions in discourse to be made. As a law of *physics,* its content is existential and contingent.

3. *Denotative and Connotative Terms.* The logical difference between these two kinds of terms is once more that between terms of subject-content, which has existential reference, and terms of predicative and conceptual import. Terms are denotative when they refer, directly or indirectly (as in propositions of a relation of kinds) to existence. Common nouns, demonstratives, and verbs that denote change or action are denotative. Mill revived the scholastic term "connotation" (giving it, however, a different and confused meaning) to designate the adjectival contents which constitute the meaning of a generic term, stating that connotation determines the *meaning* of such terms. According to this view one and the same term is both denotative and connotative, with some definite exceptions to be noted hereafter. Thus, "ship" is denotative in respect to its application to an indefinite number of objects, while its connotation consists of the traits which any object must possess in order that the term *ship* can be warrantably applied to it. The confusion here involved is not particularly subtle. It is between *characteristics* which *are* the meaning of *ship* as a *denotative* term and the *characters* which ground, inclusively and exclusively, the logical capacity of traits to describe a kind. The first is *de facto.* It states the set of traits which are in empirical fact used as the ground of calling an object a ship instead of, say, a canoe or yacht. When questions arise as to whether or not a certain object is of the kind "ship," a definition of what it is to *be* a ship is demanded. Suppose the definition consists of the following (multiplicative) conjunction of characters; floating on water, having curved sides, of sufficient capacity to transport a considerable number of goods and persons, and being used regularly for commercial transportation of goods and passengers. Such a term is not descriptive of traits which form the meaning of *ship;* they are prescriptions of the traits an object *should* have *if* it is to be a ship. The terms in

question are all abstract. They define *shipness;* they do not describe existential *ships.*

When connotation is restricted to the *meaning* of a denotative term (as it must be when a term is said to be both denotative and connotative) exactly the same thing is said twice. *Ship* as a term *denotes* primarily a set of traits and secondarily denotes a kind of objects because they are marked by these traits. When it is said that connotation determines the *applicability* of a set of traits to describe the kind, inquiry has moved into another logical dimension, that of abstract universals. If "connotative" means something other than descriptive, then the same term cannot have both denotation and connotation. Existential terms are denotative; abstract terms are connotative. Every denotative term is related to a corresponding or conjugate connotative term as far as its denotative capacity is *warranted*—substantially the scholastic use of connotation. If instead of *ship,* whose meaning is more or less conventional, we had taken a scientific term, such as *chemical element,* or *metal,* the dependence of grounded denotative application upon defining conceptions of *being* chemically simple and being metallic would be obvious. When a descriptive term is said to possess connotation in addition to denotation, not only is there bald repetition but no place is left for *attributive* terms or abstract universals. The word "connotation" should either be dropped or be reserved for the latter.

The following quotation from Mill, whose loose use of the word "attributes" to designate both characteristics and characters is unfortunately followed by writers who do not agree with his basic postulates, illustrates the confusion discussed. When it is cleared of confusion, the quotation exemplifies both the difference and the relation of descriptive terms and prescriptive "connotative" terms. "The word *man* denotes Peter, Jane, John and an indefinite number of other individuals, of whom, taken as a class (kind) it is the name. But it is applied to them because they possess, *and to signify that they possess,* certain attributes. These seem to be corporeity, animal life, rationality, and a certain external form, which for distinction we call the human." [1]

According to his official doctrine, the "connotation" ought to be

[1] Mill, *Logic,* Book I, Ch. 2, Sec. 5.

simply the set of existential qualities which constitute the meaning of the general term "men." In that case, however, the concrete word "men" simply possesses a dual *denotation;* namely, one pointing both to certain qualities used as marks and also to the objects having these qualities. It is accordingly significant that Mill actually illustrates connotation by means of *abstract* words, *corporeity,* *rationality,* which are not possessed properties of the objects in question, but which do have the force of indicating what qualities (namely, possession of a body and of power to reason) *must* be traits of objects if the name *men* is properly applied to them. For existent objects no more *are* or *have* corporeity and rationality than a sunset is or has *redness.*

Mill's denial that proper names are *connotative* is thus correct on the basis of the interpretation of connotation just given (namely, that it belongs to abstract terms) and incorrect on the ground of his own theory. For proper names are certainly not abstract; there is nothing about them which determines the ground and right of their applicability to singulars. But since Mill has identified connotation with the *meaning* of a word, his denial signifies that proper names have no meaning whatever. At the same time, he assigns meaning to generic terms, which, according to him, are only collections of singulars. However, aside from this inconsistency, denial of *meaning* to a proper name deprives it of that denotative force with respect to a singular which Mill nevertheless holds it does possess. If such words as *London, Rocky Mountains,* (which certainly are not names of abstract attributes) had no meaning, they would not be symbols or names at all. They would be mere noises having no application to one thing more than to any other. To all appearances, Mill's position rests upon a confused mixture of two different things. There are *causes* why the proper name "London" is applied to a given singular thing; there are no reasons, in the sense of logical ground, for its application. As to *rationale* the word lacks meaning. Moreover, while there are causes why the *object* to which the proper name is applied is what it is, there is no logical ground for its having just the qualities it does in fact have. On the other hand, while there is no logical ground (but only historical causes) for the general term "horse" as a *word* being used to designate a kind of objects, there *is* logical ground or reason for the selection of the special set of traits employed to describe horses *qua* a kind. In the sense of rationale or ground, the term or name "horse" has a *kind* of meaning which "London" does not have. But London or any proper noun does have a referent and it consequently has meaning in the sense of designating the distinctive traits which mark off and identify the singular to which it refers.

Mill's essential error has been revived in another form by writers on logic, who are critics of Mill's views in general, in their denial that "this" has descriptive qualification. I shall not repeat the criticisms already made of the view which holds to a sharp logical distinction between the demonstrative and the descriptive. But two arguments that are advanced in support of the separation may be referred to. One of them is the confusion (previously pointed out) between an indeterminate descriptive qualification and a determinate one, as in the case of dispute whether "it"—an object seen at sea—is a mountain or a cloud. That such cases occur cannot be doubted. But their occurrence does not prove that *"it"* is *wholly* lacking in meaning. It only shows that its qualities, so far as yet observed, do not suffice for a grounded proposition as to its kind. The case does not differ, save in degree, from a case in which the object is warrantably affirmed to be a mountain, while a question still exists as to what kind of a mountain it is. It should be evident that unless there are *some* observed qualities constituting, in the instance cited, means for identification of "this"—there is no ground for holding that the two persons who differ as to the kind of which *this* is, are referring to one and the same "this." Unless they are, it is obvious that both propositions may be valid. Every existential inquiry into existential qualities as a basis for inference involves during its process exactly the same indeterminate descriptive qualification that is found in the demonstrative *this*. The only difference is that "this" has a relative minimum of descriptive determination.

Another reason offered in support of the notion that purely demonstrative terms are *merely* denotative, or have no "meaning," proceeds from the side of descriptive terms. For there are descriptive terms which lack demonstrative reference, such as glass-mountain, the present king of France, etc. There is again no doubt as to the correctness of the fact brought forward, but again it does not show what it is intended to prove. No *contradiction* would be involved if perchance the objects referred to did exist. A glass-mountain might be manufactured, and there have been kings of France. All that descriptions not having demonstrative application show is that at a *given time* observation cannot disclose any object answering to them. What is more important is that such descriptions are inherent in a large number of important inquiries. Take, as a comparatively trivial instance, the question whether or not a sea-serpent exists. Obviously, investigation cannot proceed without some description of the term. Again, let it be the question of whether the ether or atoms actually exist. Unless these terms have a descriptive content there is absolutely nothing to direct observation in the attempt to determine whether there are existences answering the description. Another instance is to be found in the case of inventions, plans and intentions prior to their execution, indeed at any time short of their final completion. They are in this stage without determinate demonstrative reference and yet they are necessary to the operations which will render such demonstrative reference possible. We conclude, therefore, that neither of the arguments offered gives any ground for modifying the position that there is a strictly conjugate relationship between generic terms (which are admitted to have meaning) and singular terms, whether the latter are proper names or demonstratives such as *this* and *it*.

5. *Extension, Intension, and Comprehension.* Traditional theory has held that some terms have both intension and extension, just as it has been held that some terms are both denotative and connotative. This doctrine seems to be a hold-over from the Aristotelian logic. For in that system, definition is existential, being a grasp of the essence which determines a species. Intension is then a suitable name for the definition, while the species determined by the definition has extension. After abandonment of the ontological basis of this position, confusion was introduced into logical doctrine by identifying extension with denotation, and intension with connotation in disregard of the basic consideration, viz., whether the terms involved are existential or conceptual. The confusion is increased and in practice supported by (1) the

ambivalence of the word *object*, which has the signification both of existential things and of strictly conceptual and mathematical entities, and by (2) failure to distinguish between *designation* and denotation. Combination of the two confusions is found in such a sentence as the following: "Conic sections connote certain characters or attributes and denote all the objects that have these characters. The objects denoted by conic sections are the members of the class conic sections." In such a statement, *object* means non-existential entities. The fact that only existences can be denoted is ignored, the ignoring being covered up by using *denoting* as a synonym for *designating*. Any intelligible word designates something; otherwise it is a mere combination of sounds or visible marks, not a word at all. *Xypurt*, for example, designates nothing whatever in the English language. It is not a word. Denotative or existential terms and attributive or conceptual words are alike in designating something: they both have signification, for the meaning of words used can be understood. The important logical matter is the difference in *what* is designated.[2]

Modern logicians recognize the difference in logical form between a singular affirmed to be one of a kind and kinds as related members of a more extensive kind. They accordingly recognize that difficulties arise when the extension of a term is said to cover both of these cases. They have, however, been unwilling to admit that the "difficulties" in question amount to violation of logical integrity, and hence they still go on speaking of the range of singular *objects* denoted as the extension of a term. Thus in the case of a *ship*, it is said that its extension is that of all *objects*, past, present and future, to which the term *ship* applies. This conclusion both follows from and perpetuates the identification of denotation and extension. Logically, it gives the same force or form to a singular and to a kind, since various kinds of ships (sloops, schooners, steamboats, war vessels) are also said to be the extension of the term: this in spite of explicit recognition, in another connection, of

[2] The distinction made earlier between signifying and meaning is at least a help in avoiding confusion. The meaning of words and symbols is different from the signifying power of the existential things that are designated by the words, and only words that have existential meaning in the sense of intent or reference are denotative, while all words are designative, or are "names" of either existential or conceptual subject matter.

the difference between the propositions, say, *Hitler is a Nazi* and *Italians (or Germans) are Fascists.*

Aside from confusion in logical theory, the confusion is materially important. For were the genuine difference consistently recognized, it would compel recognition that (1) extension is a property of some denotative terms (namely those terms that refer to kinds instead of to singulars); that (2) denotation and extension are not two names for the same logical form or function, and that (3) non-conceptual terms have neither denotation (although they designate) nor extension. The extension of ship is simply and strictly the *kinds* of ships that exist or have existed or will exist; it is not singular ships, although the latter are *denoted* by *ship.* The definition of ship, or *being* of the ship-*character,* on the other hand, has no extension. The definition permits of different *ways of being* that union of interrelated characters which *define* ship. But these different ways are not the characteristic properties of different kinds of ships. The example is perhaps not well chosen since there is no abstract term, *shipness,* in use. Let us then take a mathematical term as such. Conic sections are circles, ellipses, parabolas and hyperbolas. As a linguistic expression, the sentence is grammatically of the same form as one about kinds of ships, flowers, metals or any existential kind. But as mathematical terms, the words have non-existential force. Hence, circle, ellipse are not kinds of conic sections, but are ways of being the abstract universal in question. *Conic section* is a multiplicative conjunction of the characters of conicity and sectionality; *circle* is circularity, etc. *Circle, ellipse,* etc. do not constitute the extension of the term in question, for they *are* the category (abstract universal) "conic sectionality" when that is made determinate.

What has been said indicates the need for a distinctive word to designate the scope of the necessary conceptual contents of an abstract universal or "class" in the sense of category as distinct from the range of applicability of a denotative term. The use of the word *comprehension* for this purpose is arbitrary as far as the mere word is concerned. It is not arbitrary as far as a distinct logical form, demanding some word by which to designate it, is concerned. Right-angled, scalene and isosceles constitute, conjunctively and disjunctively, the logical scope or comprehension of triangularity. Such comprehension is necessary and therefore must be differentiated from the contingency of extension of kinds.[3]

It is not necessary to say much in addition about *intension*. It is now used in at least three ways: To designate "meaning" in the sense (1) of the signification of words of whatever logical form words may be; (2) as a synonym for the set of characteristics constituting the descriptive force of a denotative term; and (3) as a synonym for the logical import of a connotative or attributive abstract term. It is an arbitrary matter to which of the three uses the application of the word *intension* is confined in a given context. But in the interests of logical consistency it is far from being arbitrary that it be restricted to one, and only one, application in the same treatise. There are available the symmetrical terms *connotation* (attribution) and *comprehension* with respect to universals. Hence the use of *intension* to pair with extension in the case of denotative terms is suggested by linguistic symmetry, and also by the fact that otherwise there is no distinctive term to designate the differential kind of meaning which belongs intrinsically to denotative terms; namely, a set of conjoined traits employed to describe a kind. In any case, some linguistic device is required to avoid the ambiguity otherwise attached to the word *meaning*, and to differentiate the characteristic logical forms, of description and definition. The two pairs, *extension* and *intension* for use in connection with denotative terms—and *comprehension* and *definition* (for use in connection with connotative terms) meet the needs of clarity and completeness.

6. *Collective Terms.* The ambiguous nature of the word "collection" has been pointed out in discussion of the quantitative phase of propositions. *Collection* is applied indifferently to an indefinite aggregate of units, illustrated by a heap or pile; to a group of units limited by description, as a regiment, and to a qualitative whole in which the characteristics of units comprised are modified by the whole of which they are parts—as when it is affirmed, "The first regiment of New York fought bravely at the battle of Chateau Thierry," in which it is not necessarily involved

---

[3] Cf. the earlier remarks about circles and brackets as modes of symbolization of two logical forms; *ante,* pp. 306–7.

that every individual soldier was brave. The old puzzles about the last straw which broke the camel's back, or the particular hair by losing which a man becomes bald, are further illustrations of a qualitative meaning.

The subject of collective terms is of special importance in relation to the general position that is taken for two reasons. One concerns certain difficulties which have arisen in the logic of mathematics. It is said, for example that numbers form an infinite collection in the sense of aggregate. This notion tends to assimilate numbers to existential objects to which the word collection is usually applied and in the case of which units are theoretically capable of enumeration. Puzzles then arise which would not arise if it were recognized that number (*being* number, as distinct from *a* number) is an operative formula for *determining* aggregates and collections, but it is not itself a finite collection, nor an infinite aggregate. Even if it be necessary to define number in such a way as to permit or prescribe an infinite aggregate as a mode or way of being number, it follows in no way that number as *defined* is itself any kind of a collection or aggregate.

The second reason is connected with certain alleged paradoxes. There is the example of the "self-representative series." The map of England is said to constitute a reflexive serial collection. A map is drawn of England. It is asserted that in order to be complete the map must itself include the map drawn, a condition which requires drawing another map and so on in a non-terminating collection of maps. But drawing the map is an existential operation. As such it takes place at a given date. There is nothing in the act of drawing or in its product to require the drawing of another map. If, for some *practical*, non-logical reason, it is desirable to draw another map of England on which the old map is represented, that action is another temporal occurrence. The supposed paradox arises only when there is a shift from the existential to the conceptual. When the phrase "drawing a map" stands for something purely conceptual, or a mode of operation, it is a definition or a formula for an operation to be executed. In this case the number of maps to be drawn and the objects they are to be maps of are indeterminate as far as the conception is concerned. *A* map or a collection of maps thus depends upon conditions and operations that are existential in nature and hence are not "implied" by the conception.

There is also the alleged paradox in the case of the soldier barber who is ordered by his superior officer to shave all the men and only the men in his company who do not shave themselves. It is then asked, is the barber himself comprised in the collection of men to be shaved? If he is one who does belong in the collection of those who do not shave themselves, he disobeys the order if he does not shave himself. In case, however, he obeys the order and does shave himself, he is one who shaves himself, and hence equally disobeys the order. The appearance of contradiction vanishes the moment reference to time and date is introduced, and since the act of shaving a given person is existential, such a reference must be introduced implicitly in the context or else explicitly. When the act of shaving is interpreted existentially and temporally, the command is unambiguous and there is no difficulty in determining how it is to be obeyed. If the barber is one who has not *in the past* shaved himself, then he obeys the order by *now* shaving himself; if he has shaved in the past, he obeys the order by *now* abstaining from shaving himself.* The contradiction alleged to exist arises only when the existential and the conceptual are confusedly identified.

So-called reflexives are said to involve a self-representative and hence non-terminating collection. Similar analysis applies. Take, for example, such seemingly reflexive relations as "love of love," "hate of hate." The *love* and *hate* forming the first member of each pair are concrete nouns, having existential reference. They designate acts performed at some time or place, whether once or repeatedly. The *love* and *hate* which are second members of the paired terms are of a different form. They are identifiable with the first named members only verbally. For they designate abstract characters, which, of course, are conceptual, not existential. Change the wording to read "love of benevolence" and "hatred of malevolence" and any shadow of a reflexive relation and of a self-

---

* Cf. P. W. Bridgman, *Scripta Mathematica*, Vol. II, p. 113. The interpretation given above is not identical with that of Bridgman but he shows clearly that the temporal quality of acts of shaving is the reason there is no paradox.

representative collection disappears. "Hating" is a concrete act; "hate" as the object of the act is abstract.

A collection is distinguished in form from both a kind and from a class in the sense of category. A dictionary is, from one point of view, a collection of words. At a given place and time, the number of words is definitely enumerable, although a dictionary may exhibit increase or decrease in the number of words forming the collection in subsequent or former editions. Like a postage stamp collection, it is capable of variation in number at different times, but at a given time it has just the number of units which it does have. The generic terms applying to a *kind* of objects, applies to *all* of an *indefinite* number of objects marked by specified characteristics, but while it is indefinite, instead of definite, in the number of singulars to which it refers, it is ideally completely determinate as to the set of characteristics it denotes. A category is constituted by the interrelation of two abstract universals, each of which may be complex. Hence, once more, number is not a collection but is a formula for operatively determining collections, while *a* number, 2 or 1700, is a collection satisfying the conditions prescribed by the definition of number. The collection, however, is not a collection of *objects* or existential singulars but is a collection of *operations:* namely, the operations which determine, according to the definition of number in the abstract, units. Thus 2 means that the operation which constitutes 1 is performed twice.

7. *Particular Terms.* The word "particular" is ambivalent. It is sometimes a synonym for *"certain"* in its sense of *definitely specified,* as in the phrase "the particular man of whom you are speaking." In this usage, "particular" is a synonym for "singular," and there is nothing further to be said of its logical meaning. The logical force of "particular" as distinct from singular, is found when the word is applied to existential materials which have not as yet been ordered with respect to their status as evidential data. At an early stage of inquiry, there may be an accumulation of observed materials whose relevancy and force in respect to the problem in hand is uncertain. They are fragmentary and partial, and in this capacity are particular. As a rule, the plural form "particulars" designates *possible* data while the word "particular" designates a specified determinate existential subject-matter.

I return, in closing, to a point already discussed, now taking it up in its wider theoretical bearings. There is a controversy as to the intension of singular terms. Mill, as we have seen, holds that proper names have no "meaning," while other logicians hold that demonstratives have no meaning except as expressly qualified by a descriptive term. Jevons, on the other hand, says "Logicians have erroneously asserted that singular terms are devoid of meaning in intension, the fact being that they exceed all other terms in that kind of meaning." [4]

With respect to Mill's contrary position, we may cite in addition to what has already been quoted, his statement that proper names, like the mark made by the robber in the story *Arabian Nights*, are "simply marks used to enable individuals to be made subjects of discourse." If a word is understood simply in the sense of sounds or visible marks employed, then it is true of *any* word that it is either "simply a mark used" to enable something, whether a singular or a kind, to be used as a subject of inquiry, or else an indicator of something to be said about them during the course of inquiry—the latter being the case in words which designate conceptual material. But *as* a word or symbol, every word has the meaning, either in intension or comprehension, of that which it stands for—its referent. That an existential term, denoting a singular, enables that for which it stands to be a subject of discourse and inquiry, is possible only because it already has some differentiated and differential intension; otherwise it would be so completely indeterminate that it could not identify and mark out anything in such a way that the latter could be the subject of one mode of discourse or one inquiry in distinction from thousands or millions of other predications that would be possible. When Mill admits that a "mark" has a special *intent* he admits in effect what he denies in words.

It follows that Jevons' position is the only one that can be taken. What is demonstratively denoted by a proper name is inexhaustible in its meaning or intension, instead of being lacking in all such meaning. Take London, England, for example, as a conventional mark enabling a singular object to be the subject of discourse and inquiry. Its meaning in intension is first of all topographical, but it extends far beyond physical location and area. Its meaning in in-

---

[4] W. S. Jevons, *Principles of Science*, p. 27.

tension is historic, political, cultural; it includes a past, a present and potentialities not yet realized. What *is* true of its intension is that it cannot be completely circumscribed at any given time by any set of descriptive qualifications; i.e., its meaning in intension is inexhaustible. The same statement holds in principle of any singular term, for such a term denotes a spatio-temporal career.

The wide theoretical bearings that were mentioned render the particular point at issue a critical one for logical doctrine. It links up with the view that the subject-matter of the logical subject of judgment is a discriminated determination of certain elements within a larger qualitative situation, the material in question being selected to describe a problem and to provide conditions which test any proposed solution. Secondly, it links up also with the doctrine that singulars and kinds are determined in correspondence with each other, there being no singular which is not of some kind (or having characteristics which descriptively determine a kind), and no kind which is not ultimately a kind of existential singulars. Thirdly, it is consistent with the denial of atomic particulars and atomic propositions. For the ultimate ground of belief in atomic terms and propositions is the idea that demonstratives lack all descriptive qualification. It also discloses the gratuitous nature of that doctrine of names which holds that in an ideal language every singular would have its own unique name standing in one-one correspondence with it. It also points to the fallacy in the doctrine that while the conception of kinds and of generic propositions has a place in logical theory, the theory about the latter should be so formal as to provide no place for concrete existential subject-matters. Current logical formalism in logic claims to be allied exclusively with non-existential propositions such as are exemplified in mathematics, while at the same time it recognizes propositions of existential import, covering up the inconsistency by confusing the two modes of the general, the generic and the universal.

Part Four

THE LOGIC OF SCIENTIFIC METHOD

CHAPTER XIX

LOGIC AND NATURAL SCIENCE:
FORM AND MATTER

IT is commonplace that logic is concerned in some sense with form rather than with matter. Such words as "and, or, any, only, none, all, if, then, is and is not" are not material constituents of propositions. They express ways in which material is arranged for logical purposes, no matter how "logical" is defined. Such sentences as "John loved Mary" and "Peter disliked Joan" have the same form but different material contents, while "Two plus two equals four," and "The sum of the three interior angles of a triangle is two right angles" are of the same form in spite of the difference of material content.[1] Again, the proposition "Carnegie is wealthy" and "Millionaires are wealthy" are of different forms, since the first proposition is about a singular as one of a kind, and the other is about a relation of kinds.

The intrinsic place of form in logical subject-matter is more than a commonplace. It states the character which marks off logical subject-matter from that of other sciences. It provides the fundamental postulate of logical theory. Recognition of this fact does not, however, settle the question of what the relation of form and matter is; whether there is any relation, what it is, or whether there is complete absence of relation. This problem is so fundamental that the way in which it is dealt with constitutes the basic ground of difference among logical theories. Those which hold there is no relation between form and matter are formalistic. They differ among themselves; some hold the doctrine that forms constitute a realm of metaphysical possibilities; others that forms are syntactical

---

[1] "Material" as used in the connection above is not to be identified with *existentially* material. Conceptual subject-matter is material in a non-existential proposition.

relations of words in sentences. The opposed type of logical theory holds that forms are forms-of-matter. The differential trait of the variety of this type of theory expounded in this book is that logical forms accrue to subject-matter in virtue of subjection of the latter in inquiry to the conditions determined by its end—institution of a warranted conclusion.

1. *Introduction.* There is no need to repeat or summarize here the arguments that have been adduced in support of this position. It is pertinent, however, to repeat, with some expansion, a point earlier made; namely, that the idea in question (that forms accrue to material which did not possess them in its original form) is a *vera hypothesis*, not a conception invented to serve the *ad hoc* need of a special logical theory. There are many instances in which original crude material takes on definitive form because of operations which order that material so that it can subserve a definite end. Indeed, this sort of thing happens wherever original raw materials are re-arranged to meet requirements imposed by use of them as means to consequences. The supervening of form upon matter did not await the rise of logic. It would be truer, on the contrary, to say that logic itself had to wait until various arts had instituted operations by means of which crude materials took on new forms to adapt them to the function of serving as means to consequences.

Of the numerous illustrations which might be given, two will be selected as exemplary, namely, legal forms, and esthetic forms. The formal nature of juristic conceptions is notorious, so much so that many times during the history of law there has been good ground for complaint that forms of procedure had become the controlling factor at the expense of substance. In such cases, they ceased to be forms-of-matter and were so isolated that they became purely formalistic—a fact which perhaps contains an instructive lesson for logic, since it is clear that legal forms should be such as to serve the substantial end of providing means for settling controversies. More-over, the objective aim is to provide in advance, as far as possible, means for regulation of conduct so that controversies are not so likely to arise. *Rules for ordering* human relations, by prescribing the ways in which transactions should be conducted, exist in order to avert conflicts, to settle them when they occur and to obtain redress for the injured party. These rules of law provide multifarious examples of the ways in which "natural" modes of action take on new forms because of subjection to conditions formulated in the rules. As new modes of social interaction and transactions give rise to new conditions, and as new social conditions install new kinds of transactions, new forms arise to meet the social need. When, for example, a new type of industrial and commercial enterprise required large capital, the form known as limited liability supervened upon the forms constituting the legal rules of partnership.

A simpler example is found in the legal form known as contract. Agreements between persons who combine their activities for a joint end in which one person promises to do something to contribute towards reaching the end and the other person agrees to do something else, are examples of "natural" or crude modes of action. Such reciprocal engagements must have arisen at an early period in social life. But as agreements multiplied and the problem of their execution became pressing, as business became less and less a matter of direct barter and more and more a matter of agreement to exchange goods and services at a future time, certain forms arose to differentiate among kinds of reciprocal engagements. Some of them were treated as mere promises, failure to execute which brought no enforceable penalties, while others were such that failure to execute them imposed a liability upon one party and conferred an enforceable claim upon the other party.

There is nothing in the mere act of promising which differentiates one kind from the other. Certain purely formal traits had to be added to the making of a promise in order to render it enforceable; say, a seal, and evidence of a "consideration." The sum of these forms define a contract. But while the conception of contract is purely formal, it is (1) a form-of-material, and (2) it accrued to prior non-formalized material in order that the ends served by that material might be attained on a wide scale in a stabilized way. As commercial transactions became more complex, sub-kinds of contract arose, each kind of transaction having its own distinctive *formal* traits.

Men did not wait for the rise of logical theory to engage in inquiry in order to reach conclusions, any more than they waited for the law of contracts to make reciprocal promises. But experience in inquiry, as in conduct of business transactions, made it evident that the purpose for which inquiry is carried on cannot be fulfilled on a wide scale or in an ordered way except as its materials are subject to conditions which impose formal properties on the materials. When these conditions are abstracted, they form the subject-matter of logic. But they do not thereby cease to be, in their own reference and function, forms-of-subject-matter.

That the objects of the fine arts, of painting, music, architecture, poetry, the drama, etc., are what they are as esthetic objects in virtue of forms assumed by antecedent crude materials is too obvious for argument. No one acquainted with the material is at any loss to distinguish between Doric and Gothic forms in architecture or between symphonic and jazz forms in the arrangement of tonal material. Similarly, in respect to land, there are forms of record, etc., that have to be conformed to in order to give ownership a legal status. No one has any doubt about the difference between this sort of form with respect to land and that which makes a landscape an esthetic object. Poetry is marked off from prosaic description by some special form. That its material existed independently of and prior to artistic treatment, and that the relations by which that material takes on esthetic form (rhythm and symmetry for example) also exist independently, is undeniable. But it requires the deliberate effort which constitutes art, and the deliberate efforts constituting various arts, to bring the antecedent natural materials and relations together in the way that forms a work of art. The forms that result are capable of abstraction. As such they are the subject-matter of esthetic theory. But no one could construct a work of art out of the forms in isolation. Esthetic forms very definitely accrue to material in so far as materials are re-shaped to serve a definite purpose.[2]

2. *The Failure of Formalism.* The issue of strict logical formalism, of any theory which postulates forms apart from matter, or logical forms versus forms-of-matter, comes to a head in the question of the relation of logic to scientific method. For if formalistic logic is unable to deal with the characteristics of scientific method, a strong, if indirect, confirmation of the position

[2] What I have said in *Art and Experience*, in chapter VII, on *The Natural History of Form* can be carried over, *mutatis mutandis*, to logical forms.

taken in this volume is obtained. It would at first seem as if pure formalism should lead those who accept that doctrine to abstain entirely from any reference whatever to method in the natural sciences, since that method is truistically concerned with factual materials. Such, however, is not the case. Formalistic logic is not content to leave the topic of method in the existential sciences severely alone. Belief in some sort of connection is usually expressed by the phrase "logic *and* scientific method." Another expression conveying the idea of connection is the phrase "applied logic."

Both expressions serve to beg the issue, or at least to disguise the fact that there is an issue. In the case of the seemingly innocent phrase "applied logic," the real issue is whether or not the expression has any meaning at all when logic is defined in terms of forms entirely independent of matter. For the issue is precisely whether such forms *can* be applied to matter. If they cannot, applied logic is a meaningless term. For the question is not whether logical forms are applied, in the sense of being used, in inquiry into existential subject-matter, but whether they could be so used *if* they were purely formalistic. The fact that investigation into natural phenomena, when it is scientifically conducted, involves mathematical propositions, certified purely formally, may be cited, for example, as an instance of "applied" logic. The fact is not only admitted, but, as has been shown in the course of previous discussions, is necessary. The admission proves nothing, however, as to absence of relation between form and matter. It but raises the problem of the *conditions* under which the application or use of non-existential propositions in determination of propositions having material content and import takes place.

It is precisely on this fundamental matter of conditions of application that the formalistic theory breaks down. It would seem to be evident in the very nature of the case that a form which is completely indifferent to matter is not applicable to any one subject-matter rather than to another, much less capable of indicating in any selective way to *what* matter it shall be applied. If the matter in question were completely determined as formed matter *when it is given*, the problem would not arise, and it may be argued with a certain show of plausibility that such is the case in mathematics. But with respect to the subject-matter of the natural sciences, no such plea can be made. Either logical forms have nothing at all to do with it (so that the question of applicability does not arise) or their application is such as to introduce into, or cause to supervene upon, the original subject-matter those properties which give it scientific standing. It is not easy to see how this supervention can take place unless logical forms are capable of somehow selecting just that specific subject-matter to which they should apply in any given scientific investigation, and are also capable of arranging or ordering that subject-matter so that conclusions of scientific validity are arrived at. For the minimum meaning that can be assigned to "application" in physical inquiry is selection (involving elimination) and arrangement. The brunt of the issue, moreover, is not faced until it is recognized that in any case the problem of *what* existential materials are to be selected and of how just *those* materials are to be ordered, is a *differential* one. For purely in the abstract, forms if they apply to *any* one subject-matter, apply equally and indifferently to *all* subject-matters, while in natural inquiries there is always the problem of determining some *special* materials in some *special* order. Whatever may be thought of this general argument, it at least serves to define what is meant by the necessity of determining the *conditions* under which pure and empty forms are applicable.

Discussion recurs, accordingly, to this problem. It is admitted that non-existential propositions, in the way of hypothetical universals, are necessary in order to arrive at fully grounded conclusions in natural science. This consideration is conclusive against traditional empiristic logic (of the type of Mill) which holds that a sufficient number of singular propositions will "prove" a generalization. But refutation of this position is far from substantiating the doctrine of the *merely* formal character of such propositions as they are used in natural science. For the crux of the problem is how in any given case the universal propositions employed acquire that *content* which is a condition of their determinate applicability. It is not enough that the propositional function "If Y, then X" should be seen to be a required form for reaching any scientifically grounded conclusions. It is necessary that Y should be given a *determinate value* such that X may also be given a determinate value. In addition, it is an acknowledged principle that no universal proposition "implies" singulars, so that in any case there is no direct transition from universal to existential propositions. Suppose, for example, that, in some unexplained way, the purely formal "If Y, then X" has acquired content, as in the following: "If anything is human, then it is mortal." It is one thing to hold that such a proposition has directive force in instituting operations of controlled observation that determine whether any existing object has the characteristic traits describing the kind "human" from which it may be warrantably inferred that anything of this kind is "mortal." But logically it is a very different thing to hold that, apart from its operational function in instituting controlled observation, it is applicable to existence. In short, we are brought to the conclusion that *application* is a matter of existential operations executed upon existential materials, so that in the natural sciences at least, a universal proposition has a purely functional status and form.

In the above illustration, it was assumed that somehow or other the purely formal propositional function "If Y, then X," has acquired some content so that Y has the meaning "human" necessarily related to the value "mortal." It is evident without argument that unless definite values are "insertible," the formal propositional functions have no application *even operationally* to any one existential subject-matter rather than to another. In what way then are these special values given to X and Y? Why in a specific inquiry can we not substitute the values that would give the proposition "If angelic, then mortal"? Or, "If diseased, then immortal"? Such illustrations, capable of indefinite multiplication, make it clear that the necessary relation in question is one of *contents* having a certain *form*, not one of mere forms apart from content. The question recurs with added force: How can pure forms acquire related contents? What are the logical conditions under which they acquire those contents without which the application to existence, that marks inquiry in the natural sciences, is impossible?

Suppose that somehow the propositional form "$y\phi x$" (or yRx) has in some unspecified way gained enough content so that it is expressed as "x is assassinated." Ignoring the problem of how the material content "assassinated" was introduced, the question still remains why one value rather than any other of an indefinite number of possible values is given to *x*. It is doubtless a matter of common knowledge that Julius Caesar and Presidents Lincoln and Garfield were assassinated, and that Cromwell and George Washington were not. But how did it become a matter of public information? It would be absurd to say that it became such because of the form of the propositional function. The alternative is the obvious one that it was established by observation and record. The conception of "assassination," exclusively distinct from other modes of dying, is necessarily involved. Logically, the disjunctive form just noted, and the hypothetical proposition "If such and such differential characteristics, then this specific kind, *assassination*," are logically necessary. But they are conditions *to be* satisfied, not inherent properties; and they can only be satisfied by means of extensive and complex existential operations performed upon existential materials.

The assumption that *pure* forms constitute the required application is one more instance of confusion of the functional and directive force of a formal logical relation in prescribing conditions to be satisfied with an intrinsic structural property. Take the example frequently used in contemporary logical texts, "X is mortal," which, it is said, becomes a proposition when *Socrates* is "substituted" for X. Now either "Socrates" is here an empty symbol, devoid of content and reference, or (1) it has meaning and (2) that meaning is such as to be existentially applicable. If it is a formal symbol, nothing is gained by substituting it for X. If it has meaning in application, the meaning does not follow from the propositional function save by means of observations and observable records which determine (1) that an object, Socrates exists (or has existed at some definite place-time) and (2) that this object possessed the characteristics describing the kind *men*.

The propositional function "X is man" is then an expression of highly equivocal form. As soon as it is stated in its proper form (as a hypothetical universal), it is evident that operations indicated by the formula as a rule for something to be done, are necessary to determine the existence of an object satisfying the conditions laid down in the function. "X is human," in other words, formulates a *problem:*—that of discovering the object or objects that are such as to possess the properties prescribed by the term "human"—a condition which requires that the meaning of "human" be already determinate. It follows that existential "application" necessarily (1) involves an existential *problem* with reference to which the *contents* of the non-existential propositions have been selected and ordered, and (2) the operational use of the formally non-existential proposition as a means of observational search for objects that satisfy the conditions it prescribes.

It is pertinent to repeat in this context the point which has been repeatedly made about doctrinal confusion of the two forms of the general proposition, namely the generic and the universal. For this confusion is absolutely indispensable for direct passage from universal propositions to propositions about a singular as of a kind and to propositions about a relation of kinds. The usual line of reasoning in support of the confusion runs about as follows: A general proposition (in the sense of generic) such as "All men are mortal," in the sense that "Each and every man who has ever lived, who is now living or who will ever live, has died or will die" (evidently a proposition of existential import) is said, quite correctly, not to refer to any specific singular but to *any* one of an indefinite number of singulars, the existential range of which includes many singulars not now capable of observation. It affirms, in other words, a connection between the set of traits which describes *mankind* and the set of traits which describes the kind *mortal;* or those subject to the occurrence of the event, *dying.* It is also affirmed (correctly) that ultimately the warrant for asserting this connection is a proposition which affirms that the characters "*being* human" and "*being* mortal" are necessarily interrelated. Short of such a proposition, the proposition in its existential force is at best a generalization, in the sense of an *extension,* of what has been observed in some cases to an indefinite number of unobserved cases. Such an extension is "empirically" confirmed by observation of a large number of events actually occurring. But it is, in theory, open to nullification as a generalization at any time, as much so as is the proposition "All swans are white." What takes the proposition out of this precarious form is, as a matter of fact, biological and physiological investigations which indicate a necessary interrelation between the characters that *define* "living" and those which *define* "dying"—as conceptual structures.

So far there is no confusion. But the fact that the proposition "All men are mortal" does not refer to any *specified* singular as such, or to any one man rather than to any other, is illegitimately interpreted to mean that it does not refer to *any* singular whatever. The proposition is then converted into the non-existential proposition, "*If* human, then mortal." The conversion is illegitimate because it is one thing, logically, to make propositions about traits or characteristics which describe a kind in "abstraction" from any *given* singular of the kind, and a radically different thing to make a proposition about abstractions *qua* abstract. The absence of specific reference to one singular rather than another is no ground for a proposition free from *any* existential reference. There is no logical road from "No *specific* singular" to "No singular *whatever*," in the sense of abstraction from existential reference as such. Yet this is the impossible road taken by logical doctrine when it assimilates the form of generic propositions to those of universals.

The fact that in the context of discussion of logical forms it is expressly pointed out that singular and generic propositions—all propositions of the *I* and *O* form—have existential reference, while no universal of the *A* or *E* form has existential reference, shows that the confusion in question is not an accidental slip, or a case of occasional carelessness. The confusion is inherently essential to any doctrine which (1) holds that logical forms are formal in the sense of being independent of content, factual or conceptual, and yet (2) are capable of material application—as is inherently involved in the methods of the natural sciences if the latter have any connection at all with logic. In spite of the appearance of the word *all* in the proposition "All men are mortal" (as a proposition referring to each and every singular of the kind described by the sets of distinguishing traits that determine respectively the kinds "human beings" and "subject to death"), the proposition is logically an *I* proposition—a fact recognized in the doctrine expressly stated (in another context) that *I* and *O* propositions alone refer to existence.[3]

---

[3] A conspicuous case of the confusion in question is found in the treatment of the null class. That the kinds *Indian Popes, Emperors of the United States,*

I recur to the earlier statement that while scientific method is not possible without non-existential *if-then* propositions, and while such propositions are necessary conditions of scientific method, they are not its *sufficient* conditions. An hypothesis concerns what is *possible*, and a proposition regarding possibles is indispensable in inquiry that has scientific standing. The hypothesis is formulated in an abstract *if-then* proposition. It then formulates a rule and method of experimental observation. Consequences of the execution of the indicated operations define *application* in the only logically coherent sense of that conception. One indispensable *condition* of application in the case of method in natural science is, therefore, that the *contents* of the hypothetical proposition be themselves determined by prior existential inquiries in such a way that the contents are capable of directing further operations of observation. Moreover, even in such cases, the fallacy of affirming the antecedent because the consequent is affirmed is committed, unless independent operations of extensive observation have affected the affirmed relation of contents with a *probability coefficient.* The validity of any such coefficient is conditioned upon the nature of other existential propositions and their material consequences.

The case of ordered discourse in which all propositions are, as such, non-existential in import, and which form a series in virtue of the implicatory, as distinct from the inferential, function affords at best but a seeming exception to the principle that forms are forms-of-matter. For the sequential order of any such series is determined in all cases, in which the final proposition has applicability, by material conditions. Theoretically or in the ab-

have no members, and are instances of a "null class" is a statement having radically different logical form from expressions like, say, *circular-square,* or *vicious-virtue.* The first is an instance of contingency; up to a given date, no such singular has existed or, if it has existed, has not been observed. The second set of examples express necessary exclusion of an instance, since the related conceptions contradict each other. The case of vicious-virtue is perhaps especially instructive. There can be no doubt that there occur actions which conventionally are called virtuous but which, from the standpoint of some ethical theories, are inherently vicious and vice versa. This fact does not signify that the definitions of vice and virtue are compatible with each other, but that from the standpoint of one ethical theory the definitions of vice and virtue held by its adherents are incompatible with the conceptions held by adherents of another ethical theory.

stract, an indefinite variety of series of implicatory propositions is possible—as in mathematics. But—as appears in mathematical *physics*—mathematical implicatory series, in all instances in which applicability enters as a condition, have their contents and their order (in determining a final hypothetical proposition) controlled by the observed existential conditions that form the problem requiring a generalized solution. Otherwise, contents would be taken and ordered in such an indeterminate way that even if the order were necessary with respect to rigor of implication, there would be no assurance whatever of any kind of final applicability. We are again forced to the conclusion that formal relations state conditions to be materially satisfied.

The arguments adduced show incontestably that pure forms, where "pure" means "completely independent of relation to meaning-contents" (factual and conceptual) cannot possibly determine application in the sense in which application is necessary in the natural sciences. There is one especial instance frequently given in recent logical treatises which is supposed to prove that a universal proposition is capable of direct determination of an inference regarding existential matters. It is, accordingly, worth examining, since this will disclose the typical fallacy involved in all instances of the doctrine in question. The example referred to is the following: From the *if-then* proposition "If there are more inhabitants in a town than there are hairs on the head of any inhabitant of that town, then some two (or more) inhabitants have the same number of hairs on their heads." There is, of course, no possible doubt that *if* the conditions stated in the antecedent clause are satisfied, then the state of affairs set forth in the consequent clause will follow. But as far as an *existential* proposition about a person or persons in any actual town is concerned, the proposition only raises a question: Are the conditions satisfied?

This question is one of material fact. It can be answered only by independent operations of observation that are directed by the *if-then* proposition in question. This proposition, when so employed, renders it unnecessary to count the hairs on the head of every person in a town. It is necessary only to have a dependable estimate of the number of hairs on the head of the bushiest-haired person that can be found and also have a dependable estimate of the number of inhabitants of the town. Given these existential data, the inferred proposition that *some* two persons do (or do not) have the same number of hairs on their heads will be warranted. The conclusion that they do *not* have, would be more likely in the case of a hamlet where there are only a few inhabitants. Observational data would suffice in the case of a very large city like London or New York to warrant the existential proposition that two or more (unspecified) persons do have the same number of hairs on their heads. But it would do so not because that proposition is "implied" by the hypothetical proposition in question, but because of determination by observations of existential data, taken in connection with the hypothetical proposition as the rule for their selection and ordering.

A similar mixing of propositions of two different logical forms is found in the notorious case of Epimenides and Cretans as liars. Epimenides who is a Cretan, according to an existential proposition, affirms that "All Cretans are liars." Hence, it is argued, a contradiction or "paradox" inevitably arises. Unless Epimenides speaks the truth, it does not follow that All Cretans are liars, and if he speaks the truth, then the proposition follows that "Some Cretans tell the truth" and hence the proposition that "All Cretans are liars" is false. Only a little analysis is required to show that if the proposition "All Cretans are liars" is a *generic* proposition, meaning that a disposition to lie is one of the characteristic traits that mark off Cretans as a kind from other kinds of Greeks (or of human beings), it does not follow that every Cretan is *necessarily* a liar and that he always lies. For the trait of lying describes a Cretan only in conjunction with other circumstantial, or temporo-spatial, conditions which are contingent since they are existential. In other words, if the proposition is generic, some Cretan may sometimes tell the truth, and there is no contradiction. On the other hand, if the ambiguous term "all" is interpreted in the sense of a *necessary* relation between *being* a Cretan and *being* a liar, or as the contents of a universal, instead of a generic, proposition, it poses a question as far as any existential proposition is concerned. If Epimenides tells the truth when he says "All Cretans are liars" then by definition he is not in fact a Cretan. For denying the consequent denies the antecedent. If on the other hand, it is found, by adequate observation of existential data, that he is lying then it is necessary to revise the hypothetical universal proposition in question—a state of affairs that always occurs when application of a universal proposition to existential condition is found to yield data that are not in accord with the requirements of the universal. The conclusion of the analysis is that only a mixing of the two forms, the generic and the universal, produces the alleged contra-diction.[4]

Exactly the same analysis applies to the existential conclusion that in a country having a monogamous system, it can be inferred that the number of husbands and wives is equal without having to go through the tedious process of enumeration of the actual number of husbands and wives. For independent operations of ob-servation are required to determine whether a given country has or has not a monogamous system. The same holds in the case of the inference that in a given hall the number of seats and the num-ber of persons may be determined to be equal without counting the number of either. For again, it requires independent observa-tion to determine that every seat is in fact occupied. The source of fallacy in all these instances is that, first, cases are taken whose materials have been *prepared* by prior existential operation, and, secondly, that the way in which they were prepared is ig-nored, the ignoring being here equivalent to denial.

The discussion, so far, has supported the doctrine that logical forms are forms-of-matter on a negative ground: namely, the contradictions that exist upon the alternative basis. The positive support of the doctrine is the fact that in scientific inquiry, specific contents, factual or conceptual, as well as forms in which they are ordered, are determined in strict correspondence with each other. An attempt to justify this statement at this juncture would be to repeat the analyses and conclusions of the whole two pre-vious Parts. Instead of engaging in this superfluous task, the point of issue will be approached by consideration of the principle that is present in analogous subject-matters. The basic category of

---

[4] A similar analysis applies to the alleged paradox of the "autological" and the "heterological." In one set of propositions, the words have to do with a con-ception or a category and in the other case with a *word*, which is existential. These "paradoxes" occur only when the logical ambiguity of "class" (as meaning both kind and category) is taken advantage of.

logic is *order*. It is also the basic category of all the arts. The universal order of material contents in every intelligently directed procedure is that of means-to-consequences; actual existential ma, terials providing the "stuff," while the status of the material *as* means requires operations of selection and of re-arrangement so that special interactions may be instituted to effect the consequences intended. At the outset, when a certain result is desired, some existing material in its "natural" or crude state may be used —as a stick conveniently at hand is used to pry a stone. In such a case, required operations of observation are directed merely to selection of a suitable stick. But when need for a certain kind of consequence is recurrent, it becomes advisable to select just the materials that lend themselves to formation of the tools that most expeditiously and economically effect the intended end in a great variety of temporal-spatial circumstances. Materials are then selected and shaped to be *levers*. At a certain level of culture, the lever may be simply a crowbar. But as need develops that consequences be brought about in a widened variety of circumstances, the principle of leverage is expanded and refined to include a variety of physical devices, which, scientifically stated, avail themselves of the law of momenta to obtain mechanical "advantage." An expert mechanic thus becomes acquainted, even apart from comprehension of a scientifically formulated law, with a variety of contrivances all of which are levers because, in spite of their different sizes and shapes, they have the functional relation of being means to a specified distinctive kind of consequence.

Every tool, appliance, article of furniture and furnishings, of clothing, every device for transportation and communication, thus exemplifies practically and existentially the transformation of crude materials into intentionally selected and ordered means so that they are *formed-matter;* or, stated from the side of form, so that there are forms-of-matter. Form and matter may become so integrally related to one another that a chair seems to be a chair and a hammer a hammer, in the same sense in which a stone is a stone and a tree is a tree. The instance is then similar to that of the cases in which prior inquiries have so standardized meanings that the form is taken to be inherent in matter apart from the function of the latter; or (as in the case of some of the formalistic arguments which have been criticized) matter is treated as if it were itself purely formal—a conclusion drawn because integration of form and matter is so completely accomplished.

These instances exemplify the principle stated in the first part of this chapter; namely, that forms regularly accrue to matter in virtue of the adaptation of materials and operations to one another in the service of specified ends. They are here brought forward, however, for a different but related purpose—namely, to illustrate the principle that in all cases of formed-materials, form and matter are instituted, develop and function in strict correspondence with each other. Every tool (using the word broadly to include every appliance and device instituted and used to effect consequences) is strictly *relational*, the relational form being that of means-to-consequences, while anything which serves as effective means has physical existence of some sort.

1. The abstract relation of means-consequence may be formally analyzed. It involves correspondence of material and procedural means, a correspondence illustrated, in the field of tools, utensils, articles of dress, etc., in the fact that materials and techniques are reciprocally adapted to each other. Technical processes of reshaping raw materials are invented so that they are capable of reshaping the crude material to which they are applied to make the latter function as means. The processes must be such as to be capable of just those modes of application that are suited to the materials with which they deal. Techniques once initiated are capable of independent development. As they are perfected, they not only transform old materials expeditiously and economically, but they are applied to crude materials previously not capable of use as means. The new formed-matter thus produced leads to further development of techniques and so on indefinitely, with no possibility, from the theoretical side, of setting a limit.

2. Any technique or set of procedural means must satisfy certain conditions of order so that it possesses *formal* properties. The crudest technical procedure in reshaping crude material has, of necessity, a definite *initiation, termination* and an *intermediation* that connect the two limits. It has the formal properties of first, last and intermediates—the latter being so essential as to define even the word "*means*." The ordered transitive relation of *first*,

last and *middle* operations is *formal* and capable of abstraction because it constitutes a necessary *interrelation* of characters. Change any one of them and the others are necessarily also modified. Generalize the point here made and there emerges the conception of *serial order* as an order necessary to matter *qua* formed-matters from the point of view of all intelligent activity.

3. Because of the first point mentioned (the conjugate correspondence of material and procedural means or techniques), the serial order of procedure determines formal relations in the materials to which the techniques are applied. Even the crude primitive techniques employed to effect objective consequences brought about a crude differentiation between characteristic properties of materials. Certain materials were found to be "good for" the techniques by which clothing was produced; other materials for making utensils in which to store or to cook materials, etc. As techniques of smelting developed, characteristic differences in mineral materials were automatically, so to say, noted in such a way as to mark off different kinds of metals. The principle here exemplified is generalized in the statement that differential characteristics, describing different kinds, are instituted when and only when materials are adjudged as means in connection with operations to accomplish specified objective consequences. An accomplished end, say, clothing, is generic. But it comes about that different kinds of clothing are appropriate to different seasons, occasions, and social castes. Different materials are such as to be "good for" these differential ends: one kind for winter, another for summer; one for war and another for peace; one for priests, another for chiefs, and another for "common" people. Kinds are distinguished and related in strict correspondence with each other.

Were we to recur to the considerations adduced in the chapter on the biological matrix of inquiry, we should note that the formal relations of serial order are prefigured in organic life. There are needs (in the sense of existential tensions); these needs can be satisfied only through institution of a changed objective state of affairs. Effectuation of this close, or consummatory state, demands an ordered series of operations so adapted *to one another* that they are co-adapted to arriving at the final close. If we compare these natural organic cases of means in ordered relation to a consequence one difference of importance appears. The "end" in the case of the relation of activities and material conditions is, in the case of the former, an end in the sense of a close or termination. In the case of the latter, there is an *additive* character. The objective close in being foreseen and intended, becomes an end-*in-view* and thereby serves to *direct* intelligent selection and arrangement of techniques and materials. But there is a common pattern of relationship.

Upon the practical side, the considerations which have been brought forward are so familiar as to be commonplaces. They may seem, therefore, not worth noticing in the discussion of logical theory. But they are pertinent because they bring out a number of points that are fundamentally significant in logical theory. The main considerations may be recapitulated as follows: (1) The accruing of forms to matter in the case of inquiry is not a gratuitous hypothesis. (2) Whenever materials become formed-materials, there is involved a definite order, the serial. (3) This order, being formal, may be abstracted and be formulated in such a way that its implications are developed in discourse. (4) There is continuity of development from the orderly relations of organic life through the deliberately ordered relations of the cultural arts to these characteristic of controlled inquiry.

It is important, in this connection, not to confuse the categories of potentiality and actuality. Crude materials must possess qualities such as permit and promote the performance of the specific operations which result in formed-matter as means to end. But, (1) these qualities are but potentialities, and (2) they are *discovered* to be the potentialities which they are only by means of operations executed upon them with a view to their transformation into means-to-consequences. At the outset, these operations of transformation may be random and "accidental." In the progress of culture, they become so controlled that they are experimental in the scientific sense of that word. The first point is illustrated in the fact that with the emergence of animal life certain materials became *foods*. We may then say that these materials *were* foods all the time and even that they are intrinsically or "by nature" *foods*. Such a view confuses potentiality with actuality. Looking back, we can validly affirm that these materials were *edible*. But they are not foods in actuality until they are *eaten and digested*, i.e., until certain operations are performed that give crude materials those new properties which constitute them of the special kind *foods*. The second point is illustrated in the fact that the difference between edible, non-edible, and poisonous properties was discovered only by processes of trying and testing. Even tribes regarded as primitive have found ways of instituting technical operations which transform stuffs that are poisonous in their crude state into means of nourishment. That qualities *qua* potentialities are ascertained by experimental operations is proved by the fact that with extension and refinement of physico-chemical operations the range of things that are edible has been indefinitely extended. Whether, for example, the attempt to produce milk "artificially" will succeed or not is wholly a matter of available techniques, not a theoretical matter save in the sense that some theory is necessary to *guide* practical effort.

This relativity to operations of the qualities that constitute the characteristic traits which describe kinds, together with the relativity of the discovery of the latter to execution of operations, is fatal, as we saw earlier, to the classic doctrine that inherent natures or essences define kinds. But it has another important bearing upon logical theory. The previous discussion has been limited to doctrines that make a sharp separation between form and matter. But there still exist logical theories which assign *direct* ontological status to logical forms, although in a different way from that of Aristotelian logic. These theories rest upon a basis of fact. For they recognize that logical forms can apply to existential material only in a thoroughly ungrounded, external, arbitrary fashion unless material as existential has its own intrinsic capacity for taking on these forms. But this valid insight is misinterpreted by means of the precise confusion of potentiality with actuality just mentioned. Existence in general must be such as to be *capable* of taking on logical form, and existences in particular must be capable of taking on *differential* logical forms. But the operations which constitute controlled inquiry are necessary in order to give actuality to these capacities or potentialities.

The particular way in which in recent theory, logical forms

are given *direct* existential status (instead of indirect status through their functions in inquiry) is a metaphysical interpretation of *invariants*. The use of certain mathematically formulated constants in physical inquiry is an illustration, as far as it goes, of the meaning of an invariant in its logical sense. If we generalize what is involved, logical forms are invariants. For example, there is no ordered discourse apart from the implicatory relation as a constant, and there is no grounded inference apart from the invariant formal relation of conjunction of traits to descriptive determination of kinds. But it does not follow from the fact that "invariants" are necessary for the conduct of inquiries that yield warranted knowledge that they are therefore necessary in and to the *existence* which knowledge is *about*. Under the guise of a valid principle, namely, that logical forms have existential reference, there is slipped in quite another principle; namely, a particular metaphysical conception about existence, and this special *pre*conception is then used to settle the meaning of logical invariants. Thereby logic is rendered heteronomous; or dependent upon a metaphysical principle not itself arrived at by logically determined methods. In scientific procedure, moreover, an invariant is such in relation to a specified set of operations, while the view criticized assumes that invariants are such absolutely.

The external character of the metaphysical assumption is strikingly evident in that by definition it concerns existence, whereas inquiry into existence can only arrive at conclusions having a coefficient of some order of *probability*. And it is obvious that conceptions of a *probable* invariant and an immutable structure are self-contradictory. Moreover, the conception is gratuitous. For the necessary operational presence of invariant forms in arriving (through inquiry) at warranted conclusions is completely explicable on the ground of competently controlled conduct of inquiry itself. Assumption of a one-to-one correspondence between the forms of authentic knowledge and the forms of existence does not arise from necessary conditions within the logic of inquiry. It proceeds from some outside epistemological and metaphysical source.

The net conclusion of both the critical and constructive portions of the foregoing discussion is that the phrase "logic *and* scientific method" has no valid meaning when "and" is taken to mean an external relation between the two terms. For scientific method both constitutes and discloses the nature of logical forms. It constitutes them in the actual practice of inquiry; once brought into being, they are capable of abstraction:—of observation, analysis and formulation in and of themselves. In connection with this conclusion, it is pertinent to summarize briefly the outcome of some previous discussions.

1. The history of actual scientific advance is marked by the adoption and invention of material devices and related techniques: —of complex and refined forms of apparatus and definite related techniques of using apparatus. Even in the last half-century, astronomical science has been revolutionized by invention and use of such material instruments of inquiry as the spectroscope, bolometer, ultra-violet glass, chemical emulsions in photography, use of aluminum instead of mercury for coating mirrors, and the techniques which have made possible construction of lenses eighty inches in diameter and mirrors having a diameter of two hundred inches.[5]

2. The new data thus instituted do much more than provide facts for confirming and refining old conceptions. They institute a new order of problems whose solution requires a new frame of conceptual reference. In particular, it was by the use of new instruments and techniques that changes and relations of change were disclosed in what had previously been taken as fixed; a process that has gone on at an accelerated rate since the seventeenth century. This change in the nature of data was both the source and the product of the universal adoption of the experimental method and of the new order of conceptions demanded by its successful execution.

3. Upon the conceptual side, this scientific revolution was accompanied by a revolution in mathematical conceptions; again,

---

[5] Cf. *ante*, pp. 252–3. The following passage is worth citation as one of the comparatively few instances of recognition, from the side of theory, of the importance of this point: "The reason why we are on a higher imaginative level [in science] is not because we have finer imagination but because we have better instruments. In science, the most important thing that has happened in the last forty years, is the advance in instrumental design. . . . These instruments have put thought on a new level." A. N. Whitehead, *Science and the Modern World*, p. 166.

partly as cause and partly as effect.   As long as Euclidean geometry was taken to be the exemplary model of mathematical method, the underlying categories of mathematics were such as to be applicable only to structures fixed within certain limits.   The logic of deduction from first, and immutable truths then remained supreme, wherever the necessity for general principles was acknowledged.   Cartesian analytics, the calculus, and subsequent developments were called for by the radically new emphasis placed in scientific inquiry upon correlations of change, while independent development of mathematical conceptions disclosed in their application to existence new, more refined and extensive problems of correlated change.

In the meantime, the development of a genuinely empirical theory of logic, one in accord with actual scientific practice, was seriously retarded and deflected by adherence to an order of ideas that had developed in the prescientific epoch.   The incompatibility of this conceptual framework with the actual procedures and conclusions of scientific inquiry strengthened, by reaction, the position of the non-empirical *a priori* school.   Mill's logic, as representative of the earlier type of empiricism, is a noteworthy combination of genuine concern for scientific method as the sole source of valid logical theory with a misinterpretation of that method, which is due to an adherence to notions about sensations, particulars, and generalizations, that were formulated before the rise of modern scientific method.   The outcome was his denial of the importance of conceptions; reduction of hypotheses to a secondary "auxiliary" position; the idea that mere particulars can "prove" a generalization, etc.

This chapter, in both its critical and constructive phases, is, then, preparatory to detailed examination of the logic of scientific method, as that is exhibited in the mathematical and in the natural sciences.   In a certain sense, the order of exposition of topics in this treatise is the reverse of the order in which their contents have actually developed.   For, as just indicated, the special logical interpretations which have been advanced represent the conclusions of analysis of the logical conditions and implications of scientific method, while in the interpretations that form the previous chapters they have been taken up, for the most part, on the ground of their logical status as such. The following chapters thus serve both as an explicit formulation of the ultimate foundations of the views previously expressed, and as a test of their validity.

Because of the critical role of mathematics in physical science and because also of the peculiarly formal character of mathematical subject-matter, the logical conditions of mathematical discourse will be taken up first in order of the topics that are discussed.

CHAPTER XX

MATHEMATICAL DISCOURSE

THE ABILITY of any logical theory to account for the distinguishing logical characteristics of mathematical conceptions and relations is a stringent test of its claims. A theory such as the one presented in this treatise is especially bound to meet and pass this test. For it has the twofold task of doing justice to the formal character of the certification of mathematical propositions and of showing not merely the consistency of this formal character with the comprehensive pattern of inquiry, but also that mathematical subject-matter is an outcome of intrinsic developments within that pattern. For reasons suggested in the closing sentence of the last chapter, the interpretation of the logical conditions of mathematical conceptions and relations must be such as to account for the form of discourse which is intrinsically free from the *necessity* of existential reference while at the same time it provides the *possibility* of indefinitely extensive existential reference—such as is exemplified in mathematical physics.

I. *Transformation as a Fundamental Category.* The end of inquiry (in the sense in which "end" means both end-in-view, or controlling intent, and terminating close) is institution of a unified resolved situation. This end is accomplished by institution of subject-matters which are respectively material means and procedural means—factual data and conceptual meanings. These instrumental subject-matters are instituted by operations in which the existential material of a given problematic situation is experimentally modified in a given direction. Conceptual subject-matters, consisting of possibilities of solution, are at the same time so constructed as to direct the operations of experimental selection and ordering by which transformation of existential material toward the end of a resolved situation is effected. The conceptions that represent possibilities of solutions must, moreover, if inquiry is controlled, be propositionally formulated; and these propositions must be developed in ordered series so as to yield a final general proposition capable of directing in operations definitely applicable to the material of the special problem in hand. Otherwise, there is an inference so premature as to yield an ungrounded proposition.

In short, ordered discourse is *itself* a series of transformations conducted according to rules of rigorous (or necessary) and fruitful substitution of meanings. Such transformation is possible only as a system of interrelated abstract characters is instituted. Common sense conceptions, for example, do not satisfy the conditions of systematic interrelation. Hence the change of content they undergo in science as they are modified to satisfy this condition. *Transformation* of conceptual contents, according to rules of method that satisfy determinate logical conditions, is thus involved both in conduct of discourse and in the formation of the conceptions that enter into it even when discourse is intended to have final existential application.

The logical principle involved may be restated in the following ways: (1) The subject-matter or *content* of discourse consists of *possibilities*. Hence the contents are non-existential even when instituted and ordered with reference to existential application. (2) As possibilities, they require formulation in symbols. Symbolization is not a convenience found to be practically indispensable in discourse, nor yet a mere external garb for ideas already complete in themselves. It is of the very essence of discourse as concerned with possibilities. In their functional capacity, however, symbols have the same logical status as existential data. For this reason they are themselves subject to transformations. Historically, the operations by which symbol-meanings are transformed were first borrowed from and closely allied to physical operations—as is indicated in the words still used to designate rational operations; in gross, in such words as *deliberation, pondering, reflection*, and more specifically in *counting* and *calculation*. As meanings were modified to satisfy the conditions imposed by membership in an interrelated system, operations were also modified to meet the requirements of the new conceptual material. Operations became as abstract as the materials to which they apply and hence of a character expressed, and capable only of expression, in a new order of symbols.

In the chapters preceding the present one, we have been concerned with the relation of meanings and propositions in discourse where discourse is conducted in reference to some final existential applicability. In discourse of this type application is suspended or held in abeyance but relationship to application is not eliminated in respect to the content of the conceptions. When, however, discourse is conducted exclusively with reference to satisfaction of its *own* logical conditions, or, as we say, for its own sake, the subject-matter is not only non-existential in immediate reference but is itself formed on the ground of freedom from existential reference of even the most indirect, delayed and ulterior kind. It is then mathematical. The subject-matter is completely abstract and formal because of its complete freedom from the conditions imposed upon conceptual material which is framed with reference to final existential application. Complete freedom and complete abstractness are here synonymous terms.

Change in the *context* of inquiry effects a change in its intent and contents. Physical conceptions differ from those of common sense. For their context is not that of use-enjoyment but is that of institution of conditions of systematic extensive inference. A further new context is provided when all reference to existential applicability is eliminated. The result is not simply a higher degree of abstractness, but a new order of abstractions, one that is instituted and controlled only by the category of abstract relationship. The necessity of transformation of meanings in discourse in order to determine warranted existential propositions provides, nevertheless, the connecting link of mathematics with the general pattern of inquiry.

The effect of change of context upon the intent and contents of operations was exemplified in some of the illustrations that were adduced in the previous chapter. Categories of selection and order, having an implicit esthetic quality, are involved in the writing of history. These categories when liberated from their original context gave rise to the historical novel. Carried further, they give rise to the "pure" novel with its distinctive contents. In similar fashion, music did not create in either nature or in speech sounds and their ordered arrangement. Music, however, developed the potentialities of sounds and their cadenced arrangement in activities having their own distinctive subject-matter. An analogy with development of mathematics is not forced. Numerical determinations first arose as means of economic and effective adjustment of material means to material consequences in qualitative situations marked by deficiency and excess.[1] But not only was there nothing in the operations that were involved to obstruct development on their own account, but they invited such development.

The complete execution of the abstraction involved was a slow historical process. Doubtless numbers were first closely connected with things. For example, 2, meant two fingers or two sheep, and, as the word *geometry* still suggests, geometrical conceptions were associated with physical operations of measuring physical areas. Greek mathematicians and philosophers effected a partial liberation from existential reference. But abstraction was not complete. Conceptions of arithmetic and geometry were freed from reference to particular things but not from all ontological reference. For they were supposed to refer to the metes and bounds existing in nature itself by which nature was an intelligible structure and by which limits were set to change. Since geometry was the science of these existential cosmic "measures," number was geometrically conceived. The story of liberation of mathematical subject-matter from any kind of ontological reference is one with the story of its logical development through a series of crises, such as were presented by irrationals, negatives, imaginaries, etc.

II. *The Two Types of Universal Propositions.* The foregoing introductory remarks are intended to indicate that the category of transformation extends through the whole pattern of inquiry from (1) existential transformations that are required in order to warrant final judgment, to (2) meanings in discourse, and to (3) the formal relations of completely abstract subject-matters, in which transformation as abstract possibility takes the form of transform*ability* in the abstract. As a consequence of the last named development, two logical types of universal propositions

[1] See, *ante,* pp. 209–10.

must be distinguished. In the course of previous discussions it has been held that a physical law, such as is expressed as a relation of abstract characters, is a universal hypothetical proposition. For example, the law of gravitation is a formulation of the interrelation of the abstract characters mass, distance and "attraction." But while the contents of the proposition are abstractions, nevertheless, since the proposition is framed with reference to the possibility of ultimate existential application, the contents are affected by that intent. Such hypothetical universals do not exhaust the possible existential affairs to which they may be applied, and as a consequence *may* have to be abandoned in favor of other hypothetical universals which are more adequate or appropriate to the subject at hand. This is illustrated by the change from the Newtonian law of gravitation to the Einsteinian formulation. Although both are hypothetical universals in this sense, each is an empirically significant contrary of the other. In such propositions (including all those of mathematical physics) the strictly mathematical phase resides in the necessary relation which *propositions* sustain one to another, not in their contents.

But in a mathematical proposition, such as $2 + 2 = 4$, the interpretation to be put upon the contents is irrelevant to any material considerations whatever. The final applicability of a physical law, even when stated as a universal hypothesis, demands that some preferred and therefore some limiting interpretation be placed upon the terms or contents that are related. The contents of a mathematical proposition are freed from the necessity of any privileged interpretation. Take the physical law of the parallelogram of forces, as that provides the basis of calculations ultimately applicable in existential determination. The status of "forces" in that law affects the meaning of "parallelogram"; it limits the otherwise mathematical conception to subject-matters having properties of direction and velocity. That is, it requires what was called a preferred or privileged interpretation, which is restrictive. The contents of a mathematical proposition, *qua* mathematical, are free from the conditions that require any limited interpretation. They have no meaning or interpretation save that which is formally imposed by the need of satisfying the condition of transformability within the system, with no extra-systemic reference whatever. In the sense which "meaning" bears in any conception having even indirect existential reference, the terms have no meaning—a fact which accounts, probably, for the view that mathematical subject-matter is simply a string of arbitrary marks. But in the wider logical sense, they have a meaning constituted exclusively and wholly by their relations to one another as determined by satisfaction of the condition of transformability. This type of universal hypothetical proposition is therefore logically certifiable by formal relations, because formal relations determine also the terms or contents, the "material," as they cannot do in any universal proposition having ultimate existential application. The type of relation which subsists between *propositions* in mathematical physics becomes here the determinant of the contents.

To summarize, transformation of meanings and their relations is necessary in the discourse that is conducted to take ultimate effect in existential transformations. The involved operations of transformation are capable of being themselves abstracted; when abstracted and symbolized, they provide a new order of material in which transformation becomes transform*ability* in the abstract. Control of transformations that take place in this new dimension of subject-matter is exercised solely by reference to satisfaction of conditions of transformability in the abstract.

III. *The Category of Possibility.* This theory of mathematical subject-matter continues the emphasis that has throughout been placed upon operational determination of the subject-matters of inquiry. The logical import of this operational determination in this particular context may be brought out by contrasting the operational interpretation of possibility (with respect to transformability) with another theoretical interpretation of its nature. This other theory differs in holding to an ontological as over against an operational interpretation of possibility, for it relates mathematical (and logical) forms to a Realm of Possibility conceived to have ontological status. The realm of possibility is indefinitely more extensive than the realm of actuality, and, since what is actual must be first possible, it provides the ultimate logically limiting ground for whatever is actual. The applicability of logic and mathematics to existence is accordingly explained to be a special instance of the general relation of the realm of possible

Being to that of actual Being. This theory is here brought under discussion because it affords, by way of contrast, opportunity to bring out more explicitly the implications of the functional-operational interpretation of possibility. For the question does not concern the basic importance of that category but its interpretation.

It is not a simple matter to find illustrative material such as will take the discussion out of the domain of direct clash of philosophical theories into the domain of logic proper. A point of departure may be found, however, in the question of the relation a map of a country bears to the country of which it is a map. The illustration is but a point of departure, for clearly it cannot be supposed to provide a direct analogy. For the country mapped is an example of the existential Realm of Being, and the map refers to the country of which it is the map as to an existence. The force of the illustration, as analogical, resides somewhere else; namely, in the *isomorphism* of the *relations* of the map and the country, independently of the existential nature of the relations of the latter.

That the isomorphism in question is one of relations is evident in the fact that it does not exist between a point marked on the map and an element of the country mapped, town, river, mountain, but between the relations sustained by the former and the relations sustained by the latter. Relations of up-down in the map are isomorphic with relations of north-south in the country, and those of right-left with those of east-west of the country. Similarly, relations of distance and direction of the map are isomorphic with those of the country, not literal copies of actual existences. The illustration will be used to indicate that the isomorphic relation which subsists between the relations of the map and those of the country, or between *patterns* of relation, should be interpreted in a functional and operational sense.[2]

A beginning may be made by noting the ambiguity of the word *relation*. It stands not only for existential connections, for logical relations between the terms of a proposition, and for reference or applicability of the proposition to existence—but also for relation-*ship*.[3] The first set of ambiguities does not concern the argument

---

[2] In other words, the issue concerns the *meaning* of isomorphic patterns, not their existence or importance.

[3] For the former, see *ante*, pp. 54–5. For the latter, *ante*, pp. 330–2.

regarding isomorphism in the case of mathematics. For while on general logical principles it is necessary to distinguish the existential connections of the country from the logical relations of the map as a proposition, and both of these from the reference which the map has to the country, the distinctions are not relevant to the present issue, since the order of Being with which mathematical relations are said to be isomorphic is non-existential. Nevertheless, two points about the "relation" (reference) of a map to the country mapped will be made because of their bearing upon the nature of isomorphism.

1. The relations of the map are similar (in the technical sense of that word) to those of the country because both are *instituted by one and the same set of operations*. As far, then, as this case of similarity of relations is an illustration of isomorphism, it throws no light on the ontological isomorphism said to subsist in the case of mathematics. For that doctrine is at the opposite pole. It does not hold that operations that determine the relations of mathematical subject-matter also determine those of the "Realm of Possibilities." The position here taken does hold, however, that the operations of transformability which determine mathematical subject-matter are, or constitute, the Realm of Possibilities in the only meaning logically assignable to that phrase.

The statement that the relations of the map are similar to those of the country mapped because both are instituted by one and the same set of operations is readily seen by noting the fact that both are products of execution of certain operations that may be summed up in the word *surveying*. The elements of the country are certainly existentially connected with one another. But as far as knowledge is concerned, as far as any propositions about these connections can be made, they are wholly indeterminate until the country is surveyed. When, and as far as, the country is surveyed, a map is brought into being. Then, of course, there is a common pattern of relations in the map and in the country as mapped. Any errors that result in the *map* from inadequacy in the operations of surveying will also be found in propositions about the relations of the *country*. The doctrine of structural (in the sense of non-operational) similarity of the relations of the map and those of the country is the product of taking maps that have in fact been perfected through performance of regulated operations of surveying in isolation from the operations by which the map was constructed. It illustrates the fallacy that always occurs when propositions are interpreted without reference to the means by which they are grounded.

2. Given the map as a pattern of relations, the "relation" of the the pattern to that of the country mapped is functional. It is constituted through the intermediation of the *further* operations it directs—whose consequences, moreover, provide the means by which the validity of the map is tested. The map is instrumental to such operations as traveling, laying out routes for journeys, following movements of goods and persons. If this consideration is employed with respect to mathematical subject-matter, it must, of course, be noted that the further operations which the two respective subject-matters direct are of different forms. In the case of mathematics the operations and consequences are not existential as they are in the relation of the map to traveling, etc., and their consequences. But as far as *development* of mathematical subject-matter as such is concerned the analogy concerning the *functional* use of operations is precise. The reference of mathematical subject-matter that is given at any time is not ontological to a Realm of Possibilities, but to further operations of transformation.

As far as the map is usable as an illustration of mathematics, the isomorphic relation is definitely exemplified in the relation to one another of maps that are drawn upon different projection systems. The pattern of relations of a map drawn upon the Mercator projection is isomorphic with that of maps drawn upon conic, cylindrical and stereographic projections, while theoretically still other isomorphic projection-systems are possible. There is a morphological enlargement of polar regions in the Mercator style of map; in the cylindrical, their shape is distorted, while areas are correct; in the stereographic, areas are correctly patterned but the scale is not constant throughout all parts of the map, etc. When the directive function of the map is left out of consideration it must be said that no map is "true," not only because of the special "distortions" mentioned but because in any case a map represents a spherical upon a plane surface. On the functional interpretation, any map in any system is "true" (that is, valid) if its operational use produces the consequences that are intended to be served by the map.[4] Considering only the relationship of their patterns, there is isomorphism because the relations characteristic of one are transformable inclusively and exclusively into the relations of every other.

What is involved in the last paragraph, as far as illustration of mathematical subject-matter is concerned, introduces the topic of the ambiguity in the term relations and relational with respect to the distinction of form between *relatives* and *relationships*. Terms are related to each other in the sense of being *relative* whenever they involve, in addition to the specific relation designated, singulars or kinds which have traits and relations over and above the relation which is specified: when, that is, the relation in question does not exhaust the significance of the related terms. *Father* and *son* are relative terms whether applied to two given singulars or to two kinds. But the singulars who are fathers and sons have many other traits and relations. Indeed, they are related to each other only *because* they have other properties. But *paternity-sonship* is a term in which the "relation" exhausts the meaning of the terms. The difference is that expressed linguistically respectively by "concrete" and "abstract" nouns. Furthermore, there is no *necessary* relation such that the man who is related as a father is also related as a brother. The question of whether he is a brother is a question of fact to be determined by observation. But there is possible a *system of relationships,* such that *within the system* paternity and brotherhood are necessarily related, while also both are interrelated, by the very structure of the system, with uncleship, cousinship, and so on, as in an abstract genealogical table which exhaustively includes every relationship in a system of *possibilities* of kinship. In the ordinary Mercator map, if the polar regions were taken to be *relative* (in the sense defined) to equatorial regions, there would be misrepresentation. But given the coordinates which define the projective system, they have a necessary *relationship* within the system. When mathematical

[4] Interpretation of "truth" as correspondence in terms of literal reproduction would demand that a "true representation" be another globe just like the earth itself. Such a reproduction would be useless for the purpose representation fulfills. It would, in fact, only duplicate the problems of the original.

subject-matter is said, then, to consist of relations of relations, the statement is ambiguous. In the case of singulars and of kinds, "relations of relations" always involve reference, implicit or explicit, to materials (of singulars and kinds) whose existence or non-existence can be determined only through observation. Without such reference to elements as terms of the relations that are related, it (relations of relations) is an absurd conception. But relationships by their very nature are interrelated in a system—the nature of the system being determined in mathematics by a set of postulates.

A system of relationships defined as being of a given order—as in the case of a map projection or an abstract genealogical table—constitutes, therefore, the ground of operations of transformation within that system. Indeed, this statement is too weak in that it fails to note that the system of interrelated meanings is *so* defined as to make possible a set of operations of transformations in which, on formal grounds—those determined by the postulates of the system—any given transformation is logically necessary. In a weakened sense, the relationships of maps drawn on different projective systems and the relationships of the abstract genealogical system are mathematical in quality. But mathematics proper is constituted by abstraction of the operation of *possible* transformation (transformability) so that its subject-matter is universalized in a way which is not found in the instances cited. While it is not claimed that this operational-functional interpretation of isomorphic patterns of relationships *disproves* the interpretation of mathematics that refers it to an ontological ground, it is claimed that it renders that interpretation unnecessary for *logical* theory, leaving it in the position of any metaphysical theory that must be argued for or against on *metaphysical* grounds.

IV. *The Postulational Method.* The previous discussion is meant to indicate that and how the general pattern of inquiry is reflected in mathematics—the function of abstraction which is involved in all existential inquiry being itself abstracted and universalized. Further discussion will attempt to show in more specific terms how the pattern is exhibited in the postulational method of mathematics.

1. The initiation of every inquiry springs from the presence of

some given problematic subject-matter. In its early history, problems of strictly existential subject-matter provided the occasion for mathematical conceptions and processes as means of resolving them. As mathematics developed, the problems were set by mathematical material as that itself stood at the given time. There is no contradiction between the conceptual, non-existential nature of mathematical contents and the existential status of mathematical subject-matter at any given time and place. For the latter is an historical product and an historical fact. The subject-matter as it is at a given time is the relatively "given." Its existing state occasions, when it is investigated, problems whose solution leads to a reconstruction. Were there no inconsistencies or gaps in the constituents of the "given" subject-matter, mathematics would not be a going concern but something finished, ended.

2. As was intimated in an earlier context, material means and procedural means operate conjugately with each other. Now there are material means, having *functionally* the status of data, in mathematics in spite of their non-existential character. They constitute the "elements" or "entities" to which rules of operation apply, while the rules have the function of procedural means. For example, in the equation $2 + 3 = 5$, 2 and 3 are elements operated upon, while $+$ and $=$ are operations performed. There is no inconsistency in the identity between the *logical function* of existential data and mathematical elements or entities and the strictly non-existential character of the latter. On the contrary, the condition of transformability which mathematical contents must satisfy demands that there be "data" which are determined exclusively and exhaustively by reference to the operations and rules of operations executed or to be executed with and upon them.

In any existential inquiry also, material data are selected and ordered with reference to operations to be performed, the latter being possibilities formulated in hypothetical propositions. But the qualities which are selected and ordered as evidential traits are selected from out of a total existential situation and are themselves existential. Hence they are capable of only a specific and limiting interpretation, since anything existent is spatially and temporally circumstantial and local. Consequently, as we have seen, the *contents* of physical non-existential generalizations are determined with reference to final existential applicability; the fact that they are formulated so as to be as comprehensive as possible (as applicable to the widest possible range of existences) does not eliminate their final determination in terms of existential applicability. The generalizations instituted do eliminate reference to all existential qualities and circumstances that might restrict the applicability of the generalization; but such elimination is compensated for, and, indeed, is constituted, by selection of more generic extensive existential traits.[5] The conceptual nature of the material data of mathematics means that they are determined exclusively and wholly in reference to the possibility of operations of transformation, the latter constituting procedural means. This property is all one with that freedom from specific and hence limiting interpretation that has already been mentioned.

Discussion is thus brought to explicit consideration of the postulational method of mathematics. Any scientific system, when logically analyzed and ordered, is found to involve certain propositions that are, for that system, primitive. These primitive propositions are postulates in that they state *demands* to be satisfied by the derived propositions of the system. In the systems of natural science, the demands to be satisfied involve (1) elements determined by controlled or experimental observation and (2) operations which are capable of existential execution. The primitive propositions which are the postulates of a mathematical system are, as has been shown, free from both of these conditions. For their contents with respect to both elements and methods of operation are determined exclusively with reference to transformability.

The postulates of a mathematical system, in other words, state elements and ways of operating with them in strict conjugate relation each to the other. Take, for example, such a postulate as the following: "If *a* and *b* are elements of the field *K*, then *ab* ($a \times b$) are elements of K." The postulated elements are *a*, *b*. The postulated operations are represented by "and" and by "$\times$"

---

[5] The concrete bearing of this determination is considered later with reference to M, T and L, as standard conceptual means of selecting and ordering data. Ch. XXIII, pp. 481–3.

or *ab*. The primitive proposition does not first postulate certain elements, and then by means of another primitive proposition postulate a certain operation in two separate postulates. The elements and the operations are laid down in a single postulate in logical dependence each upon the other. *a* is defined to be such that if the operation designated by *and* is applicable, then the operation symbolized by $\times$ is necessarily applicable. The elements are instituted in relation to the operations by which they are related and the operations and their rules are determined in reference to the elements. The operations which are introduced by the postulates are specified in no other way than by the combinations into which they are permitted to enter by the postulates. For example, the operation denoted by "$\times$" is any operation whatsoever, provided only that it satisfies the conditions of commutativity, associatativity, and distributivity with respect to the operation denoted by "$\times$."

For this reason description and definition, which are of different logical forms in the case of existential material, coincide with respect to the elements or material data of mathematical subject-matter, as do also inference and implication. The elements are what they are *defined* to be; constituted by definition and nothing but definition. The methods of operation, which are postulated in conjugate relation with the elements are, on the other hand, *resolutions* rather than definitions. Neither the definitions nor the resolutions can be identified with axioms in the traditional sense of self-evident truths. The resolution concerns methods of procedure to be strictly adhered to, and the definition posits elements to be operated with and upon by these specified methods of combination, yielding transformations stated in the theorems that follow. There is no other control of their meaning, which means that the control is strictly formal. They are not controlled, as in the early logical philosophy of mathematics, by extra-systemic reference to some "essence."

Every scientific system is constituted by a *set* of postulates, which in logical ideal are independent of one another, or that do not overlap as to operations to be performed. For a *combination* of operations is the only way in which development in discourse can take place. The postulate mentioned above is a way of setting forth the principle that any element subject to the condition of logical summation is also subject to that of alternation. Another postulate, namely, that if a is an element of the field K, then $\bar{a}$ is also an element, states that any posited element that can be affirmed is also subject to the operation of negation, thereby fulfilling the logical condition of the conjugate relation of the functions of affirmation and negation. Since the constituent primitive propositions of a set of postulates prescribe a complex of operations by means of which the results of one operation may be combined with results of other operations, postulates in one system may appear as theorems in another system and *vice-versa*. For the sole ultimate logical condition to be satisfied is that the postulates define elements and prescribe ways of dealing with them in combinations of operations such that theorems follow which satisfy all the conditions of formal conjunction-disjunction.

Any single operation taken by itself is indefinitely recurrent or non-terminating. This is true of even a physical operation like walking or chopping wood. Single operations do not provide the conditions of their own termination. They are brought to a close only when cut across or intercepted by an operation of an opposite direction. In other words, a combination of operations and of their results may be called *interceptive*, a typical, although limiting, instance being the relation of affirmation and negation already mentioned. At this point, however, we are concerned with the indefinitely iterative nature of any operation in and of itself. For this character gives the ground for what has been called "mathematical induction." Its nature is illustrated by the following: The sum of the first n odd integers is n^2. For this property holds for the case when n is equal to 1; and we can show that if this property holds for $n = k$ it also holds for $n = k + 1$. Consequently, it holds for every value of n, since every value of n can be obtained from 1 by the recurrent operation of adding 1. Because of inability to derive this principle from other propositions, it has been held, as by Poincaré, to be an "intuition of the mind." In fact, it is a formulation of the inherently recurring nature of any operation until it is intercepted by combination with another operation or is delimited by a field like the transfinite numbers in which operations do not have the inductive property.

It is neither a postulate nor an intuition, but a partial description of the nature of the operations that are postulated in a given system.

Combination of operations that are integrated with another and also intercepted by a limiting operation, yields in the case of the system of numbers, numbers which are sums (or products, differences), and which, in virtue of the integration of operations, are also integers.[6] Thus 748 which is a sum, or a difference or a product with respect to the operations by which it is instituted is also a number which may be treated as itself an integer in further operations. Were it not for the principle illustrated in this commonplace instance the indefinite because abstract transformability characteristic of mathematical subject-matter would not exist.

1, $\frac{1}{1}$, 1×1, $\sqrt{1}$, 1^1, $\sqrt{\dfrac{1 \times 1}{1}}$, are products of different operations and with respect to the operations by which they are instituted are distinct, as is perhaps more obvious in the case of 1 as the limiting sum of the infinite series $\frac{1}{2}$, $\frac{1}{4}$, $\frac{1}{8}$, . . . But further operations may operate with any one of these results either with or without reference to the operations by which it was instituted according to the exigencies of the problem in hand, if only the postulates of the system are not violated. If this were not so, the conditions of abstract transformability could not be satisfied, for barriers would be set up such as once were supposed to exist in the case of "irrationals."

This principle is the basis of the operations of contraction (simplification) and expansion (composition) which play such a role in mathematics. The operative combination of a variety of operations is symbolized by a vinculum or bracket. The result of the combination of operations may be represented by a simple expression which can then be operated with and upon without reference to the complex of operations symbolized by the contents within a parenthesis. This simplification is another exemplification of the principle that transformability is the ultimate logical category, and that all mathematical operations must be such as maintain

[6] I owe to Dr. Joseph Ratner the point that a "transfinite" number is such because the operations by which it is instituted are non-integratable. By definition it is not an integer. This does not mean that operations of transformation cannot be executed with and upon transfinites.

or promote transformations with respect to the postulates of the system.[7]

Within a given system, accordingly, *equivalence* is always an end-in-view or object to be attained. In accordance with the position previously set forth, as an end-in-view it functions also as a means in discriminative ordering of the conditions of its attainment. In mathematics, equivalence takes the form of an *equation*. In existential inquiry, equivalence and substitutability are effected with reference to final existential applicability and are hence limited by the condition thus imposed. In mathematics, since equivalence (equations) is the end-in-view to be attained within a given system and an operative rule in discriminative ordering of elements, differences in the operations by means of which contents in the system are determined are irrelevant with respect to further operations (as they are not in discourse intended to yield universal propositions that are existentially applicable), *provided their results* so satisfy the condition of a finally attained equivalence or equation that they are capable of being taken, either in simplified or expanded form, as the material of further operations of transformation.

Equivalence is the end-in-view *within* the system determined by a given set of postulates. When different sets of postulates determine different systems, the conditions for satisfaction of equivalence as between them are not found. But universal transformability demands that the theorems of any one system be *translatable* into the theorems of the other systems. This reciprocal translatability is effected through institution of isomorphism; that is, isomorphism (like that of maps of different projection systems) is to transformability *between* systems what equivalence is to transformation *within* a system. The institution of inter-systemic

---

[7] The reader who is familiar with current logical literature may have noticed that the canons discussed in Chap. XVII were limited to identity, contradiction and excluded middle, while it is now usual to include along with them reiteration, association, distribution, simplification, absorption, composition, etc. The omission of the latter was deliberate. For the first three canons represent conditions to be satisfied in final *judgment* while the others mentioned belong to the calculus of *propositions*, stating rules of abstract transformability of propositions. Hence, their applicability is relative to the postulates of a given system. Commutation with respect to combination of vectors has, for example, a distinctive mathematical content.

transformability requires, however, the institution of a new system as intermediary. It is as if translation of Greek, Latin, German, French, English, etc., into one another required the institution of a new language or set of symbols. For example, the distinctive results of algebra and geometry were rendered isomorphic by institution of analytic geometry. It is characteristic of the abstract universality of the transformability category in defining mathematical subject-matter that the institution of any given mathematical system sooner or later sets the problem of instituting a further branch of mathematics by means of which its characteristic theorems are translatable into those of other systems—a consideration that helps to explain the indefinite fertility of mathematical developments.

Interceptive combination of operations determines the important mathematical category of periodicity or grouping. The original historic source of periodic arrangement was doubtless existential. It has been surmised, for example, that the first name for 2 was derived from some natural grouping, such as the wings of a bird, and the name for 3 from, say, the symmetrical arrangement of leaves in trefoil. However this may be, there is no doubt that the periodic grouping constituting our decimal system was derived by suggestion from the existential fact of ten fingers and/or ten toes. While the decimal system is conventional in historic origin, some form of periodic grouping (independent of course, of existential considerations) is necessary, not conventional. Unless combinations took the form of recurrence of *groupings* of operations (or were it limited to recurrence of operations in their severalty) there would be no integration of operations already performed. While grouping is especially conspicuous in the recurrent position of 10 in our decimal system, the principle is exemplified in any number, say 2. Otherwise there would be simply a non-numerical succession as in the successive ticks of a clock when they are not integrated in relation to one another. In an infinite series, periodicity is dependent upon the partially non-integratable character of the operations by which it is instituted, and conversely any number as an integer is an integration of operations that express and determine some periodicity of arrangement. The concepts of line, plane, solid, with their subcategories, are examples of integrated groupings. If *prima facie* the same statement does not seem to hold of the conception of a point, the identity appears when the complete relativity of its conception to that of lines, planes and solids is noted. Indeed, it may be said that the mathematical point, like the mathematical instant, makes explicit the conception of abstract intervalness involved in abstract periodicity.

The conclusions reached may be applied to the interpretation of zero and infinity. The conjugate relation of affirmation and negation (identification-demarcation, inclusion-exclusion) in determination of any completely warranted conclusion has been repeatedly pointed out in the context of different logical topics. This condition cannot be completely satisfied in existential inquiry because the existential conditions of any inferred proposition do not constitute a closed system. Hence, the probable, as distinct from necessary, nature of such propositions. Mathematical subject-matter is so formally instituted that the condition is fulfilled. The positive and negative are completely conjugate with each other, so that it might be said that a primary standing rule is that no operation should do anything that another operation cannot undo. 0 is not, then, a symbol for sheer nullification of operations, nor yet, as in the case of the null class in existential propositions, a symbol of a kind that is empty at a given time. It is a symbol for the complete and necessary balance of operations of identification-demarcation, inclusion-exclusion. This conjugation finds a simple expression in such an equation as $a - b = 0$.

The positive logical function performed by 0 is that without it operations that effect complete transformability are lacking. In the series of integers, for example, negative numbers have no legitimate warrant without 0, which, as a number, introduces the function of direction. A better example is found in analytics in which 0 is the point of origin of all vectors within the system. With respect to it, as the center of a system of co-ordinates, free generalized possibility of operations in all directions is instituted, with results that are so determined that they are related contents within a defined system of transformations. On the other side, 0 as the symbol of the center of a coordinately determined system, is a symbol for the completely integrated relation that affirmative and negative functions sustain to each other.

The infinite in the sense of the non-terminating is a symbol for the intrinsically recurrent nature of any operation whatever taken in its severalty. The infinitude of number or the infinitude of a line (as distinct from lines as *segments* characteristic of Euclidean geometry) is not then *an* infinite number or *an* infinite line. In modern mathematical philosophy, another and more generalized meaning is given to the conception of the infinite. The meaning is that of correspondence, and in particular that of the correspondence of a proper part to the whole of which it is a part Since the category of correspondence is involved in the possibility of transformation (in the case both of equivalence within a system and isomorphism between systems), a logical problem arises as to whether correspondence in this definition of the infinite is to be interpreted operationally or in some other way. In its operational sense, the doctrine that infinity means that sets are "equal" to proper parts of themselves sets forth the possibility of operational institution of correspondences of an isomorphic nature. It might almost be interpreted to stand for "correspondence" in the abstract.

"Equal" does not mean in this instance the *equivalence* which is the end-in-view and the control of operations *within* a given system. For example, 7 in the series of odd integers corresponds to 4 in the series of all integers even and odd. The correspondence is genuine, as it is in the case of 9 to 5, 11 to 6, etc. While it is correct to say that the odd numbers in question are but a "part" of the "whole" set consisting of both even and odd numbers, it does not follow, however, that the *relation* between the two sets is that of whole and part in the sense in which "whole" and "part" relation is exemplified within the set of all integers. The succession of odd numbers *is* a part of the whole set of integers since it occurs by the very operations that determine that set. But *as the* set of odd numbers they are determined by a different operation and as such they are *not* a part of the other set. Taking the relation as one of "whole-part" in its usual sense is like saying that a map of England existing in that country is a "part" of the "whole" country, while its significant relation is that of isomorphism. That one-to-one *correspondence* between constituents of the two sets should be capable of being instituted is a special example of transformability. The number of *operations* to be performed in ordering odd numbers is always the same as the number of *operations* involved in *some* number of the set of odd and even numbers taken together, as in the instances of 7 and 4, 9 and 5, and so on. But in the case of 1, 2, 3, 4, etc., as parts, say, of 10 as a whole, although the difference between them *as parts* is a matter of integration of operations, *the method* of operation is not the same as that which discriminates the 1, 3, 5, 7 of the set of odd numbers. Hence these numbers are operationally different from the 1, 3, 5, 7 of the other set of integers. The correspondence between them (although it is not one of equivalence) can be regarded as that of isomorphism. As in the case noted above of isomorphisms generally, it institutes the possibility of a new order of mathematical conceptions. The category of infinity may thus be regarded as a formulation of correspondency in the abstract.

I conclude this part of the discussion by reference to the meaning of "functions" in physical and mathematical inquiry respectively. When it is said that "the volume of a gas is a function of temperature and pressure," it is affirmed that any existential variation in volume is correlated with variations in temperature or/and pressure. The formula is arrived at and tested by operations of experimental observation. Hence it is contingent, so that Boyle's formulation (cited above) was further refined to meet newly ascertained facts in Van't Hoff's formulation. Given the formulation of the function, special values can be given to volume, pressure and temperature only by means of independent operations of existential observation. The values do not "follow" from the formula in the sense of being implied by them. In the case of the proposition $y = x^2$, any operation which assigns a value to either x or y *necessarily* institutes a corresponding modification of the value of the other member of the equation, and the operation of assigning a value is determined wholly by the system of which the equation is a part, and is not dependent upon extra-systemic operations, such as those of observation. Hence the logical impossibility of interpreting the form of physical generalizations (which *are* formulable as functional correlations) by carrying over into them the form of propositional and mathematical functions.

An illustration of what is implied in the foregoing paragraphs may be drawn from interpretation of points and instants by the method of "extensive abstraction." A point in the mathematical sense cannot be "abstracted" in the sense of selective prescission from relations of physical lines, places or volumes. A point is of a different logical dimension from any physical area, however minute the matter may be. Nor is a point a *mere* negation of extension. Aside from the logical difficulties attending the *merely* negative, or negative "infinitation" in any case, the point serves a positive function. It is no more mere absence of extension than 0 is the mere absence of number. It is a strictly relational (not relative) term. In the literal sense of "extensive," it cannot be derived by abstraction no matter how extensive. *Point* designates a relation*ship*, and the relation*ship* of enclosing-enclosed cannot be logically instituted by any selection out of the relations of things enclosed in and enclosed by one another; though this latter relation may *suggest* the abstract relationship. It bears the same relation to enclosed and enclosing physical volumes that fatherhood does to those who are fathers. The statement "A line is *composed* of points" is only a way of saying that operations of interception may be combined with the operation that institutes a mathematical line such that points are determined, while the statement "a line is composed of an infinite number of points" is only a way of saying that the complex operation in question is such that, like any operation in this domain, it is not terminating.

V. *The Possibility of Existential Reference.* It was stated at the outset that a logical theory of mathematics must account both for that absence of *necessity* of existential reference which renders mathematical propositions capable of formal certification, and for the generalized *possibility* of such reference. Up to this point we have been occupied with the first of these two considerations. The use of arithmetic in ordinary commercial transactions and the role of mathematics in physical science suffice to show that applicability is a possibility and that the possibility is actualized on a wide scale. Two points will be made with respect to the matter of possibility.

1. The first point is that applicability is indefinitely comprehensive precisely *because* of freedom from the necessity of application. That the range of existential applicability of mathematical subject-matter is in direct ratio to its abstractness is shown by the history of physical science in its relation to the history of mathematical science. As long as Euclidean geometry was supposed to have direct ontological reference, the application of geometry in physics was highly restricted, and when it was applied it usually led physics into wrong paths. Riemannian and Lobachewskian geometries not only freed geometry from its alleged existential reference (assumed not only by the ancients but by Kant in his theory of a connection of geometry with space and of space with an *a priori* form of conception), but in so doing it provided instrumentalities for development of the physical theory of general relativity. Highly important developments in the special theory of relativity and the theory of quanta would not have been possible without a prior independent development of branches of mathematics which, at the time of their origin, had, like tensor algebra and the algebra of invariants, no imaginable physical bearing.

Such examples as these, which might be greatly multiplied, are not matters of coincidence. Without an idea, in itself a possibility and in so far abstract, existential transformations are brought about only by organic instrumentalities. The limited range of the activities of lower animals illustrates the result. The more extensive the domain of abstract conceptions and the more extensive and abstract the operations by which they are developed in discourse, the more instrumentalities there are for possible ways of performing the physical operations which institute data as appropriate grounds for extensive systematic inference. How far these possibilities are *actualized* at a given time depends upon the state of physical knowledge at that time and particularly upon the physical instruments and techniques then available. But the possibilities are there awaiting occasion for their operative manifestation.

The Alexandrian mathematicians, it has been pointed out, had in their possession all the conceptions that were needed for attack upon problems of velocity and acceleration of motion. Hence theoretically they might have anticipated some of the leading conceptions of modern physics.[8] But Euclidean geometry exercised compulsory restrictive influence, and this influence rested on the supposed necessity of interpreting mathematical conception in terms of ontological essences. The resulting restriction of numbers to geometrical ratios assigned specific contents to axioms and definitions and thereby to all theorems, so that space, time and motion could not be conceived in that freedom from qualitative considerations that is required in order to render them capable of free mathematical treatment, a treatment that led to an immense widening of application.

2. Reference of mathematical conceptions to existence, when it does take place, is not direct. That reference is made by means of existential operations which the conceptions indicate and direct is a basic principle of this work. What is here added is that in many cases the mathematical conceptions are instruments of direction of *calculation* by the *results* of which interpretation and ordering of existential data is promoted. In such cases, there is no direct application, even of an operative kind, to institution of data. Irrational numbers, for example, are not obtained by any process which involves only direct physical measurement. Such numbers are not the direct results of such operations, irrespective of whether these operations are conducted within the framework of conceptions which involve the irrational numbers or not. Irrational numbers are not *descriptive* of the immediate outcome of operations of measurement. But irrationals do make possible the use of methods of calculation whose results facilitate the *ordering* of experimental results. The same statement holds for continuous functions. Neither they nor irrationals permit of interpretation in terms of direct operational application even in those cases where, through the medium of calculations they make possible, they enter into final formulation of existential propositions. Such instances as these are conspicuous illustrations of the functional, non-descriptive, character of mathematical conceptions when used in natural science. They are logically significant as special evidence

[8] The reference is to an essay by George H. Mead on "Scientific Method" in the volume *Creative Intelligence*. The entire passage, pp. 179–188 should be consulted, since it provides, as far as I am aware, the first explicit formulation of the connection between absence of necessary existential reference and the extensive possibility of such reference.

of the intermediate and instrumental status of universal propositions. Unless this interpretation is given to the results of many
calculations, the propositions that result have to be denied validity
because nothing corresponding to their contents can be found to
be existential.

The considerations here adduced have an obvious bearing upon
the nature of test and verification (See *ante*, p. 157). They prove
that in the practice of inquiry verification of an idea or theory is
not a matter of finding *an* existence which answers to the demands
of the idea or theory, but is a matter of the systematic ordering of
a complex set of data by means of the idea or theory as an instrumentality.

CHAPTER XXI

SCIENTIFIC METHOD:
INDUCTION AND DEDUCTION

W HATEVER ELSE scientific method is or is not, it is concerned with ascertaining the conjunctions of characteristic traits which descriptively determine kinds in relation to one another and the interrelations of characters which constitute abstract conceptions of wide applicability. The propositions which result are generalizations of two forms, generic and universal; one existential in content, the other non-existential. The methods by which generalizations are arrived at have received the name "induction"; the methods by which already existing generalizations are employed have received the name "deduction." These considerations at least delimit the field of discussion. Any account of scientific method must be capable of offering a coherent doctrine of the nature of induction and deduction and of their relations to one another, and the doctrine must accord with what takes place in actual scientific practice.

With respect to both induction and deduction, the logical terrain is still occupied with remnants, some more or less coherent and some more or less of the nature of debris, of logical conceptions that were formed prior to the development of scientific method. There is, accordingly, no field of logical subject-matter in which the need of thoroughgoing reform of theory (the theme of an earlier chapter) is so urgent as in the case of induction and deduction. It has become traditional to repeat the statement that induction goes from particulars to the general and deduction from the general to the particulars. The extent to which these conceptions are valid, i.e., in harmony with scientific practice, is not critically examined. The result too frequently is that actual scien-

tific procedure is forced into the straitjacket of irrelevant preconceptions. Escape from this procedure depends upon analysis of
induction and deduction from the point of view of actual methods
of inquiry.

The traditional and still current conceptions of induction and
deduction are derived from Aristotelian logic, which, as has been
shown, was a systematization of logical forms on the basis of
certain cosmological beliefs. Since the actual progress of scientific
inquiry has led to an abandonment of these underlying beliefs concerning the structure of Nature, it might be antecedently expected that the doctrines about induction and deduction, which
are found in Aristotelian logic, will be so irrelevant to existing
scientific practice as to be the source of confusion and uncertainty
when they are employed as rubrics of interpretation. Discussion
will not, however, be based upon this antecedent probability. I
shall first set forth briefly the original Aristotelian doctrines in
respect to its cosmological foundation; then give a brief summary
of how induction and deduction are to be understood on the basis
of logical principles already developed in this treatise, and, finally,
present an independent analysis.

I. *Induction and Deduction in Aristotelian Logic.* The conception of induction as a procedure that goes from particulars to the
general, and of deduction as the reverse movement, has its origin
in the Aristotelian formulation. More important than the mere
question of its historical derivation, is the fact that the Aristotelian
conceptions were relevant to, and grounded in, the subject-matter
of natural science *as that subject-matter, the structure of nature,
was then understood.* There is no need at this point to expound
at length the characteristic features of the conception of Nature
entertained by Aristotle. The distinction between immutable Being, existing at all times in identical form, and the mutable, which
in its mutability is convincing proof of partial and incomplete
Being, provided the ground of the distinction made between induction and rationally complete, scientific demonstration or deduction. Since the immutable was constituted by fixed species,
each of which was defined by an essence, it followed that strictly
scientific or demonstrative knowledge consisted in a classificatory
ordering of fixed species, in which inclusive species hierarchically

determined included species of a more limited range. This ordering is effected in the demonstrative syllogism. Scientific knowledge of changing things is, on the contrary, possible only when
and as these things are caught and placed within the fixed limits
constituted by essences that define species. The result here was
also expressed in the syllogism, but in a contingent syllogism as
distinct from the rational necessity of the demonstrative syllogism.[1]

1. *The Deductive.* In each of these forms, the deductive is
identified with the syllogistic. Given the underlying cosmological
assumptions, there is genuine meaning in the conception of going
from the general to the particular. In the case of the demonstrative syllogism, the movement is from the more to the less inclusive,
where "particular" is to be understood in a strictly logical sense:—
as equivalent to the more specific in its distinction from the universal inclusive species. In the case of the contingent syllogism,
"particular" has a different meaning. Anything which is mutable
is particular in the sense of being partial, incomplete. Now the
objects of sense perception are observed things in their severalty
in distinction from the species to which they belong. They are,
as just noted, truly known only when and as they are subsumed
under universal propositions which state the inherent nature of
species. As thus subsumed, they "follow" as particulars from the
general.

At this point, I shall briefly indicate the difference between
this conception of rational demonstration and that which is in
accord with present scientific practice. Mathematical discourse
is now the outstanding exemplar of deductive demonstration; but
(1) no mathematician would regard it as logically important to
reduce a chain of related mathematical propositions to the syllogistic form, nor would he suppose that such reduction added
anything to the force of his demonstrations; and (2) such deductions *do not* necessarily proceed from the more general to the less
general even with respect to conceptions; while (3) as has already
been shown (and, indeed as is generally acknowledged), it is

---

[1] To express the contingent nature of this form of syllogism, Aristotle frequently uses the expression "dialectic syllogisms." Their conclusions are true as
a rule, "upon the whole," usually, but not always, since they are not derived
from subject-matters which are themselves necessary.

impossible to proceed directly from a universal proposition to one about an existential particular or singular. It is true (with regard to the second point) that sometimes in mathematical reasoning the final proposition has less scope or "comprehension," a narrower range of applicability, than do the preceding propositions from which it "follows." When, for example, an ellipse is defined as a curve so moving that its distance from a fixed line bears a constant ratio to its distance from a fixed point, the logical movement is from a conception of wider applicability to one restricted by introduction of a special limiting condition. But when the properties of an ellipse are defined by reasoning from the properties of a conic section, the logical movement is from the narrower to the wider range of applicability. When the equilateral is derived from the equiangular, there is neither gain nor loss in comprehension or scope. The fact is that about mathematical reasoning, as an example of deduction, no general statement whatever can be made as to the breadth of the premises in relation to that of the conclusion. Such differences as may be present depend upon the special methods used and the nature of the problem dealt with. So much, in general, for the irrelevancy of the Aristotelian conception of deduction to modern scientific practice.[2]

2. *The Inductive*. With respect to the formulation of the inductive procedures of ancient and modern science respectively there exists a *verbal* similarity. Both start from scattered data (or particulars) and move toward institution of generalizations. But the similarity does not extend beyond the vague formula of "going from particulars to generals." For (1) particulars are conceived in radically different ways and (2) the process of "going," or the way in which generals are arrived at from particulars, is very different. The nature of inductive procedures in present day science is the special subject of later analysis. But, apart from the conclusions of this analysis, a survey of the Aristotelian conception of induction suffices to show its intrinsic unfitness to serve the logical conditions of present science. The cosmological theory of Aristotle postulates that every knowable thing is of some kind or

---

[2] The important difference, not touched upon in the above paragraphs, is that the status and force of general propositions in the classic scheme represented a direct notation of an inherent static structure, or essence, while in mathematics (as we have just seen) such propositions are operational.

species. Even sense-perception is a mode of low-grade knowledge in so far as what is seen, heard and touched is apprehended as being of a kind. The very lowest grade of knowledge, mere sensation, directly apprehends qualities determined by "sensible forms," such as, in touch, hard-soft. Sensation and sense-perception are modes of knowledge in which "matter," the principle of change and hence of lack of Being, predominates, as, e.g., when the dry changes to the wet. In general, the "particular" which is "known" in sense perception is subject to generation and dissolution, to "birth" and "death," as a tree grows from seed, decays and vanishes. *Recurrent* perceptions then constitute experience. In persons who are happily constituted by natural endowment, who have the scientific and philosophic *nisus* or potentiality, the form is gradually apprehended *as such*, first as subduing matter, and finally as completely free from any connection with matter. Definition and classification are thus instituted and there is scientific knowledge on the basis of rational apprehension or notation; in short, the universal is grasped in its own inherent nature. This process constitutes in the classic scheme the "going" from particulars to the universal which is induction. "Forms" which are immutable, necessary and universal, are present from the first in qualities and objects of sensation and sense perception. Induction is but the process by which these forms are so *elicited* from entanglement in "matter" that they are perceived, by reason, in their own essential nature, "reason" being defined precisely as this actualization in knowledge of pure forms of Being.

"Induction" on this basis is a psychological process, although not in the subjective sense of "psychological" which has controlled so much of modern speculation. The process in question is rather biological, and the biological is an actualization of the cosmological. It is, accordingly, perhaps better to think of it as a *pedagogical* process, in which certain select persons in whom the potentiality of reason is brought to actuality by means of the forms that are implicit in objects of experience, are *led up to* or *induced* to apprehend universals which have been necessarily involved all the time in sense qualities and objects of empirical perception. *Epagoge*, the word translated by our word "induction," is then precisely the process of being *led or brought up to* apprehension of fixed and essential forms in and of themselves.[3] It is unnecessary, even apart from the detailed examination of inductive procedures which is later undertaken, to point out the marked difference from induction as it is now commonly understood. The only similarity is the expression "going from particulars to the general," but the sense of every term in the verbal formula is different.

II. *The Nature of Induction on the Ground of Prior Analyses.* Before engaging in analysis of induction from a material point of view I shall give a brief *formal* statement of its nature in the light of previous discussion.

1. Particulars are *selectively* discriminated so as to determine a *problem* whose nature is such as to indicate possible modes of solution. This selective redetermination of perceived objects and their qualities necessarily involves experimental transformation of objects and qualities in their given "natural" state, whereas in the classic logic they are taken "as is." According to the latter theory, any modification experimentally produced is itself of the nature of *change.* It falls, accordingly, in the domain of inferior partial Being. Hence, it would be self-contradictory to treat experimentation as a means of attaining knowledge of what "really" is. Moreover, from a socio-cultural point of view, transformations of given objects and qualities occur in the activities of the lower class of artisans, mechanics and craftsmen. Such activities and processes are, therefore, ruled out from the start as merely "empirical" and "practical," and hence connected with desire and appetite, with need and lack. They are sharply distinguished from knowledge, which is "theoretical" and inherently self-sufficing: a direct grasp of Being in its finality and completeness.

---

[3] The best account known to me of the theory of induction actually held by Aristotle is that of Joseph. He says, "There are two passages where the *passive* verb takes a *personal* subject; as if it were meant that in the process a *man* is brought face to face with the particulars, or perhaps brought, and, as we should say, *induced,* to admit the general proposition by their help." In some other cases, as he points out, the conclusion is spoken of as that which is induced. (Joseph, *Logic,* p. 378;—italics not in original). Were it stated that the man in question is brought face to face with particulars in the way which induces apprehension of general form as a result, there would be no logical difference between the cases in which it is said that a person is induced and those in which it is said the conclusion is induced. The process is in any case one of natural *e*-duction or eliciting, rather than of induction as it occurs in modern scientific method.

2. The particulars of observations which are experimentally instituted not only form the subject-matter of a *problem* so as to indicate an appropriate mode of solution, but are also such as to have *evidential and testing* value with respect to indicated modes of solution. Operations are deliberately performed that experimentally modify given antecedent objects of perception so as to produce *new* data in a new ordered arrangement. Institution of new data, which are relevant and effective with respect to any conclusion that is hypothetically entertained, forms the most indispensable and difficult part of inquiry in the natural sciences. Objects and qualities as they naturally present themselves or as they are "given," are not only *not* the data of science but constitute the most direct and important obstacle to formation of those ideas and hypotheses that are genuinely relevant and effective.

The primary meanings and associations of ideas and hypotheses are derived from their position and force in common sense situations of use-enjoyment. They are expressed in symbols developed for the sake of social communication rather than to serve the conditions of controlled inquiry. The symbols are loaded with meanings that are irrelevant to inquiry conducted for the sake of attaining knowledge as such. These meanings are familiar and influentially persuasive because of their established associations. The result is that the historic advance of science is marked and accompanied by deliberate elimination of such terms and institution in their stead of a new set of symbols constituting a new technical language. The progress of every science—physics, chemistry, biology, and even mathematics—in general and in particular, is evidence both of the difficulty and the necessity of instituting data of a new order.

Any *special* illustration offered may, accordingly, hinder rather than help precisely because of its limited nature. But I venture to cite a typical case: Consider how the development of astronomic science was arrested because the earth *as an object of direct perception* seemed fixed, while the sun was perceived to move across the heavens every day, and to move, together with the "erratic" planets, from north to south and back again during each yearly period. Consider the enormous obstructions which had to be removed before present astronomical conceptions could be reached along with the extensive and refined institution of *new* data of observation, dependent upon inventions of new instruments and techniques. It was not for lack of ingenuity in ordering data but because of what were taken to be data that astronomical theory was so wide of the mark for many centuries. It should be evident, without argument, that any theory which fails to take as basic in its conception of induction experimental operations of transformation of given objects of perception, and institution of new orders of data, is radically defective.

3. The operations by which the given material of common sense qualitative situations is reconstituted (so as to provide subject-matter that delimits a problem and that is also evidential) have been shown to be those of affirmation and denial in correspondence with each other. The prepared outcome is a set of inclusive and exclusive factual materials which reciprocally condition and support one another. That scientific inquiries search out relevant data for their problems by means of experimental determination of identities and differences is a matter of common knowledge. At this point, therefore, it is only necessary to note the complete agreement of this recognized scientific procedure with the logical requirements of the theory which has been developed. It is also to be noted that the operations of inclusion and exclusion are active and existential (not "mental") and that they substitute qualities which are products of *interactions* for qualities that are perceived directly.

III. *Inductive Scientific Procedures.* The material of the two previous sections is designed to show first the inadequacy of traditional logic to furnish the principles by which induction is actually effected, and then to set forth certain aspects of inductive procedure which follow formally from the position taken in this treatise. I come now to the analysis of those scientific procedures to which the name "induction" may be applied if the word has any application at all. For the question is not about the meaning of a word, even of a word that has been sanctioned by long usage, but of the actual procedures by which generalizations are established in the natural sciences. Moreover, generalizations are of two forms: There are those which institute a relation of including and included kinds, and there are those which institute universal *if-then* propositions as hypotheses and theories. Any adequate account of scientific methods as the means by which warranted generalizations are achieved must, therefore, be applicable to both of these two forms. This consideration is, in effect, a warning in advance of the impossibility of making a sharp division between "induction" as the operations by which *existential* generalizations are established, and "deduction" as the operation concerned with the relations of universal propositions in discourse. As far as physical inquiry, at least, is concerned, induction and deduction must be so interpreted that they will be seen to be cooperative phases of the same ultimate operations.

I begin with a summary statement of the conclusions to be reached regarding the distinctively inductive and deductive phases of inquiry, and their interrelation, or functional correspondence, with each other. (1) The inductive phase consists of the complex of experimental operations by which antecedently existing conditions are so modified that data are obtained which indicate and test proposed modes of solution. (2) Any suggested or indicated mode of solution must be formulated as a *possibility*. Such formulation constitutes a hypothesis. The *if-then* proposition which results must be developed in ordered relation to other propositions of like form (or in discourse), until related contents are obtained forming the special *if-then* proposition that directs experimental observations yielding new data. The criterion for the validity of such hypotheses is the capacity of the new data they produce to combine with earlier data (describing the problem) so that they institute a whole of unified significance. (3) The nature of the interrelation or functional correspondence of these two phases of inquiry directly follows. The propositions which formulate data must, to satisfy the conditions of inquiry, be such as to determine a problem in the form that indicates a possible solution, while the hypothesis in which the latter is formulated must be such as operationally to provide the new data that fill out and order those previously obtained. There is a continued to-and-fro movement between the set of existential propositions about data and the non-existential propositions about related conceptions.

This formulation agrees up to a certain point with current statements about scientific inquiry as *hypothetical-deductive* in nature.

But it emphasizes two necessary conditions which are usually slurred in statement of that position: (1) The necessity of observational determinations in order to indicate a relevant hypothesis, and (2) the necessity of *existential* operational application of the hypothesis in order to institute existential material capable of testing the hypothesis. These conditions place the hypothetical-deductive stage of inquiry as intermediate. When this stage is taken in isolation from the initial and terminal stages of inquiry (concerned with existential observations), it is disconnected from its occasion in problems, and from its application in their solution. It is probable that in the current formulation of the position, these stages are taken for granted or are "understood." But it is necessary to state them explicitly in order that the hypothetical-deductive stage may be relevant and controlled in its contents and their order of relation. Otherwise it is assumed (a) that existential propositions are "implied" by universal propositions, and (b) that affirming the antecedent when and because the consequent is affirmed, is valid. (3) The conjugate relation of the inductive and deductive is exemplified in the correlative nature of inference and proof, where "proof" means *ostensive* demonstration. That it is highly uneconomical from the practical point of view to separate the two functions of inference and test is clear without extensive argument. Economy alone makes it important that the material *from* which an inference is drawn should also be such as far as is possible to test the inference that is made. For it is important that the inference drawn should be such as to indicate *what* new kinds of data are required and give some suggestion as to *how* they are to be obtained. But the importance of including within one and the same set of methodic procedures the operations which produce material that is both evidentially indicative and probative is much more than a matter of practical economy. It is logically necessary. For an "inference" that is not *grounded* in the evidential nature of the material from which it is drawn is *not* an inference. It is a more or less wild guess. To say that an inference is *grounded* in any degree whatever is equivalent to saying that the material upon which it is based is such as to be a factor in warranting its validity: not in its isolation but in connection with the new data obtained as consequences of the operations to which the inference, as an hypothesis, led. The progress made by inquiry in any branch may, then, be measured by the extent to which it has succeeded in developing methods of inquiry that, at one and the same time, provide material data having conjunct inferential and testing force.[4] *Satisfaction of this condition provides the definition of inductive procedures.*

After this introductory material, I come to the main theme: analyses of inductive procedures from the material standpoint. The material taken for purposes of initial illustration will be the inquiries that have led to a generalization about the formation and nature of *dew*. Common sense observation suffices in this case to identify, for the most part, the singular phenomena to which the name "dew" is given. Certain traits sufficiently characteristic to mark off the phenomena as a kind, that is different from other kinds, are easily and recurrently observable. Such traits are the time when drops of dew are found, their position and distribution on the ground, their shape, etc. The *chief* problem regarding the phenomena was not to discover identifying traits. It was to determine the including *kind* within which the kind *dew* is included. From the time of Aristotle, and probably much earlier, the accepted idea was that dew is a subkind of the more extensive kind *rain;* in other words, that drops of dew *fell.* This belief was entertained till the early days of the nineteenth century.

It is noteworthy, on one side, that such an inferential conclusion was virtually inevitable as long as immediately given qualities were supposed to suffice in fixing a kind; and, on the other side, that the change in the conception of kind took place only after certain general conclusions regarding conduction and radiation of heat had been instituted. For these generalizations demanded that the existential traits employed to determine descriptively a kind should be conceived in terms of modes of interaction not in terms of directly perceived qualities. (1) The new conception regarding dew was suggested after specific traits that are consequences of heat, conduction and radiation between bodies of different tem-

---

[4] As has been remarked, the word "proof" is unfortunately ambiguous, being often used exclusively for demonstration in *discourse*—which at best, in existential inquiry, is but intermediate.

perature had been ascertained to be connected with traits of bodies as solid, liquid and gaseous. The new hypothesis as to dew was directly suggested by *this* subject-matter, not by any data previously observable. (2) The obvious observable qualities then assumed the status of conditions of a *problem* to be solved, losing that of traits that could be depended upon for a solution. For conceptions of radiation and conduction, of heat, of pressure, are strictly *relational* in content, being constituted as connections of modes of change. (3) Finally, while generalizations regarding temperature and pressure were sufficiently warranted to be accepted in general, their bearing upon the phenomena of dew was doubtful and hypothetical. It was a highly plausible hypothesis that dew is explicable by these conceptions. The hypothesis was capable of development in discourse in such a way that deduced propositions were in close harmony with observed phenomena. Absence of the sun's heat at night means lowering of temperature of the atmosphere. This reduction of temperature, in turn, according to recognized laws, means that moisture in the atmosphere is condensed and deposited upon near-by objects. This conclusion could be arrived at in discourse. Upon the basis of the old logic, the inherent "rationality" of the conclusion would have led to its immediate acceptance and affirmation. The scientifically important thing in the logic of scientific inquiry is that it was treated simply as an *hypothesis* to be employed in directing operations of observation, an idea to be tested or "proved" by the consequences of these operations. There were certain conditions postulated in the content of the new conception about dew, and it had to be determined whether these conditions were satisfied in the *observable* facts of the case.

The hypothesis assumed, for example, the presence of invisible vapor in the atmosphere sufficient in amount to account for the dew deposited. Elaborate experimental observations were conducted to see if this condition was fulfilled. The observations showed that dew is deposited most copiously upon substances that were known, by independent observations and measurements, to have poor conducting and good radiating capacity; as far as possible, numerical correlations were established between the independently ascertained capacities of radiation-conduction and measured amounts

)f deposited vapor. It had also to be determined by experimental observation that, other things being equal, the amount of change in the temperature of the air and the amount of change in the temperature of the things upon which vapor is deposited, bear a constant ratio to each other. Experiments were also conducted in which variations of temperature artificially produced were correlated with appearance of drops of moisture on glass and polished sheets of metal.

Even so, while the inference was plausible that dew is of the kind that accorded with the hypothesis entertained, what was "proved" was that dew *might* be formed in this way. It was not shown to be the *only* way in which it could be formed. The conditions of agreement, constituted by multiple satisfaction of the function of affirmation, were strongly confirmative of the hypothesis. But until the conditions of negation (exclusion) were conjunctively satisfied, there existed the fallacy of affirming the antecedent because the consequent was affirmed. While the nature of the case forbids *complete* satisfaction of the logical requirement, operations of variation and elimination of conditions were undertaken so that the inferred conclusion would have a high order of probability. These limiting conditions were experimentally produced, while certain familiar cases, like the lesser amount of dew on windy nights, the effect of the presence of clouds, etc., had, as far as they went, the power to effect eliminations.[5]

1. Before taking up another case as illustrative, it is worth while to summarize certain conclusions that emerge from the analysis so

[5] While a comparatively simple case has been chosen for illustrative material, the formulation is greatly simplified in comparison with actual scientific investigations; and this qualification would still be present in lesser measure if as many pages were taken to describe actual experimental observations as there are sentences in the above account. There is nothing more deceptive than the seeming simplicity of scientific procedure as it is reported in logical treatises. This specious simplicity is at its height when letters of the alphabet are used. They are an effective device for obscuring the fact that the materials in question are already highly *standardized*, thus concealing from view that the whole burden of inductive-deductive inquiry is actually borne by the operations through which materials are standardized. It is not too much to say that this symbolic device, although unconsciously adopted, arises from the doctrine (later dealt with in some detail) that induction is a process of inferring from "some to all," and then becomes the chief support of that fallacious doctrine. And, it may be said, Mill is far from being the only sinner in this matter.

far. The outstanding conclusion is that inductive procedures are those which *prepare* existential material so that it has convincing evidential weight with respect to an inferred generalization. The idea that induction consists in *going* from "some" cases (whether "some" means logically, one or several) is at best trivial. For as soon as inquiry has determined existential data which suffice to warrant a conclusion, the latter is already arrived at. There is no further "going" involved. If, on the other hand, the material data from which the generalization is inferred have not been prepared through prior experimental observations, no number of cases, no matter how extensive, will ground an inference, or occasion anything other than a more or less happy guess. The operations that prepare the material must be so directed by ideas (as hypotheses), as to satisfy, conjunctively and disjunctively, the functions of affirmation-negation. This satisfaction is obtained only through operational comparisons and contrasts. These operations, experimentally performed, disclose agreements in phenomena that are materially or existentially independent of one another, and they check the agreements (identities) obtained by systematic eliminations, or ascertainment of differences. The inductive phase of inquiry, if induction has any meaning certifiable in terms of actual scientific practices, can be defined here only in terms of operations of transforming antecedently given material of perception into *prepared* material. When the material is so prepared as to satisfy the conditions named, the work of induction is done and over with. The generalization is *ipso facto* reached.

2. The operations of experimental observation which prepare standardized materials need direction by conceptions. Until the conceptions in question are formulated as hypotheses and their meanings developed in ordered discourse, observation and assemblage of data are carried on at random—though even then there is at least some vague anticipation or guess which leads to the observation of some phenomena in preference to others. In any case, the value of these more or less indeterminate explorations lies in their power to give rise to suggestions which will direct more determinate experimental observations. The development in discourse of the directive conception that is involved provides the sole verifiable material for identifying the deductive phase of

cientific method. The functional correspondence of deductive
and inductive phases of scientific method is thus evident, while it
may be worth while to note, once more, that what "scientific
method" means is adequate satisfaction of logical conditions imposed by control of inquiry.

In the case of scientific method just analyzed, the problem of
generalization involved concerns primarily the institution of a
generic proposition. The *main* problem is to ascertain the related
kind to which phenomena of dew belong. Generalizations of the
type of the universal hypothetical were involved, such as laws of
temperature and pressure. But they were taken as already established, so that the main problem was to decide whether the
phenomena of dew was of the *kind* that is determined as a
special instance of application of these laws. The illustrative case
now to be considered is one in which primary emphasis falls upon
determination of a generalization in the sense of a law, the determination of a kind being secondary. The case in question is
that of malaria. Inquiries have determined it to be a kind,
marked by special differentia, within the extensive kind of parasitic
diseases. But the chief scientific (as distinct from practical) importance of the conclusion resides in the confirmation thereby
afforded to a general theory about a whole category of diseases.

The conception of the cause of malaria long entertained is
expressed by the literal signification of the word: namely, *bad air*.
This conception had a certain practical value for it had consequences, like closing windows at night, which had some influence
on the actual production of the disease. But its scientific value
was virtually nil. It did nothing to further inquiry into the
nature of the illness; it had no power to order the phenomena
exhibited in the course of the disease. It merely pigeon-holed
them by subsuming them *en gros* under the conception adopted.
While in logical form the idea of causation that was held seemed
to constitute an hypothesis, its content was incapable of performing the operative function which defines being an hypothesis.
The symptoms of recurrent fever and chills were so pronounced
that there is no reason to suppose that failure to understand the
nature of the disease often occasioned failure to identify cases of it.
But for scientific purposes the identification led nowhere. More-

over, this failure is characteristic of every attempt to arrive at a law by collecting cases as they happen, comparing them, and then "abstracting" so-called common properties. The result of such a procedure is simply to repeat, under the caption of a *word*, what is already known about singular phenomena, explanatory power being attributed in effect to the word.

Scientific understanding of the phenomena of malaria could hardly have commenced until *some* diseases were known to be of parasitic origin—an example of the value of hypothesis and of deduction from it in scientific inquiry. But the hypothesis had a *material* content that was derived from knowledge of what happened in some *existential* cases; it was not *merely* formal. Moreover, regarded as a generalization that might lead from known cases to as yet unknown cases, it did not yield a *conclusion*. It was an hypothesis by which to direct further observations and experiments. It was at first (that is, prior to such operational use) only a suggestion—a *mere* idea, expressing an indeterminate possibility. Deduction from the hypothesis was required in order to put it in a form which increased such operative applicability. But it was incapable of determining in and of itself a conclusion as to the nature of malaria. Even Laveran's discovery (by microscopic examination of the blood) of parasites in the blood of a malarial patient, was not sufficient. It failed to show the origin of the parasites and failed to decide whether they were causal factors or merely accompaniments or products of the disease.

Moreover, at that period it had also been discovered that some diseases had a bacillic origin, and this suggestion seemed so applicable to the case of malaria as to reduce the force of the suggestion that came from Laveran's discovery. As a mere matter of *formal* theory, one hypothesis was as good as the other, illustrating again the impotency of mere deduction to decide an issue. However, the conception of parasitic origin gradually acquired sufficient force to direct systematic observations of the actual course of the disease in connection with recurrent search for parasites in the blood. It was thereby discovered that changes in the progress of the disease corresponded closely to changes in the life-history of the parasite, and that different forms of parasites were found at different stages of the disease. These findings were easonably adequate to establish belief in the parasitic nature of the disease. They did not suffice to show the source of the parasite so hat the problem of its nature or character was only partially olved. The discovery that another disease, filiarsis, was due to he bite of a mosquito, *suggested* that mosquitoes were the active actor in introduction of the parasite in the case of malaria. This uggestion was used as a working hypothesis in further observaion of mosquitoes. Ross discovered that when a mosquito sucked he blood of a patient already suffering from malaria, new forms, inally becoming free, developed in the body of that insect. Later ne discovered that mosquitoes of the anopheles variety that fed on the blood of malarial patients, developed pigmented cells that were identical with the blood parasites of the human host at an early stage of the disease.

Logical conditions for scientific determination of a law or universal proposition were, however, not yet fully satisfied. Certain conditions for exclusion of alternative possibilities had to be met. For example, it had to be shown that other varieties of nosquitoes did *not* carry or introduce the parasite and that the pite of the anopheles did *not* produce the characteristics marking he disease when they had previously fed only on the blood of nealthy patients. Even then, when these possibilities had been eliminated, the scientific work was not complete. Experiments were performed upon human beings by which it was shown that f the anopheles bit a malarial patient, and after a *definite* time (which was identical with the time independently shown to be required for the development of the parasite in the body of the mosquito) bit a healthy person, the latter developed the characteristic traits of the disease in question. On the negative side, experiments were undertaken to show that persons completely protected against the bite of the anopheles did not develop the disease even in regions in which malaria was rife. Negative conditions were further fulfilled when it was shown that measures which prevented the anopheles from breeding, such as putting oil on the water in which it bred, draining swamps, etc., led to the disappearance of the disease. Finally, it had long been empirically known that taking quinine gave a certain immunity from malaria and was a specific remedy when the disease was contracted. The hypothesis as to inherent connection between the development of the disease and of the parasite of the mosquito in the blood was clinched when this empirical fact was experimentally shown to follow from the relation between chemical properties of quinine and the condition requisite for maintenance of life on the part of the parasite. A universal proposition of the "if-and-only-if, then" was finally grounded as far as any such proposition is capable of conclusive grounding.

The theoretical conclusion which emerged from examination of the previous instance need not be repeated here. The point there made about the futility of the "from some to all" formula may, however, be amplified. The content and validity of the general proposition hangs wholly upon the contents of the singular propositions by which it is grounded. This grounding depends in turn upon the nature of the operations by which these contents are instituted. When it is affirmed that inductive inference proceeds from what happens in some cases to what is true of all cases, the phrase "all cases" must, of course, be limited to all cases of specified *kind*. But if the kind is already determined in the "some" cases from which the inference is said to proceed, the alleged inference is a matter of pure tautology, since a kind *is* the kind which it is.[6] Stated positively, everything depends upon what is determined to happen in "some" cases. If there is any reason for believing that what is then found is *representative*, then the generalization is *ipso facto* already instituted. If it is not representative, then there is no warranted inference in any case.

We arrive again at the conclusion that "induction" is a name for the complex of methods by which a given case is determined to be representative, a function that is expressed in its being a *specimen* or *sample* case.[7] The problem of inductive inquiry, and the precautions that have to be observed in conducting it, all have to do with ascertaining that the given case *is* representative, or is a sample or specimen. There is no doubt that *some* cases, several or many, have to be examined in the course of inquiry: this is necessarily

[6] The same criticism applies when the inference is said to hold of all "similar" cases, the question of similarity being the point at issue.

[7] The words "specimen" and "sample" are not exact equivalents. The difference in their meanings will be considered later. For the purpose of the present point, they are, however, taken as sufficiently synonymous.

involved in the function of comparison-contrast within inquiry. But the validity of the inferred conclusion does not depend upon their number. On the contrary, the survey and operational comparison of several cases is strictly instrumental to determination of what actually takes place in any *one* case. The moment any *one* case is determined to be such that it is an exemplary representative, the problem in hand is solved. It is customary to infer from examples and illustrations; from what Peirce calls diagrams or "icons." That course has been frequently followed in the course of previous discussions. But it should be clear without argument that the entire value of such a mode of inference depends upon whether or not the case is genuinely exemplary and illustrative. If this point is here again emphasized, it is because the issue involved is decisive as to the nature of inductive procedure.

3. Up to this point, the current view that the object of scientific inquiry is establishment of *general* principles and laws, factual and conceptual, has been taken for granted, since there is no doubt that institution of such generalizations is an integral part of the work of the natural sciences. But it is often further tacitly assumed or expressly declared that institution of generalizations *exhausts* the work of science. This statement denies to science any part in determination of propositions referring to singulars as such. It is admitted, of course, that propositions about singulars as of a kind are required in order to reach a generalization, and also that any proposed generalization must be tested by ascertaining whether observation of singular occurrences yields results agreeing with its requirements. But when the generalization is once reached, it is assumed that singular propositions have served their whole logical purpose. This assumption is equivalent to denial that use of a generalization to determine singulars has scientific purport. It is, of course, recognized that generalizations *are* so employed, for example, by engineers and medical men. But this use is regarded as extra-scientific or merely "practical." This mode of conception both reflects and supports the invidious distinction between theory and practice, the alleged difference being expressed in a fixed logical difference between "pure" and "applied" sciences.

I shall not dwell here upon the fact that the invidious distinction in question is wholly an inheritance from a conception of logical method and forms which was appropriate to ancient cosmology, and which is now abandoned in the practice of science. Nor shall I do more than suggest its arbitrary character, since there is no way in which the *procedures* used by the competent engineer or physician in solving problems of determination of singular cases logically differ from the procedures used by another group of men in establishing generalizations.[8] The point to be noted here is that this conception rules out of the domain of science many subjects that are ordinarily termed sciences. History, for example, is to a very large extent concerned with establishing what happened at a given time and place. The question is not so much whether or not history in the large is a science, or even whether or not it is capable of becoming a science. It is whether the *procedures* employed by historians are precluded from having scientific quality. The fact that the doctrine criticized logically involves this denial is at least a comment upon it which demands consideration. The question of the scientific status of history is, however, the subject of so much controversy that this example may not seem convincing. What, then, about geology and the biological sciences? The question does not involve slurring over the importance of generalization in these fields. It calls attention to the fact that these sciences are largely occupied with determination of singulars, and that generalizations do not merely *grow out* of determination of singulars but that they constantly function in further interpretation of singulars.

The fact seems to be that uncritical adherence to Aristotelian conceptions has combined with the prestige of physics, especially of mathematical physics, to generate the conception that physics is not only the most advanced form of scientific inquiry (which it undeniably is), but that it alone is scientific in nature. From a popular standpoint, application of physical generalizations, as in the technologies of the electric and chemical engineer and in the methods used by "medical science" (if the term be allowed), appeal chiefly because of their practical consequences. But from a logical standpoint the applications are integral parts of the verification of the generalizations themselves. The drainage of swamps where anopheles mosquitoes breed is prized because it helps to

[8] See on this point, K. Darrow, *The Scientific Renaissance*, Chap. I.

eliminate malaria. But from the scientific standpoint it is an experiment which confirms a theory. In general, wide social application of the results of physics and chemistry provides added test and security for conclusions reached.

The issue involved is a far-reaching one. Dogmatic restriction of science to generalizations compels denial of scientific traits and value to every form of practice. It obliterates, logically, the enormous difference that exists between activities that are routine and those that are intelligent; between action dictated by caprice and the conduct of arts that embody technologies and techniques expressing systematically tested ideas. Even more to the point is the fact that it involves logical suicide of the sciences with respect even to generalizations. For there is no ground whatever upon which a logical line can be drawn between the operations and techniques of experimentation in the natural sciences and the same operations and techniques employed for distinctively practical ends. Nothing so fatal to science can be imagined as elimination of experimentation, and experimentation is a form of doing and making. Application of conceptions and hypotheses to existential matters through the medium of doing and making is an intrinsic constituent of scientific method. No hard and fast line can be drawn between such forms of "practical" activity and those which apply their conclusions to humane social ends without involving disastrous consequences to science in its narrower sense.

4. Some of the topics discussed in this chapter may seem somewhat remote from the topic of induction. If so, the seeming is superficial. For in the present state of logical doctrine the theory of induction is basically compromised by erroneous conceptions proceeding from two sources. On the one hand, there is the influence of a logic that was formulated before the rise of modern science, and on the other hand, there is the influence of the empiristic logic that endeavored to make logical theory correspond to the procedures of modern science. The two influences combined to support the conception that induction is a process which infers from what happens in some observed cases to what happens in all cases, unobserved as well as observed. When these theories are critically analyzed, the sole element of truth in them is found to be the fact that all inference involves *extension* beyond the

scope of already observed objects. Interpretation of this undeniable fact by both theories ignores the outstanding fact of scientific inductive inference:—namely, controlled reconstitution of the singulars which are the ground of generalizations. This reconstitution is so effected as to determine what goes on in the way of interaction in a *singular* case. Inference from *one to all* is completely and exclusively determined by prior experimental operations through which the *one* has been determined to be an exemplary specimen of an order of interactions or of functional correlations of variations. This order, when it is ascertained, *is* the generalization. As far as the order of variations is such as to be included within a more extensive order of changes, the result is a generalization in terms of a *relation of kinds*, since the interactions in question determine the observable characteristics which in their conjunction describe kinds. As far as the order of interactions is abstracted, it is capable of apprehension by means of development of the symbols forming an if-then universal proposition in discourse. The outcome is generalization in the form of a non-existential law or principle, which through execution of the operations it formulates organizes existential material.

The common logical source of both forms of generalization, the generic and the abstract universal, is another instance of their conjugate relationship. The fundamental defect of traditional empiristic logic is its failure to recognize the necessity of abstract hypotheses, involving deductive relations of propositions, for control of the operations by which the singulars are instituted that sustain the evidential-testing burden. The inherent defects of the traditional (formally rationalistic) theory are (1) its failure to recognize that the procedures of experimental science transform the singulars from which inductive generalization proceeds; and (2) its failure to recognize the strictly instrumental relation borne by hypothesis to experimental determination of singulars.

The integral role of determination of modes of interaction in scientific method involves processes to which the name *causation* is applied. The distinguishing observable traits which determine a proposition that *this* is one of specified kind, and the proposition that the kind is included with other kinds in a more extensive kind, provide warranted grounds for these conclusions only as the evidential marks in question are actualizations of potentialities that are constituted by modes of interaction. The mode or way of interaction as such, when taken as an abstract possibility, forms the content of a universal proposition, of an hypothesis.

Exposition of this theme in terms of *causation* is the subject of the ensuing chapter. Very slight acquaintance with the topic of induction is needed to appreciate the fundamental role which the conception of causation has occupied in the theories which have given interpretations of inductive inference. Since the time of Mill and earlier, the problem of the nature of causation has been bound up, however, with all sorts of traditional metaphysical and episte-mological issues. The considerations adduced in this chapter will enable us to disregard most of these issues. For acknowledgment of the central place of interactions, limits discussion of the category of causation to the *logical* function performed by the conception of interactions.

CHAPTER XXII

SCIENTIFIC LAWS—

CAUSATION AND SEQUENCES

I. *Introductory: The Nature of Laws.* Since the time of Mill, the view that scientific laws are formulations of uniform and unconditional sequences of events has been generally adopted. Mill has also been followed in defining causation in terms of such sequences. The adoption of these positions does not, however, imply general acceptance of Mill's particular interpretation. On the contrary, critics of his view have no difficulty in showing that the very conception of unconditioned or necessary sequence is fundamentally incompatible with his conception that singulars as such are the ground and content of all general propositions; or, more generally, that the necessity or invariable connection that is postulated is incompatible with the relation that holds between *singulars.* Since Mill himself had acknowledged that determination of strict uniformity of sequence is ultimately dependent upon, or even identical with, determination of its unconditional nature, it is clear that the conception of laws as causal, and of causation as unconditioned sequence, requires, when it is accepted, a very different logical foundation from that provided by Mill.

Much ingenuity has been expended in attempts to show how, upon the basis of logical conceptions different from those of Mill, the idea of uniformity in *sequence* of events may be united with that of unconditionality. But it does not follow from the validity of the criticism directed against Mill's doctrine that the one offered in its place is valid, or that it in turn is free from contradiction. On the contrary, little analysis is needed to show that the conception of a necessary (or unconditional) existential sequence of events (and any sequence of *temporal* events is ex-

istential by description) stands in contradiction to other fundamental logical principles usually accepted. For it is recognized
on all hands that only universal propositions, which are *non*-
existential in content, are necessary, and that any proposition having contents of direct existential reference are *I* and *O* propositions, neither universal nor necessary.

Yet it is evident that certain constituents of the view criticized
are sound when taken severally. Necessary universal propositions
are involved in scientific method, nor can it be denied that determination of an existential sequence is indispensable in many inquiries, as, for example, in the cases of malaria and dew discussed
in the previous chapter. It is also evident that there is some sort of
logical relation between a universal proposition, consisting of
interrelated abstract characters, and valid determination of an
ordered sequence. But it is just as evident that there is logical
distinction between the two kinds of propositions. For the latter
is existential, and as will appear in the sequel, ultimately *individual*
in reference, while the former is abstract. The doctrine criticized
thus involves a contradiction within itself. The *functional* force
of the propositions whose contents are necessarily related to each
other (functional in determining an existential sequence), is mis-
takenly ascribed to the sequence it serves to determine, as if it
were the content of the law, while to the sequence in turn is
ascribed the necessary relational property which belongs only to
the abstract *if-then* hypothetical universal proposition, by which
it is instituted.

The source of the logical confusion has been pointed out repeatedly. It occurs because generalizations of the generic and
universal form are identified with each other. Let us take a typical
scientific example. There are fundamental propositions in physics
in which time, distance and mass are interrelated with one another. The propositions which formulate these interrelations are
equations and other mathematical functions. They purport to
state necessary relations of abstract characters, and so they are
non-existential in content. The meanings of T, L, and M are determined in and by definition. As so determined, they are devoid
of material traits of date, place and mass. Inquiries into actual
changes and correlations of change have, on the other hand, con-

tents of direct existential import. They are concerned with concrete spatial-temporal courses of events. The very heart of scientific inquiry is thus to maintain the distinction *and* the functional relation (correspondence) of the two logical types of propositions mentioned—a statement in which "and" has "multiplicative" force. The fallacy vitiating the view that scientific laws are formulations of uniform unconditioned sequences of change arises from taking the function of the universal proposition as if it were part of the structural content of the existential propositions.

Neither a factual generalization as a law, nor a hypothetical universal as a law, has a sequence of events for its subject-matter. A law as a factual generalization has a set of interactions for its content. These ways of interaction are selected, affirmatively and negatively, in any given case, so that they will have as their *potential* consequences the traits which inclusively and exclusively determine a relation of kinds to one another. In logical ideal they are conjunctively so extensive in scope that any singular event that occurs can be determined to be of a specified kind, while the relation of this kind to other kinds is such that extensive inference is possible. For example, the conceptions of density, specific gravity, point of liquefaction, change to gaseous and solid state, etc. etc., are determined, one by one for, say, each and every metal in terms of some interaction of conditions. These different modes of action are then so related to one another as to determine the conjoint set of properties which respectively determine the kinds *tin, lead, silver, iron,* etc. An abstract or universal *if-then* law, on the other hand, has for its subject-matter an interrelation of *characters* such that they are integral members of a comprehensive system of interrelated characters. Ordered discourse, or "deduction," is then possible.

It is universally recognized in the context of discussion of *some* topics that the relation between the antecedent and the consequent clauses of a universal proposition is strictly formal. It is not so commonly recognized, at least in explicit statement, that with respect to such propositions in the natural sciences—as in mathematical physics—the *contents* of each such proposition are determined by reference to the availability and force of the proposition in a system of related propositions. In this way, comprehensive transitivity in theoretical ideal is a relational property of every such proposition, so that from the more basic propositions (e.g., those regarding the relations of T, L, and M) propositions of less comprehensive scope of applicability may be derived. They are then applicable to the problems set by concrete existential changes in a way in which the universal propositions of more comprehensive scope are not applicable.

II. *"Causal Laws."* The term "causal laws" is, accordingly, in spite of its general use, a figure of speech. It is a case of metonymy in which a law is designated not in terms of its own content but in terms of consequences of execution of its function. By use of such a figure of speech, a rod of metal is called a lever; a particular arrangement of a piece of wood and metal is called a hammer; a visible white material phenomenon is called sugar, etc., etc. As has been previously noted, even the objects of common sense experience are habitually designated in terms of the potential consequences of their familiar interactions with other things. Common sense, however, is given to ascribing these consequences to some "power" inherent in the things themselves (an ingredient of the popular notion of substance), and to ignoring *inter*action with other things as the determining factor. Since laws are expressly formulated as means to consequences (respectively, material and procedural means), no harm need necessarily result from describing them in terms of the existential temporal-spatial orders of sequence-coexistence, which are constituted by their operational application. But basic confusion has arisen, and is bound to arise, in logical theory when the existential orders so determined are taken to be literal constituents of the laws themselves—something which happens when they are not only *called* causal laws but are taken to be formulations of regular sequences.

III. *The Import of Sequential Linkage of Changes.* The determination of "causal" linkage between any two events is not final nor logically complete. It is a means of instituting, in connection with determination of other similar linkages, a single unique *continuous* history. As a result of scientific inquiry, events that had previously been experienced as separate and independent become integral constituents of one and the same continuous occurrence. This latter determination, then, constitutes the resolved individual qualitative situation which is the final, or terminal, conclusion. When this institution of an individual situation which is temporally and coexistentially continuous is attained, the conception of causation has served its purpose and drops out. Reference to causation recurs only when there are grounds for doubt as to whether the spatio-temporal linkage in the case of some set of events is such as in fact constitutes an existential continuum.

A building is burnt. In direct experience, as then and there constituted, this is an isolated event. The problem is to connect it with other events so that it becomes an integral part of a more extensive history. Common sense takes the problem to be resolved by reference to an "antecedent" event, say, being set afire by some one for revenge or for insurance money; or by a match carelessly dropped, etc. Science resolves the gross qualitative events taken by common sense as being sufficient for explanation into a set of interactions, each one of which is so minute that it is capable of uniting with others to form a continuous coexistential-sequential whole without gaps and interruptions. With respect to *generalization*, inquiry is content, therefore, to rest when it has determined specific modes of interaction and the universal formulae by means of which they may be related to one another. For example, generalizations are reached regarding the gravity, density, fusing point of a metal, such as are found in the scientific description of each kind. They then serve, when needed, to identify and demarcate a *given* substance as a metal of such and such a specific kind. On the side of universal propositions, gravity, heat and light are defined in terms of contents such that their relations are so formulated that deduction is possible.

The application of these generalizations is then left to be made when special conditions call for the determination of special existent phenomena. The general determinations have, indeed, been instituted with reference to availability when an occasion actually offers itself. What is added to this statement in the present context is that when so applied they determine minute and measured singulars such that they are capable of being linked together *to form a continuum which is spatially and temporally an extensive individual qualitative unity*. The very fact that generalizations of both forms are so expressly determined with reference to their capacity to perform this function, is the reason why the function gets so integrated into the content that its presence is taken for granted and then ignored—resulting finally in the complete separation of "theory" and "practice."

This formal consideration will be made more concrete by an example. A man is found dead under such unusual circumstances as to create suspicion, doubt and inquiry. Was it a case of murder, accident or suicide? The problem is one of determining traits which will enable the phenomenon in question to be securely referred to a determinate kind. The only way in which to discover and adjudge traits that will be sufficiently differential as to fix the kind is, as we ordinarily say, to find out "the cause" of the death in question. Whatever else the word "cause" may or may not mean in this context, it at least involves taking the event out of the isolation in which it first presented itself, so as to link it up with other events. As analytically transformed, it is then one constituent in a much more extensive spread of events. When it is so tied up, the "mystery" which originally surrounded it is dissipated. What is involved in the inquiry that institutes the required linkages?

1. In the first place, there is the thorough examination of the dead body and its surrounding conditions. This investigation, while strictly observational, is directed by the conceptions and techniques which the science and arts of the period make available. That these observations are directed with a view to discovering traits which are differential with respect to possible kinds of death, sudden natural death, death by suicide, by murder, by accident, becomes practically a matter of established routines. From the logical standpoint, they involve a set of disjunctive propositions, theoretically exhaustive, while the formulation of each disjunctive proposition takes the form of an *if-then* hypothesis. Then each hypothesis is developed in ordered discourse, e.g., "If natural death, then such and such related consequences." Examination of existing conditions then occurs to ascertain whether the theoretically deduced consequences are or are not actually present.

2. The resulting proposition as to the kind of death does not solve the problem with respect to which inquiries are instituted. It rather formulates it in a form that instigates and conditions further

inquiry. Suppose the proposition is: "This is a case of death by violence inflicted by some other person." The proposition instead of being final and complete is an initiation of inquiries to discover the guilty person and the conditions under which he committed the crime. The last consideration forms what is usually called "motive"; it provides the differential traits for deciding of what kind is the homicide in question: killing in self-defense, in a fit of passion, by premeditated purpose, etc. Determination of its specific kind then determines the further existential consequences in accordance with the existing system of legal conceptions as rules of action:—death, confinement in prison, release, etc.

The object in listing these various phases of the inquiry is to bring out the logical force of the obvious fact that the investigation undertaken extends its scope far beyond examination of the dead body and its immediately surrounding conditions. For the necessity of instituting such investigations as ascertain the dead man's previous state of health; his movements during the period prior to the time at which his death is fixed; his relations with other persons, such as his enemies, the persons who would benefit by his death; the antecedent activities of other persons to whom suspicion points; etc., is that the necessity proves the incomplete and partial logical status of the inferential propositions made regarding the *kind* of death that has occurred. Stated in positive terms, this determination is a condition of further inquiries that relate the facts that have been ascertained with a set of other connected facts so that the resulting complex of related events forms an individual spatial-temporal continuum.

It remains to indicate the bearings of these considerations upon the conception of *causation* as it operates in scientific inquiry. A common conception, derived from loose common sense beliefs, is that an event can be picked out as *the* antecedent of *the* event in question, and that this antecedent is its cause. For example, it would be said that *the* antecedent of the death of the murdered person is a shot fired from a revolver by another person. But examination shows that this event is not temporally antecedent, leaving out the matter of its being *the* antecedent. For the mere firing of the shot is not sufficiently close in temporal sequence to be a "cause" of death. A shot may have missed the man entirely.

Only a bullet which actually enters some vital part of the organism in such a way that the organic processes cease to function is "causally" connected with the occurrence of death. Such an event is not an antecedent of the event of dying, because it is an integral *constituent* of that event.

The intellectual processes by which the common sense conception of the cause of an event (as a selected antecedent event) are arrived at, may be described as follows: The start is made with the fact of death. This phenomenon in its perceived isolation sets the problem of discovering its connection, spatial-temporal, with other events. The problem concerns an existential singular case, not the institution of a generalization, although it cannot be solved without the use of generalizations as means. The first step in determination of its connections is the discovery that a bullet entered some vital part of the organism and that the bullet was shot by another person. So far, so good. The analysis begins to go astray when it is overlooked that such determinations form the *content* of an event that then takes the place in inquiry of the gross event originally observed. The latter is now described in terms of a set of interactions into which the event of dying, as originally perceived, has been analytically resolved.

Analysis into these interactions is effected by means of applications of certain generalized conceptions which are conclusions of prior inquiries, such as conceptions, on one side, of physical laws of velocity etc., regarding the bullet, and, on the other side, standardized conceptions regarding physiological processes. These generalizations are about contents of traits and characters that are logically related to one another. They are *not* about temporal sequences. The event of the entrance of the bullet into, say, the heart, is now a constituent element in the singular event of dying undergoing investigation, not an antecedent of it.

The doctrine that causation consists of a relation between an antecedent and a consequent event is thus the result of a confused mixture of ideas of two different orders. There is the valid idea that the gross event directly perceived can be understood only through its resolution into minuter events (interactions) so that some of the minuter events become constituent elements of a spatial-temporal continuum. But, at the same time, dying is still treated as if it were a gross event consequent upon another gross event, the firing of a revolver. The combination of these two incompatible conceptions yields the notion of a relation between an event as *the* consequent and another event as *the* antecedent.

The confusion is then completed by the notion that the generalizations, by means of which the unique continuous event is ascertained, are formulations of some uniform sequence. This confusion of operational means of procedure with the existential result of their application thus represents a mixture of the common sense conception of causation as a relation of two independent events, and the scientific resolution of what happens into a single continuous event. It does mark a refinement of the common sense notion. But it retains its inherent inconsistencies. For there are no such things as uniform sequences of *events;* while, on the other side, when a generalized conjunction of characteristics or characters is substituted for "events," the property of sequentiality is eliminated.

Before discussing this point further, something will be said about the historical origin of the idea. The fact that gross qualitative objects (which are the objects of direct perception) are separated from one another by their singular qualitative natures, led, when philosophical reflection set in, to the feeling that something was required to bridge the gap between them. The lighting of a match is over with, for example, before the burning match is applied to a piece of paper so that the paper begins to burn. The burning match and the burning paper are two distinct qualitative objects. The conception of a *force* was introduced to get over the difficulty constituted by this qualitative gap. The match was supposed to have a certain calorific power. Similarly, a living body was said to die because the vital spark, or some life-giving force, had fled. Finally, forces were generalized. The force of gravity caused things to move downwards; that of levity caused them to move upwards; the force of electricity caused rubbed pieces of amber to attract pieces of paper; the force of magnetism enabled a magnet to attract iron, etc. The idea of forces is indeed so deeply embedded in popular cultural beliefs that it is needless to give examples.

The intellectual source of the idea is that already stated. Events are first observed as successive; the succession by its every qualitative nature involves an interval or gap. Something outside the events is then invoked to explain the fact that the events although independent are nevertheless connected. The time came when it was seen that forces by definition are such as to be incapable of experimental observation. They were then ruled out of science along with other "occult" qualities and forms—of which they were perhaps the most conspicuous example. Then there grew up a hybrid notion which took from common sense the idea of succession and from science the idea of invariability of conjunction. To all appearance, the satisfaction obtained by getting rid of the unwelcome and unscientific notion of forces sufficed to protect the new ideas of laws as invariable sequences from the otherwise obvious criticism that the contents which are *invariably* related in a law are not events, and that their relation is not one of sequence. Once the idea was formulated (in sceptical reference by Hume and with constructive intent by Mill), it was accepted as a matter of course as the next thing to a self-evident truth.

There are reasons for supposing that the idea that scientific laws are formulations of invariable sequences is in considerable part the product of the attempt to revise in important respects the common sense use of the conception of causation without, however, abandoning the conception underlying this use. Common sense abounds in such beliefs as "A good rain will cause the seeds that have been planted to grow"; "Water quenches thirst"; "Heating iron causes it to be more malleable"; and so on indefinitely. Some of these popular beliefs, such as that changes of phases of the moon cause changes in vegetable growth, are now relegated to the category of superstitions. But there are many others constantly depended upon in practical activities. Such "generalizations" are of the nature of formulations of habitual expectations; they are of the sort into which Hume resolved the entire conception of causation. As formulations of expectations they do concern a relation of succession between antecedent and subsequent events. But the formulation of an expectation, no matter how practically useful nor how often confirmed, is not of the order of a law. From the standpoint of scientific inquiry, these expectations are but material of *problems*. Why is it and how is it, for example, that they can be depended upon in practice? The answer can be given only in objective terms that ground the expectations. The statement of a habit of action has to be transposed into a statement of a relation of objective subject-matters.

Take such a non-scientific belief as is expressed in the proposition "Taking arsenic into the system causes death." In linguistic form it is a generalization and it is about a sequence that is taken to be at least fairly uniform. But scientific inquiry proceeds by introducing qualifications. The amount of arsenic taken has to be specified; the dose of arsenic has to be of sufficient quantity. The conditions of the system into which it is taken have to be determined. For some persons by repeatedly taking small doses in increasing amounts become immune to doses that would be fatal to other persons. The presence or absence of "counteracting conditions" has to be taken into account, since, for example, death may not follow if an antidote be taken.

The proposition that results when inquiry is carried only to this point is not of a uniform sequence, but is of some such form as "Taking arsenic into the system under certain conditions *tends* to produce death." There is still a statement of a problem rather than a final scientific conclusion. The business of scientific inquiry in solving the problem is to discover existential grounds or reasons that warrant the propositions so far made. Their determination effects a radical change in the content and form of the propositions that constitute statement of a problem. The change from the popular belief and the partial scientific proposition to a determined scientific generalization is not just a matter of taking away certain elements and adding on others. It involves institution of existential material of a new type. In this change, gross qualitative events and immediately observed qualities such as form the content of the ideas of arsenic and of death are transformed into a determinate set of *interactions*. The result is a law, and the law states a relation of traits that describe a specified kind. These traits are logically *conjunctive-disjunctive*. There is no element of sequence in their relations to one another. The conception that a law is a formulation of a uniform (or invariable) *sequence* seems, accordingly, to be an attempt to retain some elements of the popular conception in combination with some elements of the scientific conception, without taking account of the radical transformation wrought by the scientific formulation in the material of the popular belief.

Determination of the interactions which yield the traits that constitute the non-temporal conjunction forming the scientific conception is effected, moreover, through experimentation. It would require several pages in a treatise on chemistry to set forth the experiments, with the apparatus and techniques that are involved, which are required in order to warrant the conjunctive-disjunctive set of traits which are the content of the scientific generalization. Now experiments that institute the required set of related traits are dependent upon hypotheses formulated in *if-then* propositions. It would require a chapter or chapters in a chemical treatise to set forth explicitly the conceptions and interrelations of conceptions that are directly and indirectly involved in the conduct of the experiments by which the law or generalization in question is warrantably arrived at. It is hardly necessary to add that the content of these hypothetical propositions, as physical laws, does not include any reference to sequences. For they state a relation of characters, preferably in mathematical equations. While the latter have ultimate existential reference, through the possible operations they direct, they are non-existential (and hence non-temporal) in their content.

In spite of what has been said, the notion that a scientific law is about a sequence will probably persist in the minds of many readers. It may be objected, for example, that the theory presented goes contrary to the *fact*, since causal sequences *are* found in scientific propositions about natural events. For example (to develop the objection), in a case in which poisoning is suspected, symptomatic traits are looked for which are indicative of the action of some poison, say arsenic. If the traits are found, then further inquiries are undertaken in order to determine a definite sequential order—such as an antecedent purchase of arsenic and an antecedent opportunity for some one to administer a dose of it. The final conclusion is validated, it will be said, in just the degree in which a close sequential order of events is established.

Now what has been said in no way contravenes the *facts* here stated. On the contrary, it is the only view that provides a consistent logical interpretation of them, as well as having power to indicate the exact place at which and the way in which sequential determinations do enter in and function. For the instance cited concerns a *singular* event, and the *event* is unique in its singularity, occurring at one and only one time and place, so that at any rate, there is no recurrence in the event in its singularity. Moreover, not only are no two deaths by arsenic poisoning identical in time and place of occurrence, but there are always specific *qualities* in which they differ. Laws (of both types) are instrumental in determination of the sequences that, as established in inquiry, form the content of the scientific account of what happened in the singular case. But the laws, while they are necessary means of determining sequences in given singular cases, are not of sequential contents, and the singular events determined by them are not recurrent.

What recurs is the *kind* of event, say, *death* as an including kind of deaths by poisoning, by assassination, from typhoid fever, etc., as subkinds. The view that is being criticized attempts to meet the facts of the situation by saying it is true that events do not recur but only certain traits or features, and hence the sequence which is affirmed to constitute the law holds between these traits or features. The element of constancy is certainly undeniable.[1] Otherwise, there would be no such conjunction of traits as describes a kind. But the more the soundness of this affirmation of constancy is admitted (or insisted upon) the clearer it becomes that the uniform or constant relation in question is not a temporal and sequential one. For the traits are *logically*, not temporally, conjoined. They are selected and ordered (related to one another) by means of the operations that resolve a gross qualitative occurrence into a definite set of interactions. The law or generalization that expresses the conjunction of traits determined by these interactions contains no temporal and *a fortiori* no sequential relations.

The statement made above about sequences was to the effect that laws, whether of traits determining a kind or of characters in an *if-then* formula, are instrumentalities in determining, through operations they prescribe and direct, the ordered sequences into

---

[1] The fallacy is that previously noted: confusion of constancy of evidential function with existential recurrence.

which gross qualitative events are resolved. It was also intimated that this resolution explains the actual locus and function of the so-called causal sequences. Before considering this point, I shall, however, illustrate the logical conditions that are involved in formulation of a law by consideration of another instantial case, that of the observed succession of days and nights. Their succession comes as near to being invariable as can possibly occur in the case of gross events. Yet even if one event was taken to be the "cause" of the other by the members of some savage tribe, as soon as scientific attempts to interpret the succession began, the succession was taken to set a *problem*, not as providing the content of a law. The Ptolemaic theory was based upon taking the perceived fixity of the earth and the movement of the sun as the ground for inference. The theory then explained the succession of days and nights in terms of the relations to each other of the general characters of revolution and stationariness. It was a law *of* successive events only in the sense that it was a law *for* them—not in the sense that the succession provided its content. The Copernican theory also took succession as a problem (including, however, a greater variety of successions along with that of day and night and the successive positions of the sun during the solar year, etc.), as the *problematic* subject-matter under investigation. It sought for a generalization that would cover all the planets and the successive positions of their satellites, as well as a variety of other observed successions. The astronomical laws that resulted applied to an enormous variety of kinds of successions, including many that were observed only because of the new order of conceptions. The laws, on the side of hypotheticals, were stated, as by Newton, in the form of equations, free from elements in temporal succession. On the factual or generic side laws consisted of conjunct traits of extension in time and space, which were themselves conceived not as changes but as means of determining the relations of actual changes. The Newtonian formula of gravitation comprehended the Copernican conceptions and the laws of Kepler in a more comprehensive theory.

Analysis from any point of view of the nature of the laws of science bears out the conclusion that they are means, through the media respectively of operations of reasoning (discourse) and of observation, for determining existential (spatial-temporal) connection of concrete materials in such a way that the latter constitute a coherent individualized situation. The functional nature of laws is recognized in a partial way when it is said they are means of prediction. But they are means of *pre*diction only as far as they operate as means of *pro*duction of a given situation, through transformations of antecedent problematic material brought about by the operations to which they give direction. A prediction, say, of an eclipse, is itself an *if-then* proposition. If certain operations are performed, then certain phenomena having determinate properties will be observed. Its hypothetical character shows that it is not final and complete but intermediate and instrumental. This statement does not mean that the event that is *describable, if it be known*, as an eclipse, happens because of the execution of the operations. Its bare occurrence is not the issue. What is predicted is that a phenomenon marked by certain specified traits will be *observable* at a given time and place. The prediction is not, then, a completely warranted proposition until the required operations are performed and are found to have as their *consequence* the observed material whose occurrence has been predicted.[2]

Another point of view from which the problem may be approached is that of the "plurality of causes." Deaths, as gross qualitative events, have many antecedents or "causes." But no given death in the concrete can have a plurality of possible causes; while, in the case of doubt, a plurality of *hypotheses* assists in determining what the single sequential continuum is of which it is a part. Nor do the laws which respectively describe the kind *death* and which *define*, through an interrelation of abstract characters, *what* death is in the abstract vary, as far as they are valid, from time to time and from place to place. The conjunct traits which have been used to describe death and its sub-kinds have changed historically; as science advances they may be expected to change in the future. But the change is made for the sake of obtaining a set of characters that will be applicable *without* change. The

---

[2] "Prediction in science involves a specification of *what steps to take* if we wish to observe a regularity of nature. . . . Predicting where a planet will be at a certain date is equivalent to prescribing where to put a telescope at a particular time if we wish to see it. It is, therefore, a recipe for correct conduct." Hogben, *Retreat from Reason*, p. 49, italics not in original text.

ame statement holds of the definition of death in the abstract. Mill's statement that "It is not true that one effect must be connected with only one condition, or assemblage of conditions," holds when, and only when, "death" is taken at large, as a blanket term. There is no actual case of dying which is of this vague nature. On the conceptual side, the aim of scientific method is to arrive at a comprehensive conjunctive-disjunctive system of related kinds such that it may be determined of just what kind is any given death. This system constitutes a plurality of hypotheses such that each hypothesis is a rule for the performance of specific experimental observations. The consequences of all taken together yield the summative and alternate logical traits which describe a kind, positively and exclusively. The significance for logical theory of "plurality of causes" is, then, the demonstration it affords that the traits which are used to determine a popular common sense kind are indeterminate, since they arise from relatively non-discriminative operations. Such traits as the cessation of breathing, the temperature of the body, suffice to show that a death has occurred. They throw no light upon the kind of death that has taken place.

Scientific inquiry proceeds by regarding the change in question as a complex of interactions that are ascertainable, severally and in their conjunction, by analytic experimental operations. Traits that are the differential consequences of these operations decide the kind of death that has occurred. The particular inclusive-exclusive set of interactions involved is systematically related by means of universal propositions to other modes of interaction. If, for example, *this* dying is inferred to be a case of typhoid fever, the discovery of a certain bacillus as an interacting condition, makes possible inference about preceding events of such a form that inquiry is directed in a search for data confirming the inference. The inference is possible because there is a generalization in which the presence of this bacillus in a human organism is related to its presence in drinking water, milk, etc. The conception that this relation is a sequential one arises, to repeat, from confusion of the content of the generalization with the content of actual existential histories which are determinable by its operational use. The existential subject-matter to which the generalization is ap-

plied is thereby *constituted* a temporal historic continuum, an
every such sequence is just what it *individually* is.

IV. *Propositions of Ordered Sequences.* I return now to th
question of the actual locus and function of propositions about
ordered sequences. If an ordered sequence is not the content of
law or generalization, of what kind of a proposition is it the con
tent? The means of answering this question have, of course, bee
set forth in the previous discussion, and it only remains to assembl
them. Ordered sequences are the subject-matter of proposition
in which the succession of gross qualitative events is resolved int
the constituents of a *single continuous event.* It has not escaped th
notice of writers on the methods of physical inquiry that experi
mental inquiry resolves gross qualitative changes, which are di
rectly observed, into sets of very minute changes. The theoretica
interpretation of the fact noted has, however, been vitiated by th
notion that the effect of the resolution is simply to substitute a mor
complete and much more accurate generalization regarding
sequential order for the loose generalizations regarding causal se
quences that are entertained by common sense. The proper in
terpretation is, on the contrary, that the minute changes in question
are such as, by instrumental operational application of generaliza
tions consisting of non-temporal relations of events, enable event
that are qualitatively unlike to become constituents of a single
continuous event.

The qualitative unlikeness of gross observed events constitutes
as was earlier pointed out, an apparent gap between them. Such
generalizations about traits as are determined by conceptions of *interaction* provide the means for overcoming these gaps; and the
more minute, or "elementary," the modes of interaction which are
ascertained, the more complete is the elimination of gaps, and the
smoother are the singular (and ultimately) individual temporal-
spatial existential continua that are the final outcomes of scientific
knowledge of events.

These considerations justify the theoretical conclusion that
causation as ordered sequence is a *logical* category, in the sense
that it is an abstract conception of the indefinitely numerous existential sequences that are established in scientific inquiry:—established by means of the use of generalizationed propositions as laws

For when events are taken strictly *existentially*, there is no event which is antecedent or "cause" any more than it is consequent or "effect." Moreover, even when an event is taken to be an antecedent or a consequent (an interpretation which is purely arbitrary from an existential point of view in isolation from the procedures of inquiry), it has an indefinite number of antecedents and consequents with which it is connected, since every event is existentially connected with some other event without end. Consequently, the only possible conclusion upon the basis of an existential or ontological interpretation of causation is that everything in the universe is cause and effect of everything else—a conclusion which renders the category completely worthless for scientific purposes.

The same point may be stated in other words by saying that no event comes to us labelled "cause" or "effect." An event has to be deliberately *taken* to be cause or effect. Such taking would be purely arbitrary if there were not a particular and differential problem to be solved. Given the problem of resolving a gross and indeterminate succession of observed qualitative events into a single continuous history, there is sufficient and necessary ground for taking one event as "effect" or consequent, and some other as antecedent or "cause." For the former is, for inquiry, the terminal event of the history under determination and the latter is an initial or intervening event in the same history. The events in question are discriminatively selected from out of a total welter of events in which there is no such thing as either an existential beginning or an existential close. Events as existences neither begin nor cease just because an inquirer is concerned with them. The evidence is conclusive that the category of causation accrues to existential subject-matter as a logical form when and because determinate problems about such subject-matter are present. The problems can be solved only by methods that select and order more elementary and minute changes as interactions that constitute, in their linkage with one another, a unique history with its own beginning, career and termination. While the category is logical, not ontological, it is *not an arbitrary* logical postulate.[3] For only through its use can antecedent existential subject-matters be trans-

---

[3] The word "logical" is of course to be understood in the sense of accrual within inquiry, not in an *a priori* or Kantian sense.

formed from a problematic into a resolved unified situation. The determination of a sequential order of changes is the goal of every scientific investigation that is occupied with *singular* phenomena. The institution of just such temporal-spatial continuities is the *ultimate* objective of any existential inquiry. When the objective is realized, there is *judgment*, as distinct from propositions as means of attaining judgment.

V. *Causal Propositions.* What has just been said gives the clew to the kind of propositions that may properly be said to have causational content in distinction from that of ordered temporal or historical sequential events. For there is involved in what was said the relation of means to consequences. Propositions that deal explicitly with subject-matters that are connected with one another as means to consequences have a claim to be called causal propositions in a distinctive sense. It is frequently pointed out that common sense employs causation in a practical and prospective reference. Every intelligent act involves selection of certain things as means to other things as their consequences. If iron is to be worked it must be heated; if a room is to be illuminated, a lamp is lit or a button is pressed; if a fever is to be cured, a certain treatment is employed, and so on indefinitely. The intended consequence is the *effect* in relation to which the means used are *causative*. In general, practical inquiry begins with an end to be accomplished and then searches for the means by which it may be achieved. The conception of *effect* is essentially teleological; the effect is the end to be reached; the differential means to be employed constitute its *cause* when they are selected and brought into interaction with one another.

The import of the causal relation as one of means-consequences is thus prospective. Once established, it is employed retrospectively. If in order to kill a man, a bow and arrow are employed, then, when a man is found dead with an arrow in his heart, death is called the effect and the shooting of the arrow the cause. There is no need to repeat the analysis and criticism that has already been given. What may and should be noted is that in all inquiries in which there is an end in view (consequences to be brought into existence) there is a selective ordering of existing conditions as means, and, if the conditions of inquiry are satisfied, a determination of the end in terms of the means that are available.[4] If the name "causal proposition" has any reference at all, it is to propositions of this kind.

The theory about causal laws that has been criticized holds that scientific propositions about causation differ from those just illustrated by having a strictly retrospective reference, and thus are purely "theoretical." That fact that experimentation enters into determination of every warranted proposition is sufficient to prove the incorrectness of this view. Doing and making are involved. The kind of doing and making is that which determines means—material and procedural—of effecting a prospective end, a unified situation, as a consequence. This unified situation is the ultimate (although not proximate) goal of every inquiry. Hence causal propositions (in the sense of propositions whose content is a relation of conditions that are means to other conditions that are consequences) are involved in every competently conducted inquiry. To bring about, to produce, to make, to generate, is to effect, and that which serves this purpose is a cause in the only legitimate existential sense of the word.

It is true that retrospective survey is more explicit and more extensive in scientific inquiry than in common sense inquiries. However, the retrospective reference is present in the latter for conditions can be estimated or adjudged in their capacity as means only on the basis of what has taken place in the past. It is also true that in the case of scientific propositions the *prospective* reference is the more extensive and, logically, the more explicit. Take, for instance, the case of a generic proposition. It is a proposition that has a form that enables it to be applied in *every* future occasion of inquiry when certain conditions are ascertained to be present. Moreover, the propositions which result from its operational application have inherent logical import. For they are the means by which the generic proposition in question is tested and, whenever found inadequate, is revised and reformulated.

In short, all propositions about policies to be pursued, ends to be striven for, consequences to be reached are propositions about subject-matters having the formal relation *means-consequences*, and are, in the sense defined, causal propositions. Propositions as

[4] See, *ante*, pp. 9–10, 104–7.

to what it is better to observe and what conception it is better to form and employ enter into the conduct of every inquiry; more scrupulously and extensively so in scientific inquiry than in those of common sense. They do not appear explicitly, however, in the final conclusions. But there are propositions which explicitly concern this relation, and if the term "causal propositions" has any proper reference it is to such propositions. Causation in any existential, non-categorial, sense is practical and teleological through and through.

Conclusion. The view that the category of causation is logical that it is a functional means of regulating existential inquiry, not ontological, and that all existential cases that can be termed causal are "practical", is not a view that will receive ready acceptance. But there was a time when species and essences were also conceived to be ontological. There was a time when purpose or end was taken to be an ontological property of Nature. Again, there was a time when *simplicity* was thought to be an ordering principle of Nature. Nothing in science happened save relief of inquiry from incubi when these notions were so changed that they were understood to be directive methodological principles of inquiry—logical rather than ontological. There is no risk in predicting a similar thing will happen with the conception of causation. Already difficulties have arisen in actual scientific findings which have caused some persons to believe that the whole idea or causation must be thrown overboard. But this is a mistake. The conclusion to be drawn is that the ontological interpretation is to be abandoned. Recognition of the value of the causal category as a leading principle of existential inquiry is in fact confirmed, and the theory of causation is brought into consonance with scientific practice. The institution of qualitative individual existential situations consisting of ordered sequences and coexistences is the goal of all existential inquiry. "Causation" is a category that directs the operations by which this goal is reached in the case of problematic situations.

CHAPTER XXIII

SCIENTIFIC METHOD AND
SCIENTIFIC SUBJECT-MATTER

S
INCE CONCLUSIONS form a body of organized subject-matter, and since this body of subject-matter attains scientific standing only because of the methods that are used in arriving at them, the systems of facts and principles of which science materially consists should disclose properties that conform to conditions imposed by the methods. Examination of some of the main features of natural science should, accordingly, provide a test of the account that has been given of the logic of method. Preliminary to a survey of subject-matter I shall summarize some of the outstanding conclusions concerning method that have a direct bearing on interpretation of scientific subject-matter.

THE LOGICAL VERSUS EPISTEMOLOGICAL

I. *The Significance of Experiment.* The experimental phase of method is an overt manifestation of the fact that inquiry effects existential transformation of the existential material that instigates inquiry. Experimentation is not just a practical convenience nor yet a means of modifying states of mind. No other ground than that of transformation of a problematic situation into a resolved one, can be found for the necessary function exercised in inquiry by experiment.

1. Experiment is required in order to institute the *data* which warrant inferred propositions. Without deliberate variation of given existential conditions, the latter as given neither circumscribe nor describe the problem to be solved by inquiry, nor provide material that adequately tests any proposed solution. Consequently, it may be expected, even in advance of detailed con-

sideration of actual scientific subject-matter, that the latter will have the distinctive properties that must mark data which are prepared to serve as the ground of warranted systematic inferences. In other words, the subject-matter will necessarily be marked by important differences from the subject-matter of any direct perceptual field.

2. Since *conceptions* serve as the directive procedural means of operations of experimentation, the system of ideas, conceptions and categories constituting scientific subject-matter will have the characters that have rendered them capable of instituting the operations by which material is discriminated and ordered. Hence, the laws or principles constituting scientific subject-matter will have a distinctive or differential character.

3. Experimentation endeavors to eliminate from antecedently given subject-matter any and all material that is irrelevant to determination of the definite problem which is involved in the situation, and that hence is obstructive to the mode of solution demanded. In addition to elimination, experiment also provides new existential materials with a view to satisfying these conditions. Negation-affirmation, exclusion-inclusion, demarcation-identification are thus inherently necessary functions in scientific method. Hence once more, we can anticipate in advance that scientific subject-matter will be so differentially determined as to satisfy the conditions of conjoint negation-affirmation.

II. *The Alleged Epistemological Problem of Scientific Subject-Matter.* Before directly taking up the subject-matter of natural science with a view to showing how it satisfies these logical conditions of the method of inquiry, I shall discuss a matter which would be irrelevant to the topic in hand if the position that has been set forth were generally accepted, but which is germane in the present state of philosophical opinion. On the ground of the position taken in this treatise, there is no *general* problem involved in the fact that the content (material and procedural) of scientific subject-matter is very different from that of the fields of direct perception and of common sense. It *must* differ in specified respects if it is to satisfy the conditions of controlled inquiry in resolution of problematic situations. Problems do arise. But they are specific problems of inquiry; they have to do with the particu-

r transformations that need to be effected in respect to the ma-
rial of particular problems. But on the ground of any other
neory than the one set forth there is a general problem to which
ne name *epistemological* is usually given. Hence I shall state
ome reasons for holding that the philosophical problems to which
ne name of epistemology is given, are (when epistemology is re-
arded as anything else than a synonym for *logic*) gratuitous and
rtificial; that such "problems" disappear when the characteristic
eatures of scientific subject-matter are interpreted from the
andpoint of satisfaction of *logical* conditions set by the require-
nents of controlled inquiry. I shall take two cases as exemplary
illustrations; one of them being concerned with the difference be-
ween the material of ordinary perception and the existential
ontents of scientific subject-matter; and the other being con-
erned with the nature of *conceptual* subject-matter in its relation
o the existential world.

1. Within the field of direct perception there are points of light
een in the heavens. By means of telescopic instruments, other
ots of light, not ordinarily perceptible, are disclosed. In both
ases, there is the specific problem of drawing inferences from
hat is perceived in order to account for what is observed by plac-
ng it in an extensive temporal-spatial continuum. As a conclusion
f inquiry, these specks of light are finally affirmed to be suns of
ystems situated so many light-years away from the observer on
is planet. Now, in itself, or immediately, the speck of light is
ust the quality which it is. The alleged epistemological problem
rises when the quality in its immediacy as a directly given sense-
atum is set in opposition to the object (subject-matter), the dis-
nt sun, which constitutes the scientific conclusion. It is pointed
ut, for example, that the speck of light exists here and now, while
ne object, the sun, may have ceased to exist in the period which
as elapsed since the light left the sun and "arrived" at the observer.
Hence the "problem" arises of a radical discrepancy between exis-
ntial material and scientific objects—this particular case being
ken as strikingly exemplifying the difference found between
nem as a result of every scientific undertaking.

When the theory of knowledge is framed on the ground of
nalysis of the method of inquiry employed in scientific practice,

or on logical grounds, the alleged problem simply does not presen itself. The visible light is taken as an *evidential datum* fron which, in conjunction with other evidential data, a grounded in ferred proposition is to be drawn. *It*, the light now existing, doe not purport to be a sun or to "represent" a sun: it presents a *prol lem*. An elaborate system of techniques of experimental observa tion, directed by an equally elaborate conceptual structure, resul in establishing an extensive temporal-spatial continuum, and b placing the light in a definite position in this system solves th problem presented by the existing datum. Within this inferre continuum, a sun, so many light-years distant, is determined to l the initial constituent and a light now and here existent to be th terminal constituent. There are many special problems and specifi inquiries arising in the course of this determination. But ther is no general problem of the alleged epistemological type. Fron the standpoint of inquiry and its method, the problem and i method of solution are of the same sort as when a geologist, on th ground of the traits of a rock here and now existent and here an now perceived, infers the existence of an animal of a certain speci living so many hundreds of thousands of years ago. No inferenc is possible from the observed rock *in isolation* to the object in ferred. But when it is ordered, by means of a complex conceptu: structure, in conjunction with a multitude of materially indepenc ent data, the inferred proposition is taken to be warranted. I both of the instances given, the difference in subject-matter be tween what is observed here and now and the subject-matter c the scientific object is inherent in satisfaction of conditions of cor trolled inquiry. A general philosophical problem of the "episte mological" type could and would arise only if they were nc different in subject-matter.

2. The necessity for a system of related conceptions (state propositionally) for discriminative institution of relevant data an for ordering them, has been mentioned in the case just discusse The instance now to be discussed involves interpretation of thes conceptions on the basis of the logic of inquiry in its contrast wit the epistemological interpretation. The "problem" which occa sions the epistemological interpretation arises when and because is supposed that conceptions, in general and in particular, *ought* t

e in some fashion descriptive of existential material. The idea that they should be descriptive is the only view possible when the strictly intermediate instrumental function, operatively realized, of conceptions is ignored. The difference in subject-matter of the existential and the scientifically conceptual is illustrated in the following quotation from Planck: "The physical definitions of sound, color and temperature are in no way associated with immediate perceptions due to the special senses, but color and sound are defined respectively by the frequency of wave lengths of oscillation, and temperature is measured theoretically on an absolute temperature scale corresponding to the second law of thermodynamics, or, in the kinetic theory of gases, as the kinetic energy of molecular motion. . . . It is in no way described as a feeling of warmth." [1]

What is here stated holds universally of the subject-matter of scientific conceptions in their contrast with the subject-matter of existential material. Now, unless conceptual subject-matter is interpreted solely and wholly on the ground of the function it performs in the conduct of inquiry, this difference in dimensions between the conceptual and the existential creates a basic philosophic problem. For the only possible alternative interpretations are either the (highly unsatisfactory) view that the conceptions are mere devices of practical convenience, or that in some fashion or other they are descriptive of something actually existing in the material dealt with. From the standpoint of the *function* that conceptual subject-matters actually serve in inquiry, the problem does not need to be "solved"; it simply does not exist.

The alleged epistemological problem is closely connected with the ambiguity of "abstraction" that has previously been noticed. For if conceptions are, in any assignable way, *descriptive,* then they must be derived by "abstraction" in the sense in which abstraction means selective discrimination. Take the case of *smooth* and *smoothness*. Smooth*ness*, as an instance of a scientific conception, is not capable of observation and hence not of selective discrimination. For complete absence of resistance and friction nowhere exists in nature. As a scientific conception, smoothness is stable only in a mathematical equation. The conception is

---

[1] Quoted by Stebbing, *A Modern Introduction to Logic,* p. 405.

undoubtedly *suggested* by observation of variations in degrees of friction found in nature. But *derivation* by means of suggestion is of a different dimension from *logical* derivation. "Abstraction" in the sense in which it yields an abstract universal proposition is of a different logical form from the selective discriminations by means of which generic propositions about kinds are instituted. In the words of Peirce: "It is important to relieve the term 'abstract' from staggering under the double burden of conveying the idea of precission as well as the unrelated and very important idea of creation of the *ens rationis* . . . this hypostatic abstraction that gives mathematics half its power."[2] Recognition of the logical difference in the two operations to which the name *abstraction* is given makes clear the non-existential nature of the content of propositions about relations of conceptual subject-matters. In fixing attention upon their function in conduct of inquiry it eliminates the alleged epistemological-metaphysical problem.

One more illustrative instance will be considered. It concerns the nature of points (and instants) as conceptions of mathematical physics, a problem also previously discussed. The importance of the conceptions of points and instants is so manifest that it does not have to be argued for. But anything that can be observed in existence is extended in time and space, no matter how minute the extension may be. Upon any basis except the functionally instrumental status of the subject-matters that are defined as points and instants, there arises the "problem" of *deriving* them from existential material. The long accepted method of derivation (by discriminative selection) was that a point is arrived at by selective abstraction of a limit fixed by intersection of two lines. Since the mathematical idea of a line as free of thickness was already in existence, this limit was held to be the representative of the mathematical point, and the latter to be the conceptual description of the existential fact. When the inherent difficulties in this conception became evident, the relations of a set of, say, boxes to one another such that there was a series of enclosing and enclosed volumes, was taken as the existential source from which the conception of a mathematical point is derivable. That the relation*ship* of enclosure-enclosed may be taken to define a point is not denied. The

[2] Peirce, *Collected Papers.* Vol. V, p. 304.

matter at issue is that a relation*ship* is of a different logical dimension from the *relations* which a set of enclosing and enclosed *objects* bear to one another. It is an abstraction *as such*. It may be "derived" by way of *suggestion* from the material mentioned but it is in no way logically important that it be so derived. Logically speaking, the particular way in which it is suggested is indifferent. The point at issue concerns the function of the conception in inquiry. Its justification is to be found in the consequences that follow from its operational use. Theories about its derivation in the sense of its origin may have psychological interest. But they are logically irrelevant—*unless* it is assumed that conceptual subject-matter must in some way or other be representative in a descriptive way of existential subject-matter—an idea which ultimately goes back to Aristotelian logic and to the state of science under which this logic was formulated.

III. *Subject-matter with Respect to the Inquiry-Continuum.* The subject-matter of science notoriously undergoes revision from time to time, almost day by day, with respect to details and at historic intervals quite fundamentally. This fact is interpreted by one logical school as evidence that the only secure and genuinely logical factor is *formal*. This formal character is said to be certified in turn by reference to some ultimate fixed *a priori* truth as a final premise. Even Mill, although he held that the conception of the Uniformity of Nature is inductively arrived at, held that it was a principle that had to be placed as an ultimate premise under all inductive processes. Officially, however, he belongs to the school that holds that probative value resides exclusively in existential *material*.

The problem that then arises with reference to the relation of subject-matter to form seems to me insoluble except on the ground of the continuity of inquiry. For that alone explains the actual relation that form and subject-matter bear to one another in the revision of scientific subject-matter. The problem involved is indicated by the following quotation from Peirce: "No determination of things, no fact, can result in the validity of probable argument; nor, on the other hand, is such argument reducible to the form which holds good whatever the facts may be." [3] Here we

---

[3] *Op. cit.*, Vol. V. p. 217.

have, if not a dilemma, yet certainly the materials of a problem.

For if neither matter nor form affords the warrant for generalized propositions about existential subject-matter, what is the connection between them by which reasonable warrant for inductive conclusions *is* provided? The answer is indicated in a further quotation from Peirce in which he says: "The justification of it [a probable conclusion] is that though the conclusion at any given state of the investigation may be more or less erroneous, yet the further application of the same *method* must correct the error." [4] Or, as he states the matter in another connection, "We cannot say that the generality of inductions are probably true, but only that in the long run they approximate the truth. We only know that by accepting inductive conclusions in the long run our errors balance each other." [5]

Taken in connection with Peirce's theory of leading or guiding principles of inquiry, the implications of these passages are that the formal element is provided by *method*. The relation of form and matter is that of the connection of methods with the existential material instituted and ordered by methods. Furthermore, the question of relation of method to material is a *long run* issue. For in what has been called the experiential continuum of inquiry, methods are self-rectifying so that the conclusions they yield are *cumulatively* determined. It follows that the validity of existential propositions is a matter of *probability* and that the order of probability possessed is a function of continuity of inquiry. These considerations supply the ground of transition to the first topic to be discussed regarding scientific subject-matter proper.

PROBABILITY AND ITS CONNECTION WITH FREQUENCY

It was shown earlier that existential generic propositions are not *necessary*. For they are grounded in observational material. The experimental operations by which this material is selected and ordered have, as their logical ground and intent, satisfaction of exhaustive inclusion-exclusion in a conjunctive-disjunctive system. But the logical conditions are *directive principles and ideals*. They guide experimental operations in determination of existential sub-

---

[4] *Ibid*, p. 90; italics not in original.
[5] *Ibid*, p. 218.

ject-matter, but the nature of the subject-matter is such that their realization can only be approximated, not completely effected. Hence all such propositions are of some order of probability. This section of the discussion of subject-matter is concerned, then, with the discussion of the probability-property of existential propositions with reference to its connection with the category of the long run in inquiry. Negatively, the position taken is contrary to any theory that interprets probability on the ground of ignorance or any "subjective" factor. For it is held to be a manifestation of the very nature of the existential material that is dealt with. On the positive side, the category of probability is held to admit of logical interpretation only in terms of frequency. For if warranted existential conditions are determined in the *continuity* of inquiry, by means of which errors in special cases tend to cancel one another out, some mode of frequency interpretation is involved. The discussion that follows is not, then, directed to a technical development of the conceptions of probability and frequency, but is intended to show their inherent connection with the position already developed concerning the methods of natural science. The discussion will, accordingly, be conducted on the basis of a number of illustrative instances of probability propositions.

1. Take such a proposition as "It is probable that Julius Caesar visited Great Britain." Ignorance undoubtedly enters into the class of propositions of which this is a specimen; not ignorance in general, but ignorance as a name for a specifiable insufficiency of the *data* at hand. For there is an absence of records bearing specifically upon the particular inferred proposition. In spite of the absence of these specific data, the proposition as to probability has some logical standing; complete abstinence from making any inference whatever is not logically required. Upon what ground can such propositions be justified? One view is that they rest ultimately upon an "intuition" of the *form* of probability as such.

It certainly cannot be argued that the probability-form in question rests upon ascertained *material* grounds of the given case, for by description they are lacking. It is also clear that the proposition is logically different from such a proposition as "It is probable that Julius Caesar visited Great Britain such and such a number of times during his various campaigns," for in the latter proposition a frequency-ratio is explicitly involved, while in the given case there is no frequency-coefficient in the data. How shall such propositions logically be accounted for?

The interpretation here advanced is that the *kind of situation* involved is such as, in the *continuum* of inquiry, to warrant a probability proposition. The probability in question is purely qualitative. It cannot be assigned a measured numerical index, even roughly. Its measure is qualitative and is naturally expressed in some such form as "All things considered, it is more likely than not." The frequency factor is not found in the data of this particular case any more than it appears in the proposition itself. It resides in the qualitative similarity of the total situation to other qualitative situations (qualitative because not analyzed or capable of analysis into definite material data) which in the long run (more frequently than not) have been found to yield conclusions that can be depended upon. The frequency factor might, then, be expressed in some such form as the following: "More often than not inferences drawn from the kind of situation of which this is a specimen have turned out to be fruitful in spite of absence of adequate material data." The frequency factor, in short, belongs to the *method* that is employed in this type of case.

This manner of interpretation provides a simple explanation of the "intuition" which is said to be involved. In a *psychological* sense there is something that may be called intuitive. The method employed is embodied in a *habit* operating in the case of those qualitative situations that are assimilated to one another with respect to the inferences drawn from them. The habit, in this case as in other cases of habit, is depended upon until conditions definitely block it. We may say then, either that the "intuition" is of the quality of the situations involved and of the qualitative similarity of *this* situation to others from which inferences have been drawn; or, more directly, that it is a sense of the habit that is operating. But it is the *method*, not the intuition, that gives to such propositions whatever logical standing they possess.

2. I turn now to another kind of proposition which is like the one just considered in being about a singular, but is unlike it in that (1) it is based upon definite data of observation which, more-

over, are gathered and ordered with special reference to institution of a proposition as to the probability of a specified event; and in that (2) the data are ordered and interpreted by means of *explicit* conceptual, or theoretical, propositions. The prediction of the probability of the kind of which tomorrow's weather will be is an exemplary specimen. The data in this case are provided by observation of existing conditions with respect to such matters as temperature, direction and velocity of winds, rain and clouds, over a wide range of territory and for a long period of time. The *significance* of the data thus obtained, what they point to, does not, however, reside in the mere facts in their isolation. They are ordered in relation to one another by a systematized conceptual structure (of which the conception of areas of high and low pressure is an instance), while the indicative force of the data thus ordered is determined by certain physical *laws*, of which formulae regarding relations of heat, pressure and motion are examples.

These physical laws have the form of universal propositions since their content is an interrelation of abstract characters. No one would dream of supposing that as such they "imply" the state of weather that will probably be found the next day in some specified area. They are not descriptive but instrumental. They are operatively applied, in the first place, in deciding the special sort of data to be observationally procured—the particular occurrences that are to be discriminated out of the total welter of events actually occurring; and, in the second place, in interpretation of what the recorded events *signify*. Neither of these applications could be made on the basis simply of the data of a particular day's observation. The latter are significant in connection with the record of similar observations made in the past. The forecasts are dependable in the measure in which there is a record of what has taken place over wide areas during extensive periods of time. While the proposition is *about* a singular, *frequency-distributions* of conjunctions that have been observed in the past are the decisive factor in determining the special application of conceptual material to the case in hand.

The case thus illustrates not merely the instrumental function of theory, and of calculations and discourse that are derived from theoretical conceptions, but also has a definite bearing upon the nature of the category of probability. On one side, it shows that the probability in this instance is based upon *knowledge* of what has actually taken place with respect to frequency-distributions, not upon ignorance. Positively—and this point is the crucial one —it indicates why and how any such proposition is affected with a probability coefficient. It is due to the fact that the data (here and in any case) are existential events and qualities *discriminatively selected* from out of a total existential perceptual field; selected on the ground of their evidential value with respect to a special problem—that of determining what will take place at some specified time and place.

It is a simpler matter to predict the occurrence of an event in the case of an astronomical phenomenon like an eclipse of the moon than it is of tomorrow's weather in, say, San Francisco. For in the former case, it is easier to select certain conditions as relevant to the inferred proposition and to rule out others as irrelevant. Greater approximation can be made in other words to a *closed system*, so that the probability in the case of prediction of an eclipse is of a higher order. But nonetheless there is a certain arbitrary or contingent element in the case of the proposition about the time and place of an eclipse. For, to take an extreme example, there is no *theoretical* justification for the proposition that the moon will even be in existence at the time to which the prediction refers. The probability that it will be in existence is of a very high order. But there is no logical necessity in the matter. The proposition is after all grounded in existential spatio-temporal conjunctions arrived at in past inquiries. It is therefore subject to a condition inherent in the very nature of existential conditions. For the existential conditions are such that a different conjunction may occur in the future from those whose occurrence in the past is the ground of the prediction. The probability coefficient, in other words, is rooted in the nature of the existential conditions, not in the *attitude* of the inquirer towards them.

The connection of probability with determination of frequency-distributions of existential conjunctions is evident in the fact that even if it were infallibly assured that the data employed are both genuinely existential facts and are exhaustive as far as the past is concerned, their *evidential bearing* upon a new case is not thereby completely guaranteed. *If* the conditions remain exactly the same, *then*, tautologically, the predicted issue is like the past cases. But the content of the *if* clause is existentially contingent; it has not the logical force of the *if* clause in a universal hypothetical proposition.

Suppose the objection is raised that after all it comes back to ignorance, since if, *per* what is practically impossible, the state of the universe as a whole were known, the contingency and the probability factor would vanish. This supposititious objection involves two factors, which, when they are made explicit, throw light upon the issue involved. In the first place, there is the assumption that the universe *is* a complete and closed *whole*. This proposition is purely metaphysical. It does not rest upon empirical evidence. It is brought in from outside of logic and then used to justify a certain logical doctrine. In the second place, even if the metaphysical assumption is made, it does not apply to what happens *at a particular place and area at a specified time*. Even if the universe were a closed and complete unconditioned whole, and even if, *per* the practically impossible, it were completely known, the only proposition which would follow would be one about the state of the universe as a whole at subsequent times. The problem, however, is that of ascertaining what is likely to happen in a specially designated locality at a specially designated date. Determination of this matter depends upon knowledge of what is taking place in *other* localities at *other* local times. The ordering and interpretation of this knowledge depends upon extensive records of observations of conjunctions that have occurred in a great number of other areas at a great number of times— which takes us back to probability grounded in actual existences and to the frequency interpretation.

The positive logical import of these considerations is that any determination of data is a matter of a *selection* which is controlled by reference to evidential function in a *determinate* problem. The discriminatively selected character of data *as* data is inherent in the very nature of inquiries that are concerned with existences. It does not arise from any source outside the logic of the case—such as any psychological-epistemological state of affairs due to limitations of the faculties and knowledge of the inquirer. Since the necessity for selection of the material that provides evidential data is intrinsic, inferred propositions are subject to the existential conditions thereby imposed. The probability-character follows, and also the place of propositions about frequency-distributions in deciding the order of probability belonging to a given proposition. For ascertained conjunctions of this type provide the ultimate ground for the selection of some existences and qualities rather than others to serve as data.

3. We now come to the instances in which propositions are overtly *about* frequency ratios, with respect to their probability. Throwing of a coin or of dice with respect to the probability of heads or tails, or of a certain numbered face of a die, appearing a given number of times in a series of throws, is the case that will be examined. In *subject-matter*, the case differs from those already considered in that (1) the existential data are relatively definite and complete, and in that (2) deduction from conceptions plays a more important role. In the case of a series of throws of dice, the existential conditions are determined in a way that satisfies to an unusual degree the logical conditions of inclusion-exclusion. The coin has but two sides; the die but six faces; and the conditions are such that but one side, to the exclusion of others, can be thrown at any given time. When these conditions are postulated and it is also postulated that the coin or dice are homogeneous in composition (or are not loaded), and that the successive acts of throwing are such that the peculiarities which affect the result in one case are offset, in the long run, by the peculiarities of other acts of throwing (or that the mechanism for throwing is not crooked), the mathematical theory comes into play and the ratio of frequencies in a succession of throws can be theoretically calculated.

Given the conditions in question as final, it is possible for mathematical theory, in ordered discourse, to reach certain propositions about what will *necessarily* occur as a matter of frequency-distributions in an *indefinite* series of throws. But no one today would hold that these propositions "imply" what will existentially take place, or that the theory guarantees that the conditions postulated actually exist. They are *if-then* propositions necessarily related to one another. But they do not guarantee that the conditions of the *if* clause existentially obtain. This is a matter-of-fact capable of determination only by independent operations of experimental observation. The point here made may be technically stated as follows: The probability of A *or* B with respect to C is equal to the probability of A with respect to C *plus* the probability of B with respect to C *minus* the probability of A *and* B with respect to C. This is a proposition in the *calculus* of probability. On the frequency interpretation, it is a proposition whose contents have a necessary relation to one another. But the propositions that the probability of A or B with respect to C is ¾ and that the probability of A or B with respect to C is ½, are factual in nature. They are dependent upon factual information for their content.

The important logical consideration is that from the *mathematical* point of view the calculated frequency-distributions represent the *limit* of a mathematical infinite series, while the ratio of existential distributions is a matter of a long-run *finite* series. Suppose, for example, that at the close of *n* throws (*n* being a finite number), actual results have a one-hundred-percent agreement with theoretically arrived at conclusions. The fallacy involved in stopping at that point and saying the theoretical conclusion is now completely verified is evident. For the very next throw would upset "verification" by complete agreement to an extent dependent upon the number of previous throws. It is, accordingly, impossible to give *descriptive* value to the mathematical conceptions and propositions. They have instrumental and functional status. What applies in this case of conditions, so prepared in advance as to come as close to a closed system as is possible, applies *a fortiori* to cases in which prior preparation of existential conditions cannot be instituted in the same degree.

4. I now come to the type of case represented by life-expectancy tables of an insurance company, with respect to the office they serve. Here, too, the subject-matter is not the probability of a singular event but of the probable frequency ratio of events of specified kinds to events of the kind in which they are included as subkinds. The inclusive kind is constituted by the conjunction of traits that describe the kind *deaths*. The included kinds are deaths differentiated from one another, within the in-

clusive kind, by the age, within certain prescribed limits, at which deaths occur. A physician examining John Smith may form a proposition concerning the probable length of time John Smith has to live. As an insuree, John Smith is simply one of a collection of singulars marked off by the trait of being of the same age. As one of a kind *qua* kind, not *qua* a singular, he has a certain probable life-expectancy. The propositions are: that of persons of a given age, a certain ratio die within the next year, a certain other proportionate number within the next two years, and so on.

Both the data from which inferences are made, and propositions inferred from them, are matters of frequency-distributions. The validity of the data depends upon the extensive character of past observations and the completeness and accuracy of records. They are materially checked by the fact that life-insurance companies have now been operating for a long time, and hence have a more selected prepared set of data upon which to draw than are provided by records of deaths in general. It is a commonplace that the actuarial phase of the business is mathematical in character. But the slightest analysis shows that the mathematics in question functions instrumentally, not descriptively. As far as the sub-jective theory is concerned, it is obvious that the more extensive and accurate the knowledge of relevant data, the more accurate are the probability propositions formed.

5. It is perhaps advisable to say something about a question more or less often discussed, namely, the probability that a given *theory* or a given law is "true." According to the position here taken it is meaningless to speak of the degree of probability of a given law or theory save as that phrase is an elliptic or shorthand (and also awkward) way of pointing to the probability-coefficients of the subject-matters between which the laws, as means of transi-tion, enable relations to be instituted. Some laws are more com-prehensive than others; they apply to a wider range of cases. If the degree of probability of a law had any literal meaning, it would seem to apply only to the relative frequency of the valid applica-tion of less comprehensive laws within the total system of laws of which they are members. It is difficult to find a case in which such a determination would have any importance. If it did have meaning, it would exemplify the principle already stated, viz., that

the probability of a theory is measured by the relations its consequences sustain to those of other theories in the continuity of inquiry.

In terminating this phase of the discussion of subject-matter, it is pertinent to recur to the intent of this chapter. Its purpose is to show the connection of the characteristic features of the body of propositions that form the subject-matter of existential science with the account previously given of the logic of method. The discussion of probability is intended, then, only to indicate that and how, the probable character of scientific propositions about singulars, collections and kinds bears out conclusions that were reached as to method, not to provide a technical discussion of the whole subject. Its most intimate connection is with the discussion of propositions having existential reference found in Chapter XV.

CASES AS REPRESENTATIVE

The net conclusion of the discussion of the inductive phase of inquiry was that it is concerned to institute a case that is *representative* of various phenomena in such a way that it warrants a general proposition; or, negatively stated, that induction is not a matter of inferring from some to all. Upon the side of subject-matter, this conception of method accounts for the role played by the category of specimens and samples. After checking propositions by experimental variation of conditions, the following proposition is affirmed: The melting point of *this* substance is 125° C. This proposition in conjunction with other propositions of independent material contents leads to the generalization "Anything having this set of conjoined traits is sulphur": that is, it is a *case* of the *kind* denominated sulphur. The determination of singulars as *cases* of a generalization or law is the result of operations of selection and ordering of traits that have the function of being determinately significant; that is, representative. The statement that "the phenomenon is a case of a law," is elliptic. It cannot be interpreted to mean that laws are inherently and ontologically embodied in phenomena, or that the phenomena are "implied" by the law. It means that a certain selected and ordered set of conjoined traits is, or is taken to be, an adequate ground from which to make a generalization, which when formulated, has the form of a law; and that, given the law, the case thus constituted is a secure ground for inference.

At this point, it is pertinent to distinguish the cases that are samples, from those which are specimens. A case is a *specimen* when its content is so constituted that its *kind* permits inferences to be safely made from it to traits and objects which are not there and then observed. This thing, for example, is determined to be a specimen of rye, wheat or oats when it is ascertained to be marked by a certain conjunction of distinctive traits. Its character as a specimen would not warrant inference to things and properties outside the kind—for example, to things that are temporally and spatially contiguous. When, however, the material in question is determined to be a fair *sample*, the material becomes something more than an exemplary case or specimen of a kind. A given thing is a sample only when it is determined to be an element in a homogeneous continuum. Whether or not a portion of grain selected from a bin is or is not a sample of the contents of the bin is a different question from whether or not it is an adequate specimen of the kind *wheat* or of some subkind of wheat. It is a fair sample only if homogeneity has been instituted by mixing, say, all the contents of the bin so thoroughly that any given handful will present in *proportionate distribution*, all the constituent grains in the bin. It then becomes *representative* of them in the sense that inference can be made from it to the properties of any other handful, no matter of what kind or combination of kinds it is, or from what part of the bin it is taken.

Determination of cases as samples thus has a distinctive logical function. The scope of inferences from what I have called specimen cases is subject to a definite restriction. For determination of singulars as being of a kind is dependent upon selection and ordering of *qualities*. The qualities are not, as we have seen, taken in their immediacy, for they are selected and ordered as marks or signs of interactions of which they are consequences. The establishment of a specified *interaction* is identical with determination of a correlation of changes or variations, and the formula of an interaction in law or generic proposition is not in its content a formulation of a notation of observed qualities. But *reference* to the qualitative necessarily remains. This reference is not such as to obstruct measurements of phenomena or calculations based on measurements, since the very content of the law is such as to promote and direct those measurements of selected material that render calculations possible. But it does get in the way of applicatory use of abstract universal propositions or of mathematical formulae as such. For kinds are *hetero*geneous, being marked off on the ground of qualities; even subkinds within an inclusive kind are demarcated by distinctions having qualitative reference. Hence the application of calculations is restricted to relations *within* kinds. Institution of a spatial-temporal continuum such that any portion of it is *homo*geneous with every other portion is equivalent to institution of a *new type of kind* which is existentially so inclusive that its contents are related to one another not as qualitatively distinct kinds but as special interactions within a complex single scheme of interactions, the latter being stated in terms free from reference to anything but properties common to every interaction. The bearing of this change upon the subject-matter of natural science forms the special theme of the next section.

THE STANDARDIZED CONCEPTIONS OF SCIENTIFIC SUBJECT-MATTER

I. The subject-matter of physical science is constituted as far as is possible in terms of constituents which lend themselves to numerical measurements of such a sort that the measurements in question are capable of systematic relation with one another; i.e., comparisons that determine identities and differences which are also numerically formulated. It is not enough just to measure. The measurements must be such, in scientific ideal, as to be statable in terms that are systematically comparable with one another; that is, to be relatable in calculations.

1. This end is effected in scientific inquiry through the categories of space, time and mass so correlated with one another as to enable changes that occur (which themselves are numerically measured) to be stated in terms of differences of motion as an inclusive category. For determination of change as motion means formulation of it in terms of numerically measured mass in con-

junction with numerically measured time and distance or "length." M, T, and L, are standard means of determining the units in which physical phenomena are measured, since it is by their use that any change is capable of formulation in terms of velocity and acceleration of motions having vectorial properties. They are the means by which homogeneity of data is established such that any portion of a space-time continuum may be taken as a sample of a system of interactions. Free interchange of data is thus made possible with respect to extensive inferential functions.

On the negative side, this statement implies that the status of the conceptions is logical, not ontological. Existential interactions must have *potentialities* such that they are capable of formulation in terms of motions defined by application of the conceptions, M, T and L. Nevertheless, the classic formulation in terms of qualitative changes, in which change of spatial positions and the time taken in the course of this change were of no particular importance, was a more faithful *descriptive* rendering of the direct field of perception than is modern physical science. Interpretation on the basis of kinds of which particular objects are more or less complete specimens, is also much closer to what on its face is the report of common sense, than is the idea of a homogeneous spatial-temporal continuum. But "science" that was constructed in these terms did not lend itself either to fruitful theoretical development or to extensive practical control of qualitative change. Constructive development of science has taken place through treating the material of the perceived world in terms of properties that accrue to natural objects on the ground of their function in promoted and controlled processes of systematic inquiry; that is, in terms of properties that are logical, rather than directly ontological. Mass, time and length, as conceptions, are contents of universal propositions whose application to existence is functional.

2. Statement in terms of a homogeneous spatial-temporal continuum makes possible extensive systematic ordering of propositions in discourse as well as institution of measured data in extensive inference. The elimination of qualities as the ground of scientific propositions made, as has been said, measurements and calculations on the basis of those measurements possible. But

measurements and calculations do not of themselves alone provide the means of completely systematic *interpretation or ordering* of the data obtained. For the conjugate relation of data and conceptions (which has so often been pointed out) requires for complete organization of data a corresponding system of interrelated conceptions capable of exclusive and inclusive (exhaustive) application. The conceptions of mass, time and length in their interrelations with one another satisfy this condition. Transformation of contents that are stated in their terms is possible in discourse without limitation; or at least, it is the logical ideal that the ultimate categories of physical inquiry be such that this unrestricted transformability is possible. Phenomena as qualitatively unlike as those of heat, light and electricity, are capable of statement in equations that are capable of indefinite deductive development.

3. Nevertheless, there is a twofold convention involved in selection of M, T and L, as standardized conceptions. One of them, a minor one from the standpoint of the present theme, was previously discussed. The selection of a bar of platinum, kept in a certain place under specified conditions, to serve as the unit of measurement of lengths, is obviously a matter of social agreement. But, as already indicated, while the particular content is a matter of agreement, its function is not conventional, since the operation of measurement is of such intrinsic importance that some effective means must be found for its execution.

There is another and conceptual convention that has direct logical import. The fact that M, T and L are logical rather than ontological in nature indicates that there is no existential necessity for choosing them. Mass, energy and density might, for example, have been selected, in which case length and time would have been derivatives. There are those who believe that, because of development of quantum physics, mass, electric charge and angular momentum will sometime become the standard conceptions. The facilitation and control of inquiry is the criterion by which standard conceptions are instituted—a further indication that their status is that of procedural means, as well as of the fact that the convention involved is not arbitrary.

The discussion of the present topic will be concluded by recurring to the correlation of inductive and deductive operations in scientific inquiry. The subject-matter of physical science exhibits in overt form the meaning of this correlation. Existential determinations, which are inductive, are made in such a way as to enable mathematical conceptions and relations to function effectively in deductively ordered discourse. In and of itself, the existential world is such that an unlimited variety of selective discriminations is possible. A problem decides the selection which is actually instituted in any given case. In what is called *common sense*, the problem is that of some use-enjoyment. In science, the generic problem is promotion of controlled inquiry. Since the required control can be obtained only through the intermediation of abstract interrelated conceptions, inductive existential determinations are conducted with constant reference to institution and application of conceptions deductively interrelated with one another, while the conceptions are chosen and ordered with reference to ultimate existential application.

This consideration qualifies the meaning of induction and deduction in their methodological significance. As far as *processes* of inquiry are concerned, there is no difference between induction and deduction. Sagacity in evaluation, scrupulous care in notation and record, cherishing and development of suggestion, a keen eye for relevant analogies, tentative experimentation, physical and imaginative shaping of material so that it takes the form of a diagrammatic representation, are all demanded whether the subject-matter is observational or conceptual; that is, whether the *function* of the subject-matter in question is inductive or deductive. The distinction between induction and deduction does not lie then in the processes of inquiry but in the *direction* which the processes take—according as the objective is determination of relevant and effective existential data or relevant and effective interrelated conceptions. A man traveling from New York to Chicago and from Chicago to New York may use the same route and the same means of transportation in each trip. His intended destination and his direction of movement make the difference. The case is not different as far as processes involved in induction and deduction are concerned.

The notion that there is one *logic* of induction and another of deduction, and that the two logics are independent of each other, is an expression of a certain stage of intellectual history. It developed at the time when the classic logic was still supposed to provide the norm of *demonstrative* discourse, and yet was found to be inadequate for purposes of existential inquiries. It was then retained as a valid logic of deduction and was supplemented by superimposition of an inductive logic supposed to formulate the methods employed in physical investigations. In consequence, both the so-called deductive and inductive logics suffered in their own contents. The isolation of each from the other made it impossible to state either of them on the ground and terms of the functions they respectively performed. The attempt to obtain a complete logic by addition of two distorted and defective logics is impossible of execution.

It is pertinent to quote the following passage with reference to the actual import of the more recent developments of the logic of the deductive function. "The new logic offers the deductive procedure, not as a method of proof, but as a method of analysis. Instead of taking the field of arithmetic or of logic as one in which indispensable premises are to lead to previously uncertain or undiscovered conclusions by a process of demonstration, it takes the generally accepted facts of arithmetic, or of logic, as a problem for analysis and orderly arrangement. In the process of making such an analysis and reconstructing our facts upon the basis of its results, we may—and most frequently do—come upon some previously unsuspected facts or principles which are required by those more commonly recognized. But in general we accept the results of previous experience; the need is not so much to substantiate as to understand the results." [6] There are two considerations implied in this statement that are pertinent to the present discussion. The *processes* involved in the work of analyzing and reordering accepted material cannot, it seems to me, be any different from those involved in any strictly existential inquiry. Thorough familiarity with material, sagacity in discrimination, acuteness in detection of leads or clews, persistence and thoroughness in following them through, cherishing and developing suggestions that arise, are required in one as in the other. There are no set rules to be fol-

[6] C. I. Lewis, "On the Structure of Logic and its Relation to Other Systems," *The Journal of Philosophy*, Vol. XVIII (1921), p. 514.

lowed. The only "rule," it might be said, is to be as intelligent and honest as lies within one's power. The other implication is that logic—and mathematics—has at any given time a body of subject-matter which, in a historical sense, is existential, and with which it works. The forms that result from the analysis and re-ordering are relative to the subject-matter at hand. Change from a theory of deduction as rational *demonstration* (a theory characteristic of the classic theory), to such an interpretation as that quoted above, did not itself arise or proceed from formal logical considerations. On the contrary, the change in the formal conceptions of logic was conditioned by the fact that change had occurred in the methods used in inquiry and consequently in the subject-matter arrived at. Analytic examination and reordering of the subject-matter of method and conclusions resulted in a new and immensely fruitful knowledge of forms and formal relations. But forms are still relative to the continuum of inquiry from which they derive, and to which they are still relevant even when they are abstracted and independently formulated.

CHAPTER XXIV

SOCIAL INQUIRY

T HE SUBJECT-MATTER of social problems is existential. In the broad sense of "natural," social sciences are, therefore, branches of natural science. Social inquiry is, however, relatively so backward in comparison with physical and biological inquiry as to suggest need for special discussion. The question is not whether the subject-matter of human relations is or can ever become a science in the sense in which physics is now a science, but whether it is such as to permit of the development of methods which, as far as they go, satisfy the logical conditions that have to be satisfied in other branches of inquiry. That there are serious difficulties in the way is evidenced by the backward state of social inquiry. One obvious source of the difficulty lies in the fact that the subject-matter of the latter is so "complex" and so intricately interwoven that the difficulty of instituting a relatively closed system (a difficulty which exists in physical science) is intensified. The very backwardness of social inquiry may serve, then, to test the general logical conceptions that have been reached. For the results of discussion of the topic may show that failure to act in accord with the logical conditions which have been pointed out throws light on its retarded state.

I. *Introduction.* Certain conclusions already arrived at form an introduction to the discussion.

1. All inquiry proceeds within a cultural matrix which is ultimately determined by the nature of social relations. The subject-matter of physical inquiry at any time falls within a larger social field. The techniques available at a given time depend upon the state of material and intellectual culture. When we look back at earlier periods, it is evident that certain problems could not have arisen in the context of institutions, customs, occupations and in-

terests that then existed, and that even if, *per impossibile*, they had been capable of detection and formulation, there were no means available for solving them. If we do not see that this conditioning, both negative and positive, exists at present, the failure to see it is due to an illusion of perspective. For since conceptions standardized in previous culture provide the ideational means by which problems are formulated and dealt with, even if certain problems were felt at a particular period (past or present), the hypotheses required to suggest and guide methods of their solution would be absent. "There is an inalienable and ineradicable framework of conceptions which is not of our own making, but given to us ready-made by society—a whole apparatus of concepts and categories, within which and by which individual thinking, however daring and original, is compelled to move." [1]

a. The impact of cultural conditions upon social inquiry is obvious. Prejudices of race, nationality, class and sect play such an important role that their influence is seen by any observer of the field. We have only to recall the story of astronomy and of more recent incidents in the doctrine of evolution to be aware that in the past institutional vested interests have told upon the development of physical and biological science. If they do not do so at present to anything like the same extent, it is in large measure because physics has now developed specialized subject-matters and techniques. The result is that to many persons the "physical" seems not only relatively independent of social issues (which it is) but inherently set apart from all social context. The appearance of absence of conflict is to some extent a function of this isolation. What has actually happened, however, is that the influence of cultural conditions has become indirect. The general type of physical problems that are uppermost determines the order of conceptions that are still dominant. Social tendencies and the problems attending them evoke special emphasis upon certain

---

[1] Cornford, *From Religion to Philosophy*, p. 45, quoted by Stebbing, *A Modern Introduction to Logic*, p. 16n. The latter author adds: "No thinker, not even the physicist, is wholly independent of the context of experience provided for him by the society within which he works." While this is especially true of the relation of a given physicist to the smaller society of scientific workers within which he works, it is also true that the activities of this group as a whole are determined in their main features by the "context of experience provided" by the wider contemporaneous community.

orders of physical problems rather than upon others. It is not possible, for example, to separate nineteenth century devotion to exclusively mechanical conceptions from the needs of industry in that period. "Evolutionary" ideas were active, on the other hand, in dealing with cultural-social material before they were applied in biology. The notion of the complete separation of science from the social environment is a fallacy which encourages irresponsibility, on the part of scientists, regarding the social consequences of their work.

b. That physical science and its conclusions do as a matter of fact exercise an enormous influence upon social conditions need not be argued. Technological developments are the direct result of application of physical science. These technological applications have profound and extensive consequences upon human relations. Change in methods of production, distribution, and communication is the chief determining condition of social relationships and, to a large extent, of actual cultural values in every advanced industrial people, while they have reacted intensively into the lives of all "backward" peoples. Moreover, only an arbitrary, or else purely conventional point of view (itself a cultural heritage from earlier periods), can rule out such consequences as these from the scope of science itself. The convention in question posits a complete separation between "pure" and "applied" science.[2] The ultimate ground of every valid proposition and warranted judgment consists in some existential reconstruction ultimately effected. When the logician or philosopher is faced by the reconstructions resulting from physical discoveries, it is not possible for him to say, like Canute to the tide, "Thus far shalt thou go and no further."

2. One of the points discussed in an earlier chapter concerned the experiential continuum and the continuity of inquiry. This

---

[2] "The only valid distinction between pure and applied research in natural science lies between inquiries concerned with issues which *may eventually* and issues which *already do* arise in the social practice of mankind." Hogben, *Retreat from Reason*, p. 8. The following passage from the same author is pertinent to the earlier remark concerning the tendency toward intellectual irresponsibility bred by isolation of the field of physical inquiry from the needs and possibilities inhering in the "social practice of mankind." "The education of the scientist and technician leaves him indifferent to the social consequences of his own activities." (*Ibid*, p. 3)

expressed the principle of the "long run" phase of knowledge connected with the self-developing and self-correcting nature of scientific inquiry. Just as the validity of a proposition in discourse, or of conceptual material generally, cannot be determined short of the consequences to which its functional use gives rise, so the sufficient warrant of a judgment as a claimant to knowledge (in its eulogistic sense) cannot be determined apart from connection with a widening circle of consequences. An inquirer in a given special field appeals to the experiences of the community of his fellow workers for confirmation and correction of his results. Until agreement upon consequences is reached by those who reinstate the conditions set forth, the conclusions that are announced by an individual inquirer have the status of an hypothesis, especially if the findings fail to agree with the general trend of already accepted results.[3] While agreement among the activities and their consequences that are brought about in the wider (technically non-scientific) public stands upon a different plane, nevertheless such agreement is an integral part of a *complete* test of physical conclusions wherever their public bearings are relevant.[4] The point involved comes out clearly when the social consequences of scientific conclusions invoke intensification of social conflicts. For these conflicts provide presumptive evidence of the insufficiency, or partiality, and incompleteness of conclusions as they stand.

3. The conclusion that agreement of activities and their consequences is a test and a moving force in scientific advance is in

---

[3] C. S. Peirce is notable among writers on logical theory for his explicit recognition of the necessity of the social factor in the determination of evidence and its probative force. The following representative passage is cited: "The next most vital factor of the method of modern science is that it has been made social. On the one hand, what a scientific man recognizes as a fact of science must be something open to anybody to observe, provided he fulfills the necessary conditions, external and internal. As long as only one man has been able to see a marking upon the planet Venus, it is not an established fact. . . . On the other hand, the method of modern science is social in respect to the solidarity of its efforts. The scientific world is like a colony of insects, in that the individual strives to produce that which he himself cannot hope to enjoy." —*Dictionary of Philosophy and Psychology*, Vol. 2, p. 502.

[4] The "agreement" in question is agreement in activities, not intellectual acceptance of the same set of propositions. (Cf. ante, pp. 51–4.) A proposition does not gain validity because of the number of persons who accept it. Moreover, continuity of inquiry as a going concern must be taken into account rather than the exact state of belief at a given moment.

harmony with the position that the ultimate end and test of all inquiry is the transformation of a problematic situation (which involves confusion and conflict) into a unified one. That it is much more difficult to accomplish this end in social inquiry than in the restricted field of physical inquiry is a fact. But it is not a fact which constitutes an inherent logical or theoretical difference between the two kinds of inquiry. On the contrary, the presence of *practical* difficulties should operate, as within physical inquiry itself, as an intellectual stimulus and challenge to further application.

4. That social inquiry must satisfy the conjoint conditions of observational ascertainment of fact and of appropriate operational conceptions may seem too evident to require explicit statement. For they are obviously conditions of all scientific achievement with respect to existential subject-matter. But the failure to satisfy the requirement of institution of factual and conceptual subject-matter in conjugate correspondence with each other is such a marked characteristic of the present estate of the social disciplines (as is shown in some detail later) that it is necessary to make the point explicitly. On the positive side, the necessity of this conjugate relation indicates the most important way in which physical science serves as a model for social inquiry. For if there is one lesson more than any other taught by the methods of the physical sciences, it is the strict correlativity of fact and ideas. Until social inquiry succeeds in establishing methods of observing, discriminating and arranging data that evoke and test correlated ideas, and until, on the other side, ideas formed and used are (1) employed as *hypotheses*, and are (2) of a form to direct and prescribe operations of analytic-synthetic determination of facts, social inquiry has no chance of satisfying the logical conditions for attainment of scientific status.

5. One further point will be mentioned before we come to discussion of social inquiry in its own terms. The wide field and intricate constitution of social phenomena, as compared with physical phenomena, is more than a source of practical difficulties in their scientific treatment. It has a definite theoretical import. For the existential conditions which form the physical environment enter at every point into the constitution of socio-cultural phenomena. No individual person and no group *does* anything

except in interaction with physical conditions. There are no consequences taking place, there are no social events that can be referred to the human factor exclusively. Let desires, skills, purposes, beliefs be what they will, what happens is the product of the interacting intervention of physical conditions like soil, sea, mountains, climate, tools and machines, in all their vast variety, with the human factor.[5] The theoretical bearing of this consideration is that social phenomena cannot be understood except as there is prior understanding of physical conditions and the laws of their interactions. Social phenomena cannot be attacked, *qua* social, directly. Inquiry into them, with respect both to data that are significant and to their relations or proper ordering, is conditioned upon extensive prior knowledge of physical phenomena and their laws. This fact accounts in part for the retarded and immature state of social subjects. Only recently has there been sufficient understanding of physical relations (including the biological under this caption) to provide the necessary intellectual instrumentalities for effective intellectual attack upon social phenomena. Without physical knowledge there are no means of analytic resolution of complex and grossly macroscopic social phenomena into simpler forms. We now come to discussion of the bearing of logical principles of inquiry upon distinctive social subject-matter.

II. *Social Inquiry and Judgments of Practice.* It was shown in the course of earlier discussions that there are judgments which are formed with *express* reference to entering integrally into the reconstitution of the very existential material which they are ultimately about, or concern. It was also shown that the judgments in which this phase is explicit—namely, judgments of practice and historical judgments,—are special instances of the reconstructive transformation of antecedent problematic subject-matter which is the end-in-view and the objective consequence of all inquiry. These considerations have a peculiar bearing upon social inquiry in its present condition. For the idea commonly prevails that such inquiry is genuinely scientific only as it deliberately and systematically abstains from all concern with matters of social practice. The special lesson which the logic of the methods of

[5] This consideration is fatal to the view that social sciences are exclusively, or even dominantly, psychological.

physical inquiry has to teach to social inquiry is, accordingly, that social inquiry, *as inquiry*, involves the necessity of operations which existentially modify actual conditions that, as they exist, are the occasions of genuine inquiry and that provide its subject-matter. For, as we have seen, this lesson is the logical import of the experimental method.

Physical inquiry to a considerable extent and mathematics to an even greater extent have now reached the point where problems are mainly set by subject-matter already prepared by the results of prior inquiries, so that further inquiries have a store of scientific data, conceptions and methods already at hand. This is not the case with the material of social inquiry. This material exists chiefly in a crude qualitative state. The problem of institution of methods by which the material of existential situations may be converted into the prepared materials which facilitate and control inquiry is, therefore, the primary and urgent problem of social inquiry. It is then to this phase of the logic of social inquiry that further discussion will be particularly directed.

1. Most current social inquiry is marked, as analytic examination will disclose, by the dominance of one or the other of two modes of procedure, which, in their contrast with one another, illustrate the separation of practice and theory. On the practical side, or among persons directly occupied with management of practical affairs, it is commonly assumed that the problems which exist are already definite in their main features. When this assumption is made, it follows that the business of inquiry is but to ascertain the best method of solving them. The consequence of this assumption is that the work of analytic discrimination, which is necessary to convert a problematic situation into a set of conditions forming a definite problem, is largely foregone. The inevitable result is that methods for resolving problematic situations are proposed without any clear conception of the material in which projects and plans are to be applied and to take effect. The further result is that often difficulties are intensified. For additional obstructions to intelligent action are created; or else, in alleviating some symptoms, new troubles are generated. Survey of political problems and the methods by which they are dealt with, in both domestic and international fields, will disclose any number of pertinent illustrations.

The contrast at this point with methods in physical inquiry is striking. For, in the latter, a large part of the techniques employed have to do with determination of the nature of the problem by means of methods that procure a wide range of data, that determine their pertinency as evidential, that ensure their accuracy by devices of measurement, and that arrange them in the order which past inquiry has shown to be most likely to indicate appropriate modes of procedure. Controlled *analytic* observation, involving systematic comparison-contrast, is accordingly a matter of course in the subjects that have achieved scientific status. The futility of attempting to solve a problem whose conditions have not been determined is taken for granted.

The analogy between social practice and medical practice as it was conducted before the rise of techniques of clinical observation and record, is close enough to be instructive. In both, there is the assumption that gross observation suffices to ascertain the nature of the trouble. Except in unusually obscure cases, symptoms sufficiently large and coarse to be readily observable sufficed in medical practice to supply the data that were used as means of diagnosis. It is now recognized that choice of remedial measures looking to restoration of health is haphazard until the conditions which constitute the trouble or disease have been determined as completely and accurately as possible. The primary problem is, then, to institute the techniques of observation and record that provide the data taken to be evidential and testing. The lesson, as far as method of social inquiry is concerned, is the prime necessity for development of techniques of analytic observation and comparison, so that problematic social situations may be resolved into definitely formulated problems.

One of the many obstructions in the way of satisfying the logical conditions of scientific method should receive special notice. Serious social troubles tend to be interpreted in *moral* terms. That the situations themselves are profoundly moral in their causes and consequences, in the genuine sense of moral, need not be denied. But conversion of the situations investigated into definite problems, that can be intelligently dealt with, demands objective *intellectual* formulation of conditions; and such a formulation demands in turn complete abstraction from the qualities of sin and righteousness, of vicious and virtuous motives, that are so readily attributed to individuals, groups, classes, nations. There was a time when desirable and obnoxious physical phenomena were attributed to the benevolence and malevolence of overruling powers. There was a time when diseases were attributed to the machinations of personal enemies. Spinoza's contention that the occurrence of moral evils should be treated upon the same basis and plane as the occurrence of thunderstorms is justifiable on the ground of the requirements of scientific method, independently of its context in his own philosophic system. For such procedure is the only way in which they can be formulated objectively or in terms of selected and ordered conditions. And such formulation is the sole mode of approach through which plans of remedial procedure can be projected in objective terms. Approach to human problems in terms of moral blame and moral approbation, of wickedness or righteousness, is probably the greatest single obstacle now existing to development of competent methods in the field of social subject-matter.

2. When we turn from consideration of the methods of inquiry currently employed in political and many administrative matters, to the methods that are adopted in the professed name of social science, we find quite an opposite state of affairs. We come upon an assumption which if it were made explicit or formulated would take some such shape as "The facts are out there and only need to be observed, assembled and arranged to give rise to suitable and grounded generalizations." Investigators of physical phenomena often speak and write in similar fashion. But analysis of what they *do* as distinct from what they *say* yields a very different result. Before, however, considering this point I shall discuss a closely connected assumption, namely the assumption that in order to base conclusions upon the facts and only the facts, all *evaluative* procedures must be strictly ruled out.

This assumption on the part of those engaged, in the name of science, in social investigation derives in the minds of those who entertain it from a sound principle. It springs, at least in large measure, from realization of the harm that has been wrought by forming social judgments on the ground of moral preconceptions, conceptions of what is right and wrong, vicious and virtuous. As has just been stated, this procedure inevitably prejudices the institution of relevant significant data, the statement of the problems that are to be solved, and the methods by which they may be solved. The soundness of the principle that moral condemnation and approbation should be excluded from the operations of obtaining and weighing material data and from the operations by which conceptions for dealing with the data are instituted, is, however, often converted into the notion that all evaluations should be excluded. This conversion is, however, effected only through the intermediary of a thoroughly fallacious notion; the notion, namely, that the moral blames and approvals in question *are* evaluative and that they exhaust the field of evaluation. For they are *not* evaluative in any logical sense of evaluation. They are not even judgments in the logical sense of judgment. For they rest upon some preconception of *ends* that *should* or *ought* to be attained. This preconception excludes ends (consequences) from the field of inquiry and reduces inquiry at its very best to the truncated and distorted business of finding out means for realizing objectives already settled upon. Judgment which is actually judgment (that satisfies the logical conditions of judgment) institutes means-consequences (ends) in *strict conjugate relation* to each other. Ends have to be adjudged (evaluated) on the basis of the available means by which they can be attained just as much as existential materials have to be adjudged (evaluated) with respect to their function as material means of effecting a resolved situation. For an end-in-view is itself a means, namely, a procedural means.

The idea that "the end justifies the means" is in as bad repute in moral theory as its adoption is a commonplace of political practice. The doctrine may be given a strictly logical formulation, and when so formulated its inherent defect becomes evident. From the logical standpoint, it rests upon the postulate that some end is already so fixedly given that it is outside the scope of inquiry, so that the only problem for inquiry is to ascertain and manipulate the materials by which the end may be attained. The hypothetical and directive function of ends-in-view as procedural means is thus ignored and a fundamental logical condition of inquiry is violated. Only an end-in-view that is treated as a *hypothesis* (by which discrimination and ordering of existential material is operatively effected) can by any logical possibility determine the existential materials that are means. In all fields but the social, the notion that the correct solution is already given and that it only remains to find the facts that prove it is so thoroughly discredited that those who act upon it are regarded as pretenders, or as cranks who are trying to impose some pet notion upon facts. But in social matters, those who claim that they are in possession of the one sure solution of social problems often set themselves up as being peculiarly scientific while others are floundering around in an "empirical" morass. Only recognition in both theory and practice that ends to be attained (ends-in-view) are of the nature of hypotheses and that hypotheses have to be formed and tested in strict correlativity with existential conditions as means, can alter current habits of dealing with social issues.

What has been said indicates the valid meaning of evaluation in inquiry in general and also shows the necessity of evaluative judgments in social inquiry. The need for selective discrimination of certain existential or factual material to be data proves that an evaluative estimate is operating. The notion that evaluation is concerned only with *ends* and that, with the ruling out of moral ends, evaluative judgments are ruled out rests, then, upon a profound misconception of the nature of the logical conditions and constituents of all scientific inquiry. All competent and authentic inquiry demands that out of the complex welter of existential and potentially observable and recordable material, certain material be selected and weighed *as* data or the "facts of the case." This process is one of adjudgment, of appraisal or evaluation. On the other end, there is, as has been just stated, no evaluation when ends are taken to be already given. An idea of an end *to be* reached, an end-*in-view*, is logically indispensable in discrimination of existential material as the evidential and testing facts of the case. Without it, there is no guide for observation; without it, one can have no conception of what one should look for or even *is* looking for. One "fact" would be just as good as another—that is, good for nothing in control of inquiry and in formation and settlement of a problem.

3. What has been said has direct bearing upon another assumption which underlies a considerable part of allegedly scientific social

inquiry; the idea, namely, that facts are just there and need only to be observed accurately and be assembled in sufficient number to warrant generalizations. A *generalization* in the form of a *hypothesis* is a *prerequisite* condition of selection and ordering of material *as* facts. A generalization is quite as much an *antecedent* of observation and assemblage of facts as it is a consequence of observing and assembling them. Or, more correctly stated, no generalization can emerge as a warranted conclusion unless a generalization in the form of a hypothesis has previously exercised control of the operations of discriminative selection and (synthetic) ordering of material to form the facts of and for a problem. To return to the point suggested earlier: What scientific inquirers *do*, as distinct from what they say, is to execute certain operations of experimentation—which are operations of doing and making—that modify antecedently given existential conditions so that the results of the transformation are facts which are relevant and weighty in solution of a given problem. Operations of experimentation are cases of blind trial and error which at best only succeed in *suggesting* a hypothesis to be later tried except as they are themselves directed by a hypothesis about a solution.

The assumption that social inquiry is scientific if proper techniques of observation and record (preferably statistical) are employed (the standard of propriety being set by borrowing from *techniques* used in physical science), thus fails to observe the logical conditions which in physical science give the techniques of observing and measuring their standing and force. This point will be developed by considering the idea, which is current, that social inquiry is scientific only when complete renunciation of any reference to *practical* affairs is made its precondition. Discussion of this fallacy (fallacious from the strictly logical point of view) will start from a consideration of the nature of the *problems* of social inquiry.

III. *Institution of Problems.* A genuine problem is one set by existential problematic *situations*. In social inquiry, genuine problems are set only by actual social situations which are themselves conflicting and confused. Social conflicts and confusions exist in fact before problems for inquiry exist. The latter are intellectualizations in inquiry of these "practical" troubles and difficulties. The intellectual determinations can be tested and warranted only by doing something about the problematic existential situations out of which they arise, so as to transform it in the direction of an ordered situation. The connection of social inquiry, as to social data and as to conceptual generalizations, with practice is intrinsic not external. Any problem of scientific inquiry that does not grow out of actual (or "practical") social conditions is factitious; it is arbitrarily set by the inquirer instead of being objectively produced and controlled. All the techniques of observation employed in the advanced sciences may be conformed to, including the use of the best statistical methods to calculate probable errors, etc., and yet the material ascertained be scientifically "dead," i.e., irrelevant to a genuine issue, so that concern with it is hardly more than a form of intellectual busy work. That which is observed, no matter how carefully and no matter how accurate the record, is capable of being *understood* only in terms of projected consequences of activities. In fine, problems with which inquiry into social subject-matter is concerned must, if they satisfy the conditions of scientific method, (1) grow out of actual social tensions, needs, "troubles"; (2) have their subject-matter determined by the conditions that are material means of bringing about a unified situation, and (3) be related to some hypothesis, which is a plan and policy for existential resolution of the conflicting social situation.

IV. *Determination of Facts in Social Inquiry.* This topic has, of necessity, been anticipated in the foregoing discussion which has shown that facts are such in a logical sense only as they serve to delimit a problem in a way that affords indication and test of proposed solutions. Two involved considerations will, however, be explicitly dealt with.

1. Since transformation of a problematic situation (a confused situation whose constituents conflict with one another) is effected by interaction of specially discriminated existential conditions, facts have to be determined in their dual function as obstacles and as resources; that is, with reference to operations of negation (elimination) and affirmation, the latter being determination of materials as positively agreeing with or reinforcing one another. No existing situation can be modified without counteracting ob-

structive and deflecting forces that render a given situation con-fused and conflicting. Operations of elimination are indispensable. Nor can an objectively unified situation be instituted except as the *positive* factors of existing conditions are released and ordered so as to move in the direction of the objective consequence desired. Otherwise, ends-in-view are utopian and "idealistic," in the senti-mental sense of the latter word.

Realistic social thinking is precisely the mode of observation which discriminates adverse and favorable conditions in an existing situation, "adverse" and "favorable" being understood in connec-tion with the end proposed. "Realism" does *not* mean appre-hension of the existing situation *in toto*, but selective discrimina-tion of conditions as obstructive and as resources; i.e., as negative and positive. When it is said "We must take conditions as they are" the statement is either a logical truism or a fallacy which then operates as an excuse for inaction. It is a truism if it is understood to mean that existing conditions are the material, and the only material, of analytic observation. But if it is taken to mean that "conditions as they are" are *final* for judgment as to what can or should be done, there results complete abnegation of intelligent direction of both observation and action. For condi-tions in any doubtful and undesirable situation are never all of a piece—otherwise there would be no conflict or confusion involved —and, moreover, they are never so fixed that no change in them can be effected. In actual fact, they are themselves changing any-how in *some* direction, so that the problem is to institute modes of interaction among them which will produce changes in the direc-tion that leads to the proposed objective consequence.

2. That conditions are never completely fixed means that they are in process—that, in any case, they are moving toward the production of a state of affairs which is going to be different in *some* respect. The purpose of the operations of observation which differentiate conditions into obstructive factors and positive re-sources is precisely to indicate the intervening activities which will give the movement (and hence its consequences) a different form from what it would take if it were left to itself; that is, move-ment toward a proposed unified existential situation.

The result of taking facts as finished and over with is more serious in inquiry into social phenomena than it is with respect to physical objects. For the former phenomena are inherently historical. But in physics, although universal conceptions are defined and kinds are described in reference to some final existential application, they are free from the necessity of any immediate application. Every social phenomenon, however, is itself a sequential course of changes, and hence a fact isolated from the history of which it is a moving constituent loses the qualities that make it distinctively social. Generic propositions are indispensable in order to determine the unique sequence of events, but as far as the latter is interpreted wholly in terms of general and universal propositions, it loses that unique individuality in virtue of which it is a historic and social fact. A physical fact may be treated as a "case." Any account of, say, the assassination of Julius Caesar assuredly involves the generic conceptions of assassination, conspiracy, political ambition, human beings, of which it is an exemplifying case and it cannot be reported and accounted for without the use of such general conceptions. But treatment of it as just and merely a case eliminates its qualities that make it a social fact. The conceptions are indispensable but they are indispensable as *means* for determining a non-recurring temporal sequence. Even in physics "laws" are in their logical import ultimately means of selecting and linking together events which form an individual temporal sequence.[6]

It was just affirmed that social phenomena are historical, or of the nature of individual temporal sequences. Argument in support of this assumption is superfluous if "history" is understood to include the present. No one would dream of questioning that the social phenomena which constitute the rise of the papacy, the industrial revolution, the rise of cultural and political nationalism, are historical. It cannot be denied that what is now going on in the countries of the world, in their domestic institutions and foreign relations, will be the material of history in the future. It is absurd to suppose that history includes events that happened up to yesterday but does not take in those occurring today. As there are no temporal gaps in a historically determined sequence, so there are none in social phenomena that are determined by inquiry for the latter constitute a developing course of events. Hence, al-

[6] See, *ante*, pp. 445–7.

though observation and assemblage of materials in isolation from their movement into an eventual consequence may yield "facts" of some sort, the latter will not be facts in any social sense of that word, since they will be non-historical.

This consideration reinforces the conclusion already drawn: Inquiry into social phenomena involves judgments of evaluation, for they can be understood only in terms of eventuations to which they are capable of moving. Hence, there are as many possible interpretations in the abstract as there are possible kinds of consequences. This statement does not entail carrying over into social phenomena a teleology that has been outmoded in the case of physical phenomena. It does not imply that there is some purpose ruling social events or that they are moving to a predetermined goal. The meaning is that any problematic situation, *when it is analyzed*, presents, in connection with the idea of operations to be performed, *alternative* possible ends in the sense of terminating consequences. Even in physical inquiry, what the inquirer observes and the conceptions he entertains are controlled by an objective purpose—that of attaining a resolved situation. The difference between physical and social inquiry does not reside in the presence or absence of an end-in-view, formulated in terms of possible consequences. It consists in the respective *subject-matters* of the purposes. This difference makes a great practical difference in the conduct of inquiry: a difference in the kind of operations to be performed in instituting the subject-matters that in their interactions will resolve a situation. In the case of social inquiry, *associated* activities are directly involved in the operations to be performed; these associated activities enter into the *idea* of any proposed solution. The practical difficulties in the way of securing the agreements in actual association that are necessary for the required activity are great. In physical matters, the inquirer may reach the outcome in his laboratory or observatory. Utilization of the conclusions of others is indispensable, and others must be able to attain similar conclusions by use of materials and methods similar to those employed by the individual investigator. His activity is socially conditioned in its beginning and close. But in physical inquiry the conditioning social factors are relatively indirect, while in solution of social problems they are directly involved. Any hypothesis as to a social end must include as part of itself the idea of organized association among those who are to execute the operations it formulates and directs.

Evaluative judgments, judgments of better and worse about the means to be employed, material and procedural, are required. The evils in current social judgments of ends and policies arise, as has been said, from importations of judgments of value from outside of inquiry. The evils spring from the fact that the values employed are not determined in and by the process of inquiry: for it is assumed that certain ends have an inherent value so unquestionable that they regulate and validate the means employed, instead of ends being determined on the basis of existing conditions as obstacles-resources. Social inquiry, in order to satisfy the conditions of scientific method, must judge certain objective consequences to be the end which is *worth* attaining under the given conditions. But, to repeat, this statement does not mean what it is often said to mean: Namely, that ends and values can be assumed outside of scientific inquiry so that the latter is then confined to determination of the means best calculated to arrive at the realization of such values. On the contrary, it means that ends in their capacity of values can be validly determined only on the basis of the tensions, obstructions and positive potentialities that are found, by controlled observation, to exist in the actual situation.

V. *Conceptual Subject-matter in Social Inquiry.* This theme was necessarily touched upon in the consideration of the first point, the nature of problems. It was also treated in the foregoing section regarding "fact-findings" that are carried on in isolation from conceptions of an end to be attained. For it was pointed out that such conceptions, while they need to be tested and revised in terms of observed facts, are required to control the selection, arrangement and interpretation of facts. Consideration of the present theme will, accordingly, be confined for the most part, to pointing out the logical mistake of those methods that treat conceptual subject-matter as if it consisted of first and ultimate, self-validating truths, principles, norms. As so often happens with contrary one-sided views, the defects of the factual, so called "positivistic" school and of the conceptual school, provide arguments by which each evokes and supports the views of the other. It cannot be said that the conceptual or "rationalistic" school pays no attention whatever to facts. But it can be stated that it places its entire emphasis upon conceptions, so that facts are subsumed directly under "principles," the latter being regarded as fixed norms that decide the legitimacy or illegitimacy of existing phenomena and that prescribe the ends towards which endeavor should be directed.

There can be no doubt that in some form or other the past history of social thought has been dominated by the conceptual approach. There have existed (to mention merely some outstanding phases) first, the conception, in classical, moral and political theory of ends-in-themselves that are fixed in and by Nature (and hence ontological and cosmological); secondly, the doctrine of "Natural Laws," which itself assumed a variety of forms in successive epochs; thirdly, the theory of intuitions of *a priori* necessary truths, and, finally, as in contemporary thought, the doctrine of an intrinsic hierarchy of fixed values. It is no part of the present task to examine these various historical manifestations of identification of ends having objective status with *a priori* conceptual material. An illustration, exemplary as to the logic involved although not exemplary as to its material, will be given.

Classical political economy, with respect to its logical form, claimed to be a science in virtue, first, of certain ultimate first truths, and, secondly, in virtue of the possibility of rigorous "deduction" of actual economic phenomena from these truths. From these "premises," it followed, in the third place, that the first truths provided the norms of practical activity in the field of economic phenomena; or that actual measures were right or wrong, and actual economic phenomena normal or abnormal, in the degree of their correspondence with deductions made from the system of conceptions forming the premises. The members of this school, from Adam Smith to the Mills and their contemporary followers, differed of course from the traditional *rationalistic* school. For they held that first principles were themselves derived inductively, instead of being established by *a priori* intuition. But once arrived at, they were regarded as unquestionable truths, or as axioms with respect to any further truths, since the latter should be deductively derived from them. The actual content of the fixed premises was taken to be certain truths regarding human nature, such as the universal desire of each individual to better his condition; the desire to do so with the least effort (since effort constituted cost in the sense of pain to be minimized); the impulse to exchange of goods and services in maximum satisfaction of wants at least cost, etc.

We are not concerned with the question of the validity or invalidity of the content of these premises. The point at issue concerns the import of the logic of the method involved. The net consequence of the procedure of classic economics was reinstatement of the older conception of "natural laws" by means of a reinterpretation of their content. For it was concluded that the "laws" of human activity in the economic field, which were theoretically deducible, were the *norms* of proper or right human activity in that field. The laws were supposed to "govern" the phenomena in the sense that all phenomena which failed to conform to them were abnormal or "unnatural"—were a vicious attempt to suspend the working of natural laws or to escape from their inevitable consequences. Any attempt to regulate economic phenomena by control of the social conditions under which production and distribution of goods and services occur was thereby judged to be a violation of natural laws, an "interference" with the normal order, so that ensuing consequences were bound to be as disastrous as are the consequences of an attempt to suspend or interfere with the working of any physical law, say, the law of gravitation.

Discussion of this position is concerned only with its inherent logic, not with the fact that its practical product was a system of *laissez-faire* "individualism" and a denial of the validity of attempts at social control of economic phenomena. From the standpoint of logical method, the conceptions involved were not regarded as *hypotheses* to be employed in observation and ordering of phenomena, and hence to be tested by the consequences produced by acting upon them. They were regarded as *truths* already established and therefore unquestionable. Furthermore, it is evident that the conceptions were not framed with reference to the needs and tensions existing at a particular *time* and *place*, or as methods of resolving ills *then* and *there* existing, but as universal principles applicable anywhere and everywhere. A strong case might be made out for the position that if they had been framed and interpreted on the ground of applicability to conditions existing under specified spatio-temporal conditions, say, in the first half of the nineteenth century in Great Britain, they were to a considerable extent directive operational hypotheses relevant to those historical conditions. But the method that was employed forbade an interpretation in specified spatio-temporal terms.

In consequence, the three indispensable logical conditions of conceptual subject-matter in scientific method were ignored; namely, (1) the status of theoretical conceptions as hypotheses which (2) have a directive function in control of observation and ultimate practical transformation of antecedent phenomena, and which (3) are tested and continually revised on the ground of the consequences they produce in existential application.

A further illustration of the demands of logical method may be found in other current theories about social phenomena, such as the supposed issue of "individualism" versus "collectivism" or "socialism," or the theory that all social phenomena are to be envisaged in terms of the class-conflict of the bourgeoisie and the proletariat. From the standpoint of method, such conceptual generalizations, no matter which one of the opposed conceptions is adopted, *pre*judge the characteristic traits and the kinds of actual phenomena that the proposed plans of action are to deal with. Hence the work of *analytic* observations by which actual phenomena will be reduced to terms of definite problems that may be dealt with by means of determinate specified operations is intrinsically compromised from the start. The "generalizations" are of the nature of all-or-none contradictory "truths." Like all such sweeping universals, they do not delimit the field so as to determine problems that may be attacked one by one, but are of such a nature that, from the standpoint of theory, one theory must be accepted and the other rejected *in toto*.

One of the simplest ways of grasping the logical difference between social inquiry that rests upon fixed conceptual principles and physical inquiry, is to note that in the latter the theoretical controversies which exist concern the *efficacy* of different conceptions *of procedure*, while in the former they are about the question of an alleged intrinsic truth or falsity. This attitude is generative of conflict in opinion, and clash in action, instead of promoting inquiries into observable and verifiable facts. If one looks at the early stage of what is now the body of facts and ideas that constitute physics, chemistry, biology and medicine, one finds that at some earlier period controversy in those fields was also mainly about the intrinsic truth and falsity of certain conceptions. As these sciences have advanced in genuine scientific quality, doubt and inquiry have centered upon the efficacy of different *methods* of procedure. The result has been that instead of a state of rigid alternatives of which one must be accepted and the other rejected, a plurality of hypotheses is positively welcome. For the plurality of alternatives is the effective means of rendering inquiry more extensive (sufficient) and more flexible, more capable of taking cognizance of all facts that are discovered.

In fine, fact-finding procedures are necessary for (1) determination of *problems* and for (2) provision of data that indicate and test hypotheses; while formulation of conceptual structures and frames of reference is necessary to guide observation in discriminating and ordering data. The immature state of social inquiry may thus be measured by the extent to which these two operations of fact-finding and of setting up theoretical ends are carried on independently of each other, with the consequence that factual propositions on one side and conceptual or theoretical structures on the other are regarded each as final and complete in itself by one or another school. With reference to the conceptual framework, some additional considerations are appended.

1. Directing conceptions tend to be taken for granted after they have once come into general currency. In consequence they either remain implicit or unstated, or else are propositionally formulated in a way which is static instead of functional. Failure to examine the conceptual structures and frames of reference which are unconsciously implicated in even the seemingly most innocent factual inquiries is the greatest single defect that can be found in any field of inquiry. Even in physical matters, after a certain conceptual frame of reference has once become habitual, it

tends to become finally obstructive with reference to new lines of investigation. In biology and in the social disciplines, law, politics, economics and morals, the danger is more acute and more disastrous. Failure to encourage fertility and flexibility in formation of hypotheses as frames of reference is closer to a death warrant of a science than any other one thing.

2. With respect to social subject-matter in particular, failure to translate influential conceptions into *formulated* propositions is especially harmful. For only explicit formulation stimulates examination of their meanings in terms of the consequences to which they lead and promotes critical comparison of alternative hypotheses. Without systematic formulation of ruling ideas, inquiry is kept in the domain of opinion and action in the realm of conflict. For ultimately the only logical alternative to open and aboveboard propositional formulation of conceptual alternatives (as many as possible) is formation of controlling ideas on the ground of either custom and tradition or some special interest. The result is dichotomization of a social field into conservatives and progressives, "reactionaries" and "radicals," etc.

3. One of the chief practical obstacles to the development of social inquiry is the existing division of social phenomena into a number of compartmentalized and supposedly independent noninteracting fields, as in the different provinces assigned, for example to economics, politics, jurisprudence, morals, anthropology, etc. It is no part of a general logical theory to indicate special methods and devices by which existing barriers may be broken down. That task is the business of inquirers in the several fields. But a survey from the logical point of view of the historical development of the social disciplines instructively discloses the causes of splitting up social phenomena into a number of relatively closed compartments and the injurious effects of the division. It is legitimate to suggest that there is an urgent need for breaking down these conceptual barriers so as to promote cross-fertilization of ideas, and greater scope, variety and flexibility of hypotheses.

4. The practical difficulties in the way of experimental method in the case of social phenomena as compared with physical investigations do not need elaborate exposition. Nevertheless, every measure of policy put into operation is, *logically*, and *should* be

actually, of the nature of an experiment. For (1) it represents the adoption of one out of a number of alternative conceptions as possible plans of action, and (2) its execution is followed by consequences which, while not as capable of definite or exclusive differentiation as in the case of physical experimentation, are none the less observable within limits, so they may serve as tests of the validity of the conception acted upon. The idea that because social phenomena do not permit the controlled variation of sets of conditions in a one-by-one series of operations, therefore the experimental method has no application at all, stands in the way of taking advantage of the experimental method to the extent that is practicable. Suppose, for example, it is a question of the introduction of some legislative policy. Recognition of its experimental character would demand, on the side of its contents, that they be rendered as definite as possible in terms of a number of well thought out alternatives, or as members of a disjunctive system. That is, failure to recognize its experimental character encourages treatment of a policy as an isolated independent measure. This relative isolation puts a premium upon formation of policies in a comparatively improvised way, influenced by immediate conditions and pressures rather than by surveys of conditions and consequences. On the other side, failure to take into account the experimental nature of policies undertaken, encourages laxity and discontinuity in *discriminative* observation of the consequences that result from its adoption. The result is merely that it works or it does not work as a gross whole, and some other policy is then improvised. Lack of careful, selective, continued observation of conditions promotes indefiniteness in formation of policies, and this indefiniteness reacts in turn to obstruct definiteness of the observations relevant to its test and revision.

Finally, it may be pointed out that the present state of social inquiry provides a test of the adequacy of general logical theory, and in this respect furnishes confirmation of the validity of the general theory which has been developed. To consider in detail its value as a test of logical theories held regarding facts and conception and their relation to each other would be to repeat what has already been said. A word may be added about its value as a test of formalistic logical theories. A logic of forms in isolation from matter is confined in social inquiry to the function of forms in locating formal fallacies in discourse, especially in giving warning against the confusion of words having emotional immediate practical effect, (so called "expressive sentences") with those having objective meaning. This purging of reasoning from formal fallacies is a valuable service. But it rarely requires any elaborate formal scheme to enable them to be detected. The important fallacies are the material ones. They spring from lack of proper methods of observation on one hand, and, on the other, from lack of methods for forming and testing hypotheses. With respect to these material concerns, formalistic logic is necessarily silent. The silence is sometimes defended on the ground that propositions about social matters and about what is to be done with respect to them involve valuations (which is correct), and then holding that propositions about values are pseudo-propositions, expressing *merely* resolutions to act in certain ways. That an element of practical resolution exists need not be denied; it is found also in every conception as to how to operate in physical science. The point which is important is that formalistic logic provides no possible ground for deciding upon one practical policy rather than another, and none for following out the consequences of a policy when put into operation as a test of its validity. The net effect is to throw the very field in which intelligent control is of the utmost importance wholly outside the scope of scientific method. There are those to whom this result will present itself as a *reductio ad absurdum* of the theory in question. In any case, the formalistic position is very likely to provoke a reaction that contributes to strengthening the theory of fixed *a priori* schemes of value, known by direct rational intuition. For any denial of the possibility of application of a scientific method is bound to encourage resort, in a matter of such importance, to use of non-scientific and even anti-scientific procedures.

I conclude discussion of the topic of the logic of social inquiry by referring again to the point which is fundamental in the foregoing discussion—its intrinsic reference to practice. This reference has been shown to be involved in determination of genuine problems, in discriminating, weighing and ordering facts as evidential, and in formation and test of the hypotheses that are entertained. I add a few words upon the special topic of *understanding* facts. Understanding or interpretation is a matter of the *ordering* of those materials that are ascertained to be facts; that is, determination of their *relations*. In any given subject-matter there exist many relations of many kinds. That particular set of relations which is relevant to the problem in hand has to be determined. Relevant *theoretical* conceptions come into play only as the problem in hand is clear and definite; that is, theory alone cannot decide what set of relations is to be instituted, or how a given body of facts is to be understood. A mechanic, for example, understands the various parts of a machine, say an automobile, when and only when he knows how the parts *work together;* it is the way in which they work together that provides the principle of order upon and by which they are related to one another. The conception of "working together" involves the conception of consequences: the *significance* of things resides in the consequences they produce when they interact with other specified things. The heart of the experimental method is determination of the significance of observed things by means of deliberate institution of modes of interaction.

It follows that in social inquiry "facts" may be carefully ascertained and assembled without being understood. They are capable of being ordered or related in the way that constitutes understanding of them only when their *bearing* is seen, and "bearing" is a matter of connection with consequences. Social phenomena are so interwoven with one another that it is impossible to assign special consequences (and hence bearing and significance) to any given body of facts unless the special consequences are of the latter *differentially* determined. This differential determination can be affected only by active or "practical" operations conducted according to an idea which is a plan. Social phenomena are not unique in being complexly interwoven with another. All existential events, as existential, are in a similar state. But methods of experimentation and their directive conceptions are now so well established in the case of physical phenomena that vast bodies of facts seem to carry their significance with them almost on their face as soon as they are ascertained. For prior experimental operations have shown what their probable consequences will be under specified conditions to a high degree of accuracy. No such state of affairs exists with reference to social phenomena and facts. A like state of affairs can be brought into existence, even approximately, only as social facts are related together and hence understood, on the basis of their connection with differential consequences that are effected by definite plans of dealing practically with the phenomena:—the plans, once more, being hypotheses directive of practical operations, not truths or dogmas.

CHAPTER XXV

THE LOGIC OF INQUIRY AND PHILOSOPHIES OF KNOWLEDGE

A TWO-WAY CONNECTION exists between logic and philosophical systems. On the one hand, the history of philosophy shows that every main type of philosophic system has developed its own special interpretation of logical forms and relations. Indeed, it is almost a convention to divide philosophy in general and special systems in particular into ontology or metaphysics on one side and a corresponding epistemology or theory of knowledge, on the other side. From another point of view, logic, esthetics and ethics are the traditional main branches of philosophy. It is not accidental that spiritualistic and materialistic, monistic, dualistic and pluralistic, idealistic and realistic philosophies have evinced predilections for one or another type of logical doctrine; and as they have become aware of the relations between their first principles and their methods, have developed a type of logical theory consonant with their theories of nature and man. It is to the credit of each main type of philosophy that it has attempted to make explicit its underlying logic.

It is, however, the other line of connection with which this chapter is concerned. In order to gain adherents and to endure, a philosophical system must not only maintain a reasonable degree of internal dialectical consistency but must square itself with some phases and conditions of the *methods* by which the beliefs that are entertained about the world have been reached. It does not suffice that a system have a consistent logic of discourse. It must also have a considerable measure of plausibility in application to things of the world if it is to gain and hold adherents. It follows that every main philosophical theory of knowledge must not merely avoid fallacies from its own standpoint, but must borrow its leading principles from some phase of the logical pattern of inquiry in order that its conclusions may seem to avoid *material fallacies*. More than meticulous consistency in discourse is required to produce and sustain recurring types of philosophies of knowledge. The fact that there is a limited number of types and that they do recur in history (with modifications of subject-matter appropriate to the culture of an epoch) of itself suggests that they have laid hold of some features of the logic of competent inquiry as the ground of their appeal. Wishful thinking may enter into the special features selected; these may be chosen in order to support in advance certain conclusions rather than others. But the logical features cannot be themselves invented *ad hoc*. If they were, the theories would be paranoic constructions.

The purpose of this chapter is, then, to consider some of the main types of epistemological theory which mark the course of philosophy with a view to showing that each type represents a selective extraction of some conditions and some factors out of the actual pattern of controlled inquiry. It will be shown that this borrowing is what gives them their plausibility and appeal, while the source of their invalidity is arbitrary isolation of the elements selected from the inquiry-context in which they function. They will not be criticized, then, on the ground that they violate all conditions of inquiry as means of attaining knowledge, but on the ground that the selections are so one-sided as to ignore and thereby virtually deny other conditions which give those that are selected their cognitive force and which also prescribe the limits under which the selected elements validly apply.

To undertake a complete exposition of the selected logical characteristics that make each typical theory of knowledge just what it is would demand a book, not a chapter. The pattern of inquiry, in and by which knowledge is instituted, fixes attention, however, upon the logical conditions that knowledge must satisfy, and thereby furnishes us a clew that will guide us through the maze of theories. If the theories are not wholly arbitrary but are one-sided emphases selected from the total context of the pattern, the pattern presents us with the total set of logical conditions out of which some are extracted and then set over against one another.

This possibility of selection has been actualized. The result is the various types of epistemological theory that mark the history of thought. While the material of further discussion is, then, necessarily critical and controversial the purpose is not controversial. It is to throw light upon the directing logical motif of each system and also to provide indirect confirmation of conclusions already set forth.

1. The pattern of inquiry involves actively cooperating divisions of labor between perceptual and ideational subject-matters. Emphasis upon one of these conditions at the expense of the other will necessarily result in conflicting theories of knowledge. Those who make one factor supreme and final will necessarily attempt to explain the other in its own terms or else to explain it away. Moreover, the inadequacy of each view will also necessarily give renewed life and vigor to the opposed theory. The history of thought from Greek times on is marked by the continued controversy between sensationalistic empiricism and abstract rationalism.

2. Again, the pattern of inquiry is marked both by the presence of immediate qualitative elements which determine the problem of inquiry; which determine the material that is relevant; and which test any proposed solution; and by mediate factors. Here again, one-sided selection is possible.

While the theory of immediate *knowledge* has been discussed and rejected, yet that discussion does not fully cover the points which are relevant to the issue in hand. For there are theories that admit that the processes of mediation are preliminary to obtaining knowledge but are themselves extra-logical; e.g., the theories which hold that induction and inference are merely preparatory psychological adjustments. On the other hand, there are theories whose recognition of the necessity of mediation leads them to the conclusion that in the final object of knowledge everything stands in mediated relation to everything else. From this point of view the only genuine object of knowledge is the universe as an unconditioned whole so that what ordinarily passes for knowledge, science included, is only of "phenomena" or appearances, since they are fragmentary bits of ultimate "Reality." Although the final conclusion is metaphysical, in modern times the metaphysical conclusion is reached by what purports to be a critical examination of the conditions of the possibility of knowledge. The difference between idealistic and realistic theories of knowledge ultimately depends upon the attitude taken towards immediate and mediate elements in knowledge.

3. There is the question as to the relation between form and matter. One aspect of this question has also been already discussed; namely, the view that logic is concerned with forms to the exclusion of matter. But, again, this view does not exhaust the issue. There are theories, such as traditional rationalism, which hold that forms completely determine the ultimate matter of knowledge; there are other theories which hold that while forms, as essences, are wholly independent of material existence, yet from time to time some of them descend and lay hold of existence as a mere flux and thus render it, in so far, knowledge. One type of traditional rationalism, absolute idealism, holds that logical forms are characteristic only of human knowing and are completely absorbed within the material of absolute knowledge.

This aspect of the issue calls attention to the fact that various permutations and combinations of the various conditions of the total pattern of inquiry exist, so that (apart from the view that forms are characteristic of a realm of abstract possibilities), the issue of form and matter has historically operated as a qualifying factor of other theories, rather than as an independent basis of theories. For example, denial of the necessity of logical forms is characteristic of both traditional empiricism and materialism, and different views as to their nature play an important role in producing the difference between monistic, dualistic and pluralistic theories.

I. *Traditional Empiricism and Rationalism.* These theories of knowledge may be considered together as each offers a typical case of selective emphasis of one of two subject-matters that are formally involved in any complete act of inquiry. Empiricism in all its varieties has insisted upon the necessity of perceptual material in knowledge; historical rationalism has held that only conceptual subject-matter is capable of providing knowledge in its full sense. There is no need to repeat here the previous analyses which have shown that the distinction and relation between observed data and directive ideas represent a functional division of labor within inquiry in order that the latter may meet the logical requirements of warranted assertibility. It is for this reason that the controversy is interminable. Each type of theory of knowledge has flourished in virtue of the weakness of the other. The special characteristic of traditional empiricism is its extreme immediatism. It engaged in one-sided selection of perceptual material, but it also interpreted this material in an unqualified particularistic way. It held that the immediately given consists of qualitative discrete atoms that have no intrinsic connection with one another. Our earlier discussion has shown that the immediately given is an extensive qualitative *situation*, and that emergence of separate qualities is the result of operations of observation which discriminates elements to serve as means of delimiting the special problem involved and as means of providing tests for proposed solutions. In other words, they are functional distinctions made by inquiry within a total field for the sake of control of conclusions. Traditional empiricism thus affords a striking exhibition of what happens when genuine conditions in the pattern of controlled inquiry are isolated from their context and in consequence are given a non-functional interpretation.

The development of this type of empiricism with its denial of the reality of relations (except those of external contiguity) led to that type of modern rationalism which selected the relational function and made relations the center and heart of all knowledge. Since this rationalism admitted the premise of sensationalism—that qualities as such are discrete unitary elements—the necessary presence of relations in knowledge was attributed to the "synthetic" activity of "thought" as an independent factor. Such rationalism was hard put to it to account for the presence of elements to be related, and, as we shall see in the sequel, this serious difficulty was a chief factor in transforming an earlier rationalism into later idealism. No careful reader of Mill's *Logic*—the typical representative of logical empiricism of the type in question—can fail to be struck by the continually recurrent contrast between his official doctrine of independently given disconnected sensory qualities and his constant falling back upon objects which are groups or sets of related qualities. The reader of T. H. Green's devastating critique of sensationalistic empiricism, on the other hand, is equally struck by his recurrent embarrassment when he is obliged to deal with the "elements" which "thought" relates.[1]

Kant, with his earlier leanings to the rationalistic side, began a new departure when he affirmed that conception without perception is empty and perception without conception blind, so that a union of the two is required for any knowledge of nature. However, his doctrine held that the two materials proceed from two different and independent sources, not seeing that they emerge as cooperative conjugate functions in those processes of inquiry by which problematic situations are analyzed with a view to transformation into unified situations. In consequence, Kant was not only compelled to have recourse to an artificial mechanism to bring two entirely different kinds of subject-matter into connection with one another, but to conclude (given his premises) that the perceptual material, while necessary, gets completely in the way of knowledge of things as they "really" are, so that everything which can lay claim to be knowledge is but of phenomenal appearance.

It is worth noting that development of the particularism of traditional empiricism led, when it was applied in the social field, to an atomic "individualism" which dissolved all intrinsic ties of association, leaving only self-interest in economic matters and coercion in political affairs to hold human beings together. The way in which one-sided empiricism evoked one-sided rationalism and provided it with its chief arguments is especially conspicuous in this field. "Organic" theories of the state with subordination of all human relations to the political nexus was the logical response to atomic individualism. This philosophy supplied the groundwork for a revival of authoritarianism and provided one of the theoretical foundations of modern totalitarian states. On the other hand, the historic involvement of democratic theories of the state with the older "individualistic" atomism has been a chief source of the grow-

---

[1] Not till the time of William James was the common premise of both sensationalistic empiricism and the type of rationalism in question openly challenged by denial that the empirically given consists of disconnected elements. See his *Principles of Psychology*, Vol. I, pp. 244–248. It may be recalled in this context that realistic logical atomism also rests upon acceptance of the doctrine of disconnected elements as ultimate, although not mental, data and consequently must introduce a formal *a priori* rational logical factor to explain the existence of generalizations. (See, *ante*, pp. 147–151.)

ing weakness of "liberal" national and local communities.

Popular positivism with its claim to be strictly scientific is an offshoot of traditional empiricism and, like its parent, has done valiant service in pointing out and rooting out the harmful presence in common sense and science of conceptions for which no confirmatory experiential meaning or test can be found.[2] This positivism has the advantage, however, of freedom from entanglement with highly dubious psychological theories about sensations and the involved epistemological doctrines concerning particulars. It is quite willing to admit that generalizations are valid provided they have the sanction of science. But it inherited from traditional empiricism its contempt for general ideas and for theories that pretend to be anything else than summary records of ascertained facts. Its logic has no recognized place for hypotheses which at a given time outrun the scope of already determined "facts," and which, indeed, may not be capable of verification at the time or of *direct* factual verification at any time.

Popular positivism's one-sided grasp of the method of inquiry is evident when it is noted that the history of science shows that many hypotheses have played a great role in the advancement of science which were at the time of their origin purely speculative, and would have been condemned by a consistent positivism as merely "metaphysical"; e.g., the ideas of the conservation of energy and of evolutionary development. The history of science, as an exemplification of the method of inquiry, shows that the verifiability (as positivism understands it) of hypotheses is not nearly as important as is their directive power. As a broad statement, no important scientific hypothesis has ever been verified in the form in which it was originally presented nor without very considerable revisions and modifications. The justification of such hypotheses has lain in their power to direct new orders of experimental observation and to open up new problems and new fields of subject-matter. In doing these things, they have not only provided new facts but have often radically altered what were previously taken to be facts. Popular positivism, in spite of its

---

[2] The word "popular" is introduced because many of the criticisms passed upon positivism do not apply to some of the more carefully formulated newer types.

claims to be strictly scientific, has been in some respects the heir of an older metaphysical view which attributed to ideas inherent truth-falsity properties. A sense for the actual pattern of inquiry will assign to ideas as ideas the intrinsic function of being operational means. On this ground alone, the positivistic theory of knowledge falls short. This criticism also applies to any form of positivistic theory that confines the scope of logic to transformation of pre-existing materials with no provision for production of new hypotheses whose operative use supplies new materials which reconstruct those already at hand. It applies to "logical positivism" as far as that theory limits logical theory to *trans*formation of propositions in separation from the operations by which propositions are formed.

II. *Realistic Theories of Knowledge.* A distinction was made earlier between subject-matter, content, and objects in inquiry.[3] As a broad term, "subject-matter" is that which is investigated, the problematic situation together with all material relevant to its solution. The word "content" is used in a restricted sense. It designates the subject-matters, existential and conceptual, which are provisionally taken and used in the course of investigation. They may be genuinely objective in their reference, but their value as the material and procedural means of reaching a resolved situation is conditional, or else hypothetical until the transformed situation is instituted. For they may be genuinely objective in some context and yet not be capable of functioning to effect the transformation required in the given situation. An object, logically speaking, is that set of connected distinctions or characteristics which emerges as a definite constituent of a resolved situation and is confirmed in the continuity of inquiry. This definition applies to objects as existential. Since, and when, sets of interrelated abstract characters emerge and are recurrently confirmed in conjugation with such existential objects, ideational or "rational" objects come into being.

Now such objects, existential and ideational, are constantly used in further inquiries. Indeed, the continuity of inquiry depends upon their being taken and used as means in subsequent inquiries. Old objects may undergo modification through the tests which are

[3] See, *ante*, pp. 119–20.

put upon them in new problems—just as the set of related distinctions which once were taken without question to be objects have altered with progress in scientific knowledge. Primarily, however, the objects instituted in continued previous inquiries are accepted "as is," just as tools that have repeatedly proved effective are employed in new undertaking. Now when this direct taking and using is treated as itself a case of knowledge, the "realistic" philosophy of knowledge is the logical outcome. The objects that are used *are* known objects. If, then, the operations of inquiry through which they have been instituted *as* known are ignored, there is a selective emphasis upon one phase of the actual pattern of inquiry which, while valid as far as it goes, is so one-sided as to yield a fallacious theory. The act of *referring* to an object which is a *known* object only because of operations quite independent of the act of referring is taken to be itself a case of representative knowledge for the purpose of a theory of knowledge.

The necessary presence of definite objects repeatedly and familiarly employed as means to further knowledge gives the realistic theory its plausibility; a plausibility so great that any other theory seems like a departure from common sense made only to meet the exigencies of some preconceived theory. That stones, stars, trees, cats and dogs, etc., exist independently of the particular processes of a knower at a given time is as groundedly established fact of knowledge as anything can well be. For as sets of connected existential distinctions, they have emerged and been tested over and over again in the inquiries of individuals and of the race. In most cases it would be a gratuitous waste of energy to repeat the operations by which they have been instituted and confirmed. For the individual knower to suppose that he constructed them in his immediate mental processes is as absurd as it would be for him to suppose that he created the streets and houses he sees as he travels through a city. Nevertheless, the streets and houses *have* been made, although by existential operations exercised upon independently existing materials, not by "mental" processes. When once instituted, objects, like streets and houses, are directly used in new undertakings.

It is at this point that confusion as to the nature of the "given" adds plausibility to the realistic theory.[4] Existences *are* immediately given in experience; that is what experience primarily *is*. They are not given *to* experience but their giveness *is* experience. But such immediate qualitative experience is not itself cognitive; it fulfils none of the logical conditions of knowledge and of objects *qua* known. When inquiry occurs, these materials are given *to be* known—a truistic or tautological statement, since inquiry is the subjection of the given experience to operations of inquiry with the intent of institution of objects as known. The realistic theory of knowledge thus represents a merger of two considerations both of which in themselves are valid. One of them is the necessity (just mentioned) of referring to objects already known in conducting operations of inquiry to arrive at further knowledge. The other consideration is the fact that inquiry always depends upon the immediate presence of directly (but non-cognitively) experienced existential subject-matters. Were the assertions of the realistic theory of knowledge confined to this latter point, it would be as naive and as groundedly a matter of common sense as it professes to be. But by mixing this field of non-cognitive, directly enjoyed and suffered, subject-matter with an act of direct reference (taking and using) to objects already known (known as the consequence of prior tested and testing operations of inquiry) the realism that results, is misplaced.

So far I have been dealing with realistic theories of the direct, or as they are sometimes called "monistic," variety. The confusion of two different things just mentioned, arising from mixing them in a blend which is then alleged to be the simple and single act of knowing, results in certain difficulties, of which the existence of errors, mistakes, illusions and delusions is a significant aspect. The consistent realist of the type just criticized is compelled logically to attribute independent subsistence—if not existence—to the subject-matter of all false knowledge as well as of true, thus obliterating the distinctive logical meaning of knowledge. For by this theory false knowing is also a case of the direct referring or "pointing" by the knowing subject to subject-matters that are what they are in independence of operations of knowing. I shall not go into this point by way of further criticism, since it

[4] Cf. *ante*, pp. 124, 228.

is the logical consequence of the confused merger pointed out. I refer to it in connection with another type of realistic theory, so-called dualistic or "representative" realism.

According to this view, the direct or given object of cognition is always a mental state, whether "sensation" or "idea," and the existential physical object is known through a mental state taken to be a representation of an external object. As in the case of other theories under examination, the present discussion is concerned with this view only as far as it has a basis in the actual pattern of inquiry. It is due to extraction of the *inferential* phase of inquiry, while the isolation of this phase from the total inquiry-context results in conversion of functional values into the kind of ontological existence that is then called mental. In inquiry, immediate qualities are discriminated with reference to use as signs or indications of a possible inferred conclusion. For example, a pain is directly had. It is interpreted as a toothache, and thereby judged to be a singular of a specified kind. The pain, in conjunction with a set of other observable qualities, is taken to constitute an *object* of which it is an evidential mark. In this capacity, the pain-quality *represents* an object. Now if its special function in inquiry is ignored, this representative function is hypostatized. The pain is then taken not just for what it is, namely a quality which at first has a problematic or doubtful reference, but as a mental existence which somehow represents a physical object. By a figure of speech its representative function in resolution of a problem is converted into *a* representation.

The same line of consideration applies to ideas as distinct from direct qualities. An idea as it operates in inquiry is the possible significance of given qualities that are problematic in their significance. As such, it has representative capacity since it stands for a possible solution. Being a possibility, it is not immediately accepted if genuine inquiry occurs, but is employed as a directive of further operations of observation that yield new data. If its operative function is ignored, then the idea is also taken to be inherently a *mental* representation of an object. In the illustration just given, a pain *suggests* a toothache. Premature judgment (so premature that it is not judgment at all in a logical sense), accepts and affirms the suggestion. But inquiry uses it to initiate and direct additional observations which determine whether or not other qualities exist which are the describing characters of a toothache. In this capacity, the suggestion of a toothache *is* an idea, a possible hypothetical meaning. It is representative, but is not *a* representation. Its hypothetical status is what is meant by calling it an idea. But this status is a logical property not an ontological property that can be set over against the object as a mental existence.

The basic fallacy in representative realism is that while it actually depends upon the inferential phase (as defined) of inquiry, it fails to interpret the immediate quality and the related idea in terms of their functions in inquiry. On the contrary, it views representative power as an inherent property of sensations and ideas as such, treating them as "representations" in and of themselves. Dualism or bifurcation of mental and physical existence, is a necessary result, presented, however, not as a result but as a given fact. Failure to place the representative capacity of immediate qualities as signs and of meanings as possible significances in their context in inquiry leads to their being supposed to be psychical or mental existences, which are then endowed with the miraculous power of standing for and pointing to existences of a different order.

With reference to the matter of errors, false beliefs and hallucinations, representative realism accounts for their occurrence in *general* without being compelled to resort to peopling the realm of Being with all kinds of subsistences, which are said to be pointed to by the knowing subject just as real things may also happen to be pointed to. According to the representative theory, the possibility of mistake is inherent in the very nature of sensations and ideas as representations. Being of a different order of existence from the external objects they represent, there is no assurance that they will be taken to be the representation of just the external things of which they are in fact the mental surrogates. This conception, while it accounts for the abstract possibility of errors and falsities, is impotent to explain the difference between true and false beliefs in any particular case. To decide, for example, whether a given idea is a representation of a sea-serpent or a whale, of a ghost or a sheeted figure, the theory is obliged to go outside the idea and outside of everything that examination of the idea will disclose. It is obliged to have recourse to ordinary competent operations of inquiry, and these operations are wholly independent of the alleged nature of the idea as a mental representation. Now the important thing is always the validity or invalidity of the *specific* interpretation assigned to an immediate quality and to a suggested meaning. Since to determine this question, representative realism must have recourse to the normal operations of inquiry, it is useless and irrelevant in the one matter that is of logical importance. It would be simpler and more direct, to say the least, to begin and continue with consideration of the operations of inquiry which are what is finally depended upon. If this were done, the whole conception of qualities and ideas as modes of mental existence would automatically drop out.

A more detailed examination would confirm the point that has been made more than once, namely, that epistemology, so called, is a mixture of logical conceptions, derived from analysis of competent inquiry, and irrelevant psychological and metaphysical preconceptions. It would confirm the validity of the position that the genuine element in every typical "epistemological" theory is logical. It may be added that if one wishes to interpret the "mental" as that subject-matter of experience which has, for the purposes of inquiry and in its conduct, a strictly conditional and hypothetical status (a status that must be given to qualities and meaning while any inquiry is still in progress) there can be no objection. But this interpretation of the "mental" differs radically from the doctrine that there is involved in knowledge an order of existence which in and of itself is psychical or mental. That there are certain existential qualities like emotions, which are referable to *persons* as a distinctive kind of existence (in the same sense in which stones, stars, oysters and monkeys, are kinds of existence with their own distinctive qualities), is a valid proposition. But this *differential* objective reference has nothing to do with the alleged subjective characters of qualities and ideas as they function in knowledge. A *person* is an object, not a "mind" nor consciousness, even though because of his capacity for inquiry he may be said to have mind.

In the case of an emotion, "subjective" is simply a synonym for *personal*. Whether such qualities as characterize hope, fear, anger, love, describe a kind of objects that are distinctively personal is a question of fact to be settled by the same methods as determine whether distinctive traits mark off clams and oysters from one another. The properties that mark *inquiry* constitute knowledge to be of a different kind from ignorance, mere opinion and delusion. A *person*, or, more generically, an organism, *becomes* a knowing subject in virtue of engaging in operations of controlled inquiry. The theory criticized holds that there is a cognitive subject antecedent to and independent of inquiry, a subject which is inherently a knowing being. Since it is impossible to verify this assumption by any empirical means, it is a metaphysical preconception which is then mixed with logical conditions to create a mode of "epistemology."

III. *Idealistic Theories of Knowledge.* There are three types of theories of knowledge to which the word "idealist" is currently applied. They may be identified as the perceptual, of which the Berkeleyan is representative; the rationalistic, and the absolutistic. The difference between the first two mentioned is constituted by interception of idealistic ontologies with the separation, already discussed, of the empirically perceived and the conceptually ideated. The third theory represents an attempt to overcome the division by reference to an experience in which the perceptual and rational are completely fused, an absolute experience.

1. *Perceptual Idealism.* In classic theory as it was maintained throughout the medieval period, a species, or the essential form which determines a species, was termed an Idea—"species" being in fact the Latin transcription of the Greek *eidos* or *idea*. The psychological trend of modern thought tended to conceive of ideas as mental states. Locke retained the notion that an idea or species is "the immediate object" of mind or thought and gave it a status set over against real external objects. Knowledge proper consisted in the relation between ideas, a relation capable of taking different forms. Locke thus provided the background of the theory of representative realism. Locke attempted to get over the difficulty of finding a ground, on the basis of his premises, for belief in the existence of a world external to the ideas by drawing a distinction between primary qualities, solidity, size, motion, which *are* properties of objects, and secondary qualities, like color,

sound, odor and pain, which are purely effects of the impact of objective primary properties upon a subject. Berkeley cut under this theory by pointing out the impossibility of separating primary and secondary qualities in perception. The consequence was denial of the existence of any material substance behind ideas, since by description it was not an object of perception. *Mind* to which ideas belong and of which they are properties was thus taken to be the only substance. Berkeley accepted Locke's theory that the object of knowledge is a *relation* of ideas. His originality consisted in interpreting this relation as one of signifying or pointing—as the qualities of smoke point to those of fire. Nature as an object of knowledge is thus a book or language, while knowledge is understanding of what is inscribed in the book. Certain ideas, moreover, are forced upon us, and the relation of indicating or signifying which holds between them is permanent and stable. The fact that primary ideas and the fixed relations existing between them are beyond our control shows that they do not originate in our minds but are the manifestation of a Divine Mind and Will.

As far as the basic assumption of the original *mental* nature of "ideas" is concerned, the criticism made of representative realism applies as well to this theory. The distinctive logical feature of perceptual idealism is the identification of the relation which constitutes knowledge with that of signifying. This aspect of the theory evidently represents a genuine apprehension of a necessary condition of controlled inquiry:—that in which qualities directly had are taken as evidential signs of something beyond themselves. The one-sided character of the selective emphasis consists in ignoring the fact that the qualities in question are discriminated from out of an inclusive field in order to serve a special function in inquiry—namely, determination of the problem to be solved. Consequently, a purely functional status of perceived qualities is treated as something inhering in them in and by their inherent nature. The theory thus affords an exemplification of what happens in the theory of knowledge when certain logical conditions are isolated from their inquiry-context.

It is worth noting that by dropping the assumption that primary "ideas" or qualities are mental, the theory can be given a purely realistic epistemological version. For then it follows that qualities and the signifying relation between them exist *in rerum natura*, and that both are directly apprehended. This version, however, neglects and denies the following traits of the inquiry-context: (1) That qualities as indicative or signifying are deliberately selected for the purpose of inquiry out of a complex that is directly had in experience; and (2) that the existence of the problematic situation to be resolved exercises control over the selective discrimination of relevant and effective evidential qualities as means. When these considerations are noted, it is at once clear that the signifying property is not inherent but accrues to natural qualities in virtue of the special function they perform in inquiry.

Take the illustrative case already mentioned—that smoke means fire. Because of the recurrence of a certain problem in common sense, this particular signifying connection becomes familiar and habitual. It may then be taken for granted and directly referred to (or taken and used) in solution of new problems as they present themselves. But (1) discriminating observational inquiries are required to determine that the qualities in question are those of smoke; they may, for example, be those of vapor. Moreover, (2) the fire which is indicated is not just fire in general but some particular fire, and the particular fires may be as different from one another as are a forest conflagration, the burning of a cigar, and the domestic cheer associated with smoke coming at dusk from the chimney of a house. Inquiry is required to determine the *kind* of object of which that which has been determined by controlled observations to be smoke, is a sign. In any case, (3) smoke is *not* the warranted sign of fire. For example, take the scientific idea of fire as combustion. In this finally warranted case, *smoke* does not appear at all. Characteristics which describe fires from a scientific point of view are such as to prove the relativity of the signifying function of objects to inquiry. The notion that this function is a relation which inheres in the structure of nature (or is structural, not functional) originates in the fact that in matters of familiar use and enjoyment past habits have instituted a relation that can be immediately referred to. Beyond a limited range of common sense uses, however, the same objects signify different things in different cultures—a fact sufficient to show that it is not an inherent structural relation capable of direct apprehension. That significance is inherent is a holdover from idealism.

2. *Rationalistic Idealism.* Classic Greek ontologies and metaphysics were realistic in their theories of knowledge. But the "real" element in Nature was taken to be the rational or ideal. Sensory qualities characterizing changing things, and change itself, were a mark of the presence of an element of Non-Being—of incomplete or imperfect Being. The development of modern physical science eliminated ideal forms and rational ends from Nature as known. In accord with the subjective tendency of modern philosophy, philosophers of the rationalistic school endeavored to reinstate the intrinsic rationality of the universe *via* the route of examination of the conditions under which knowledge is possible. These philosophers had no difficulty in showing that knowledge is not possible without the presence of conceptions, and that conceptions cannot be derived from sensory qualities either as their weakened copies or as their compounds. Rationalistic idealism was the outcome. It holds that the real world consists of a system of relations which are of the nature of an objective comprehensive Mind or Spirit, while knowing in the case of human subjects consists in piecemeal reproduction of the constitution of this objective Mind.

The theory, like the traditional rationalism of which it is the offspring, represents a selective emphasis of the ideational functions in controlled inquiry, when the latter is isolated from their operation as means of transformation of problematic situations. About this aspect of the theory, it is, accordingly not necessary to say anything further. The feature of this theory which is relevant to the present discussion is that it arrives at its final idealistic ontology by means of a logical theory of the process of knowledge. It is this phase of the theory which will be examined.

Viewed from this angle, the theory recognizes that judgment is the means of knowledge; that it proceeds by mediation, and that the movement of judgment is towards transformation of antecedently given material in the direction of unification. *So far* it depends for its conclusion upon selection of logical conditions that genuinely mark the pattern of inquiry. But, as has just been observed, it ignores and denies the existence of individual qualitative situations whose problematic quality evokes inquiry. In consequence of this ignoring of a fundamental condition of knowledge no account is taken (1) of the existential *operations* of observation and (2) of the directive experimental function of conceptual subject-matter. Because the theory is not based upon examination of the actual practices by which knowledge is obtained, it is compelled to hypostatize "thought," whose strictly "mental" activity, according to its own immanent constitution, is then taken to be the source of both the structure of the universe and of knowledge of it. Instead of interpreting "thought" on the ground of examination of the actual operations of inquiry, as they are empirically ascertained, something called *thought* is postulated at the outset as an independent original all-inclusive activity or force. The purely metaphysical or empirically unverifiable nature of this assumption is acknowledged by the theory itself in its insistence that thought is strictly *a priori*.

The theory must be given credit for acknowledging the necessity of mediation in attainment of knowledge. Its strong point is insistence upon the presence of *reflection* (which is the mediating aspect of inquiry) in all knowledge and an accompanying implicit or overt criticism of all immediate theories of knowledge. But, for the reason just stated, reflection is taken to be something which descends upon existence out of the blue and operates in a wholesale manner. The *a priori* categories or synthetic modes of conception which, according to it, constitute the structure of "thought," operate in a wholesale manner. They descend equally upon that which is finally ascertained to be valid knowledge and that which is specious and turns out to be false—as the rain from heaven descends equally upon the just and the unjust. Hypostization of "thought" into a substantial entity is the result of ignoring the operations of inquiry by which alone "thought" can be empirically identified. The hypostization precludes the theory from ability to account (given its premises) for the difference between true and false beliefs, since the categories of "thought" are equally operative in both. Now the genuine logical problem is found at precisely this point—the grounding and testing of specific beliefs as to their warrant. Since the theory in question must go outside its own set of premises in order to effect this differentiation, and since it must fall back upon the actual operations of inquiry by which beliefs are grounded and tested, it is clear that its premises are gratuitous and that the theory should begin with the considerations with which it is compelled to end.

The empirical confirmation to which the theory appears to appeal is derived from the fact that reflection or mediation *is* involved in the attainment of whatever can claim to be knowledge as distinct from mere opinion. But it ignores the fundamental considerations which define reflective operations and which constitute their actual force in inquiry:—The occurrence of existential problematic situations, and the occurrence of existential operations which are directed by ideas and whose consequences test the validity of ideas. The theory thus radically misconstrues the *unification* towards which inquiry in its mediate reflective phase actually moves. In actual inquiry, movement toward a unified ordered situation exists. But it is always a unification of the subject-matter which constitutes an individual problematic situation. It is not unification at large. But because reflective operations are hypostatized into an entity of a wholesale nature called Thought or Reason, the feature of unification is generalized beyond the limits in which it takes place, namely, resolution of specific problematic situations. Knowledge is then supposed to consist in attainment of a final all-comprehensive Unity, equivalent to the Universe as an unconditioned whole—a demand which accounts for the absolute idealism which is considered below. It is true that problematic situations are such because of the existence of conditions which conflict as to their significance, thus constituting a disordered situation. Hence, a universal property of any inquiry is transformation into a situation unified or continuous in significance. But the theory under examination generalizes this movement beyond empirically verifiable limits.

Rationalistic idealism claims that the world is rational through and through since science is the disclosure of an order of uniform, because necessary, laws. Leaving out of consideration the fact that laws of uniform relations are ultimately instrumentalities for control of individualized situations, and taking the claim in its own terms, the alleged rationality of the universe as a whole is another case of generalization beyond the limiting conditions of grounded inquiry. That problematic situations are resolv*able* (though the means of attaining solutions may not be practically available at a given time) is certainly a working postulate of inquiry, and it is true that such resolution renders intelligible what was previously unintelligible. But extension of these principles beyond the bounds of a plurality of problematic situations has no warrant. The existence of problematic situations is a challenge to inquiry—that is, to operative intelligence. The idea that the intelligibility effected by scientific or controlled inquiry proves the antecedent existence of an *a priori* rational world puts the cart before the horse. Moreover, it renders the appearance of blind and unordered situations an insoluble problem save by drawing a hard and fast metaphysical line between the world of phenomenal appearances and the world in its reality. Finally, the challenge to make the world more reasonable is one that is ever-renewed, since it is a challenge to execute concrete operations at definite places and times. The working scientific faith is the belief that concern for objective continual inquiry, with assiduity and courage in its performance, is capable of becoming habitual with an ever-increasing number of human beings. The idea that the faith of science is a belief that the world is already in itself completely rational is not so much inspiration to work as it is a justification of acquiescence.

3. *Absolute Idealism.* It was noted that idealisms of the type just considered have great difficulty in accounting for the existence of immediate qualitative elements. Every theory which is derived, even at a distance, from Kant, is compelled to hold that the "categories" of *a priori* thought operate upon a given sensuous material which simply has to be accepted as given. The difficulty thus occasioned is the source of the third type of idealistic theory of knowledge. This theory takes a derogatory attitude towards abstract conceptual and reflective functions. The Absolute which is the Unconditioned Whole, the object of knowledge in its logically proper sense and the goal of human knowing, is, according to this view, a complete interpenetration and interfusion of the elements of the immediate and of the conceptual and reflective. Since what has been said about the fallacy of an all comprehensive unification applies equally to this theory, discussion will be confined to the conception of the interpenetration of the immediate

(represented by feeling and sensory qualities) and relational thought as judgment.

The gist of the criticism passed by this type of idealistic epistemology upon rationalistic idealism concerns the *relational* character belonging to judgment as such. All reflection and all judgment as such, according to absolutistic idealism, involves a self-contradictory process. For judgment proceeds in terms of relations and every relation institutes a distinction as well as a connection. Therefore, judgment, while being the only way in which human subjects can proceed, necessarily stands in the way of attaining the required goal of *final* unification. Reflection is thus said to presuppose an all-inclusive experience—an Absolute Experience—in which there is no distinction of the immediate and the mediate. This Experience is of the nature of qualitative feelings which have so completely absorbed rational and relational properties into themselves that the latter have no existence. But the material content of this ultimate whole (which is the only "Reality") is completely inaccessible to us, since *we* "know" only by means of judgment which is reflective and mediate.

This theory also rests upon one-sided selection of what actually takes place in controlled inquiry. For every resolved situation which is the terminal state of inquiry exists directly as it is experienced. It is a qualitative individual situation in which are directly incorporated and absorbed the results of the mediating processes of inquiry. As an existential situation it is had as the consummation and fulfilment of the operations of inquiry.[5] The related distinctions which are effected by the operations of inquiry exist as definite objects distinguished in inquiry and for the purposes of inquiry. But the experienced situation as a qualitative situation is not an object or a set of objects. It is just the qualitative situation which it is. It can be referred to, taken and used in subsequent inquiries, and then it presents itself as an object or ordered set of objects. But to treat *it* as an object involves confusion of two things which are experientially different: viz., an object of cognition and a situation that is non-cognitively had. Idealism of the type under consideration thus presents a selection of an undeniable aspect of every successful inquiry. But it is guilty of

---

[5] Cf., the discussion of appreciation, *ante*, pp. 174-7.

a fundamental fallacy of generalization of this aspect beyond the limits of consummatory outcomes of inquiry. For these issues are resolutions of unique existential problematic situations.

The discussions and conclusions of the present chapter are controlled by the theory of the pattern of inquiry which has been developed. Their import cannot be understood apart from that theory. They are undertaken in order to provide an indirect confirmation of the position taken in the book. I shall not repeat what has been said to the effect that selective emphases from the actual pattern of inquiry are fallacious because their material is extracted from their context, and thereby made structural instead of functional, ontological instead of logical. It is appropriate to conclude with reference to the total neglect and consequent denial of the *operational* conditions and consequences of inquiry. All of the procedures and techniques of inquiry that yield stabilized beliefs, upon both the common sense and the scientific level, are operations existentially executed. The operations of common sense are restricted because of their dependence upon limited instrumentalities, namely, bodily organs supplemented by instrumental apparatus that was invented to attain practical utilities and enjoyments rather than for the sake of conducting inquiry. The cumulative effect of these operations conducted for a practical end is to give authority to a set of conceptions made familiar in a given culture. Competent science begins when the instrumentalities employed in operations of inquiry are adapted and invented to serve the purpose of inquiry as such, involving development of a special language or set of symbols.

Theories of knowledge that constitute what are now called epistemologies have arisen because knowledge and obtaining knowledge have not been conceived in terms of the operations by which, in the continuum of experiential inquiry, stable beliefs are progressively obtained and utilized. Because they are not constructed upon the ground of operations and conceived in terms of their actual procedures and consequences, they are necessarily formed in terms of preconceptions derived from various sources, mainly cosmological in ancient and mainly psychological (directly or indirectly) in modern theory. Logic thus loses its autonomy, a fact which signifies more than that a formal theory has been crippled. The loss signifies that logic as the generalized account of the means by which sound beliefs on any subject are attained and tested has parted company with the actual practices by means of which such beliefs are established. Failure to institute a logic based inclusively and exclusively upon the operations of inquiry has enormous cultural consequences. It encourages obscurantism; it promotes acceptance of beliefs formed before methods of inquiry had reached their present estate; and it tends to relegate scientific (that is, competent) methods of inquiry to a specialized technical field. Since scientific methods simply exhibit free intelligence operating in the best manner available at a given time, the cultural waste, confusion and distortion that results from the failure to use these methods, in all fields in connection with all problems, is incalculable. These considerations reinforce the claim of logical theory, as the theory of inquiry, to assume and to hold a position of primary human importance.

INDEX